P9-AGL-803

GROUNDED
ethics

GROUNDED ethics

The Empirical Bases of Normative Judgments

Max Hocutt

Transaction Publishers
New Brunswick (U.S.A.) and London (U.K.)

This book is printed on acid-free paper that meets the American National Standard for Permanence of Paper for Printed Library Materials.

Library of Congress Catalog Number: 00-034403
ISBN: 0-7658-0026-8
Printed in the United States of America

Library of Congress Cataloging-in-Publication Data

Hocutt, Max.
Grounded ethics : the empirical bases of normative judgements / Max Hocutt
p. cm.
Includes bibliographical references and index.
ISBN 0-7658-0026-8 (alk. paper)
1. Ethics, Evolutionary. 2. Normativity (Ethics) I. Title

BJ1311 .H64 2000
171'.7—dc21 00-034403

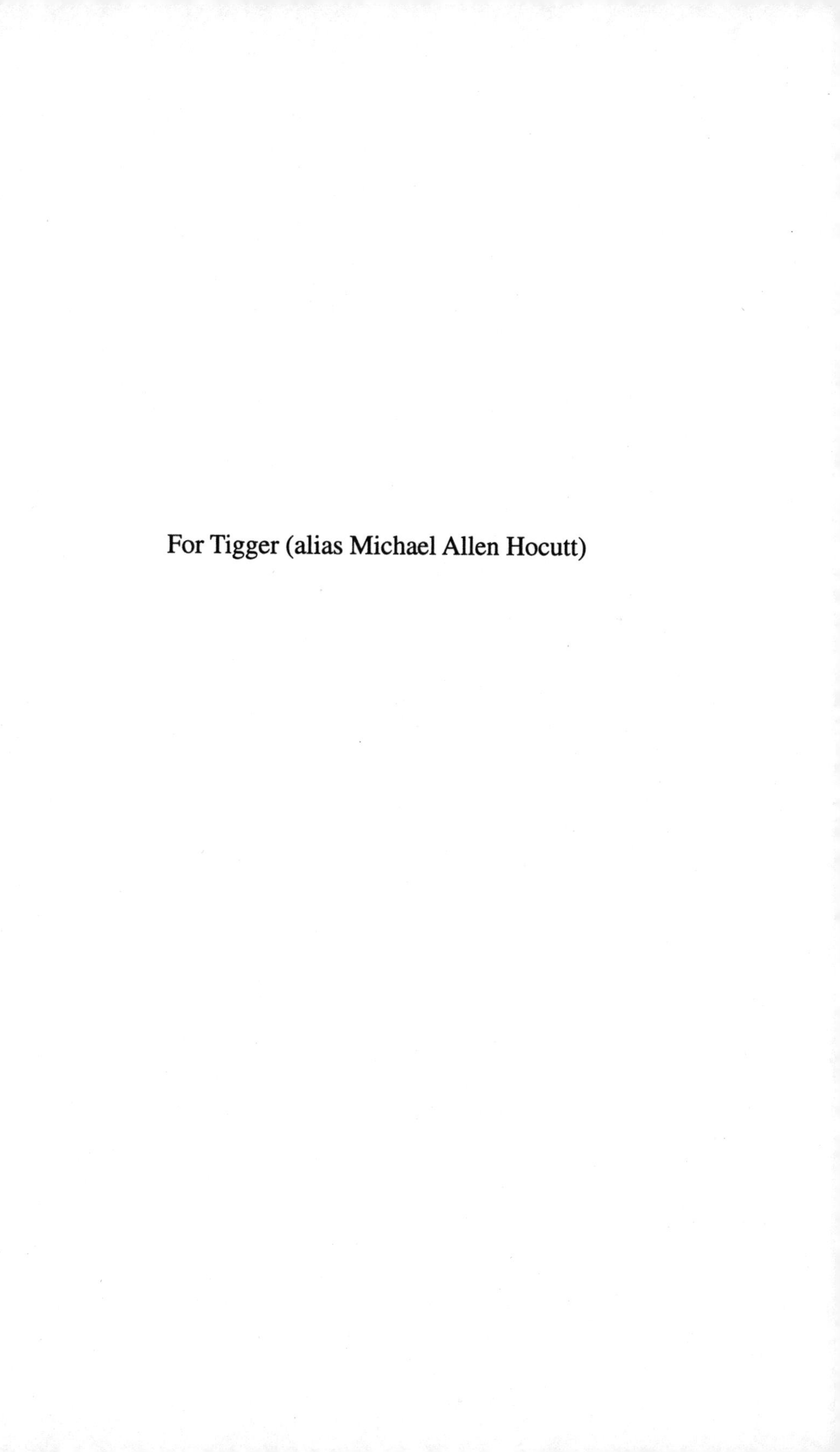

For Tigger (alias Michael Allen Hocutt)

Contents

Contents

Acknowledgments

Colleagues who have read parts of this work in draft and given me the benefit of their criticism include Wallace Matson of the University of California at Berkeley, Michael Levin of the City University of New York, Bruce Wallor of Youngstown State University, George Graham of the University of Alabama in Birmingham, Norvin Richards of my own university, and Mark Rowlands of the University of Cork in Ireland. I am especially grateful to Levin, who bucked me up and kept me going when the project seemed hopeless. I have sometimes stubbornly resisted the good advice of all these generous and wise people, but I have always tried to accommodate their objections, if not always in ways they would approve, and I am grateful for their help. I am also grateful to the University of Alabama, which twice gave me leave from teaching and administrative duties to work on this book, once at Princeton University, where I was a visiting fellow, and once at the University of St. Andrews, where I was Royal Bank of Scotland Research Fellow in the learned company of John Haldane and Gordon Graham, who made valuable suggestions.

Chapter 15, "Must Relativists Tolerate Evil" and "Reply to Sullivan" are reprinted *Philosophical Forum* and *Philosophia*.

Preface

Scientific naturalism has now triumphed in every field of inquiry except moral philosophy. Here it is still thought appropriate to cite otherworldly standards known only by such esoteric means as divine revelation and its secular relic, moral intuition. No single author can hope to change so deeply entrenched a way of thinking, but the present book is a contribution to the ongoing attempt. Its topic is what, in the trade, are called *normative judgments*, and its aim is to show that these have empirically knowable truth conditions. Against conventional wisdom, I argue that there is no transcendent reality on which to base the claims of ethics and no high road to its truths. Instead, I say, normative truth must be sought in the desires of individuals and the customs of societies.

Moral philosophy is about what people ought to do, but you will find here no instruction on how to lead your life or remake your society. This book does not *make* normative judgments; it seeks to *explain* them. Its aim is not moral and political reform but conceptual and logical clarification, the only task for which a philosopher can claim special qualification. I try to show not what you ought to do but what it means to say that you ought to do it —in other words, what must be so for the statement to be true. In my view, moral instruction is no part of philosophy proper, and intellectuals, who live in ivory towers, may be the last persons from whom you should seek advice on how to lead your life or remake your society. In the end, it must be left up to you to decide how to behave. My desire is to facilitate your doing that by clarifying the fundamental issues.

Briefly stated, my thesis is that what you *ought* (that is, *have reason*) to do is determined by your biologically based desires and by the rules of law, morality, and etiquette to which you happen to be subject as a member of some society. More briefly still: You ought to do what promises to serve your interests and comport with your group's customs. I regard as all but meaningless the question "What interests ought you to have?" In my view, interests are given by nature and made specific by nurture. So, although there is much choosing between desires, there is little choosing of desires. Empirical meaning *can* be given to the question, "What customs or conventions ought a society to have?" and the answer is roughly "Those that promise to serve the needs and fulfill the desires of its members." But what will do that cannot be known in advance. Because it will vary with circumstances, it must be learned the hard way, by trial and error.

My empiricism about these matters contradicts long-standing belief that what you ought to do is determined by transcendent but intuitively known standards of Goodness and Justice. In my view, there are no such standards. As B. F. Skinner pointed out, we call *good* what reinforces our desires, and we call *right* or *just* what we desire to reinforce. In the final analysis, then, desire is the measure of both goodness and justice, not the other way around. Rationalist belief — that we ought to desire what is antecedently know to be good and to reinforce what is antecedently known to be right—gets the cart before the horse. It also detaches normative judgments from the very things that give them such determinate meaning as they have for us, leaving them largely emotive. I hope to subvert this *a priori* philosophy by showing that the determinants of rational and moral conduct are contingent facts of the matter, not self-evident principles.

The showing, which owes much to the writings of Gilbert Harman, is offered as an alternative to two other accounts that are favored by empiricists. These are A.J. Ayer's despairing belief that normative judgments lack truth values because they express attitudes and guide conduct and J. L. Mackie's equally pessimistic belief that these judgments are false because they presuppose nonexistent standards. Against Ayer, I argue that pragmatics and semantics need not exclude each other. Against Mackie, I develop Hobbes's observation that normative judgments are indexed to their users, each person describing as good what he or his auditor prefers, each society describing as right or just what its members prefer. Following Skinner, I define the *good* as that which reinforces preference for it, the *right* (or *just*) as that for which preference is reinforced by other persons in the society. Then I note that, since what reinforces A might not reinforce B, the good is relative to persons, and since what is reinforced in S1 might be discouraged in S2, justice (or rectitude) is relative to societies. All of this enables me to show how to assign truth values to suitably relative judgments. Defining the good and the right in terms of reinforcement also makes it immediately clear how factual statements about these can motivate behavior, a difficulty for other analyses.

The claim that goodness is relative to personal preferences and rectitude to social conventions must not be confused with two other doctrines that I firmly reject. One is subjectivism—belief that there is no truth about these matters, just opinions. I hold no such view. Instead, I argue that truth, including the truth about the goodness of a thing or the rectitude of an act, is absolute, independent of opinions. It is goodness and rectitude that are relative, the first to individuals, the second to societies. My relativism amounts, then, simply to belief that well-formed statements about goodness and rectitude are either relational in form or indexed to their users. I have no use for subjectivist belief that a thing has value, or an action is right, for you if you think so. The distinction will seem paradoxical to those who believe, with Plato, G. E. Moore, and W. D. Ross that values are simple qualities, like shape. So, I try to make it intelligible by comparing goodness and rectitude to location, which is relational yet independent of opinions.

The second doctrine that I reject is the belief that one person's preferences and one society's institutions are as good as another's. In my view, this doctrine is incoherent. Necessarily, every man regards as good what comports with *his* preferences and beliefs; and every woman has the same attitude toward *her* preferences. If the preferences of other persons conflict with your own, then you necessarily regard them as regrettable if not also evil. If they do not threaten you or your interests, you need not take the same view respecting the institutions of society, your own or that of other persons, but this does not mean that you must refrain from believing either that these institutions could have been better designed or that they could be improved. On the contrary, I insist that, since a society's morality and law are man-made, they can be made well or poorly, like everything else. The only point I insist on is that evaluations presuppose values, and moral judgments presuppose moralities. We are human beings, not gods. So, contrary to Thomas Nagel, there is no "view from nowhere"—no Olympian perspective from which to make evaluations that are wholly disinterested or moral judgments that can be detached from familiar social practices.

There is, of course, such a thing as human nature, and although I do not believe that a form of conduct is desirable just because it is natural, I also do not believe that you can transgress human nature without paying a price—the greater the transgression, the greater the price. Because human beings everywhere possess a common biology, it is also true that individual needs and social customs are much alike everywhere, the differences being mostly attributable to historical accident and geographical circumstance. But, contrary to rationalist belief, we are not disembodied bits of Pure Reason. Instead, we are animals, with bodies. So, what will satisfy our needs cannot be known *a priori*. It has to be discovered by a largely biological inquiry. If you are interested in how such an inquiry might go, I recommend the writings of the sociobiologists and evolutionary psychologists. It is with inquiries like these, not with armchair reflection on the nature of Goodness and Justice, that we must begin if we are ever to have realistic hope of improving the lot of mankind. I say this, however, only to reemphasize that the present work is not such an inquiry. As noted already, its immediate aim is more modest. My citation, at the beginning of the first chapter, from biologist E. O. Wilson's *Consilience* is intended only to indicate a kinship of philosophical outlook; not to suggest that I will engage in biological speculation.

The book has two main parts. The first, which I have just described, is mostly an account of the positive doctrine—an empiricist analysis of normative judgments. Although it too contains constructive argument, the second part is mostly a polemic against rationalist belief that normative concepts cannot be defined in empirical terms, because they are about the Moral Law or other ideals of Pure Reason. Against this belief, which is premised on Platonic semantic theory, I point out that, if the Moral Law exists only as an ideal, it does not *exist* and is not *binding* in the same senses of these words as the empirically known laws and moralities of concrete societies. Against Platonic semantic theory, which treats the Good as a transcendent ideal, I marshal objections from Bertrand Russell, Wittgenstein, and Eleanor Rosch, then add a trick or two of my own. To the reply that these arguments conflict with the rationalist's intuitions, my rejoinder is that these do not have the evidentiary value that rationalists like to attribute to them. Although the rationalist regards his "intuitions" as insights into *a priori* principles of Moral Reason, the evidence comports better with the theory that they are expressions of animal instinct, socially conditioned prejudice, and personal preference—what Hume called sentiment. In the absence of independent confirmation, which is never forthcoming, it begs the question to *presume* that the rationalist's intuitions constitute evidence for the reality of entities that the empiricist has called into question.

Part III contains two chapters, one defending Part I from the charge that it is self-refecting, the other extending the ideas of Parts I and II to the concept of rights.

The writing was begun more years ago than I care to remember, at the suggestion of William Provine of the Department of Biology of Princeton University. Having read a breezy essay I had written for an anthology on *Humanistic Ethics* put together by Morris Storer for Prometheus Books, Provine wanted me to write a book for the educated reader and amateur philosopher. The main feature of this book was to be absence of technical argumentation. After Gilbert Harman of Princeton's Department of Philosophy warned me that ethics is a field in which one can not expect to change minds, I undertook to comply with Provine's request. My book would answer the philosophers' arguments, but it would be written in a readable style, and it would not address the philosophers themselves. After countless revisions, the final result has departed greatly from the original intention. Because I believe that, in matters moral and political, plain English contributes to clarity, increases precision, and helps to bring high abstractions down to earth where they can be examined more thoroughly, I avoid the usual jargon and define it when I cannot avoid it, but my commitment to argument and the desire to come to terms with my fellow philosophers has altered the book's aims and its style. The writing remains plain, and I have spared no effort to make it clear, but it is now somewhat more sober and didactic than before, as befits the topic.

I fear that I must apologize for the frequent repetition of central points. When I started, I had hoped to develop a linear outline that would make repetition unnecessary. I found as I went along that the argument had to be woven, like a rug, by a line of thought that kept crossing itself at critical points. However, these are stated briefly when used as premises, more fully when drawn as conclusions; so, perhaps the repetition is excusable after all. I hope that it will at least emphasize what is important. It should also have the advantage of enabling the book's chapters to be read in almost any order the reader pleases.

The repetition of examples has a related purpose: to remind the reader of the arguments in which these examples originally figured.

Since I am mainly interested in making points of logic and clarifying diction, not advancing empirical claims about matters of fact, the examples are offered as illustrations, not as evidence. Therefore, it seemed better that they be few. For the same reason, it seemed better that they be trite and undisputed. I do occasionally venture side comments that are more contentious.

1

Abstract*

"Ethics, in the empiricist view, is conduct favored consistently enough throughout a society to be expressed as a code of principles. It is driven by hereditary pre-dispositions in mental development—the "moral sentiments" of the Enlightenment philosophers—causing broad convergence across cultures, while reaching precise form in each culture according to historical circumstance. The codes, whether judged by outsiders as good or evil, play an important role in determining which cultures flourish, and which decline."—E. O. Wilson, Consilience, p. 240.

"If the Empiricist world view is correct, ought is just shorthand for one kind of factual statement, a word that denotes what society first chose (or was coerced to do), and then codified. The naturalistic fallacy is thereby reduced to the naturalistic dilemma. The solution of the dilemma is not difficult. It is this: Ought is the product of a material process. The solution points the way to an objective grasp of the origin of ethics."—Ibid., p. 249

I

The word *ought* has two main uses. In one, what someone ought to do is what he would be well advised to do in order to improve his chances of achieving his ends or serving his interests. This may be called a *prudential*, or *rational*, use of the word *ought*. In another use,

* The word *abstract* is here meant literally. The arguments adumbrated here are spelled out in greater detail in the chapters that follow. It is to these chapters that the reader must repair if he wishes to understand these arguments well enough to evaluate them. The purpose of this abstract is to provide a guide to the chapters that follow, not to provide a substitute for them. The chapter titles should make it clear where a particular argument is elaborated most fully; so, there is no need to clutter the text with references.

what someone ought to do is what she is required, or obligated, to do by the rules of law, morality, or etiquette to which she happens to be subject as a member of some society. This may be called a *juridical*, or *moral*, use of the word *ought.*

As Gilbert Harman has observed, the connection between these two uses is that someone ought, other things being equal, to do what there is reason for him to do; it is just that the reason may be either prudential or moral. In a third, derivative, use of the word, we say that a person ought to do not what *she* has reason to do but what *we* have reason to prefer her to do, because we think her doing it would be a good thing. Here again the central concept is *reason.*

Since ethics is about what people *ought* to do, this means that its central question is "What is a reason, and when does someone have reason to do, or prefer that someone else do, something?"

The oldest and still the best answer to this question is that a *reason* is anything that can, does, or will, serve as a *motive.* In day to day speech, we describe as a reason for an event or an action anything that can explain, or cause it. Thus, we say, the reason the lamp fell is that Sarah bumped into it, the reason Sarah bumped into the lamp is that Sam pushed her, and the reason Sam pushed her is that he was angry. To give a reason for someone to do something is, then, to say what could, or under the right conditions would, cause her to do it. In short, a reason is an actual or potential *motive.*

Specifying such a motive requires constructing what Aristotle called a *practical syllogism*, which explains conduct by postulating an appropriate combination of desires with beliefs. Thus, we say "Mary is going to the grocery store because she wants some milk and believes she can get it there." In this syllogism, the desire supplies the motive power; the belief gives it direction.

The prescriptive, or normative, counterpart to this syllogism is "Mary wants some milk and believes she can get it at the grocer, so she should go to the grocer." Here the desire and the belief are the same as before, but in this case they constitute a potential rather than an actual motive. The motive will become actual when it begins to effect the behavior in question. This simple fact shows how the normative is dependent on the descriptive.

In the examples just used, the motive was desire. There are other motives besides desire, but it is customary in moral philosophy to treat these as kinds of desire, because it simplifies the argument.

Thus, fear counts as a desire to avoid something, love as a desire to possess it, anger as a desire to destroy it, and so on. This is a loose way to talk, but it has become conventional, and there can be no objection to it so long as we satisfy the main requirement, which, to quote Hume, is to specify something with the capacity to "move the will."

For that purpose to be served, we must understand that, in behavioral contexts, talk of desires, interests, and other motives denotes not *feelings* but *dispositions*. A desire is what economists call a *preference function*, an inclination to prefer one thing to another. Thus, a desire for happiness is a disposition to prefer what you believe will make you happy, and a desire for prestige is a disposition to prefer what you believe will bring prestige.

Explaining behavior by invoking desires is pointing out how the behavior manifests the relevant disposition. Thus, we say, "Jones ate because he was hungry," understanding that hunger is a disposition to eat. Like explaining why dropped objects fall by invoking gravity, the tendency of objects to fall, this has an appearance of circularity. It is, rather, an example of fitting a case to a rule.

An illusion of circularity also attends specification of belief. Despite conventional wisdom, neither beliefs nor desires come to us labeled as such. They must be inferred from the behavior, as its most likely explanation, but we can identify the belief only presupposing a certain desire, and conversely. So, we must identify the belief and the desire together, but how are we to know whether we have identified the right combination?

The answer is that we can not, but we can know whether we have found a combination that will do the job. Since many hypotheses will do that, we can never be sure that we have found the correct one; but it is a truism of science that explanatory hypotheses always exceed the data. So, you pays your money and you takes your chances.

Given that they are such difficult entities to identify and define, why must we invoke beliefs and desires? Because, so far, that is what is *meant* by explaining behavior. To understand human behavior is just to postulate a combination of beliefs and desires from which we can infer it. Where we can imagine no combination of beliefs and desires from which to deduce the behavior in question, we find it unintelligible. Thus, the behavior of madmen surpasses comprehension.

That understanding behavior requires us to discern the beliefs and desires that motivate it has an important implication. Since what motivates A may leave B unmoved, reasons are *relative to persons*; nothing is a reason absolutely, in itself.

This conclusion is also evident from grammar. The logical form of reasons is not "R is a reason," but "R is a reason for person P to do action A." Thus, it is the bandit, not the honest citizen, who has reason to carry a gun, and it is the peace-loving Christian, not the Samurai warrior, who has reason to turn the other cheek. Reasons are personal. Mine are mine and yours are yours.

Deriding this view as *egoism*, critics have objected that it constitutes an apology for selfishness, but the objection confuses ownership with object. By all accounts, Mother Theresa's consuming passion was to improve the lot of the poor; she had little interest in her personal welfare. This entitles us to say that her motives were unselfish. No matter. These motives were distinctively *hers*. If I had wanted to give Mother Theresa a reason for doing something, I had better have shown her how doing it would serve *her* personal but unselfish ends. Telling her merely how it would have served *my* personal but selfish ends would not have sufficed. If a name for this doctrine is wanted, it is better called *internalism*.

The internalist may be thought to overlook what H.L.A. Hart called *external judgment*, meaning judgment made from the observer's point of view. Suppose I say, "Rockefeller *ought* to give us his fortune." I do not mean that Rockefeller has reason to give us his fortune. I mean that I have reason to prefer that he do so. Such a judgment is also internal—to the beliefs and desires of the observer if not also the agent.

Many philosophers have objected that this view overlooks "objective" reasons—reasons that do not depend on "subjective" beliefs or desires. This thesis is hard to evaluate, because the word "objective" is ambiguous. When Thomas Nagel uses it, he means *impersonal* reasons, reasons having no identification with any particular person. In *The Possibility of Altruism,* he claims that reasons are impersonal in the following sense: If one person has reason to do something, every person has reason to "promote" his doing it. According to Nagel, refusal to respect this principle constitutes "practical solipsism," denial in practice [if not also in words] of the reality of other persons.

The argument is fallacious. Does Smith want to kill Jones? Jones's refusal to help Smith find the gun is a denial not of Smith's *reality* but his project's *desirability*, quite a different thing. The concept of an impersonal reason is a logical and metaphysical muddle.

In another sense of the word, objective reasons exist. In support of Nagel, E. J. Bond has reminded us that there might *be* a reason that one does not *have*, or *know*. For example, suppose that Jones does not know that he could make money investing in the market. Then this fact will not motivate him. No matter. It still constitutes reason for him to invest; he just does not know it.

The premise is true but the argument fails. In the sense just defined, objective reasons exist, but we call them reasons because we can see how they would *become* motives if they were known. So, they constitute no exceptions to the principle that a reason is an actual or potential motive. Furthermore, the existence of reasons that are objective in this sense provides no support for Nagel's view. That money could be made investing in the market will motivate *Jones*, who wants money, but not *Smith*, who is indifferent to it. Even "objective" reasons are relative to persons.

Also in support of Nagel, Stephen Darwall has objected that reasons are not what *do* or what *would* but what *should* motivate behavior. At first hearing, this sounds right, but it creates a vicious circle. If "x ought to do y" means "x has reason R to do y" and this means "x ought to be motivated by R to do y," then we have used the word *ought* to define itself, making no progress.

Following Kant and Plato, Nagel also tries another tack: He argues that one can be *motivated* to do what one believes to be good, even when one lacks any *desire* to do it. This hypothesis, which attempts to disconnect reasons from desires, is mystifying. Given that a disposition to prefer something constitutes a desire for it, preference for the good must also count as a desire. If not, what should we call it, and what could it mean to say that someone was motivated to do what he lacked all desire to do? That he prefers to do what he does *not* prefer to do? Neither Nagel, Kant, nor Plato has answers for these questions.

The mistake all of these philosophers make is to suppose that we can conceive of the good as independent of desire. Plato thought so because he knew that, out of ignorance, people often make mistakes, desiring what is not good and failing to desire what is. Because knowledge that something is good can motivate us to pursue it, he concluded that you can be motivated by simple knowledge, without an accompanying desire.

Anxious, like Plato, to make morality "autonomous," Kant said the same thing about duty. According to him, you can be moved to do it by Reason alone, without the support of Desire. Just recognize that you have a duty and you will be motivated to fulfill it. Kant believed that, if recognition of duty lacked this motivating power, we could not explain why people do their duty when they would prefer, for other reasons, not to.

This reasoning has a false premise. As B.F. Skinner observed, we call *good* that which we believe will *reinforce* desire. So, there is no defining the good without mentioning desire. It is true that the *morally good*, or *right*, may not itself be reinforcing, but it will be reinforced by those who are reinforced by it. So, it too falls under the heading of what reinforces desire. We have no conception of the good or the right as something entirely independent of desire.

John Stuart Mill was right after all. Although we cannot equate the good with what is desired, we can attach no meaning to the idea that something might be good but not such as to elicit, or reinforce, desire. G. E. Moore tried to do so by saying that the good *ought* to be desired, because it *deserves* to be desired, but this idea is paradoxical. What could it mean to say that some conduct was so good it deserved to be repeated even if, having experienced it, no one would ever want to do so again?

Moore also replied that, if desire were the measure of the good, there would be no bad desires; sweet and fatty foods would be good things. The answer to this is that sweet and fatty foods *are* good things; just think of the pleasures of butter pecan ice cream! It counts as bad only because we have learned that it can be unhealthy in large quantities and because we desire good health. Although not everything desired is good, desire remains the measure of what is.

If Moore had a different opinion, it is because he assumed, like Plato, that the goodness of a thing or action is intrinsic to it, as spherical shape and, in his view, yellow color are intrinsic to a lemon. According to Moore, goodness is a "simple" quality, one that the good thing would have even if there were nobody in the world to acknowledge it or appreciate it. In short, "x is good" has the same logical form as "x is round" and, Moore believed, "x is yellow."

Nowadays, its proponents call this doctrine *moral realism.* It is also frequently called *moral objectivism.* The essence of the view is, however, that good things are good absolutely, not relatively to persons. So, a better name for it is *moral absolutism.*

Whatever it is called, the doctrine is demonstrably false. If, as just observed, the good is what reinforces preference for it, then it is relative to persons; for what reinforces A's preferences will not reinforce B's. Thus, licorice tastes good to you, bad to me. Thus, my getting the job you wanted is good for me, bad for you. If by *intrinsically* good we mean *absolutely* good, then nothing is intrinsically good. Even an act of giving one's fortune to the poor would not in the required sense be intrinsically good; just good for the poor.

The stock reply is that, since *good* and *bad* are contraries, the same thing cannot be *both* good for A *and* bad for B. This argument is usually thought to be decisive, but one might as well argue that, since *near* and *far* are contraries, the Eiffel Tower cannot be both near Jacques in Paris and far from Jack in New York.

To think in this way is to ignore the main point, which is that good is relative, like location, not absolute, like shape or color. As Hobbes said, the word *good* is an indexical term, which each of us uses "in relation to himself," to denote what *he* prefers. Hence, as "x is near" is elliptical for "x is near *me*," so "x is good" is short for "x is preferable to *me*," and what is preferable to me might be anathema to you.

It will be objected that this makes value to be a matter of opinion; so, mistake proof. Not by any means. Where the Eiffel Tower is located is an objective matter of fact, one that is independent of Jacques's, or Jack's, beliefs. The thing is not near Jacques, far from Jack, *because they think so*. They think so *because it is true*. Location is objective, independent of opinions. It is also relative. So is goodness. Licorice does not taste good to you, bad to me, because we think so. We think so because it is true.

The present doctrine is often called *subjectivism*, but the term is misleading. If a name is wanted, a better one would be *objective relativism*, or *relationalism.*

Critics may agree that the *aesthetically* good is relative to persons, but they will have a different idea about the *morally good*. According to Kant, the morally good is so independently of everything else. Thus, he held, an act of telling the truth, or keeping your promises, must count as good even when it does not reinforce your desire to do it again.

This is so, however, because people usually like to be told the truth, if not always to tell it. So, the case constitutes no counterexample. It merely highlights the need to get clear about *whose* desire is being reinforced. As observed earlier, we count as morally good not acts the doing of which reinforces the *agent's* desire to repeat them but acts which reinforce the *observer's* desire to have them repeated.

Given this explanation, it is no harder to understand why one should be moral than why one should be prudent. Why do we give up smoking despite the fact that we take pleasure in it? Because there is greater pleasure, and less pain, in having healthy lungs. Why do we do the moral thing even when we know it will be costly? Because our happiness is dependent on the good opinion and good will of others, who will think better of us if we make doing the right thing a habit.

To say so is not to say that hope for reward and fear of punishment are the only reasons to behave morally. Not so. These may be the reasons of unruly children and criminals, but well-reared adults do the right thing automatically, without worrying about reward or punishment, because they *want to*. For them, virtue has become its own reward. Doing the right act has become a habit, principle, or value. Thus, most of us prefer telling the truth, even when we know that it will cost us. If nothing else, it avoids the guilt that we would feel if we lied.

Behavioral psychologists have a name, even if they lack an explanation, for this phenomenon: They say that, in well reared adults, the desire to do the right thing becomes *functionally autonomous*, independent of the rewards that originally fostered it; so, it persists without additional reinforcement. In some cases, it may even persist in the face of punishment. Thus, men and women with strong consciences will suffer imprisonment, torture, or even death rather than violate their principles.

Still, even in these cases, a habit of doing the right thing is the result of a previous history, one in which the agent was taught by the use of suitable rewards or punishments. Furthermore, although the habit can become to some extent autonomous, it can also be *extinguished*. Even deeply entrenched conduct will change if it ceases to be rewarded or is punished severely and consistently. It never becomes completely independent of what reinforces it.

Morally good conduct includes *duty*, or *obligation*. Because it is praiseworthy even when it is not obligatory, charity counts as morally good, but it is not a duty. By contrast, lying makes one liable to condemnation, so telling the truth is a duty. The difference? Charity is something that other persons *desire,* while performance of duty, or fulfillment of obligation, is something that they *require*.

Once again, this does not mean that the existence of a requirement is the only reason to do one's duty. Not so. As the sociobiologists have emphasized, we are social creatures, who have an innate, because evolutionarily adaptive, propensity to behave as others in our group wish us to. Furthermore, as Hobbes explained, living under a system of rules with their corresponding obligations is to everyone's advantage; so, we have an interest in maintaining and complying with the rules, even when there is no immediate promise of reward or threat of punishment.

Still, what makes complying with a rule an obligation is the fact that breaking it might expose you to punishment, or to withholding of reward. Formally: person P has obligation O (or duty D) to do action A just in case P is subject, *under the applicable rules*, to an enforceable requirement to do A, and this is so just in case there is a practice of enforcing this requirement by punishing those who do not fulfill it.

We must, of course, distinguish the case where one is *obligated* to do something from the case where one is merely *obliged* to do it. As H. L. A. Hart has explained, the difference is that between being subject to a rule and being exposed to arbitrary coercion. Despite libertarian belief that taxation is thievery, there is a big difference between the two things. However obnoxious it may be, taxation is in accordance with the law; thievery is not.

This needs to be emphasized because some philosophers wrongly believe that one must agree to, or accept, an obligation to have it. They need to be reminded that the social contract is a myth. I have never agreed, formally or informally, to the scheme of taxation to which I am subject. Like most people, I have only acquiesced to it .

The obligation to pay taxes is imposed by a rule of *law*, but there are also obligations of *morality* and *etiquette*. The difference? Rules of law are made and enforced by officials of government acting in their capacities as officials, while rules of morality and etiquette are made and enforced by ordinary persons in the course of their daily lives. Thus, a law proscribing murder is enforced by officially fixed prison sentence, while rules against cheating at cards are reinforced by refusing to play.

Because different societies have different rules, what is *legal*, *moral*, and *mannerly* varies from one society to the next. Thus, polygamy is legal, moral and mannerly *in Saudi Arabia*, but it is illegal, immoral, and ill-mannered *in Selma, Alabama*. Some practices—for example, patriarchy and avoidance of incest—are universal, because rooted in a common, biologically based, human nature, but the existence of differences between societies means that what is legal or moral or mannerly in one place may not be so in another.

This view may fairly be regarded as a form of moral relativism, but it must not be confused with the view, sometimes called *cultural relativism*, that one society's institutions and customs are as good as another's. If, as is claimed here, all rules are man-made, then, it is clear, they can be made well or poorly. Hence, even the best societies often have some very bad rules. The only claim made here is that, however bad a society's rules may be, they determine what, in that society, is to count as just.

If they determine what is just, how can the rules be criticized as bad? In several ways. First, the rules can be criticized on the grounds that they do not produce the desired result, or produce results that are not desired. In other words, they do no good, or do more harm than good. Secondly, the rules can be criticized on the grounds that they contradict each other, one permitting what the other forbids, or requiring what the other makes optional. And so on. The vocabulary of evaluation is extensive, and there is no reason why we should not use all of it.

It is true, of course, that evaluations of the rules will themselves be relative—either to the preferences and principles of those affected or to the preferences and principles of observers, but on the present theory, there is no way to avoid this. It is inherent in the act of evaluation.

This view is also not to be confused with *subjectivism,* belief that right and wrong are matters of opinion. Polygamy is not permissible in Saudi Arabia because the Saudis think so, impermissible in Selma, Alabama because the Selmans think so; they think so because it is true. What makes a practice to be —that is, constitutes it as—moral or immoral in a society is its *conventions*, not its *convictions*. So, a better name for what we have in mind might be *conventionalism.*

Whatever it is called, the view will contravene what most people believe—that the requirements of morality are absolute, not relative.

Thus, the Saudi believes that polygamy is absolutely permissible, not just permissible in Arabia, and the Selman believes that polygamy is absolutely impermissible, not just impermissible in Alabama.

What this shows is merely that both the Saudi and the Selman are mistaken. Each believes that he is giving voice to a culturally transcendent and universally binding Morality when, in fact, he is voicing the rule to which he has been conditioned because it is in force in his society. No other hypothesis explains the facts so well.

Some philosophers will argue that this view is incoherent. Because the words *moral* and *immoral* are contraries, they will say that no practice can be both moral in S1 and immoral in S2. However, the words *legal* and *illegal* are contraries, as are the words *mannerly* and *ill-mannered.* Yet few people have any difficulty understanding that what is legal in one place might be illegal in another, or that what was once mannerly may no longer be so. Why should it be harder to understand the exactly analogous claim regarding morality?

G. J. Warnock once answered that there is no analogy between law on the one hand and morality on the other, because laws are *made* while morality is *recognized.* Thus, he said, we make laws against speeding in built up areas because we recognize that the practice is already objectionable without the law. Warnock allowed that a practice can be made illegal by a convention proscribing it, but he believed that nothing can be made immoral in this way.

Warnock's idea is commonplace but confused. Grant that law is made. So are morality and etiquette, but in different ways. Laws are made by officials; morality and etiquette by ordinary persons. Grant, too, that the rules of morality and etiquette have to be recognized before they can be enforced and obeyed. The same is true of the rules of law. Grant, finally, that speeding in congested areas is *objectionable* just because it is dangerous, even where there is no law against it. The practice is *illegal* only where it is proscribed by law, and it is *immoral* or *ill mannered* only where it is proscribed by the conventions of morality or etiquette. So, the analogy holds.

If this reply does not seem to meet Warnock's objections, it is because his argument presupposes an unstated belief—that there is a thing called Morality that consists not of local conventions but of culturally transcendent principles. According to medieval doctrine, these are divine commands. According to Enlightenment theory, they are innately known truths of Reason. According to both theories, human beings can recognize and comply with Morality, but they cannot alter it or replace it with principles of their own. Warnock's arguments presuppose this belief.

To give a complete answer to Warnock, we must show what is wrong with this belief.

II

In an ancient tradition that stems from Plato, ethics has to do with what *ought to be* rather than what *is*. So, it must be pursued like pure mathematics, by reflecting on previously given ideals, or concepts. If this view is right, we discover what is good not *a posteriori,* by learning what elicits or reinforces desire, but *a priori*, by contemplating a previously given understanding of *the Good*. Similarly, if this view is right, we discover what is just not *a posteriori*, by learning about the law that happens to be in force in our society, but *a priori*, by thinking about a previously given concept of *Justice*.

Proponents of this view often call it *rationalism*, but it is not belief in reason; it is belief in Reason—reason uncontaminated by experience. So, I shall call it Rationalism, and I shall argue that it is mistaken in principle. Neither the good nor the just can be known *a priori,* just by thinking about it. Instead, they must both be discovered empirically. The contrary view detaches the language of conduct from the things—individual desires and social conventions—that give this language such determinate meaning as it has for us, making it largely emotive.

Who are these Rationalists? As already noted, the first was Plato, who held that to discover what is good and just we must study not empirically known facts but previously given ideals, or concepts. These ideals can be known, Plato said, by means of a combination of *intuition*, or immediate insight, with *analysis*, or definition. Plato called this combination *Reason* and argued that the use of Reason enables philosophers to decide which things are good and which practices are just.

In the Christian Middle Ages, Plato's view was transformed into belief that the good and the just are determined by the creative act of God and can be known by means of a combination of divine revelation with God-given reason. The essence of Christian morality is the

Golden Rule, doing unto others as you would have them do unto you, because every man is equal in the eyes of God.

Hoping to avoid basing ethics on disputable claims of theology, Kant reverted to Plato's belief that the required principles are known by Pure Reason alone. The chief such principle, according to Kant, is the Categorical Imperative. Like the Golden Rule, this principle presupposes belief in the essential equality of all human beings—a proposition that is not vouchsafed by experience but is postulated by Kant as an article of moral and metaphysical faith.

Kant's line of thought has been extended by John Rawls. As Rawls points out in a lengthy footnote to *A Theory of Justice*, his "Method of Reflective Equilibrium" is essentially Henry Sidgwick's "method of intuition." Its aim is to discover *a priori* truths of Reason by reflecting, behind a "veil of ignorance," on a previously given ideal of Justice. Thus, thinkers in "the original position" are to conduct their deliberations in ignorance of all empirically known facts, in order the better to get clear about a previously given concept of justice, one that assigns equal and absolute worth to all human beings.

What is wrong with this Rationalist line of thought? Everything.

First, there is no reason to believe that intuition has the evidentiary authority attributed to it by Rationalists. In *Methods of Ethics*, Henry Sidgwick started with the hypothesis that intuitions reveal convictions that are common to the whole of mankind, but he eventually saw that this cannot be reconciled with the fact that moral feeling varies, both with individuals and with societies. Thus, the intuitions of Arabians favor polygamy, while those of Alabamians favor monogamy. This fact is best explained by the hypothesis that these intuitions, if not all of them, are socially conditioned prejudices.

In this respect, moral belief is quite unlike mathematical belief, with which Rationalists like to compare it. People do not disagree about 2+2; they do disagree, or at least they differ, about polygamy. Sidgwick's follower W. D. Ross dealt with this uncomfortable fact by claiming special authority for the intuitions of "educated men in civilized societies," but this gives up the original claim, which was that moral intuitions are expressions of a culturally universal Reason.

The really serious objection to intuitionism is, however, not that it constitutes special pleading for privileged authority (although it does) but that there is no way to confirm or refute the insights it is alleged to provide. In this respect, appeals to intuition resemble appeals to special revelation. These cannot be refuted, but there is also no obligation to accept them. Philosophers who think otherwise may no longer *be* theologians, but they still *think* like them. As Alasdair MacIntyre has said, an appeal to intuition in moral philosophy is a virtual admission that the author's argument has gone wrong somewhere.

With intuition goes conceptual analysis, the other half of Rationalist method. They are two sides of a single *a priori* method.

The main trouble with this method is that it detaches the vocabulary of conduct from the personal desires and social conventions that give it meaning. As we normally use these terms, the *good* is what elicits, or reinforces, desire; the *just* what conforms to law, or other rules. The Rationalist obscures this by claiming that (1) to behave rationally, you must pursue not what you desire but the Good, an other-worldly standard known *a priori* and (2) to behave justly, you must do what is required not by the rules of your society but by the Moral Law, another transcendent standard known *a priori*. This detaches practical language from its empirical moorings, rendering it meaningless.

Rationalist talk of equality provides a perfect illustration. We have some idea what it means to say that two human beings are equal in height, weight, strength, intelligence, business acumen, or beauty. These are all empirically discernible qualities that we know how to measure. By contrast, we have no idea what it means to assert that human beings are all "equal in the eyes of God," so, equal in some way that is essential to morality. This does not make the claim false; it makes it meaningless. How are we to understand the claim that men are equal when no one can say how? And why should people be treated equally if there is no respect in which they are equal?

Not all Rationalists are egalitarians. Plato was a resolute aristocrat, showing that Rationalism is capable of yielding any view. Plato merely had different intuitions than Aquinas and Kant, both of whom were Christians, the true source of belief in equality.

The root of Rationalism, whether egalitarian or elitist, is a mistaken view of the meanings of words. According to this view, which was first advanced in Plato's *Phaedo* as a basis for a proof of immortality, to say of an object that it is circular is to say that it resembles the ideal Circle, the most nearly perfect circle there is. Other things count as circular only by comparison with this ideal. Similarly, Plato said, things are called good because they resemble the Good, the best thing there is; and laws are called just because they resemble the Just, the most truly just thing there is.

This theory is mistaken. Predication is not comparison to an ideal. As Eleanor Rosch has shown, it is comparison to other empirically known entities. "This is circular" does not mean "This is like the [ideal] Circle." It means, "This is like that [actual] circle." "This is good" does not mean" This resembles the [ideal] Good." It means, "This resembles that [actual] good." We do not start out comparing things to a transcendent ideal. We start out comparing things to each other, then construct an ideal using the comparison. This is a fair horse; that is a better one; if it could be found, one still better would be ideal.

Owing mainly to the work of Gottlob Frege and Bertrand Russell, the defects of Rationalist semantic theory are now known to most philosophers, but the doctrine still influences their thought about morality. This is especially evident in the belief —now called *moral realism*—that a thing should count as good, or an action as just, only if it possesses an intuitively evident quality.

Early in this century, G. E. Moore claimed that, since the Good is too simple to be defined, you have to discern it directly, by means of a special kind of insight, or *intuition*. When asked why the good could not be perceived by means of the several senses, Moore said that it is a *non-natural* quality, one that can be discerned only by means of the mind. When asked why there appears to be no similarity between good music, good food, good people, and good behavior, Moore said that goodness is a *supervenient* quality, one that depends on a variety of other properties.

This line of thought refutes itself. To assert that the elements of a certain set all have a certain quality in common is to say that there is some way in which they *discernibly resemble* each other. Yet, saying that goodness is a *non-natural* quality makes it a mystery how it is to be discerned, and saying that this resemblance *supervenes* on a wide variety of different properties is not explaining but denying its reality. Hence, J. L. Mackie and A. J. Ayer were led by considerations exactly like Moore's to draw conclusions contrary to his.

John McDowell believes that the difficulties emphasized by Mackie and Ayer can be resolved by noting that goodness is a "secondary quality." Here, McDowell uses a term that was invented by Locke, who said that a secondary quality is not a *quality* but a *power*. The things that have this power resemble each other only in producing perceptions of the quality "in us." Thus, yellow objects are alike in causing us to see them as yellow, and good things are alike in causing us to prefer them.

McDowell's reply—that colors are phenomenal, if not physical, qualities of objects—does not rebut this observation; it confirms it. On any natural interpretation of this claim, a *phenomenal* but not *physical* property is one that the object appears to have but in fact does not. So, although McDowell's comparison of goodness with color has merit, it does not support, it refutes, moral realism, in two ways. First, that objects affect us in the same way does not mean that they are alike; only that our response to them is the same. Ice cream and sexual intercourse both give us pleasure, but they resemble each other in no further respect. Second, what gives you pleasure may displease me, showing that if goodness is a power to please, it is not in the thing itself but in the relation between it and the people it pleases.

Rationalist talk of justice is subject to similar criticism. According to Plato, we should describe as just what conforms not to actual but to ideal law. Aquinas agreed, claiming that law which does not conform to the ideal is not really law but only an imitation of law.

This thesis has proved to be popular, but it is also indefensible. There is no difficulty with belief that justice is what comports with law. The problem is that a merely ideal but otherwise non-existing law is not itself a kind of *law*. It is merely an *ideal* . So, it can no more determine real justice than a merely ideal horse can win a real race.

The Rationalist who thinks otherwise has overlooked the fact that we learn juridical language, as we learn other language, by reference not to *a priori* ideals but to determinate cases. In the first instance, we describe as *just* what comports with the rules that happen to be in force in *our* society—the one with which we are most familiar. By reattaching the word *just* to the rules of a merely ideal Law, one that is in fact in force in no society, the Rationalist deprives it of determinate meaning.

The standard reply is that actually existing laws may themselves be unjust, but if the expression *unjust law* has any meaning, it is that the existing law is bad in some other way, not that it is *contrary to the law*. The first claim might be true; the second is a contradiction in terms. Not that law is itself necessarily just. There is justice wherever there is law, and there is no justice without law, but law is itself neither just nor unjust. Instead, it is the measure of the justice or injustice of the practices that fall under it.

This does not mean that law cannot be criticized, only that it must be criticized in other than juridical terms. As already noted, a society's law can be criticized as more harmful than useful, as contrary to human nature, and so on. All such criticism makes sense. So does similar criticism of a society's morality and etiquette. What does not make sense is to claim that a society's law is illegal, its morality immoral, or its etiquette ill-mannered. One might as well claim that the standard meter bar is more, or less, than a meter long.

Confusion on this point has been encouraged by ancient belief in what used to be called Natural Law. According to a tradition that began with the Stoics but achieved its definitive formulation in the late Middle Ages, there are two kinds of law: conventional and natural. Conventional law, which is made by men, is sometimes bad, but Natural Law, which is made by God, is always good. Therefore, it is natural, not conventional, law that defines duty and justice for us. Or so it is believed.

The trouble with this belief is that there is no such thing as Natural Law. There are laws of nature, but these are laws only in a metaphorical sense of the word. In its original and literal sense, law consists of *socially instituted regulations*—rules imposed on human beings by other human beings. The "natural law" of gravity therefore counts as law only given anthropomorphic belief that stones fall in "obedience" to divine command. But, as we all know, this belief is false if taken literally. Stones do not fall because they have been *ordered* and are *required* to fall; they fall because it is their *nature* to fall. Falling is not their divinely imposed *duty*; it is their natural *disposition.*

Human beings are not stones, but the same is true of what even Hume called natural obligations. It is a law of nature that mothers love their children, but this is law only in a metaphorical sense of a word, and so is the "duty" that it imposes. Few parents care for their children out of duty, because they must. They do it out of love, because they want to. Such behavior therefore comes under the heading of the *natural*, not the *obligatory*. Duties are products of society, not nature.

Not that nature is irrelevant to what people ought to do, either out of self-interest or obligation. But, despite Rationalist belief to the contrary, nature is not reason alone, and its principles cannot be known *a priori,* by simple reflection. Instead, they must be earned the hard way, by a largely biological inquiry into human practices and the reasons for them. We need to understand why human beings have the desires they do—and understanding this means understanding how these desires are rooted in our biology—before we can begin to appraise the means and methods either societies or individuals employ to satisfy them. This, however, is an inquiry which has only recently begun in earnest. Therefore, few conclusions are yet justified.

Furthermore, discovering what is *natural* will not even begin to tell us what is *obligatory*, because obligation is always in part conventional; so, determined by historical accident as well as by universal biology. Thus, we are sometimes obligated to do the unnatural thing —for example, repress our desire to take two helpings of dessert or demand intercourse with every beautiful woman. The main connection between the natural and the obligatory is the price that is paid by societies with conventions that require forms of conduct that are contrary to nature, which refutes socialist belief in the infinite malleability of human beings by imposing serious limits on the ability of a group to mold individuals as it chooses. Of course, societies exist to serve our needs, which are rooted in our nature. Therefore, from a study of nature we may hope to learn something about the rules that our societies ought to have, but we cannot expect from this study to learn what rules societies do in fact have, and it is the latter that determine our obligations.

The natural is what we are inclined to do because it serves some need or instinct rooted in our biology as a result of evolutionary selection. It is, therefore, what we all *ought* to do, circumstances permitting and other things being equal. But natural inclinations determine what we are *obligated* to do only indirectly, by giving shape to the practices and institutions that happen to evolve in the particular society in which we happen to live, under the press of the circumstances that happen then to exist. In that sense, morality is a product of natural law, but this is no Higher Law. It is a Lower Law—the law of evolution, both biological and cultural.

Despite this clear logic, Rationalists continue to believe in a Higher Law, one that is binding on all men everywhere. Because they were taught by Rationalists, most men share this belief, but the evidence is against it.

This becomes clear when we analyze what it means to say that a rule of law or morality *exists* and is *binding*. If we do not confuse rules with their verbal formulation, saying that a rule of law or morality *exists* is saying that people comply with it. To add that the rule is *binding*, or that compliance with it is *obligatory*, is to add that there is a practice of enforcing it. Thus, we count ourselves obligated to do what we are required to do by the rules that happen to be in force in our various societies.

To claim that men are everywhere obligated to comply with a Higher Law is, then, to assert that some rules are everywhere complied with because they are everywhere in force. We have, however, no proof — none whatsoever—that a single Morality or Law is everywhere enforced and obeyed. Higher Law is a myth. That the myth persists is evidence not of its truth but of the hold that theological modes of thought still have on our minds.

The usual way of avoiding this objection is to assert that the Moral Law is an ideal, not an actual, law, and we ought to obey it not because we are required to do so but because doing so would be good. This reply is unsatisfactory, in several ways. First, as noted earlier, a merely ideal law or morality is not a law or morality but an ideal for law or morality. Second, it is not clear that every society ought to have the same law and morality In fact, it seems reasonable to presume the contrary—that because circumstances differ from place to place and time to time, so should practices. Third, even if it were true that everybody ought to behave in the same way, it would not follow that they were obligated to do so. As we have been at pains to emphasize, that claim has a different meaning.

Talk of a culturally transcendent and universally binding Morality or Law would have some basis if all human beings were members of the same community and subject to the same rules, but they are not. Human beings all belong to the same *species*, but they do not all belong to the same *community*, they are not all members of the same *society*, and they are not literally members of the same *family*.

To meet these objections, Kant tried to show that there is a single rule of morality, the Categorical Imperative, that every person everywhere is obligated to obey because it is built into Pure Reason. On the grounds that consistency requires it, this rule commands you not to do anything to other people that you would not want them to do to you.

Many people have found this reasoning persuasive, but it is fallacious where it is clear and unclear where it is not fallacious. What is true is that lying, cheating and stealing are usually self-defeating.

Once discovered, they are likely to be punished or repaid in kind. So, if you want to be treated well yourself, you are well-advised to treat other people well too. But this recommends *tit for tat*; not the *Golden Rule*. It shows that you ought (for reasons of prudence) to do unto others as they *do* unto you, not that you ought (as a matter of morality) to do unto others as you *would have* them do unto you.

There is a further difficulty. Though *tit for tat* might itself be regarded as a self-evident principle of reason, it alone provides no guidance to how anyone ought in a particular case to behave. Grant that I should repay kindness with kindness, cruelty with cruelty, I cannot know whether I should be cruel or kind until I know how the other fellow will behave. To provide guides for conduct, *a priori* principles must be supplemented by relevant matters of empirical fact.

Conclusion: There is no escaping the empirical. If we want a sensible ethics, we must build it from the ground up; it cannot be pulled out of some vague but pious Rationalist sky.

Part I

An Empiricist Moral Theory

2

What One Ought to Do

This chapter attempts to give empirical definitions to the words *ought*, *obligated* and their cognates and synonyms. To do this is to challenge the dogma, often mistakenly attributed to David Hume, that you cannot derive an *ought* from an *is*.[1] Lending plausibility to this venerable but erroneous myth is the fact that the word *ought* has a bewildering variety of uses, literal and figurative. These have what Wittgenstein called *family resemblance*, but no single definition fits them all.[2] So, there is an exception to every analysis. The cure for this malady is, however, not to abandon the attempt to define our terms but to distinguish various ways of using them.

Four Ways of Saying *Ought*

According to *The American Heritage Dictionary*,

x ought to Ø

can mean either :

(1) *x is obligated to Ø.*

(2) *x's* Øing *would serve x's ends.*

(3) *x's* Øing *would be a good thing.*

(4) *x can be expected to Ø.*

Examples, some due to Gilbert Harman, are

(1)' *A Christian ought to turn the other cheek.*

(2)' *The bandit ought to carry a gun.*

(3)' *Bill Gates ought to give us his fortune.*

(4)' *Jones ought to be here by noon.*

We may call these the "ought" of *duty*, the "ought" of *prudence*, the "ought" of *evaluation*, and the "ought" of *expectation*.[3]

Some (Highly Speculative) Etymology

The *ought* of duty came first. According to the *American Heritage*, the word *ought* comes from old English *aght*, or *acht*, for debt, or duty. To have a debt is, of course, to have what we can also call an *obligation*, from the Latin *ligature,* for *bond*—a metaphor for an enforceable requirement, something you must do whether you wish to or not, under threat of penalty. To be in debt or have an obligation is, then, to be metaphorically bound, literally under compulsion, to pay. In short, the word *ought* seems originally to have expressed the idea that, as a debtor, one was subject to compulsion to behave in a certain way.

It is an interesting and not altogether idle question how we got from this use of the word *ought* to its other three uses, to which the notions of debt, duty, and obligation seem foreign. Consider our four examples again. The Christian certainly has a duty to turn the other cheek, but, it seems clear, the bandit has no *duty* to carry a gun, Bill Gates does not *owe* us his money, and, we may suppose, Jones has no *obligation* to arrive by noon. How has it come to pass, then, that we use a word for debt, duty, or obligation to denote relationships that are neither of these?

An answer is suggested by Eleanor Rosch's theory of prototypes.[4] Taking a hint from Wittgenstein, Rosch has shown that words extend their meaning by analogy, beginning with a prototype. We may deploy this theory to explain the various ways of saying *ought*. Grant that the prototypical meaning of *ought* is debt, something one can be compelled to pay, by threat of censure or punishment if need be. Desire to avoid censure and punishment is a powerful motive. By analogy, then, it may be inferred that, if someone is motivated to perform an action, he must have a duty, debt, or obligation to do it. That the inference is fallacious will not prevent many people from seeing profound truth in it. Some people will even be tempted to say that the bandit has a duty to carry a gun. It is, they will solemnly intone, a duty he owes himself. In this way, even unprincipled prudence gets counted as a metaphorical form of duty—duty to oneself. I do not mean to defend this nonsensical and regrettable usage; I am merely trying to explain it.

To explain the remaining two uses of the word *ought*, we need two more analogies, both easily guessed. Begin again with the idea of a debt. The beneficiary of a debt usually regards payment as a good thing; it is something he prefers. So, the statement that somebody has a duty implies that his fulfilling it would be good, at least for the person to whom the debt is owed, if not also for the debtor. From this, it is but a small step to the converse proposition, that if doing a thing would be good, the reason must be that it is obligatory—a requirement of duty. If you doubt that anybody could be guilty of this fallacy, think of the eagerness with which many people convince themselves that they are entitled to whatever they deem beneficial. Such people are persuaded that Bill Gates does owe them his money; it is something to which they have a *right*. This explains the *ought* of evaluation.

To explain the *ought* of expectation, we need note only that people generally do what they are required to do. So, if someone has a duty, we may predict that she will fulfill it—a truth that incautious persons will confuse with its converse, the proposition that, if we can predict a person's behavior, it must be because she has a duty. To some people, this fallacious inference will seem all the more compelling if the conduct in question is desirable as well as predictable. Nobody looks a gift camel in the mouth.

These highly amateurish speculations may be completely wrong, but they are surely plausible. Many people find the analogies just described entirely convincing, fallacious though they may be from the point of view of strict logic. Particularly popular is the idea that we have obligations to ourselves—for example, to get more exercise, to save some money or spend it more carefully, to carry a gun or take advantage of others in a trade, and so on. The appeal of such thinking is its ability to lend a specious moral legitimacy to self-gratification. Duty becomes something you want to do instead of something you are required to do—a very agreeable idea.

The Metaphorical Nature of Some "Obligations"

This idea is, however, logically as well as morally objectionable. Obligation properly so-called has the form "x is obligated to y to Ø." For an obligation to exist, then, there must be at least two persons, one of whom may, under the rules, be compelled to do something for the other's benefit. But nobody can literally require, or compel, himself to do anything. So nobody can literally have an obligation of which he is also the beneficiary; for who would enforce it if he did? Yet philosophers from W. D. Ross to James Rachels have used the words *ought* and *obligated* more or less interchangeably, as if they meant the same thing.[5]

Failure to see that they do not has many causes, among them confusion about *necessity*, a notion that still causes endless confusion in philosophy.[6] That you are *obligated* to do something means that you are *required* to do it. In other words, you *must* do it—doing it is necessary.[7] But the bandit who wants to rob people *needs* to carry a gun; his doing so is necessary to his success. Necessity in both cases. If you are careful not to notice the difference between these two kinds of necessity, you may be tempted to equate them, but doing so is a serious mistake. A bandit's carrying a gun may be *prudent*; it is not *obligatory*. It may serve the bandit's ends, but—unless his fellow bandits require it of him—it is no obligation.

Obligations literally so-called are socially imposed requirements—things that you can be *obliged*, or compelled, by other people to do, whether you wish to do them for their own sake or not. Thus, you are obligated to pay taxes, and you are obliged, if not also obligated, to give your money to the bandit who has a gun to your head; but the bandit is neither obligated nor obliged to carry a gun. If he does so, it is not in fulfillment of a duty but in response to a need.

Do not reply that the bandit is obliged, or required, to carry a gun by his desire to rob people. This is animistic thinking, which personifies desire. Only other persons, or beings with wills of their own, can literally require, compel, or oblige anybody to do anything. The police can require the bandit to park elsewhere, and the growling dog can oblige him to find another route to his destination; but the bandit's desires cannot compel or oblige, they can only *cause*, him to carry a gun. To say otherwise is to take a metaphor literally —a loose way to talk.[8]

Why "Natural Obligations" are not Obligations Truly So-Called

Loose talk of this sort is at the heart of the venerable but confused doctrine of *Natural Law*. According to this doctrine, only some rather trivial obligations are imposed by other human beings; other, more fundamental, obligations are imposed by God, or by Nature. An example is a mother's "natural obligation" to care for her children. This obligation, it has been said, is imposed not by the laws of society but by the Laws of Nature, which bind mothers to their children. The depth of this bond is indicated, it is thought, by the strength of the mother's love, which may be so strong as to be irresistible.[9] It makes her solicitous regard for her progeny to be not a choice but a foreordained conclusion.

One hesitates to criticize so poetical an expression of fundamental truth, but this truth turns into a falsehood if it is taken literally. Grant that mothers care for their children because they want to. Grant, too, that this desire is rooted in their chromosomes. That solicitous mothers are literally compelled to act as they do does not follow. Instead, the contrary follows. What people do because they want to, they do of their own free will. They act under compulsion only when they act as they do because somebody has made threats. I act under compulsion if I unwillingly give the bandit my money because he is holding a gun to my head, but there is no compulsion if I willingly give money to the Red Cross out of a sense of charity, however strong. In the latter case, therefore, talk of obligation is entirely out of place.

It is also out of place in connection with motherly love. What is wrongly called the mother's natural *obligation* to care for her children would be more accurately described as her natural *disposition*, *inclination*, *desire,* or *preference*. Belief that the mother's inclination can be so strong as itself to constitute literal compulsion suffers from two faults. First, as already remarked, the mark of compulsion is not its strength but its source. "Psychological compulsions" are not literally compulsions, and although motherly love *causes* mothers to care for their children, it does not literally *compel* them to do so.[10]

Belief to the contrary makes such limited sense as it does only against the background of ancient theology. The idea was that God, who created Nature, also created her "laws" and commanded His creatures to obey them. Thus, it was thought, stones fall and mothers love their progeny in fulfillment of a natural, because divinely imposed, command. The only difference is that, because mothers have free will, they sometimes go against their natural obligations, which stones never do.

To any scientific mind, the defects of this doctrine—if you can call such a tangle of metaphors and metaphysics a doctrine—are all too obvious. Laws of nature are not in any literal sense *laws*—regulations backed up by official threat of punishment. And although stones fall and mothers love their children in accordance with these "laws," they do not do so in obedience to them. Instead, as Hume observed, what we loosely call laws of nature are ways in which things naturally, so regularly, behave. In short, natural laws are not regulations; they are regularities. More precisely, they are what the mathematicians call *functions*, meaning determinate relations between variables. The law of gravity is the function that relates mass and distance to acceleration; natural parental affection is the function that relates genetic inheritance to care of children. Falling stones and loving parents do not *obey* these "laws"; they *illustrate* them. Belief to the contrary may be good poetry; it is bad science.

True, we, if not stones, are liable to suffer if we do not "obey the laws of our nature." Parents who do not love their children are likely to find that their children do not love them, and this can be a cause of great unhappiness. This important fact has induced more than one person to say that Nature *punishes* those who disobey Her, and this striking metaphor teaches an important lesson: Going against natural inclinations is costly; the stronger the inclination, the greater the cost. The fact remains: thinking of natural inclinations as obligations is a mistake, which confuses causation with coercion; motivation with compulsion.

A related mistake is regarding as a literal form of punishment the costs of opposing natural inclinations. Literally used, the word *punishment* denotes not every unpleasant outcome, only that brought about by the deliberate intervention of other persons. Punishment is not natural but social. It is something that other people do to you.[11] The unpleasantness that results from folly ought not to be confused with the punishment that results from failure, or refusal, to do your duty to others. That the natural consequences of foolhardiness can be worse than the evils imposed by other persons is certainly true, but it does not make the cost of foolishness to be a literal form of punishment.

Ought and Reasons

If *ought* does not always mean *obligated*, what do the four ways of saying *ought* have in common? What besides etymology ties them together?

The answer appears to be *reasons*. According to Harman, our four paradigm cases can be rendered as follows:

(1)'' *The Christian has reason [of duty] to turn the other cheek,*

(2)'' *The bandit has reason [of self-interest] to carry a gun,*

(3)'' *We have reasons [of self-interest] to want Bill Gates's money.*

(4)'' *We have reasons [of fact] to expect Jones by noon.*

As these examples make clear, what distinguishes one case from another is the *kind* of reason, or *who* has it.[12] In the first of our four cases, it is a reason of duty; in the second and third, of self interest; in the fourth, of fact. In the first two cases, the reason is a reason for the *agent*; in the remaining two, it is a reason for the *observer*.

This last distinction is as important as the others. Following H. L A. Hart, Harman describes reasons that the agent has as *internal*, reasons that the observer has as *external.*[13] External reasons could also be said to be internal *to the observer*, but that is not how Harman and Hart use the word. In their lexicon, internal judgment takes the *agent's* point of view, presupposing his preferences and beliefs. By contrast, external judgment takes an observer's point of view, presupposing her preferences and beliefs. Thus (1) and (2) are internal, (3) and (4) external. When discussing the ways of saying *ought,* one needs to keep this distinction between internal and external judgment constantly in mind.

An example of the errors that result from failure to do so is the commonplace confusion of *justification* with *rationalization*.[14] To *rationalize* conduct is to say what would make it acceptable to *the agent*—to say how it would comport with *her* interests and beliefs. To *justify* conduct is to say what would make it acceptable to *observers*—to show how it would comport with *their* interests and beliefs. Thus, (1) and (2) rationalize conduct, while (3) justifies it and (4) predicts it, also from an external point of view. As we shall see, a common mistake of moral philosophers who follow Immanuel Kant is to confuse justification with rationalization.

Some Small but Important Points of Grammar

We shall undertake a more thorough discussion of reasons in Chapter 3, where we will observe that a reason is an actual or potential motive. Then in Chapter 4 we shall explain why all reasons are personal. In the meanwhile, there is a further distinction to be made. As both Harman and John Searle observe,

x ought to Ø

can mean either

A: *Other things being equal, x ought to Ø*

or

B: *All things considered, x ought to Ø.*

A means simply that there is some reason or other for x to Ø; B that these reasons outweigh, or override, reasons to the contrary.

It follows that B implies A, but not conversely. If you ought , all things considered to Ø, then you ought, others being equal, to Ø; but the converse proposition does not follow and might be false. This is so because both A and B are consistent with

C: *Other things being equal, x ought not to Ø.*

which means simply that there is some reason not to Ø and might be true even though there is greater reason to Ø. Of course, B, if not also A, rules out

D: *All things considered, x ought not to Ø.*

It cannot be the case both that you ought, all things considered, to Ø and that you ought, all things considered, not to Ø. Yet B and D are not contradictories; merely contraries: Although both statements could not be true, both could be false.

To get contradictories, we must shift the scope of the negation, denying not the predicate alone but the whole statement, as in

A': *It is not the case that, other things being equal, x ought to Ø,*

and

B': *It is not the case that, all things considered, x ought to Ø.*

A' means "There is no reason for x to Ø," B' that "The reasons there are for x to Ø do not outweigh the reasons there are for x not to Ø."

Special symbols, or differentiating subscripts, would facilitate further analysis, but I think we can usually let context resolve ambiguities, as in daily discourse. Where context does not suffice, the necessary distinctions can be made as, and in the fashion that, the occasion requires. The main point to get now is how various uses of *ought* can be defined in terms of reasons. Since these can also be regarded as empirically determinate motives, this fact takes us a long way towards giving empirical definitions of normative statements.

Special Features of the *Ought* of Obligation

Special remarks are in order for the *ought* of obligation—the claim that you ought to do something because you have an obligation to do it. In this connection, it should be noted that your having an obligation means only that you ought to fulfill it, other things being equal; not that you ought to fulfill it, all things considered. Thus, I ought, other things being equal, to tell the truth, but contrary to Immanuel Kant, I ought not to tell the truth if doing so would mean the destruction of the whole world. Considerations of duty do not always outweigh all other matters. Sometimes, duty is decidedly, and rightly, secondary. In a slave -holding society it will be a slave's duty to obey his master, but, if his life is insufferable, what he ought to do is escape.

It should also be noted that there is no distinction between what you are obligated, all things considered to do, and what you are obligated, other things being equal, to do. We do not qualify obligation in these ways. Instead, we say that a person is either obligated or not. We do recognize that obligations can have different strengths. Being obligated is not like being pregnant; you can be more or less obligated, and one obligation can be stronger than another. Thus, your obligation to support your children is stronger than your obligation to pay your debts. The strength of an obligation is proportional to the strength and probability of the coercion to comply with it. Thus, I have an obligation, enforceable by government, to pay my taxes, a weaker obligation, enforceable by my neighbors, to mow my lawn.

Another point worth noting, because it is often denied, is that it is possible to have contrary obligations. Indeed, it is a moral commonplace. Thus, A has, as a citizen, the obligation to serve in the military, but he also has, as a Quaker, the obligation not to do military service; B has, as a husband, the obligation to spend Saturday night alone with his wife, but he also has, as a friend, the obligation to spend it with the old college chum who has just come into town, and he cannot do both. Although contrary obligations cannot both be met, neither of them can be erased, only overridden, by the other. This may be thought to contradict, Kant's dictum "*Ought* implies *can*," but contrary to Kant's belief, you can have obligations that you cannot meet. For example, you can owe money that you cannot pay. That you cannot pay your debt may be thought to erase it, but only your creditor's forgiveness, or payment, can do that.

One final point. Whether you *have* an obligation is not to be confused with whether you *feel* one. I may owe you an apology even if I do not think so; or think so although it is not true. You may also have an obligation that you do not accept—for example, to keep your cat from killing the birds that eat out of my feeder. Finally, someone may have an obligation that he did not voluntarily incur. If he can do so without danger, a passing stranger is obligated to help someone in distress. That he made no prior agreement to help may be true, but the fact does not nullify his obligation. Our obligations are not determined by our opinions; they exist in the form of socially enforced rules, about which we shall say more later.

Conditional and Categorical Uses of *Ought*

Following W. D. Ross, Harman says that the *ought* of "other things being equal" is a *conditional*, or *prima facie*, use of the word, while the *ought* of "all things considered" is *categorical.* This appears to be a mistake.

At first hearing, the claim sounds right. Talk of what one ought to do, other things being equal, is clearly subject to revision; talk of what one ought to do, all things considered, appears not to be. Also, it seems natural to treat "X ought, other things being equal, to Ø" as meaning "Since Ri, x ought to Ø, " conditioning the *ought* on reason Ri, which could conceivably be set aside by a weightier reason Rj. By contrast, "X ought, all things considered, to Ø" does not so obviously condition the judgment on a particular reason Ri or so obviously leave room for this reason to be outweighed by another.

These considerations are, however, not conclusive. Although we can regard "Other things being equal, x ought to Ø" as meaning "Since x has reason Ri to Ø, x ought to Ø," we can also regard "All things considered, x ought to Ø" as meaning "Since x has reasons R1...Rn to Ø, x ought to Ø." If the first of these two statements is to count as conditioned on reasons, then so must the second; the difference is one of quantity, not kind. In fact, neither statement qualifies as a conditional. Strictly speaking, only sentences of the form "*If* p, then q" are properly described as hypothetical, or conditional. As Lewis Carroll pointed out in "The Tortoise and the Hare," however, "*Since* p, q" means "p, therefore q," which is not a statement but an argument and is composed entirely of categorical statements, having nothing *iffy* about them.

There is also no real difference with respect to revisability. Nobody but an omniscient God could literally consider *everything*. So, when we talk of what someone ought to do, *all things considered*, this must be regarded as elliptical for *everything that we know that seems to be relevant,* which is as subject to revision by changes in information as any other judgment.

Kant's Mistake

Kant's distinction between conditional and categorical uses of the word *ought* is vulnerable to similar criticism. According to Kant, judgments of prudence are conditional because premised on the agent's desires or other contingent, empirically known, facts of the matter. By contrast, judgments of duty are categorical because not premised on empirically known facts of the matter, including, in particular, the agent's desires. Thus, Kant would have said,

> I: *The bandit ought to carry a gun,*

is conditional because elliptical for

> I' *Since he wants to rob banks, he should carry a gun.*

By contrast, Kant believed,

> II: *Jones, who is a Christian, ought to turn the other cheek,*

is categorical because premised on the Moral Law, not on Jones's personal desires or on other contingent facts of the matter.

But grant that I is elliptical for I', as Kant believed. As just noted, there is nothing conditional or hypothetical about I', which is equivalent to,

> I'' *The bandit wants to rob banks; therefore, he should carry a gun.*

Kant, a poor logician, evidently mistook the *premise* of an inference for the *protasis* of a conditional. Kant also overlooked the following fact: If we can count I as equivalent to I', we can equally well count II as equivalent to

> II' *Since Jones is a Christian, he ought to turn the other cheek,*

which premises the judgment that Jones ought to turn the other cheek on the wholly contingent fact that Jones is a Christian. Kant tried to elude this conclusion by arguing that duty is universal, so absolute; but this proposition is plainly false. It is only the Christian who has the duty to turn the other cheek. The Samurai warrior is under no such obligation.

It is certainly true, as Kant avers, that an agent's duty to Ø need not be premised on the agent's desire to Ø, but it remains true that a judgment of duty, like a judgment of prudence, will have to be premised on *some* contingent fact of the matter; it cannot stand by itself. That Smith has a duty to pay taxes to the U.S. government is premised on the fact that Smith is a citizen of the U.S; that a soldier has a duty to shoot at his country's enemy is premised on the fact that he was ordered to and will be punished if does not. There is no duty—absolutely none—that is not thus conditioned, or premised, on some empirically knowable fact of the matter.

Conclusion: The distinction between the prudential and the obligatory is not located in the grammatical space between hypothetical and categorical sentences; it must be sought elsewhere.

Doing Your Duty For Its Own Sake

By focusing on issues of grammatical form, these remarks may seem to miss Kant's substantive point, which was that you should do your duty *for the sake of doing your duty*; because it is your duty.[15] If you do it for some ulterior motive, said Kant, it lacks "moral worth." Duty must be conditioned on *no* empirically determinate or discoverable fact of the matter; that is what Kant meant by calling it a *categorical* imperative.

Kant's own example will do for an illustration of this thesis. Compare a tradesman who treats his customers honestly only out of a concern for his reputation, or out of a fear of getting caught, with a tradesman who acts conscientiously, from a sense of rectitude and moral principle. Although the actions of the first tradesman may always be in accord with duty, Kant says that only the conduct of the second, conscientiously honest, tradesman has moral worth, because only it is done from a sense of duty.

This comparison has merit. A conscientiously honest tradesman is an admirable person, and he is certainly preferable to one who is honest only when he can see no opportunity to be dishonest with impunity, if only because he is more reliably honest. Unfortunately, having stated this truth, Kant went further and added a falsehood. Not only did he deny moral worth, or dignity, to the first of his two tradesman, he also denied it to a third, who treats his customers fairly and honestly out of fellow feeling. According to Kant, the actions of this benevolent third tradesman also lack "moral worth." That encomium, the highest Kant knew, belongs solely to the second tradesman, who acts from a sense of duty alone.

This famous—or should we say infamous—claim is puzzling, in two ways. First, as noted above, your duty just *is* that performance of which makes you eligible for praise and reward, neglect of which exposes you to condemnation and punishment.[16] So, it sounds self-contradictory to say that you ought to do your duty because it is your duty but not because you hope for reward or fear punishment. Second, although it is clear why he should be preferred to the first, reluctantly honest tradesman, it is not clear why the second, duty-driven tradesman, should be preferred to the third, benevolent tradesman.

The first puzzle can be partially solved if we take into account what Willard Quine has called *referential opacity*, meaning, in this context, the fact that you can desire something under one heading without desiring it under another. Thus, just as someone can desire to meet the president of the university without desiring to meet Sam Jones, who *is* president of the university, so someone can desire to do his duty, because it is his duty, without desiring to do it in fear of punishment —as Kant avers. The only trouble is that doing your duty in this referentially opaque way requires being ignorant of what makes it your duty. You must do what is described as your duty without having any concept of what that designation means. Although unthinking performance of this kind is certainly possible, one wonders what could make Kant admire it.

One also wonders how Kant could prefer duty-driven conduct, however admirable, to benevolence. Yet, as noted above, Kant also denies moral worth to the actions of a *third* shopkeeper, who treats his customers honestly not for the sake of duty but out of fellow feeling. But why we should prefer the conscientious to the benevolent shopkeeper is not obvious. In fact, there is a very good reason to prefer the latter. The duty-driven shopkeeper will do only what he thinks duty requires, no more. Actuated by a more generous motive, however, the benevolent shopkeeper may be expected to behave magnanimously. Where the one is merely honest, the other will also be kind and helpful. Kant's preference for duty seems perverse. Love is better.

Kant's analysis of duty for its own sake is also vitiated by failure to recognize what Sigmund Freud would later draw to our attention—that a motive may be unconscious. The tradesman who acts out of duty would presumably feel guilty if he lied to, or cheated, his fellows; he feels good about himself when he behaves more honorably. Such a person is indeed a paradigm of moral propriety, as Kant maintains, but it is wrong to think that fear of duty and hope of reward play no part in motivating him. To see how they do so, let us look a little deeper into the conscientious person's psyche.

Although it was not known to Kant or Freud, the psychological mechanism of guilt is now well understood. On the standard account, a feeling of guilt is a conditioned reflex—the result of previous punishment for doing something "wrong." Having stolen some cookies, the child is told that doing so is wrong and made to stand in the corner; having hit his little sister, he is told that this too is wrong and spanked, and so on. In each case the punishment activates unpleasant glandular and muscular reflexes, and, after awhile, the act of doing something wrong will activate these same reflexes, even in the absence of punishment. We call the resulting state of mind *guilt.*

A corresponding analysis accounts for the feeling that one has when, having done one's duty, one thinks "What a good boy am I!" This is how you feel when you have done something for which, in the past, you were praised or rewarded. Once an unconditioned response to the praise and reward, the feeling has, through association, become a conditioned response to the doing of duty. That it and guilt are conditioned reflexes is confirmed by the way in which they can be *extinguished.* Repeatedly do something "wrong" without being punished. Then all feelings of guilt will eventually disappear, and so will the glow of righteousness that used to follow doing something right if this is not occasionally reinforced by praise or reward.

All of this indicates that the doing of duty cannot be separated from fear of punishment or hope of reward; it can only be separated from *conscious thought* of punishment or reward—quite a different thing.

Desires and Motives

The worst feature of Kant's analysis is, however, not the shallowness of his account of motives, or even the perversity of his preference for duty over love, but his utterly mystifying belief that one can, and should, do one's duty without having any desire, or inclination, to do it. According to Kant, you are to do your duty solely because you recognize it as your duty. That recognition is supposed to suffice by itself to motivate you, without the need for any additional motive. Although this idea is the centerpiece of Kant's moral philosophy, it cannot be made intelligible, as Kant himself candidly confesses in the end.[17] How can someone be *motivated* to do what he has *no motive* to do? How can he *desire* to do what he does *not desire* to do? How can he be *inclined* to do what he has *no inclination* to do?

Contradictory as this idea sounds, Kant insisted that it must describe a possible state of affairs, else there would be no basis for his conception of morality. He had two connected reasons—both derived from Augustine by way of Luther—for thinking so. One was his belief that duty is holy, because otherworldly in origin, while desire is profane, because tied to the body. In Kant's view, then, the word *desire* applied only to base physical motives such as the desire for food and sex. It could not also apply to the purely "noumenal" motivation to do your duty, which, he thought, must have a higher source in Reason.[18] Therefore, Kant did not regard a preference for doing your duty as an instance of desire, although he was never clear what it should be called.

Kant's second reason for saying that duty needs no motive, was his belief that an action has "moral worth" only if it is freely chosen, which he took to mean that it had to lack an empirically determinate cause. In other words, to do something of your own free will, you must choose to do it without anything in the empirically known world causing you to do it. Calling this *autonomy,* Kant denied that either the tradesman who is honest out of fear of punishment or the one who is honest out of benevolence is autonomous. In Kant's view, their honesty, though in accord with duty, does not arise from a sense of duty; instead, it is the consequence of some other inclination or desire. So, it is an instance of *heteronomy,* not *autonomy;* rule by desire rather than rule by one's own will.

This is, to say the least, a puzzling idea. How can you be inclined, or motivated, to do what you have no inclination, or motive, to do? In order to take the paradox out of it, some philosophers have suggested that Kant meant *not* that the doing of duty must be unmotivated *but* that it must be motivated solely by a recognition of duty. In other words, you must do your duty because you see that it is your duty, and for no other reason. To use the terminology of Kant's faculty psychology, the Will must be moved not by Desire but by Reason. This interpretation is supported by Kant's talk of the need for "respect" of the law and of the rational persons who are subject to it. It is also supported by Kant's insistence that compliance with the law is *necessary* for all rational persons. By this he might reasonably be taken to have meant that, as a rational being, you cannot recognize the reality of the moral law without being compelled to comply with it.

But although much in Kant supports this interpretation, it raises the following question: How is there greater autonomy in being dictated to by Reason than by Desire? Autonomy was supposed to be dictation —or rather, decision—by the Will alone. There is also a further inconvenient fact: Kant often suggested that what makes conformity to the Moral Law obligatory is that you *choose* to be obligated by it; it binds you because you freely bind yourself to it. He says as much when he describes human beings as members of a Realm of Ends who are bound by the Moral Law because they make it themselves; they are its legislators. Of course, if Kant was right the Moral Law that they make is the only law that rational legislators like them *could* make, but Kant insists that it is nevertheless a law that they make freely, under the influence of no natural, or empirically discernible, inclination. In short, Kant believed that the essence of duty is *commitment*: you are bound to do only that which you *necessarily but freely* commit yourself to do as a rational being bound by nothing but Reason. It is from this mystifying idea that some people have gotten the silly idea that nobody has an obligation he does not himself agree to.

I confess that I can make neither head nor tail of all this. As Kant himself candidly but morosely confesses at the end, the whole idea is mystifying. We must do our duty of our own free will unmotivated by anything; yet we must be motivated by rational cognition of the necessity of conforming with a previously given duty, which is our duty only because we have chosen, without cause or influence, to make it so. The attempt to reconcile these contradictions has provided much amusement and some agreeable salaries to many philosophers, but I may be excused if I decline to join the game.

Free Will and Causation

What I will do is try to clear up some of Kant's mistakes. Begin with Kant's view of autonomy, which he equates with freedom of will, which he equates with transcendence, independence of the "natural" order of things—in other words, independence of causal influence.

This idea of free will, which Kant got from Luther by way of Augustine, was invented by Plato, who said that doing what you wish is being a slave to your passions; to be free, you must obey not the dictates of Desire but the commands of Reason. The idea was widely accepted by philosophers when Kant wrote, but both Hobbes and Hume had already exposed the error in it. Contrary to voluntarist belief, if you do something because you want to, you do it of your own free will. What you do against your will is what you are required to do under threat of punishment by another person. Thus, I give money to charity of my own free will, because that is what I wish to do; but I give money to the bandit against my will, because he is holding a gun to my head. Freedom is political, not metaphysical. What diminishes liberty is *coercion by others*, not *causation by your own desires*. Kant had the truth exactly backwards.

That point made, let us return to Kant's confusions about motivation. Given common use of the word *desire*, which is a portmanteau word for *motive*, little sense can be attached to the idea that a voluntary act might have no basis in desire. Even the voluntary act of unwillingly giving your money to the bandit is motivated by desire — the desire not to get shot. That you have "no desire" to give the bandit your money means only that you have no *other desire* to do so than that deriving from your desire to save your life. In other words, it means that your desire is derivative, not basic. Still, to explain voluntary behavior, we need to discover some desire—something with what Hume called a capacity to "move the will."

The problem with Kant is that he wanted us to do our duty without having anything that might be called desire, either basic or derivative, to do it. When asked how this is possible, his only answer was to say that we have free will, a capacity to make choices that are undetermined by any "natural" desire, or inclination—meaning any empirically determinate fact about the natural world. In other words, we can be motivated to do what we have no desire to do because we choose to do it of our own free will, a mysterious capacity to transcend nature. But this resort to metaphysics invokes a mystery to resolve a conundrum. Kant, who started out as a theologian, is here talking about *miracles*, a religious, not a scientific, concept. How, we need to be told, does the Will *move itself*? And what can motivate it to do so if not some desire?[19]

It is true that there are other motives—for example, fear, anger, and love—besides desire, but this is no help to Kant. As Hobbes had already explained, each of these emotions can be regarded for behavioral purposes as forms of desire—fear being a desire to escape something, anger a desire to destroy it, and love a desire to possess it. So, nothing turns on the word *desire* as such. In its commonplace usage, it is just another name for *disposition* or *inclination,* and Kant also rules out doing your duty out of any "inclination." As he himself admits, what makes his moral theory so puzzling is his suggestion—no his insistence—that you can have a motive, or inclination, to do what you have no motive, or inclination, to do.

Kant as Moralist Rather than Philosopher

If Kant was insistent about this, it is only because he feared that there was no other conceivable basis on which to found Christian morality, which he mistakenly thought it his duty as a philosopher to foster. Hume and Hobbes had tried to show that the rules of morality and law are to be accepted and complied with because of their utility, but they could not answer the moral skeptic who wanted to know why anyone should comply with the rules if he could serve his interests better by not doing so. Kant concluded that the defense of morality must not rest on circumstances that might not obtain in fact. So, he sought a basis for morality in what he called Pure Reason, detaching it from everything empirical. In short, he sought to secure morality by making it metaphysical.

The trouble was that by so doing he made it meaningless. By detaching the concept of duty from its empirical anchor—socially imposed requirements—Kant left it to drift out to sea, never to be returned again to its home port. That Kant was right about the inadequacy of empiricist arguments for behaving morally does not excuse this. Grant that there may be some person who can not only misbehave with impunity but even flourish and prosper by doing so. Hobbes and Hume could give this person no good reason why he should obey law and morality *because there is no good reason why he should do so*. On the hypothesis assumed, doing his duty will not serve the skeptic's interests. If we want to give the moral cynic a reason to behave as we wish, we must offer him not abstract philosophy but concrete social reform. The rest of us must so alter our behavior towards him that he cannot reasonably expect to prosper without doing his duty. Word magic will not do the trick. The answer to the moral skeptic cannot come from moral philosophy. It must take the form of concrete social sanctions.

If Kant thought otherwise, it is because he mistakenly believed that the business of the moral philosopher is not to understand and explain morality but to inculcate and reinforce it. This belief confuses the moral philosopher with the moralist; moral science with moralizing. The business of the philosopher is to explain morality, not to reinforce it. Explaining morality may entail explaining why people ought to comply with it *when that is so*, but it cannot be part of an unbiased attempt to understand morality to assume at the outset that this is always so, then seek justification for one's presumption in the form of an unintelligible metaphysics.

Whether Duty Overrides Desire

It is true that these remarks run contrary to Kant's belief that, for truly rational persons, moral considerations always and necessarily outweigh and override prudential considerations. Kant believed that you ought, all things considered, to do what you are obligated to do. Indeed, he believed that this proposition is analytic, true by definition. Unfortunately, it cannot be said that Kant made it clear why he thought so.

Nor has any other philosopher since Kant. Kurt Baier once tried to do so by arguing, from what he called "the moral point of view," that we ought to sacrifice our personal interests to morality because the whole point and purpose of morality is to institute rules of conduct that override personal interests.[20] But this argument begs the question. That the point and purpose of issuing a command is to override the agent's personal interests does not mean that she ought always to obey commands. Grant that this proposition would seem true if seen from "the command point of view." Why should one take up the command point of view?

Calling those who ask this question egoists, Baier replies that the egoist cannot justify to other persons acting in his own interests while disregarding theirs. This may be so, but it does not answer, it changes, the question, which was not what conduct is *justifiable* given the interests of other persons, but what conduct is *rational* given the interests of the agent. Although they are frequently blurred, these are very different questions, which it does not pay to identify.

Followers of Kant may think they can get around the distinction between these two questions by stipulating that there are *two kinds of reasons*, prudential and moral, then adding that the latter always and necessarily outweigh the former, but this is, once again, nothing but word magic. You cannot make a cat into a dog by stipulating that there are two kinds of dogs, canine dogs and feline dogs, and you cannot make irrational behavior rational by redefining what you call a *reason* so that it has nothing to do with a person's interests or motives. But that is a topic we shall pursue more fully in the next chapter.

Hume on "Is" and "Ought"

I have here tried to specify in empirically determinate terms what it means to say that someone *ought* to do something. In other words, I have tried to give the word *ought* empirical definition. More precisely, I have tried to specify the empirically determinate truth conditions of normative statements when those statements have determinate truth values.[21]

In a famous passage in *A Treatise of Human Nature*, David Hume complains,

> In every system of morality, which I have hitherto met with, I have always remark'd, that the author proceeds for some time in the ordinary way of reasoning, and establishes the being of a God, or makes observations concerning human affairs; when of a sudden I am surpriz'd to find, that instead of the usual copulations of propositions, is and is not, I meet with no proposition that is not connected with an ought or an ought not. This change is imperceptible; but is, however, of the last consequence. For as this ought, or ought not, expresses some new relation or affirmation, 'tis necessary that it shou'd be observ'd and explain'd; and at the same time that a reason should be given, for what seems altogether inconceivable, how this new relation can be a deduction from others, which are entirely different from it.

This passage is usually read as an objection to all attempts to derive an *ought* from an *is*, or norm from fact, as I have, in effect, showed how to do above. In fact, a moderately careful reader will see that Hume had no such objection. Hume's objection is not to going from "is" to "ought" but to doing so *without providing an explanation.* Although Hume rightly put great store in the distinction between prescriptive (i.e., action guiding) claims and descriptive (i.e., fact stating) claims, he nowhere says that it is impossible to derive one from the other.

It would be ironic if he had, since it is clear to even the most superficial reader that Hume was himself engaged in reducing *ought* to *is* by showing that moral judgments, as he called them, acquire their power to motivate by appealing to innate or socially conditioned *sentiments*. Thus, according to Hume, much of morality is premised on an innate *sympathy,* or feeling of benevolence, and the rest depends on the existence of socially sanctioned conventions; so, all of it is premised on preference for what Hume called *utility*, meaning a suitably enlightened regard for one's own, or some one else's, welfare. Obviously, Hume had no objection to such naturalistic, or psychological, derivations of *ought* from *is.* On the contrary, he favored them.

As Hume's animadversions against the "rationalists," make clear, the sort of thing he was complaining about was authors who claim that people ought to behave in a certain way without making clear what motive they could have to do so. Hume regarded this kind of philosophy as deeply unsatisfactory. He would have had the same unfavorable opinion of Kant's claim that we should obey the Moral Law because it is commanded by Pure Practical Reason. Assuming one could know the commands of "Pure Practical Reason," Hume would have wanted to know what could motivate anyone to comply with them.

The present chapter is merely an expression of agreement with Hume about this. It says: If you tell someone that he ought to Ø and mean more than "*We* have reason to prefer that you Ø," then you should tell him what reason *he* has to prefer Ø, and doing that means adducing some considerations that have the power to motivate him to Ø. If you fail to do this, you have not engaged in rational discourse. Instead, you have either expressed your own personal preference or made a claim that is devoid of clear meaning.

Notes

1. The source of this attribution is Hume's famous complaint against those philosophers who suddenly switch "without explanation," from talking about how things *are* to talking about how they *ought* to be. Overlooked is Hume's use of the phrase "without explanation." What Hume rejected was not the transition from the indicative to the normative but the absence of a justifying explanation for this transition. Nobody holds that you can replace the word *is* by the word *ought* without changing meaning, but Hume, a thoroughgoing empiricist, was an opponent of the idea that moral language has any meaning that resists empirical analysis. That idea is distinctive of rationalist and theist moral philosophy, which Hume opposed. This point is treated more fully at the end of the chapter.
2. "Family resemblance" was Wittgenstein's term for a set of connecting similarities. One member of the family has eyes like another, who has a nose like a third, but there is nothing that all members of the family have in common. In

Wittgenstein's view, most uses of words of daily discourse have family resemblance, yet fail to denote something they have in common. According to Eleanor Rosch, this is because we learn to use these words first in connection with certain prototypes, or paradigmatic examples, then extend usage to other cases by means of analogy, and so on. The result is that we sometimes end up using the same word in a wide variety of ways.

3. See Gilbert Harman, "Moral Relativism Defended," *Philosophical Review,* Vol. LXXXIV, No. 1, 3-22. I have spoken of duty or obligation where Harman speaks of morality because morality is not the only source of obligation, or duty, others being law and etiquette. Your obligation to be honest and honorable belongs to morality, but your obligation to pay taxes belongs to law, and your obligation to be courteous belongs to etiquette. In general, you have an obligation to perform an action where an enforceable rule of law, morality or etiquette makes you subject to punishment, or to withholding of reward, for refusal, or failure, to do so. For further discussion of the types of obligation, see chapter 7, "Rules of Morality."
4. See Rosch, editor, *Cognition and Categorization* (Hillsdale N J: Lawrence Erlbaum, 1978).
5. This mistake is perhaps most evident in standard refutations of "ethical egoism," which is usually defined as the belief that acting in one's interests is one's only *moral obligation*, a proposition that no philosopher (with the possible exception of the novelist Ayn Rand) has ever asserted. What many philosophers (e.g., Hobbes) have asserted is that one *ought*, as a matter of *reason*, always to act in the way that promises to serve one's interests. To read the latter claim as equivalent to the former is to confuse the *ought* of reason with that of morality. In other words, it is to confuse *ought* with *obligated.*
6. Just think of the illogical mess called modal logic.
7. This explains what some philosophers misleadingly call the *inescapability* of obligation, meaning that you can be obligated to do what you have no wish to do. The obligation consists in the fact that, under the rules, you are subject to an enforceable requirement to do it. The same fact also explains why knowledge that you are obligated to Ø always constitutes a reason or *motive* to Ø, even when you might otherwise prefer not to Ø. Failure to fulfill your obligations increases your liability to punishment, which everybody wishes, by definition, to avoid. Explaining these things is impossible on any view that tries to separate obligation, and duty, from liability to punishment.
8. See my "Freedom and Capacity," *Review of Metaphysics*, xxix, 2 (1975): 256-262.
9. Even Hume sometimes succumbed to the idea.
10. Confusion between causation and coercion is, of course, the source of puzzles about freedom of will. As both Hobbes and Hume pointed out, that behavior is *caused* does not mean that it is *compelled* or *coerced*; so, freedom is compatible with determinism. Thus, that I ate breakfast of my own free will does not rule out the fact that I ate it because I was hungry. What does rule out free will is causation by means of threats. If I eat because you are holding a gun to my head, I do not do so of my own free will. This distinction is blurred by those who, following Plato and Kant, define free will as a capacity to transcend desire—implying, paradoxically, that you do something of your own free only when you are doing what you do *not* want to do. Determinism certainly does rule out this kind of metaphysical "freedom"; it does not rule out the kind of freedom—namely political freedom—that matters. You are free if you are free from coer-

cion or restraint by others. You need not also be free from influence by your desires. In fact, the concept is a muddle. Freedom, as Simone de Beauvoir once observed in reply to Sartre, does not forbid us to want things.

11. This does not mean that fear of punishment is the only reason to fulfill your obligations. Not so. As children, we had to be compelled to fulfill our duties; it was not always something we did naturally. As adults, however, most of us *want* to do our duty; it has become, if not natural, then second nature. Hence, what we once did out of fear, under compulsion, we now do out of desire, willingly. Nevertheless, what makes something an obligation, or duty, is the fact that, under the rules, one can be compelled to fulfill it, by threat of censure or punishment if need be.
12. In the next two chapters, we shall explain more fully what it means to say that some person has a reason to do something.
13. H. L. A. Hart makes his distinction in *The Concept of Law* (London: Oxford University Press, 1961).
14. Followers of Kant are particularly prone to this confusion. An example is Stephen Darwall, whose views we shall discuss in a later chapter.
15. This is the oft repeated thesis of Kant's *Foundations of The Metaphysics of Morals*, the clearest of Kant's ethical writings.
16. It will be replied that Kant did not use the word *duty* in this way, and the reply will be true, if only because Kant did not use the word in any way that has clear meaning. Kant's definition of duty was "Duty is the necessity of an action executed with respect for the law." (p. 29, op. cit.) As this "definition" illustrates Kant was one of those philosophers who mistakenly thought that he could define small words that we already understand by using big words whose meaning is hopelessly obscure. It is the basis of his belief that, to define moral terms, we must have resort to abstract metaphysics. This idea gets the truth exactly backwards.
17. See the last few pages of the *Foundations of the Metaphysics of Morals*.
18. Kant does sometimes speak of a special kind of rational desire, but on his view, this ought to be a contradiction in terms.
19. In the next chapter, we shall offer an explanation of how desire motivates.
20. See Baier's *The Moral Point of View* (Ithaca, NY: Cornell University Press, 1958).
21. I have not tried to say what people *have in mind* when they make these statements, and I reject the kind of philosophy which supposes that this kind of introspective analysis of meaning is the central task of the philosopher.

3

Reasons as Causes

Smith shot his wife. He had a reason for shooting her: He hated her. He had a reason for hating her: He believed that she had been unfaithful. He had a reason for believing that she had been unfaithful: He had seen some pictures of her in the nude with another man. In short: Smith's reason for shooting his wife was that she had been unfaithful to him.

In this lurid tale are four different uses of the word *reason*. The first mentions an emotion (hate), the second a belief (that his wife had been unfaithful), the third an observation (seeing her with another man), the fourth a fact (her infidelity). The first three refer to what are sometimes called *subjective reasons*, meaning psychological states or activities. The fourth, which refers to a fact of the matter, denotes what has been called an *objective* reason. As we shall see later, objective reasons are reasons only in a proleptic and derivative sense of the word. For now, however, our question is: What makes something a reason?

Reasons as Motives

The oldest, most intuitive, and still the best answer to this question is that it motivates conduct. "Subjective" reasons (emotions and beliefs) motivate conduct directly; "objective" reasons (facts of the matter) motivate conduct indirectly, by giving rise to emotions and beliefs. Thus, Smith's emotions and beliefs were reasons because they motivated his murderous action; the fact of his wife's infidelity was a reason because, when he learned about it, it gave rise to his murderous emotions.

This account faces only one difficulty: Because they are unknown, some facts of the matter do not give rise to motives; they do not motivate conduct. Consider Jones's wife. She, too, has been unfaithful, like Smith's; but this fact has not yet caused Jones to shoot her, because he has not yet found out about it. The fact of the matter has not yet provided Jones with any motive.

No matter. To solve the philosophical problem, if not also the moral one, we need only recognize that the fact of the matter would become a cause if it were known. Let Jones discover his wife's infidelity and he too will have a motive to do as Smith did. Mere facts of the matter have no capacity to function as motives, but they can acquire such a capacity by becoming known. Hence, they count as reasons by courtesy and by an extension of terms.

As this indicates, objective reasons are parasitic on subjective reasons. Subjective reasons are primary, objective reasons secondary. Subjective reasons are reasons in the *literal,* objective in the *proleptic,* or anticipatory, sense of the word. Subjective reasons are actually functioning as reasons; they are actually motivating conduct. Objective reasons may not actually be motivating conduct, but we call them reasons because we can see how they would or could do so if they became known.

"Normative" Reasons

The preceding remarks concern the *indicative* use of the word *reason.* The word also has a *normative* use. In this use, to say that there is a reason R for X to do Y would mean neither (1) that R *was* causing X to do Y nor (2) that R *would* have this result if it were known but (3) that R *should* have this function.

To see the distinction, consider a third person, Lewis. His wife has also been unfaithful, but although he knows about it, he has not yet taken out his gun and shows no signs of doing so. Nevertheless, one might want to say that Lewis also has reason to act, meaning that he should. In this case, one would use the word *reason* in neither its indicative nor its subjunctive but in its normative sense. This distinction can be made in idiomatic English by contrasting

Descriptive: *R is X's reason for doing, believing, or feeling Y,*

with

Normative: *R is a reason for X to do, believe, or feel Y.*

Where the first of these two formulas suggests that R is in fact causing X to do, believe, or feel Y, the second formula suggests only that R should cause X to do, believe, or feel Y.

Many philosophers believe that the normative use of the word is fundamental, indicative and subjunctive uses being derivative. In their view, to give somebody a reason for doing something is to tell him why he ought to do it; the fact that he might not be inclined to do it, even after learning the reason, will then be utterly irrelevant. What matters is that he *should be* motivated by the reason, not that he *is* motivated by it. Or so many philosophers believe.[1] In the nineteenth century, this belief led philosophers to regard logic and ethics as normative sciences. Where psychology determined how people do think, logic determined how they ought to think. Where sociology determined what people in fact do, ethics determined what they ought to do.

Despite its continued appeal to Rationalist moral philosophers, this view seems to be mistaken, in at least two ways. First, it confuses the question whether something is a *reason* with the question whether it is a *good* reason. In the normative view, the expression *good reason* is a pleonasm; all reasons are good reasons; so-called bad reasons are not really reasons properly so-called. That we sometimes say, "That is no reason," meaning "That is a bad reason" lends support to this view, but there is no contradiction in the idea of a bad reason. Suppose that Phillips falsely believes his wife to be unfaithful, like Smith's. Then, he too has a reason—a bad reason—to do something. This reason counts as such as long as it has the capacity to motivate Phillips's conduct. Whether it should motivate his conduct is irrelevant. The fact that it does suffices.

Second, the normative view is viciously circular. To see this, look first at logic. Wanting to know whether one ought to believe the conclusion C, one asks whether the premises P constitute reason to believe it. According to the normative view, premises P constitute *reason* to believe conclusion C only if one *ought* to believe C given P. It follows that, to find out whether you ought to believe the conclusion given the premises, you must first find out whether you ought, given the premises, to believe the conclusion. In other words, you must go in circles, getting nowhere.

The same circle exists in ethics. Suppose that, wanting to know what you ought to do, you ask, "What have I reason to do?" According to the normative theory, a reason to do something is one that ought to determine what you do. So, you are to decide whether you have a reason to do something by first deciding whether you ought to do it. In other words, you are to get from here to there by chasing your tail.

How the Normative Reduces to the Indicative

The normative view has this problem because it gets things the wrong way around. To see this, begin with logic again and notice that, according to the indicative view, the reason you ought to believe the conclusion given the premises is simply that, if the argument is valid, the conclusion follows from the premises. Notice that this explanation no longer defines a good reason as one you ought to believe. Instead it defines both good reasons and what you ought to believe in terms of validity, which can then be defined in terms of truth and measures for securing it.[2] By such means, which are familiar to all logicians, normative logic reduces to indicative.

There are, it is true, systems of *deontic* modal logic that try to do it the other way around, by reducing the indicative to the normative. But nobody can claim that any of these has yet been proved to be as sound or as useful as straightforwardly indicative treatments; and there is no good reason to think that any of them ever will. Willard Quine of Harvard has famously argued that many systems of modal logic foster use-mention confusion while others depend on questionable belief in Aristotelian essentialism.[3] For this reason, the canonical systems of logic are all indicative. Of course, even an indicative logic can be normative in the sense that it determines the canons that ought to guide your thinking, but no indicative logic need contain normative terms among its primitive vocabulary.[4] As Charles Peirce pointed out, no logic need say "You *ought not* to believe that p and not-p." Rather, it need say only "It *is not* the case that p and not-p," while leaving it to you to recognize that you ought not to believe what is not true.

This fact suggests a way to reduce our *three* uses—the indicative, the modal, and the normative—to *one.* Let it be said that X ought to believe the conclusion given the premises. In accordance with the principle just laid down, we may regard this as a way of saying that, if X were logical in the indicative sense just explained, he *would* deduce the conclusion, because he would see that it must be true given the premises. In this translation, we get rid of the word *ought* in favor of the word *would*. That gets us from three uses down to two, the indicative and the modal. To get from the modal to the indicative, we need only recognize that logical people *are* people who *do* believe the conclusions of arguments whose premises they believe. Since we can define a logical person as one who does generally reason logically, and since we can define logical reasoning in wholly indicative terms, as indicated above, the normative and the modal uses reduce to the indicative.

Once it is effected in logic, a comparable reduction becomes available in ethics. Just speak of the *good* where we formerly spoke of the *truth*, and of *means* and *ends* where we formerly spoke of *premises* and *conclusions*; then the job is done. Thus, where we said that a person is thinking what he ought to think only if he believes whatever follows from what he believes to be true, we may now say that he is doing what he ought to do only if he does what he believes will have a result that he believes to be good. In other words, he is rational only if he uses known means to achieve recognized ends. This shows how to explain the normative *ought* in indicative terms. In principle, then, the normative *ought* can be eliminated. Of course, in practice, we shall want to make frequent use of it; but we can now do so with a good conscience. For, if any doubt arises as to its meaning, we can always replace it with its indicative definition. Since there is no satisfactory logic of the normative *ought*, this is a very useful thing to be able to do.

Despite this, that the normative can be reduced to the indicative has been repeatedly disputed. Many philosophers believe that Hume disputed it, and G. E. Moore said that it commits the *naturalistic fallacy*. However, the belief that Hume opposed reduction of the normative to the indicative is wrong; and the "naturalistic fallacy" is no fallacy. What Hume questioned was the practice of replacing the word *is* by the word *ought*. As Hume pointed out, this practice is invalid. Given only that Smith *is* in fact selfish, we may not conclude that he ought to be; or conversely. But to admit that the normative cannot *replace* the descriptive, or vice versa, is not to admit that it cannot be *reduced* to it.

Furthermore, we have just seen that it can. So, there is no fallacy in it. Moore's belief that there is fallacy in it is the product of his Platonic conviction that the normative is determined not by the actual but by the ideal. This conviction is, however, misguided. Other things being equal, you ought to do what you have reason to do, and you have reason to do what promises to improve your chances of getting what you want. So, as Hume pointed out, it is not the ideal but the actual that determines what you ought to do.

Causes as Constituents of Explanations

So far, we have learned that reasons are actual or potential motives—causes of conduct. Unfortunately, saying so is not yet saying very much; because, if reasons are causes, so is everything else. The world is not divided into two kinds of entities, causes and effects. Rather, everything you can mention is both a cause and an effect. Which of the two a thing or event counts as being depends on how it is viewed. Viewed in one way, the rain is a cause of the ground's being wet; viewed in another, it is an effect of certain meteorological conditions. In itself, it is equally *both* cause and effect, or *neither*. Causes are not a particular *kind* of thing or event; rather, they are any kind of thing or event viewed in a certain way. Therefore, to say that something is a cause—or a reason—is to indicate that we are viewing it in a certain way.

In what way is that? The best answer I know was first stated by Aristotle, in the *Posterior Analytics*.[5] It was later restated in more modern terms by Hempel and Oppenheim in a famous paper on the hypothetico-deductive method of explanation.[6] Aristotle said that a cause is the middle term of a syllogism. In more modern language: It is a constituent of an explanation. Spelled out, this means two things. First, to specify a cause of X is to answer the question "Why X?", which we normally answer by saying "Because Y." Second, this response, "Because Y" is elliptical for a syllogism, in which the cause is mentioned by the premises, the effect by the conclusion. Thus, when asked why Socrates died, we may answer "Because he drank hemlock." This answer is elliptical for something like the following syllogism:

All who drink hemlock die.

Socrates drank hemlock.

So, Socrates died.

To know that hemlock was the cause of Socrates's death is to know that some such syllogism as this is sound—that is, that it has true premises and a conclusion that follows.

Of course, this particular syllogism is not sound, because its major premise is false. Many people who drink hemlock do not die. So, we may feel better with the following, more elaborate, explanation:

All who drink hemlock of a sufficient dosage die, if they don't take an antidote.

Socrates drank hemlock of a sufficient dosage, and did not take an antidote.

So, Socrates died.

Clearly this is better. We now have true premises. Admittedly, the major premise is true only because it is tautological—a sufficient dosage being one big enough to cause Socrates's death. The syllogism would be still better if we had an independent criterion of a sufficient dosage—something like "X grams of hemlock per pound of body weight." Until we get it, we won't have a fully satisfactory explanation of Socrates's death. No matter. As Donald Davidson has urged, this is a problem about details; and the task of filling these in can be left to the empirical sciences.[7] Until the required "covering law" has been found, we must make do with rough generalizations, as above. Doing so is unsatisfactory, but we seem to have no other choice until science is finished.

In the meanwhile, we do at least now have a reasonably clear idea of what a *cause* is: In the very broadest sense of the word, it is anything that might figure in an explanation, where an explanation is a valid (or approximately valid) syllogism with true (or approximately true) premises. Furthermore, given this idea of a cause, we can now distinguish actual from potential causes without using either normative or modal notions, by invoking the distinction between a syllogism and an enthymeme. Where actual causes correspond to complete syllogisms, potential causes correspond to enthymemes, incomplete syllogisms. Thus, corresponding to the syllogism given above, there is the enthymeme:

All who drink hemlock die.

Socrates has drunk hemlock.

Therefore,...

Even if Socrates has not yet died, the existence of this enthymeme gives meaning to the claim that there is a cause for Socrates to die, viz., the fact that he has drunk hemlock. This makes sense of talk of a cause that, not yet having had its effect, is merely potential. Although we did not know it then, that was merely a way of distinguishing complete from incomplete explanations—syllogisms from enthymemes.

Reasons and Explanations

As we said earlier, reasons are causes; so, a parallel account of reasons should be possible. And it is. Consider the syllogism:

If they know about it, husbands whose wives are unfaithful shoot them.

Smith's wife was unfaithful and he found out about it.

So, he shot her.

This gives us Smith's reason for shooting his wife. By hypothesis, there was also a reason for Jones, whose wife has also been unfaithful, to shoot her—but only in the derivative sense that Jones would (or would be more likely to) shoot her if he were to learn about her infidelity. According to our present analysis, to say so is just to say that we can see how to complete the following enthymeme:

If they know about it, husbands whose wives are unfaithful shoot them.

Jones's wife has been unfaithful.

Therefore, ...

Just add to the premises the information that Jones has learned of his wife's infidelity, and you will get the conclusion that he is likely to shoot her. This gives clear meaning to the claim that there is a reason for Jones to shoot his wife, although that reason has not yet caused him to do so.

Of course, both our explanatory syllogism and the corresponding enthymeme suffer from many of the same defects as our crude explanation of Socrates's death. For one thing, it just is not true that husbands always shoot faithless wives, even when they discover their infidelity; and insofar as this is so our explanation continues to be unsatisfactory. True enough; but, as before, this is a question of detail. We can patch the hole by limiting the disposition to shoot unfaithful wives to certain *sorts* of husbands, viz., those inclined to violence. That there is need to amend our syllogism in this way means that our talk of reasons is often loose; but, as we have seen, so is our talk of causes. In practice, we count ourselves as having a fair idea of the reason for (i.e., the cause of) somebody's behavior if we know a plausible or approximately true generalization under which to fit it.

In summary: Calling something a *reason* is thinking of it as a *motive*, or *cause*, and thinking of something as a cause is thinking of it as part of an *explanation*, which is a syllogism having an appropriate covering law as major premise. This is true even when we mean reasons in the normative sense. A reason for a person to believe or do something is just the reason why he would believe or do it if he believed what follows from his premises and chose the means to his ends. There is certainly a distinction between the reasons that actually cause him to act and the ones that would do so, assuming further conditions were satisfied; but we can account for this distinction by noting the difference between complete and incomplete explanations. In cases where the explanation is complete, premises and conclusions being all filled in, we may think of it as a reason in the primary sense of the word. In other cases, where further premises must be stated before the premises will yield the conclusion, we may say that it is a reason only by courtesy, in a secondary and derivative sense of the word.

Beliefs and Desires as Reasons

We are exercising the question, What makes something a reason? We have decided that it is the capacity to function as a motive.

The main reason to prefer this view is the fact that talk of *reasons* is parasitic on talk of *reasoning*. When the reasoning in question concerns what to do, it usually takes the form that Aristotle called *practical syllogism*, meaning argument of roughly the following form:

X desires (to have, or bring about) Y.

X believes that doing A will improve the prospects for Y.

Therefore, other things being equal, X does A.

This syllogism gives two reasons for X to do A. One is X's desire; the other is his belief. The belief constitutes a reason, *given the desire*;

and the desire constitutes a reason, *given the belief.* There is no explanation without both. So both are necessary.

That we may abbreviate the syllogism by saying, "I do A because I believe that it will improve the prospects for Y," which mentions the belief but not the desire, may suggest that the desire is incidental. But the practical syllogism could as well be shortened to "I do A because I want Y," which mentions only the desire, suggesting that the belief is irrelevant. In this respect, both abbreviations are misleading. Each is valid only if regarded as an enthymeme for the unabbreviated argument, which mentions *both* the desire *and* the belief.

It would nevertheless be a mistake to say that both desire and belief are required in every case. Desire is always necessary; belief is not. We know this from the fact that reasoning about what to do also takes the simpler form,

X desires to do Y.

Therefore, other things being equal, X should do Y.

For example, suppose that X wants to dance. Then, other things being equal, that is what X should do. Notice that nothing is said here , or need be said, about X's beliefs; the argument mentions only X's desires. It is nevertheless entirely complete. This shows that desires alone, without accompanying beliefs, can constitute reasons.

In spite of this, some philosophers have held that belief is always necessary.[8] As they see it following an old tradition, Reason is the faculty for reasoning—deriving one proposition from another; but desire, which lacks propositional form, is unreasoning. So, desires cannot be reasons; that role is reserved for beliefs, or other acts of cognition. This line of thinking was influential for a long time, but it rests on a faculty psychology that can no longer be taken seriously.[9] Given that they both figure in reasoning about how to behave, both desires and beliefs are entitled to be counted as reasons. And, since the desires alone can constitute the premises of such reasoning, it seems reasonable to say that they can constitute reasons by themselves.

That desires alone, without additional beliefs, sometimes constitute reasons, suggests that beliefs alone might do so as well, without the addition of desires. But this proposition is more questionable. If we understand desire behaviorally, as not a feeling but a disposition to prefer one thing to another, then desire is an essential part of *every* explanation of conduct. It provides the *motive*; and without a motive there is no conduct. But whereas it is usually easy to see what conduct is implied given a certain desire, this is not always so given merely a certain belief. Thus, given only that you want to dance, we know what might follow. But given only that you know the next dance to be a waltz, we have no idea what to expect. This suggests that beliefs constitute reasons only when accompanied by appropriate desires. I will call this *Hume's principle*.

A frequently cited exception to Hume's principle is belief that something is good. Given that someone believes a thing to be good, we may know what behavior to expect, even if no desire is mentioned. Yes, but it is wrong to say that no desire is involved. The truth is rather that, in this case, the needed desire is already assumed to be a constituent or accompaniment of the belief. There is no believing to be good what you do not also find desirable. The idea is a contradiction in terms. Another example of the same sort is belief that something is dangerous. This usually involves desire to avoid it. People do sometimes desire what is dangerous, because they find it exciting; but in these cases, the relevant desire is a desire for excitement. Hume's principle is safe. Belief without desire is powerless to motivate conduct.

In summary: Giving the *reason* for an agent's behavior is *explaining* it, specifying circumstances that could lead us to expect, or predict, it. But we explain conduct and successfully predict it only when we supply it with a *motive*; and this is provided by the agent's desire, his disposition to prefer one thing to another. Although, speaking elliptically, we sometimes call the belief itself a reason, we also know that its functioning in this capacity is dependent on the agent's having the relevant desire; and the role of belief is not so much to motivate conduct as to aim it in the appropriate direction. The agent desires water; he believes that the alcohol in this bottle is water; so he drinks it. In a manner of speaking, his belief motivates his conduct: Without the belief, he would not drink *alcohol*. Without the desire, however, he would not drink *anything*. So, in the final analysis, it is the desire that matters.

Despite our previous discussion of the reducibility of the normative to the indicative, it will be objected that thus equating *reasons* with *motives*, and tying these to *desires*, is blurring the distinction between the *descriptive* (or normative) and the *prescriptive* (or factual). The answer to this is that, in the case of human conduct, the two things cannot be separated; and in some cases they cannot be clearly distinguished.

To see this, consider the following syllogism.

X desires (to have, or bring about) Y.

X believes that doing A will improve the prospects for Y.

Therefore, other things being equal, X ought to do A.

Here, talk about what X ought to do has replaced talk about what he does. No matter. As we noted earlier, one ought, other things being equal, to do what one has reason to do; but one has reason to do what one believes will improve the prospects of getting what one wants. So, that is what one ought to do.

There appears to be no final distinction between *explaining* conduct and *prescribing* it—Rather, description and recommendation are two sides of the same thing—explaining actual or prospective behavior by referring to actual or possible motives.

Reasons and Deliberation

In my opinion, this constitutes a satisfactory explanation and defense of the doctrine that reasons are causes; anyhow, it straightforwardly answers all the major objections to this doctrine that I know. It also, however, raises other questions. If reasons are causes, what *kinds* of causes are they? How do they differ from other causes?

This is a really hard question, because the word *reason* is used both broadly and narrowly. In the broad use of the word, all causes are reasons. In accordance with this usage, we sometimes describe as the reasons for an event everything that contributed to bringing it about. Thus, we may say either, "The stone fell because it was dropped," or "Its being dropped was the reason the stone fell." The two claims are equivalent. By contrast, in the narrow use, only consciously entertained causes count as reasons. Thus, using the word narrowly, we describe as a reason only that which does or could enter into the agent's deliberations about his behavior. In this use, there can be a cause of the stone's falling but no reason why it fell, because the stone is incapable of consciously entertaining reasons.

Given a choice, we might prefer the narrower, use—on the grounds that the broad use is too broad to distinguish the conduct of human beings from that of stones. But if we make this choice, because talk of stones having reasons seems unduly anthropomorphic, what will we do when we come to hybrid cases? Suppose that Green unconsciously picks his teeth, because there is food between them. Shall we say that Green has a reason, though an unconscious one, to pick his teeth? Or shall we also regard this as a metaphorical use of words, like our earlier attribution of a reason to the unthinking stone? This is a difficult dilemma to resolve.

The following observation may help. Ultimately, we are interested in what it means for a rational (i.e., reasoning) being to have a reason, but it is not always convenient to limit the reasons a rational being has to things that he recognizes as such. We often want to count as the agent's reasons what some observer of his behavior would recognize as such, even if the agent himself does not do so. The toothpicking case provides an example; and there are many others. In such cases, our best course may be to split the difference. In order to limit the use of the term *reason* so that it does not become coextensive with the word *cause*, we can resolve to attribute reasons only to reasoning beings, not also to inanimate objects or dumb animals. This will enable us to avoid the anthropomorphic implications of saying that stones have reasons. On the other hand, it will enable us to use the word *reason* to account for the plain fact that some behavior clearly serves ends of which the agent is not conscious.

The effect of these stipulations will be to limit our use of the word *reason* to (actual or potential) causes of the clearly purposive behavior of conscious beings. Hence, a person picking his teeth in order to remove the food that is between them may be said to have a reason for doing so; but a person picking his teeth out of nervous habit may not. If we wanted to do so, we could then broaden this usage even more and admit that purposive behavior on the part of animals can be motivated by what we call reasons. For example, if we wished, we could say that Fido's reason for barking at Susie was that she is a stranger to him. In fact, we do sometimes talk like this. Even this liberal usage would not, however, justify saying that the stone's reason for falling was that it had been dropped. As we intended, that broad usage is now definitely ruled out as too anthropomorphic.

From now on, then, we are to describe as a reason for a person (or, by analogy, an animal) all and anything that either does, would, or could cause him to do something for a given end. More formally: R is a reason for X to do Y just in case R either does or, under certain conditions C, would cause X to do Y in order to achieve E. In short: reasons are motives—causes that serve ends. So-called objective reasons count as reasons only insofar as we can see how they could become motives, by becoming known.

Reasons and Rationality

The noun *reason* and the adjective *rational* both come from the word *ratio*, which implies calculation. In the case of practical reason, reasoning for the sake of practice, this usually involves calculating means to ends; although it can also mean comparing one end to another, in order to determine which is weightier. A rational person is simply one who makes a habit of doing this—figuring out what he wants most, figuring out how best to get it, then behaving accordingly. A reason is any step in the figuring.

When we represent conduct as the result of such figuring, we *rationalize* it. As Jerry Fodor has repeatedly insisted, *rationalizing* conduct (both our own and that of others) is, so far, the only way we have of understanding it.[10] In fact, in connection with conduct, rationalizing is usually what we *mean* by understanding: Our ability to see rationality in the conduct in question is our test of whether we understand it. We understand what we can rationalize, not what we cannot.[11] Thus, to pronounce a form of conduct irrational is to declare it unintelligible; and vice versa.

This fact provides an answer to an objection that Christine Korsgaard has made to Hume's theory of reasons.[12] Korsgaard's objection is that, because even insane behavior has causes, it is impossible, on Hume's theory, to conceive of irrationality. Korsgaard seems to think that to get irrationality you would have to have someone who both believed and did not believe something, or both wanted and did not want something; then acted on these plain contradictions. But irrationality need have no particular characteristics, much less involve self-contradiction. It is an essentially negative notion: We regard as irrational behavior in which we can see no rationality. So, irrationality is the absence, not the presence, of something.

Aristotle famously *defined* human beings as reasoning (i.e., syllogizing and calculating) animals. In doing so, he appears to have overlooked (or disregarded) the plain fact (which he knew as well as anybody) that some human beings not only do very little reasoning but also have very little capacity for it. Aristotle's disregard of this fact did not mislead him, but it has caused a great deal of confusion in minds more literal than his. Thus, psychiatrists such as R.D. Laing have maintained that the seemingly irrational conduct of schizophrenics must itself be, in its own peculiar way, rational; insanity must exhibit a special kind of reason. To understand the lunatic, we need only learn his premises, or the peculiar logic that governs his deductions from these premises.

Others have deduced the contrary conclusion. Reasoning that human beings are necessarily rational, because rational by Aristotelian definition, the Nazis concluded that the insane and the mentally retarded must not be full-fledged human beings; instead, they must be beasts who look like human beings but lack the distinctively human capacity for reason. What this debate shows is merely that we do not count ourselves as understanding conduct that we cannot rationalize—explain in terms of beliefs and desires.[13] That men are rational animals is only partly an empirical proposition. It is also a transcendental postulate, one justified by the fact that it provides us with a useful model. When there is a better model, we may give this one up.

Motives as Functions

That fact acknowledged, we should now take a look at how we understand beliefs and desires. It is customary in our Cartesian era to think of these as feelings, momentary states of mind. But desire and belief thus mentalistically construed have no intelligible connection to action, which is what we invoked them to explain. Hence, given reference to a belief or desire considered as a mere feeling it is always open to someone to ask, "Just how did that particular feeling give rise to, or cause, that particular action?"

If, then, we want to understand what beliefs and desires have to do with conduct, we must learn to think of them not as *feelings* but as *preference functions*—dispositions, given a choice, to pick one thing rather than another. Thus, to have a desire for riches is not (or not merely) to *feel* a certain way about money. It is to be disposed to do what you believe will make money. And to believe that you can make money by investing is not (or not merely) to *feel* a certain way about money or investing. It is, rather, to be disposed to invest given that you desire to make money. Of course, appropriate feelings usually accompany dispositions; but we ought not to confuse the feelings, which are momentary and incidental, with the desires and beliefs, which are dispositional and essential.

To see why not, consider an analogy from physics. It is often said that gravity is the *cause* of falling. And this is right, provided it is rightly understood. It is false, however, if we understand it to mean that gravity is what Aristotle called the *efficient cause* of falling. Not so. Suppose I drop a pencil. The efficient cause of the pencil's falling is not gravity but its being dropped. In Aristotle's language, gravity is the *formal cause* of the pencil's falling—it being of the form or nature of things to fall. In modern parlance, gravity is the function that relates being dropped to falling—the rule that things fall when dropped. More generally, gravity is the rule that we describe by saying "Bodies in empty space tend to move towards each other with a velocity that is directly proportional to their masses and inversely proportional to the square of the distance between them."

We call gravity a cause only because it figures in our explanations, generally as what Hempel and Oppenheim called *the covering law*. These explanations go roughly as follows:

Covering law: *Dropped things tend to fall.*

Efficient cause: *This thing was dropped.*

Effect: *This thing fell.*

Here, gravity is the rule described in the first premise; the efficient cause the event described in the second. Conceiving gravity as an efficient cause of falling makes no sense. We have no independent test of gravity, which is detectable only in the disposition of things to fall. So, explaining their falling by reference to gravity is going in circles. Viewed as a covering law, however, gravity provides explanations by fitting events to a recognizable pattern.

The same is true of beliefs and desires. Viewed as efficient causes, they become mysteries. "How are these momentary states to be identified?" and "How do they give rise to their effects?" become unavoidable but unanswerable questions. We at least fit the conduct in question to a familiar pattern when we think of motives as dispositions—functions, covering laws. Thus, knowing that I have a passion for hot fudge sundaes explains why I ate one. But because we lack any independent description of the desire for hot fudge sundaes, referring to it provides understanding only when we understand it behaviorally, as a behavioral disposition. Thus, to desire hot fudge sundaes is to have a disposition to eat one if given the opportunity; it is to prefer eating a hot fudge sundae to doing the alternative.

As ethologist Nicholas Thompson and philosopher Patrick Derr have pointed out, this too can be represented by an appropriate syllogism:[14]

***Covering law:** I had a disposition to eat a hot fudge sundae if given the opportunity.*

***Efficient cause:** I was given the opportunity.*

***Effect:** I ate a hot fudge sundae.*

The chief advantages of this representation are (1) it makes explicit the connection between motive and conduct and (2) it gets around our inability to identify motives except by reference to conduct, as its causes. Neither of these advantages is enjoyed by the view that motives are feelings, momentary states of mind. That way of construing motives leaves mysterious both their intrinsic nature and their connection to conduct.[15]

Why Reasons are Always Personal if not Always Selfish

That reasons are constituted by beliefs and emotions, which are personal and relative, has a very important implication: Nothing is a reason absolutely, in itself, apart from its relation to some person. Instead, my reasons are mine, yours are yours, and a reason for me to do something may not be a reason for you, or anybody else, to do anything. Thus, Jones's belief that his wife had been unfaithful was a reason *for Jones* to shoot her; but it is not on that account a reason *for you, me, or anybody else* to shoot her. The logical form of reasons is not "R is a reason" but "R is a reason for person P to do action A."

This must not be misunderstood. To say that reasons are *personal* is not to say that they are *selfish.* The distinction—a vitally important one that is often neglected—is between *ownership* and *object.* St. Francis's reason for giving his money away was that he desired to help the poor. This desire was a personal desire, for it belonged to (or characterized) the saint; it was his. But, as Bishop Butler rightly emphasized, it was not on that account a selfish desire, for it was not aimed at benefiting St. Francis; he was not its object. So, although the saint's desire was personal, it was not selfish. Of course, there are selfish desires. Whether selfish or unselfish, however, all desires—indeed, all motives—are personal, owned by somebody. To say so is, in fact, to say nothing disputable. The proposition is a mere tautology.

This fact has an important implication: *That person X has reason R to do action A does not mean that different person Y also has reason R to do A.* If what we have said so far is right, what X has reason to do will depend on what *X* believes and desires; what Y has reason to do will depend on what *Y* believes and desires. But since X and Y desire and believe different things, they will have different reasons to do similar things and similar reasons to do different things. Desiring to help the poor and caring little for money, St. Francis had reason to give his wealth away, but John D. Rockefeller, who appears to have been largely indifferent to the poor, had reason to keep his wealth.

As this shows, the logical form of reasons is not simple but complex. Reasons do not have the form of simple predications; they have the form of relations. Not "R is a reason" but " R is a reason for X to do Y." This is true of even so-called objective reasons –in other words, facts of the matter. Suppose that one can make money by investing in the stock market. That is an objective fact of the matter. Will that constitute a reason to invest in the stock market? It depends on whether one wants to make money. If Smith desires to make money, then the fact that he could do it by investing in the market constitutes an objective reason for him to invest; but this objective reason is still no reason *for Jones*, who is indifferent to money.

Platonic Belief in Objective and Impersonal Reasons

Plato denied this. According to him, there is only one reason to act in a certain way, viz., the fact that doing so will be, or will achieve, a result that is, good. If Plato was right, it does not matter what one believes or desires. What matters is whether the action in question would achieve a good result. If it would, one has reason to do it; otherwise not.

This Platonic line of thought has one thing going for it: Everybody must agree that he has reason to do what promises to achieve results that he regards as good. The trouble is that what is regarded as good differs from person to person. I regard as good getting rich at your expense, you regard as good getting rich at mine. Jones regards as good beating Smith out for the professorship at All-State University; Smith regards as good beating Jones. And so on. As this indicates, the "good" that each person has reason to seek is not independent of personal desires or preferences.

Instead, as Hobbes remarked, each of us uses the word *good* "in relation to himself," to denote what he prefers or desires. So, what X regards as good, Y regards as bad. Plato believed, of course, that things are good or bad in themselves, independently of personal preferences and desires. But if there were a good that was so independently of preferences, we would have no reason to seek it. We have reason to seek only that which we believe to be good, because it seems to us to be in accord with our preferences.

To say so is not to say that the good just is that which we believe to be good; or that it is definable as what we prefer. As Plato emphasized, we sometimes make mistakes, preferring and believing to be good what turns out not to be so. This fact induced Plato to conclude that the good is objective and absolute—independent of personal preference and desire. There is an alternative view. As B. F. Skinner has pointed out, the good is not what we desire; it is what *reinforces* desire. Thus, good tasting ice cream is ice cream that you want to taste again.[16] So, although what we call good is not identical with what we desire, it is at the same time not independent of it.

Plato's line of thought also blurs the important distinction between the ideal and the rational. It is certainly true that one ought, *ideally speaking*, to do all and only what is, or would be, good, whatever that may turn out to be. But the Platonist purports to be talking about reason; and the truth of the matter is that, other things being equal, one ought, *rationally speaking*, to do all and only that which one *believes* to be good. Unless we confuse *rational* conduct with *optimal* conduct, as the Platonist routinely does, it is beside the point whether the action in question is in fact good. What matters to considerations of rationality is whether the agent believes his action to be good. If he does, he has a reason to act; otherwise not.

The belief that constitutes his reason need not also be true. It is admittedly true that, sometimes, after the fact, looking back in the light of hindsight, we talk as though one ought to have done differently, because it would have turned out better, although one could not have known this at the time. Second-guessing like this suggests that one ought always to do what is, or would be, good *in fact*, whether one *knows* it or not. In other words, it suggests that what matters is not belief but truth. But although this is what Platonists believe, it cannot be right. How, before the fact, could one manage this marvelous feat —of picking out and doing what is good without knowing what it is?

That it would be rational to do the optimal thing *if one knew what it was* is certainly true; but the fact is entirely irrelevant. It needs to be remembered that reason is not needed in a state of complete information. For an omniscient being, reason is an entirely superfluous faculty. This faculty is useful only to those of us who, being ignorant, must try to infer what we do not know from what we do know, in order to improve our chances. So, contrary to Platonic belief, the use of reason cannot presuppose full knowledge of the objective facts of the matter. On the contrary, it presupposes ignorance and subjective misinformation. When it is available, knowledge, certain truth, is good; but it is not necessary. Belief, however fallible, will suffice. It must, because it is usually all we can get.

It will be objected that, for the resulting conduct to count as rational, the belief must itself be rational, but this claim is also highly doubtful. Rationalists like to believe that all belief can be rationalized —shown to be self-evident or derived by logical means from other beliefs that are. But as skeptics from Protagoras to Popper have forcefully argued, this belief is itself neither self-evident nor derivable by logical means from beliefs that are. Instead, it is an undemonstrable faith. So, it is itself irrational by Rationalist standards.

That is why our workaday test of rationality is not usually so stringent. In practice, a belief counts as rational if it is not demonstrably irrational; and it is not demonstrably irrational if it does not obviously contravene what seem to other people in the community to be undisputable truths—the laws of logic, the superiority of the community's morality and religion, or what in the community are regarded, however wrongly, as plain facts of the matter. This shows that counting as rational generally means believing certain "truths"—namely, those that seem to the rest of the community to be both undeniable and basic. It does not show that being rational means believing no falsehoods. As we all know very well, error and rationality are perfectly compatible. Thus, it was at one time rational to believe that the earth is flat. In fact, it was at one time irrational to believe otherwise.

For the present issue, then, it does not matter whether the belief in a thing's goodness is true or false. What matters is whether the agent has this belief. If he does, he has a reason to pursue the thing; otherwise not.

Summary

Reasons are actual or potential motives, dispositions to behave in certain ways. They count as reasons because of their capacity to function in reasoning about conduct, your own or that of somebody else. So, "subjective" reasons (i.e., emotions and beliefs) are fundamental; "objective" reasons (i.e., facts of the matter) are secondary. Plato challenged this view by arguing that one has reason to do only what will result in the good, which is independent of personal beliefs and desires. The truth is rather that one has reason to do only what one *believes* will be good; but we describe as good only that which we expect to *reinforce* our preference, or desire. We have no conception of a good that is independent of desire and no reason to prefer that which we do not believe will reinforce our desires.

We started by noting a distinction between "subjective" and "objective" reasons. The implication of everything we have said so far is that reasons in the true and primary sense of the word are subjective. So-called objective reasons are reasons only in a parasitic and derivative use of the word. Thus, beliefs and desires count as reasons because they do in fact motivate conduct. By contrast, facts of the matter count as reasons only insofar as we can see how they could come to motivate conduct, by causing certain beliefs and desires. In that sense, all reasons are tinged with subjectivity. We shall explore the implications of this fact more fully in the next chapter.

Notes

1. As we shall explain in the next chapter, one such philosopher is Stephen Darwall.
2. Defined in indicative terms, a *valid* argument is one having a form which is such that all arguments of that form having true premises also have true conclusions. In other words, there are no *counterexamples* to that form of argument. For a fuller explanation, see Max Hocutt *The Elements of Logical Analysis and Inference* (Cambridge, MA:Winthrop, 1979), 153-159.

3. See Willard Quine, "Reference and Modality," *From a Logical Point of View* (Cambridge, MA: Harvard University Press, 1953), 139-160.
4. See my "Is Epistemic Logic Possible?" *Notre Dame Journal of Formal Logic* 13 (1972): 433-454.
5. For a full account, see my "Aristotle's Four Becauses," *Philosophy* 49 (1974): 355-379.
6. See Hempel and Oppenheim, "Studies in the Logic of Explanation," *Philosophy of Science* 15 (1948):135-175.
7. See Donald Davidson, *Actions and Events* (Oxford: Clarendon Press, 1980).
8. Among them, apparently, was David Hume
9. I am talking about the old idea, invented by Plato and still influential, of the mind as a sort of committee of three persons or faculties: Reason, Will, and Emotion or Passion.
10 See Jerry Fodor, *The Language of Thought* (Cambridge, MA: Harvard University Press, 1979).
11. That is why mindless vandalism and aimless violence seem incomprehensible to us. Even when we can understand the motives, we cannot see any rationality in the behavior, which does neither its victim nor its perpetrator any visible good.
12. See "Skepticism about Practical Reason," reprinted in Stephen Darwall, Allan Gibbard, and Peter Railton, editors, *Moral Discourse and Practice* (New York: Oxford University Press, 1997), 373-388.
13. We also invoke other emotions besides desire, but insofar as these enter into explanations of conduct, they can be regarded as special kinds of desires. Thus, hate is a desire to harm, fear a desire to flee, and so on.
14. See Patrick Derr and Nicholas S. Thompson, "Reconstruing Hempelian Motivational Explanations," *Behavior and Philosophy,* 20, 1(1992): 37-47.
15. A full justification for this statement would require on complete development of the behaviorist philosophy of mind that it presupposes, but part of that justification would be the way it helps us to make sense of ethics, which also has to do with conduct.
16. There are, of course, other uses of the word *good.* This remark just defines the intrinsically good. The instrumentally good is that which reinforces because it produces the intrinsically good, which reinforces. The morally good is that which reinforces because it has been reinforced by others, who are reinforced by it. More on this later.

4

Why Reasons are Personal

In the preceding chapter, I argued that reasons do not have the logical form of simple predications; they have the logical form of relations. Not "R is a reason" but "R is a reason for X to do A." It follows that what is a reason for X to do A need not be a reason for Y to do anything. Thus, Jones's belief that his wife was unfaithful was a reason *for Jones* to shoot her; but it was not on that account alone a reason *for anybody else* to do anything. Reasons need not be selfish, but they are *necessarily* personal; mine are mine, and yours are yours.

Nagel on Altruistic Reasons

The leading opponent of this view is Thomas Nagel, who first expressed his opposition in *The Possibility of Altruism.*[1] Though maddening, like all Kantian philosophy, for the obscurity of its prose at critical junctures in the argument, this influential book provides the most able exposition to be had of the doctrine of "objective"—meaning *impersonal*—reasons.[2] Therefore, we must take a close look at it.

As its title suggests, the aim of Nagel's book is to explain the conceivability of what he calls *altruism*, meaning "any behavior motivated merely by the belief that someone else will benefit or avoid harm by it" (p. 16n). The operative phrase here is "motivated merely by belief." Nagel wants to exclude motivation by desire or emotion. Suppose that, as an act of charity, philanthropist Jose decides to give his worldly goods to an orphanage. Although it is other-regarding, this compassionate and eleemosynary behavior will *not* count as an example of what Nagel calls altruism. Motivated by fellow feeling, Jose's behavior is not motivated "merely by belief"; so, it lacks the necessary "objectivity." What is wanted is regard for others, but it must not come from the heart; it must come from the head. As in Kant, you must help others because it is your duty, not because you want to.

One wonders how anyone but a socialist bureaucrat without family or friends could favor such an ethic, and I confess that I find it abhorrent: May God save us from the ministrations of such grudging but well-intentioned altruists! Nagel, however, regards this sort of thing as admirable. His task is to prove that it is also possible and rational: You can (and should) be motivated to act in ways that benefit others, even if you have no desire to do so; indeed, even if you have every desire not to do so. As Nagel puts it, "The general thesis to be defended concerning altruism is that one has a direct reason to promote the interests of others—a reason which does not depend on intermediate factors such as one's own interests or one's antecedent sentiments of sympathy and benevolence" (p. 16).

Using a charged but ambiguous word, Nagel describes such disinterested and detached behavior as "objective." As the following passage shows, the word *impersonal* would be more accurate.

> It is important that the reasons which you believe others have to consider your interests should not refer to them specifically as yours. That is, you must be prepared to grant that if you were in the position in question, other people would have as their reason to help you simply that *someone* was in need of help. (p. 83; emphasis in the original)

In other words, the beneficiary of your action must have no particular identification with you: You must not help him because he is your friend or your brother. You must help him because he is an indeterminate *someone*. There are to be no personal pronouns in the statements of altruistic reasons. Impersonality with a vengeance.

Why this insistence on impersonality? Because Nagel is afraid, like his hero Kant, to rest his hopes for other-regarding behavior on personal inclinations. As Hume pointed out, most of us care more for our families and friends than for strangers and foreigners. Hume agreed that most of us also have a natural sympathy for other people, but he admitted that this sentiment is often weak. Fearing that it is too weak, Nagel is anxious to bind us with stronger chains. He says so himself:

> It will in any case not do to rest the motivational influence of ethical considerations on fortuitous or escapable inclinations. Their hold on us must be deep, and

> it must be essentially tied to the ethical principles themselves, and to the conditions of their truth. The alternative is to abandon the objectivity of ethics. (p. 6)

Can Reasons be Independent of Desires?

As you might expect given these remarks, the centerpiece of Nagel's argument is an attack on the doctrine that reasons are premised on desires. Nagel wants to show that you can have a *reason*, and therefore a *motive*, without having a corresponding *desire.*

Though Kant defended it with vigor, this is a paradoxical claim. It has long been customary in philosophy to use the word *desire* as a portmanteau term for *motive* and think of *reasons* as motives. From this it follows that all motives are desires, by definition. So, in saying that there can be a reason that is not a desire, Nagel may seem to be claiming that there can be a reason that is not a motive.[3] Not so. Agreeing that reasons must be capable of motivating, Nagel says that practical logic (the study of what there is reason to do) and normative psychology (the study of what should, so can, motivate conduct) come to the same thing (p. 21). As he understands it, then, his problem is to show that *motives* need not take the form of *desires,* and it is this idea that is paradoxical.

To resolve the paradox, Nagel invokes a distinction between *motivated desires* and *unmotivated desires.*

> The claim that a desire underlies every act is true only if desires are taken to include motivated as well as unmotivated desires, and it is true only in the sense that whatever may be the motivation for someone's intentional pursuit of a goal, it becomes in virtue of his pursuit *ipso facto* appropriate to ascribe to him a desire for that goal. But if the desire is a motivated one, the explanation of it will be the same as the explanation of his pursuit, and it is by no means obvious that a desire must enter into this further explanation. (ibid.)

What does this mean? I can only guess. Consider the behavior of eating. Although it may be motivated (caused?) by the agent's hunger, this hunger will itself normally be caused by a period of starvation, an objective fact of the matter. Although this objective fact will itself be a cause of desire, it will itself be caused by no desire. So, it will be an "unmotivated motive" for eating. Nagel's argument appears to be that, given this unmotivated motive, we can explain the behavior in question without mentioning hunger, the motivated desire. I cannot be sure that this is his meaning, but it is the only interpretation I can think of that makes sense of his words.

Granted that this is Nagel's argument, is it sound? No. The premise is true. Starvation can certainly motivate eating, but this does not prove that there is an *action* that is not motivated by a desire. It proves merely that there is a *desire* that it not motivated by another desire. Nagel appears to have confused the motivation for the *action* with the motivation for the *desire*. Hence, he remarks, "Although it will no doubt be generally admitted that some desires are motivated, the issue is whether another desire always lies behind the motivated one, or whether sometimes the motivation of the initial desire involves no reference to another, unmotivated desire." (p. 29) Not so. The question is whether a desire lies behind every action. Pointing out that some desires are not motivated by other desires does not answer this question. It changes the subject.

Perhaps realizing this, Nagel shifts ground. Observing that we can always explain any action by postulating an appropriate desire, he complains that doing so yields explanations that are "trivial," because invented for the occasion. In his view, any behavior that we explain by invoking such *ad hoc* desires as this could be better explained by referring to the circumstances that produced it. Thus, to use the same example again, explaining that a man is eating because he is hungry is "trivial." We would provide a deeper insight into his behavior if we pointed out that he has been deprived of food for four days. When we do that, however, we refer not to his "subjective" desire for food but to its "objective" cause, a period of starvation. Nagel concludes, "Though all motivation implies the presence of desire, the sense in which this is true does not warrant us in concluding that all motivation requires that desire be operative as a motivational influence" (p. 32). [4]

Despite the obscurity of this language, I think that it makes some sense. Nagel appears to be making a point that behaviorists often make: Talk of desires and beliefs is empty because it is tautologous. If we explain the behavior of eating by invoking hunger, then go on to define hunger as a desire to eat, we end up going in circles and leave ourselves unable to differentiate eating out of hunger from eating compulsively. We would do better, the behaviorist believes, to forget about such "subjective" states as hunger and refer instead to such "objective" facts as deprivation. Nagel seems to be making the same point.

If he is, the point has merit, but Nagel is not entitled to make it because he is not a behaviorist. He himself makes free use of explanations that mention desires. Indeed, he confesses that he does not see how we could get along without them. So, he is not entitled to use behaviorist arguments. Perhaps that is why, having said that explanations invoking desires are *trivial,* he shifts without explanation to the quite different view that desires are *impotent.* Admitting that desires may always be present, he now declares that they are "causally inefficacious." Precisely what this means is also not obvious, but it may mean something like the following: Because they are mental, desires lack the power to cause behavior, which is physical. In the final analysis, then, what causes a hungry man to eat is not the "subjective" feelings of hunger that accompany his behavior but the "objective" circumstances that gave rise to it. In short, a man eats because he has been deprived of food, not because he feels hungry.

If this is Nagel's argument, it poses a false dichotomy. Grant that *feelings* of hunger do not cause eating. Hunger is to be identified not with feelings of hunger but with the inclination to eat that results from a period of deprivation. That is why it seemed circular to explain eating by mentioning hunger. We were saying, "Jones is eating because, having been starved, he now has a disposition to eat." So, there is no need to choose between attributing a man's eating to hunger and attributing it to starvation. Hunger being that condition that results from starvation, invoking a man's hunger to explain his eating is simultaneously invoking the deprivation that produced it.

Confusion about this comes from thinking of desires as *causes.* As we noted in the preceding chapter, we should, rather, think of them as *disposing conditions.* Regarded as a disposition to eat, hunger is not the sort of thing that could function as a *cause.* As Nicholas Thompson and Patrick Derr have made clear, hunger should be regarded as what Hempel and Oppenheim called a *covering law.* In Aristotle's jargon, it is not an *efficient*, it is a *formal,* cause. The efficient cause of eating is not hunger but the presence of food.[5] Hunger, the disposition to eat when you have been starved, is merely the condition of this cause's having its normal effect.[6]

Nagel's remarks about desire appear, then, to be the result of two mistakes: confusing desires with feelings and conditions with causes. These mistakes lead him to conclude that desires not only need not but also should not figure in explanations. We should explain eating by mentioning not hunger but food deprivation. The premises are false, and the conclusion does not follow. Desires are not feelings, and although it is wrong to regard them as causes of behavior, it is useful to think of them as its general conditions. We do not give the cause of eating when we mention hunger, but we do say why that cause has that effect rather than some other.

But suppose we are wrong about desire. Suppose Nagel is right. *It does not matter*. Desire is a red herring. In the final analysis, nothing depends on it. To see why not, take Nagel at his word. Explain Jones's eating by pointing out that he has been starved for four days. Make no mention of hunger. Our explanation will still refer to *Jones*. It will still have no relevance to *Smith* or *Green*, both of whom, being well fed, have neither feelings of hunger nor a disposition to eat. We still cannot explain *their* behavior, whatever it may happen to be, by pointing out that *Jones* has been deprived of food, however objective a fact that may be. So, despite our studied refusal to mention desires, our explanation of the agent's behavior will still contain a personal pronoun; it will still lack the impersonal anonymity that Nagel requires of "objective" reasons.

If an "objective" reason is one having no identification with a particular person, there is, and can be no such thing. The whole idea is unintelligible, and so, we shall soon see, is any concept of morality that depends on it.

Prudence

We have just reviewed Nagel's critique of the doctrine that reasons are personal. As preparation for his positive argument for the contrary thesis, Nagel engages in an extended discussion of prudence, defined as concern for your future. To show that reasons can be independent of personal desires, he argues that you have reason to prepare for your future even if you presently have no wish to do so. He plans, eventually, to argue by analogy that you have reason to help other people even when you may have no wish to do so. We will agree with the premise but dispute the conclusion.

Here Nagel has an example. Suppose I plan to go to Rome. Then, Nagel says, I have reason to learn Italian, because I will want to speak it when I arrive. That I may *presently* have no desire to study Italian may be true. It makes no difference. Reason still dictates that I learn Italian *now*. This seems to Nagel to show that you can have a reason to do what you have *no* desire to do.

To reinforce this conclusion, Nagel offers a *reductio ad absurdum* of its contrary. In Nagel's view, an agent who disregards his future wishes disassociates his present self from his future self, treating his future self as if it were a different person. In fact, when it comes into being, one's future self will be continuous with one's present self, both being parts of a single enduring person. Furthermore, behaving prudently depends on recognizing the fact. It is only the impulsive and irrational person who ignores desires that he will have in the future. The prudent person counts as reasons for present actions not just his present desires but also the desires that he can expect to have later.

Nagel interprets this to mean that desires are valid throughout an agent's life. We are to view ourselves not from our present vantage point in time but from a point of view wholly outside of time. Seen from this point of view, every desire will be an eternally fixed part of the temporally extended whole that is one's enduring self. One's present and future selves will be inseparable parts of this temporally extended whole. Therefore, whatever one desires at any stage of life, one should desire timelessly, at every stage. Descriptions of one's motives should be tenseless. Not "In 1999, I wanted to do X," but "In 1999, M.H. wants to do X." As Nagel puts it,

> My basic contention has been that practical judgments must share with factual judgments the property of being assimilable to the standpoint of temporal neutrality. Just as a change from a tenseless to a tensed factual judgment does not alter what is believed, but only the standpoint from which one views it, so the change from a tenseless to a tensed practical judgment does not alter what one accepts a justification for wanting, but only the standpoint from which one wants it. If the sense of practical judgments were changed, or their motivational content lost when one shifted out of the present tense, then practical reasoning would be an area divorced from the conception of oneself as equally real over time. (p. 71)

Unfortunately for Nagel's argument, this is not the way any agent views himself, or can. On this way of looking at things, my future would be as real—that is, as determinate and fixed—as my past. Everything would already be (eternally) done; all actions would have been (eternally) taken. None of us can think of himself in such terms. Because we are ignorant of what it will bring, each of us must think of the future as something yet incomplete, something to be done—something not yet fully determinate or real. For us, the future is neither fixed nor certain, and rational but fallible beings will take account of the fact in making their plans. Omniscient beings might be able to take a different view. You and I cannot.[7]

A more defensible view of time consideration in decision making is stated in Thomas Sowell's *Knowledge and Decisions.*[8] Observing that time is never free of cost and the future never certain, Sowell says that it is rational to discount the value of a future prospect by the gratification that must be deferred until it is realized. He also observes that different individuals have different *time horizons*. In other words, different periods of time govern their calculations. Thus, impulsive persons have very short time horizons. Does that make them irrational? Not by any means. Rationality is not defined absolutely, by reference to some transcendent end, but relatively, in terms of a given individual's aims. So, if the agent's aim is gratification now, in the present moment, then what achieves that is rational for him. Therefore, as Sowell observes, the conduct of a person whose decisions are governed by short term considerations "may be as rational within his time horizon as the opposite result is for those with a longer time horizon. No one has an unlimited time horizon, and there is no logically compelling objective reason for preferring one time horizon to another."

Is this denying the possibility of what Nagel calls prudence? No. Just its necessity. Despite the modest title of his book, Nagel is not trying to prove merely that people *can* act with regard for their futures. That would have been easy to show. Nagel would have needed only to point out that sometimes people *do* act with regard to their futures. Nagel is trying to show, however, that rational creatures *must* act prudently. Or, rather, he is trying to show that, since prudence is a requirement of rationality and entails giving weight to desires that one does not presently have, therefore rationality entails giving weight to desires that one does not presently have.

This argument is fallacious. Grant that it is irrational to *acknowledge* the likelihood of having certain desires without permitting your acknowledgment to influence your behavior. It will follow that a person who presently *expects* to have certain desires presently has reason to make provision for their satisfaction. What does not follow is that a person who does not presently have these desires presently has reason to make provision for their satisfaction. Nagel has proved the first claim; he has not proved the second. Yet his argument depends on it.

If Nagel thinks that the second claim follows from the first, it is because his argument presumes that one always knows what desires one will have. This presumption is built into his talk of a timeless point of view. But only God occupies such a view; so, only He has the foreknowledge Nagel requires. The rest of us do not know what the future holds. We can only make informed guesses, and these may have little relation to the eventual facts. If we are rational, our guesses will influence our conduct.

Expecting to go to Rome and wanting to speak Italian when we arrive, we will indeed try to learn the language, as Nagel avers. But if we do *not* expect to go to Rome, or care whether we can speak Italian when we arrive, what does it mean to say that we presently have reason to act as though we do? It is hard to see. We might admit that, under the hypothesis of the example, *there is* presently reason to learn Italian, even if we do not presently *know*, or acknowledge, it. As observed in the previous chapter, however, this counts as a reason only in a *proleptic*, or anticipatory, use of the word. Furthermore, even this proleptic use is relative to persons. It is because *I* will have need to speak Italian that *I* have reason to study it. There is reason for *you* to study Italian only if *you* too are going to Rome. So, if this is an "objective" reason, it is also a personal reason.

The concept of an impersonal reason remains unintelligible.

Altruism

Nagel's reply is to try to make the concept intelligible by stipulating its truth—a procedure having all the advantages of theft over honest toil, to quote Bertrand Russell. Without offering anything remotely resembling an argument in support, Nagel states in so many words,

> *If any person Q has reason R to do act A, then every person P has reason R to promote Q's doing A.*

Thus, to use Nagel's example, suppose that G. E. Moore is about to be run over by a truck. Then, says Nagel, Moore has reason to get out of the way, and everybody else has reason to "promote" Moore's doing so. This claim is the definitive expression of Nagel's view of reasons, and, in the final analysis, it is the postulate on which he bases his argument for altruism.

It is an incredible claim. Imagine that Jones wants to kill Smith. Then, given Nagel's thesis, two things follow. First, Jones has reason to kill Smith. Second, Smith has reason to "promote" his own execution. Nagel never says what he means by the word "promote," but on any obvious interpretation of the word, it is absurd to claim that someone without suicidal tendencies has a reason to promote his own death. Recognizing this, Nagel tries to soften the paradox by saying that he is talking not about *conclusive* but about *prima facie* reasons (p. 93). "X has a reason to do Y," does not mean that X ought to do Y *all things considered*; only that X ought to do Y, *other things being equal*. If, Smith's desire to live outweighs Jones's desire to kill him, perhaps Smith need not "promote" his execution with much vigor.

This qualification may dissolve the paradox, but it makes Nagel's thesis meaningless. How are we to decide which of two competing desires is objectively weightier? Jones wants to kill Smith; Smith wants to stay alive. Whose desire should count for more? Without some way of deciding, we have no way of interpreting Nagel's claim. Yet Nagel disclaims any intention of telling us how to assign weights to desires, promising to take that question up in his next book. Unfortunately, the devil is in the details; and although thirty years have passed, Nagel has not yet kept his promise to fill them in. A later book, *The View from Nowhere,* still touts the wisdom of "objectivity" in ethics; but it does not tell us how to achieve it.[9]

Or why we should try. That question is raised in the present book, but the answer is gravely disappointing. According to Nagel, each of us is "simply a person among others all of whom are included in a single world"; so, disregard for the desires of other people manifests a failure to recognize, or a refusal, to acknowledge, their "equal reality" (p. 100). In other words, it amounts to "practical solipsism," acting as though one were the only person in the world. In the end, this is the only argument Nagel has to justify his postulate that reasons are impersonal.

The argument confuses *reality* with *value*. My disinclination to promote your efforts to kill me may betray belief that you and your project are without merit; but thinking that you are deranged and dangerous is not thinking that you are unreal. On the contrary, it is thinking that you may be too real for comfort. So, the argument is a howler. If he hopes to make his case, Nagel needs to explain how I can, and why I should, be motivated by desires that I regard as real but, because they are contrary to my interests, do not count as worthy, and this he altogether fails to do.

Instead, he reverts to prudence and suggests that the argument for altruism parallels it. The idea seems to be this: Where prudence required acknowledging the "reality" of one's future self, altruism requires acknowledging the "reality" of other selves. But this analogy is faulty. What gave the argument for prudence such plausibility as it had was one's willingness not just to *recognize* the reality of one's future self but also to *identify with* it. Recognizing it as one's future self, one thinks of its interests as *one's own* interests. If the argument for altruism is to go through in a parallel way, it will be necessary not merely to *acknowledge* the existence and interests of other people but also to *identify with* them: Just as the prudent man identifies with his future self; so the altruistic man will have to identify with other persons.

The trouble with this reasoning will be obvious: There is a clear sense in which a future you is still you, but there is no clear sense in which other people are you. So, the identification needed for Nagel's argument to go through cannot be presumed. Grant that it would be irrational not to promote the satisfaction of what you recognize to be your own desires. This fact does not show that it would be irrational not to promote the satisfaction of someone else's desires. Identification with another's interests has none of the same self-evident necessity as identification with one's own interests. Nagel's altruism will have to stand on its own. It can borrow no support from the rationality of prudence.

To say so is not to deny the *possibility* of identifying with other people; just its necessity. Fathers treat the interests of their children as their own; companions in arms treat each other's interests as their own; and so on. To acknowledge these possibilities will not, however, satisfy Nagel. As we noted earlier, he is not trying merely to prove the *possibility* of altruism. Like Kant, he wants to demonstrate its *necessity*. He wants to show that it is rational to "promote" the projects of other people, even when doing so fails to advance, or even defeats, your own projects, and like Kant he altogether fails to do this.[10]

Darwall on Impartial Reason

Perhaps recognizing Nagel's failure, other philosophers have tried to buttress his argument. One who has done so is Stephen Darwall, whose book *Impartial Reason* contains a critique of what it calls the

"DBR thesis," meaning belief that reasons are personal because they derive from desires and beliefs.[11]

According to Darwall, this thesis grows from four "roots." These are (1) naturalism, belief that an agent's behavior can best be *explained* by thinking of it as a function of his desires; (2) coherentism, belief that rationality is simply *coherence* of means to ends; (3) internalism, belief that a reason for doing something must be capable of functioning as a *motive* for doing it; and (4) belief that the DBR thesis is supported by the mathematical theory of decisions. Darwall proposes to kill the DBR thesis by cutting it off from its roots.

Darwall believes that the naturalism presupposed by the DBR thesis is the result of failing to make some needed distinctions. According to Darwall, "We speak variously of the *reasons why* someone did something, of that *person's reasons* for so acting, and of the reasons that there were *for* the person so *to* act" (p. 28; emphasis in the original). Darwall says that it is important to distinguish the third use of the word, which is *normative,* or *justificatory*, from the first and second uses, which are *explanatory*, or *descriptive.* In his view, rationality has to do with reasons that *justify* an action, not also with reasons that *cause*, or *explain*, it. In other words, it has to do with the reasons why we *should* perform an action, not with the reasons why we *do*.

Darwall's complaint against the DBR Thesis is that it offers explanations when justifications are wanted, thereby obscuring the distinction between the normative and the descriptive. Thus, he says, proponents of the DBR thesis explain an agent's behavior by referring to his desires, then go on to talk as though these justified it. Yet, Darwall notes, the behavior might be unjustified even when it is motivated.

The first thing to be said about this argument is that it, too, overlooks an important distinction—that between the *normative* and the *justifiable.* Darwall uses these two terms interchangeably, but they have quite different meanings. *Justify* is a juridical term. In its original usage, it has reference to a court of law, where an action is justified by explaining not why the defendant did it but why *we*, his judges, should excuse him. As this shows, justifying conduct requires looking at it not from the agent's point of view but from *ours*. There is, however, also such a thing as *rationalizing* conduct—showing not how it can be justified but how it serves the agent's ends.[12] Doing this involves taking not our point of view, but the *agent's*. We appraise his conduct by presuming not our beliefs and preferences but his. Thus, Smith's hitting Jones in the nose will not be justified but it will be rationalized by noting that Smith got pleasure out of it. To justify his action Jones would have to show us that Smith deserved a punch in the nose, or that he was entitled to give him one.

Since a person *ought*, other things being equal, to do what is just and, in a different sense, what is rational, both justification and rationalization fall under the heading of the *normative*—that which one ought to do. But if our concern is to understand *rationality*, not *justice* or *rectitude,* then what we should seek to know is not how conduct is justified but how it is rationalized. Having equated the normative with the justifiable, however, Darwall mistakenly equates rationalization with justification. Then, he concludes that it is proponents of the DBR thesis who have overlooked rationalization. Using some graceless and redundant phrases of his own invention, he says that since the DBR thesis neglects *justificatory reasons*, it is guilty of overlooking *normative reasons.* Well, to use Darwall's ugly terminology, the reply to this is that justificatory reasons are not the only kinds of normative reasons there are. Also to be considered are rationalizing reasons.

To justify this charge, we need only remind you how defenders of the DBR thesis distinguish explaining conduct from rationalizing it.[13] Imagine a person P with desires D1...Dn. For simplicity's sake, assume that these desires are well defined, consistent with each other, and ranked in accordance with the formal requirements of some standard theory of decision, so that D1 is preferred under specified circumstances to D2, D2 to D3, D3 to D4 and so on. In good DBR fashion, we shall say that P *has reason* to perform any action A that promises to fulfill one of his desires. Observing that his desires are of different strengths, however, we shall add that P has *more reason* to perform those actions that promise to get him what he desires more strongly, and we shall also say that he has *most reason* to do what will get him what he desires most.

These simple and commonplace definitions give a proponent of the DBR thesis all that he needs to distinguish a normative from a descriptive use of the term *reason.* Very roughly: All he has to do is (1) distinguish what someone ought to do, other things being equal, from what he ought to do, all things considered, then (2) equate the latter with what he ought to do *in the final analysis.* Thus, suppose that Sam eats sweets and coffee for breakfast. We ask him why, and he replies

"Because I like them." We may retort, "Yes, but you would prefer to be slim and healthy." By making this reply, we are not denying that Sam's desire for sweets constitutes a reason for him to eat them. We are merely reminding Sam that he has a weightier reason—namely, his desire for good health—not to give in to his desire for sweets.

Darwall thinks that this blurs the distinction between the *purely* descriptive and the *purely* normative, but Darwall has confused a distinction with a dichotomy. There is a distinction between Buicks and automobiles, but every Buick is also an automobile, and, if the proponents of the DBR thesis are right, every "normative reason" is also a "descriptive reason." We explained why this is so in the preceding chapter, but we may summarize the point here: To say why a person ought to do something is to invoke a consideration that either *does*, or under given circumstances *would*, motivate his conduct; and to do this is to refer to the agent's actual or potential beliefs and desires

It is the disjunction in this last sentence that reveals why a proponent of the DBR thesis is not limited to describing. Given this disjunction, we have all the tools we need to explain not only why an agent does what she does but also why she should do something else: It is because she *would* do so if she took certain considerations into account that she is now failing to acknowledge. This shows that the DBR thesis has the terminology with which to formulate rationalizations. To explain how justification can be done in DBR terms, we need only point out the possibility of shifting from the point of view of the agent to that of an observer.

If this naturalistic account of reasons does not satisfy Darwall, it is because he wants a concept of norms—and, therefore, of reasons—that (1) severs them from all connection with desires and (2) identifies them instead with a concern for impartial justice. But this begs the question. What was wanted was an understanding of what makes conduct *rational*, not an account of what makes it *just*. That is why his confusion of rationalization with justification matters.

Irrational Ends

Darwall has a different diagnosis of the issue. In his view, the problem is that the DBR thesis accepts what he calls coherentism, meaning belief that rationality is coherence of means with ends. In

Darwall's view, this overlooks the possibility of criticizing an agent's ends (p. 15). Darwall makes the same complaint against standard theories of decision. Taking the ends as given, they limit themselves to assessing ways of achieving them. Believing that if conduct is to be rational, it must be rational through and through, Darwall objects that a proper decision theory would make provision for the criticism of ends. It would acknowledge that conduct is rational only if the end pursued is rational too.

This criticism, a common one, overlooks the possibility of criticizing an agent's ends by considering whether they cohere with each other. Suppose Smith wants both to eat hot fudge sundaes and to stay lean. *Pace* Darwall, nothing in the DBR thesis precludes noticing that these two desires are inconsistent with each other. On the contrary, since no means can cohere with both of them, the DBR thesis is committed to noticing their inconsistency if it is committed to assessing the coherence of means with ends, as Darwall acknowledges. So, Darwall has attacked a straw man. The DBR thesis does not forbid us to criticize an agent's ends. It merely forbids us to criticize A's ends on the grounds that they are contrary to B's, and it does this only when the question is the rationality, not the justice, of the conduct at issue. In short, internal criticism is permitted. It is only external criticism that is disallowed. This fact is evident in the postulates of every decision theory. These make both consistency of ends and transitivity of preferences conditions of rational behavior.

Darwall's reply to this fact is confusing if not also confused. He says that requiring transitivity as a condition of rationality is a mistake. Suppose that P prefers A to B for reason R1, B to C for reason R2, and C to A (*not* A to C) for reason R3. Assuming that these three reasons are consistent with each other, Darwall says that so must be this set of intransitive preferences (p. 68, p. 74). But suppose that X believes that p for reason R1, that q for reason R2, and that not both p and q for reason R3. Then X has the following inconsistent set of beliefs: that p, that q, that not both p and q. Yet, if R1, R2, and R3 are consistent with each other, Darwall must declare that the beliefs are consistent too, which is absurd. Darwall has shot himself in the foot.

He has also distracted us from his main point, which is that both standard decision theory and the DBR thesis lack a satisfactory account of "normative," because "objective," so "universal" reasons. Darwall believes that, in order to provide such an account, one would have to show not only how a reason *does* (or could, or would) but also how it *should* motivate conduct. And this, he says, is something that neither the DBR thesis nor any formal decision theory does. Remarking that "subjectivist" decision theories of the kind favored by proponents of the DBR thesis tell us that the agent A prefers strategy S because it leads to outcome O, Darwall observes that these theories offer no answer to the question, "Why should A prefer O?" Concluding that rational decision theory is in this respect "incomplete," Darwall proposes to complete it by offering an account of reasons that are not merely formal and subjective but "substantive" and "objective"—whatever that means.

About one thing, Darwall is right. No proponent of the DBR thesis, and no decision theorist, tells us why any reason *should* motivate us. What Darwall fails to understand is why this is so. Talk of reasons that *should* motivate us is circular. All parties to the discussion agree that

> (1) *x ought to do y*

means

> (2) *There is reason for x to do y.*

If Darwall is right, there is reason for x to do y only if this reason —call it R1—should motivate x to do y. So, (1) means,

> (3) *x ought to be motivated by reason R1 to do y.*

Given, however, that (1) means (2), (3) must mean,

> (4) *There is reason R2 for x to be motivated by R1 to do y.*

And, if Darwall is right, (4) is true only if

> (5) *x ought to be motivated by reason R3 to be motivated by R2 to be motivated by R1 to do y,*

and so on, *ad infinitum*. As this shows, to define the word *ought* using the word *reason*, then define the word *reason* using the word *ought* is to go in a circle, getting nowhere.

Nevertheless, Darwall, complains that the mistake of both normal decision theorists and proponents of the DBR thesis is to put personal preference first, reason last. So, he proposes to reverse the order, putting reason first, preference second, in order to guarantee that rational decisions are based on *rational* preferences. Declaring "a reason is a fact that motivates when rationally considered" (p. 86) he says that, "If *p* is a fact about A reflective awareness of which would move S [a rational agent] to prefer his doing A (to his not doing A), then *p* is a (presumptive) reason for S to do A" (ibid.). Then he defines a *presumptive reason* as a consideration that *would* motivate *a rational person*, because it involves pursuit of an end that is itself rational because part of a system of rational ends.

But to say this is to use the word *rational* to define the word *reason* when talk of rationality presupposes prior understanding of the concept of a reason. More circling.

Must Reasons be Rational?

This brings us to Darwall's final objection to the DBR thesis. According to him, it confuses the belief that reasons are motives with the belief that reasons are premised on desires. Darwall calls the first belief *internalism*; the second is the DBR thesis.

Darwall believes that to confuse these two claims is to overlook the lessons of David Hume. Although Hume is a hero of DBR theorists, Darwall regards him as "a prime example of a philosopher who embraces internalism but who is not committed to any version of the [DBR thesis]" (p. 52). In support of this interpretation, Darwall notes two facts. First, Hume limited the word *reason* to beliefs. When speaking "strictly and philosophically," he did not call desires reasons (p. 53). Darwall interprets this as a repudiation of the DBR thesis. Yet, Darwall observes, Hume insisted that a reason must have the capacity to "move the will" (p. 57).

In reply, it is relevant to note that the DBR thesis might be true even if Hume did not think so, but Darwall's interpretation of Hume is both unorthodox and unconvincing. There are some very good reasons why Hume is generally regarded as an advocate of what Darwall calls the DBR thesis: Hume clearly thought that behavior is motivated by beliefs and desires. He also clearly thought that, if you want to give somebody a reason for doing something, you should show him how it will help him satisfy his desires. In short, Hume accepted the DBR thesis. Before Darwall, nobody ever doubted it. It is true that Hume declined to call desires *reasons*, reserving that term for beliefs. But this fact does not prove that he thought beliefs alone sufficient to motivate conduct, in the absence of associated desires. Furthermore, this idea is hard to reconcile either with Hume's famous declaration that "Reason is, and only ought to be the slave of the passions" or with his emphasis on *sentiment* as a basis for moral judgment.

Darwall's reply is that Hume wanted us to make our judgments from an *impartial* point of view (p. 61), but Darwall has a peculiar idea about what makes a point of view impartial. In Hume's eighteenth century lexicon, a judge was impartial if he did not favor one of the parties to the dispute. According to Darwall, a judge is impartial when his reasons are not "self-centered." When is a reason not "self-centered"? When it is not selfish? No. For Darwall, a reason is "impartial " only when it is not anybody's in particular. He says,

> As its title suggests, this book seeks to vindicate the feeling of the moralist that considerations other than self-centered ones are reasons to act.... It maintains that practical reason is, at its base, *impartial* rather than self-centered. More specifically, it argues that reasons to act are grounded in principles that would be (relatively) rational to choose were a person to adopt a perspective *impartial* between agents and to select principles for all to act on. (p. 17, emphasis added)

For the moment, let us overlook the circularity of defining an impartial reason as one that is impartial. (Look again if you don't believe me.) Let us focus instead on the phrase "select principles for all to act on." Despite its opacity, this phrase makes one thing clear. We were not being overly literal in our earlier observation that Darwall is talking about appraising conduct from the disinterested point of view of a judge—someone who decides the case at hand by formulating a principle that, he hopes, will hold for all relevantly similar cases. In short, he is talking about making a judgment as to whether the agent's conduct was *just* or *unjust*, when what we wanted to know was what makes conduct *rational* or *irrational*.

Darwall makes this mistake because he has assumed what Kant tried to prove—namely, that it is always and necessarily rational to behave justly. It this assumption that leads him to conclude that "reasons to act" are necessarily impartial, because impartial by definition. This, in turn, leads him to conclude erroneously that, instead of being based on personal preferences, reasons must be based on objective facts.

Darwall conceals these errors from himself by engaging in double-talk. What sort of a fact would enjoy the necessary motivating capacity? The answer, it turns out, is facts enjoying "Nagelian objectivity," facts having "objective," "intersubjective," or "impersonal" value (p. 118). Following Nagel, Darwall says that such facts are *universal*: If a fact is a reason for someone, it is a reason for everybody (p. 118). We can learn to recognize the presence of a fact's universality and objectivity by adopting an *impartial* or *impersonal* point of view. This, Darwall says, is the view of Hume's impartial spectator, who

> expresses sentiments in which he expects all his audience are to concur with him. He must here, therefore, depart from his private and particular situation and must choose a point of view common to him with others; he must move to some universal principle of the human frame and touch a string to which all mankind have an accord and symphony. (Quoted from Hume by Darwall on p. 141)

In effect, Darwall is *defining* reasons as considerations made from what Kurt Baier called *the moral point of view* and John Rawls has called the Original Position (p. 182, p. 230). From this point of view one is to look at things not with an eye jaundiced by one's personal preferences but with an eye made clear by its intention to give due consideration to the preferences and interests of all parties. Darwall's thesis is that only this attitude is rational. But he has not proved this claim. Instead, he has merely assumed it, as if it were self-evident, then adjusted his definitions to suit his assumption, equating a rational point of view with an impartial one.

This way of proceeding begs the question. First, a reason is defined as anything that counts as a reason when seen from a rational point of view. Then a rational point of view is defined as an impartial point of view—one presupposing a principle that is rational not just for the agent but for everybody. Finally, it is concluded that nothing counts as a reason for *any* person to do something unless it counts as a reason for every person to do it. As observed already, to reason like this is just to go round and round, like a child on a carousel.

Is there no way off this carnival toy? Having ridden it for over a hundred discursive pages, Darwall finally tries to get off by discussing what he calls the *normative* aspect of reason. This concept, which was announced early, is explained late:

> To this point we have focused primarily on the motivational aspect of reasons for acting; their capacity to motivate when they are rationally considered. Equally

> central to our notion of a reason is what I call its *normative* aspect. Reasons for a person to do something are not simply facts about an action that motivate him to act. Rather they are considerations that rationally *ought* to have force for a person and that do [have force] for a person who considers them as he rationally ought. Without the normative aspect of reasons there would be nothing to distinguish reasons *for* someone *to* do something from reasons *why* he did or will do it, reasons that justify or recommend action from those that explain it. (p. 20; emphasis in the original)

Darwall eventually tries to explain this concept of a normative *reason* further, by talking of a normative *system* —a system of norms, standards, or requirements "that *must* be met" (p. 203). This is then called a Rational Normative System, and a consideration is said to be made rational by reference to this system. In short, rationality is explained by talking of reasons, which are explained by invoking rational considerations, which are defined as considerations presupposing a system of *rational* norms, and so ever on. No progress here. Just the same old merry-go-round.

There are two ways to get off this ride. One is to maintain with the Platonists that the only reason to do something is that it would achieve the good, but this way off has its own disadvantages. It would require proving that the good is independent of desire, and it would raise the problem of how anyone who does not desire the good could be motivated to pursue it. The other way to get off is to claim, with G. E. Moore and W. D. Ross that the concept of a *reason* is logically primitive and ultimate; so, indefinable. This would require saying that reasons can be known only by intuitions, the veracity of which can be confirmed by no known means, and, it would raise the problem of explaining why anybody should be moved by an intuition he personally does not have.

Conclusion: The concept of objective, so impersonal, reasons is unintelligible. It detaches the word *reason* from the beliefs and desires that give it such meaning as it has for us, leaving us grasping at the wind.

Notes

1. (Oxford: Clarendon University Press, 1970).
2. Nagel's style is deceptive. The words are small and the grammar is usually simple but both become increasingly vague as the argument reaches its climax.
3. As we shall see in the last half of this chapter, Stephen Darwall does come close to making such a claim on Nagel's behalf. At times Darwall suggests that a

reason *should* motivate, but he appears to acknowledge that it sometimes *does* not. He also defines a reason as a consideration that would motivate a *rational person*, but there is no reason why an irrational person should not have a reason to do something.

4. Bond's defense of Nagel distinguishes a *grounding* reason from a *motivating* reason (E.J. Bond, *Reason and Value*, Cambridge: Cambridge University Press, 1983, p. 57). A grounding reason is the thing's objective and possibly unrecognized value; the motivating reason is the agent's desire. Bond believes that motivating reasons are premised on grounding reasons. In other words, we desire, or prefer, something because we regard it as good. This assumes that we know how to make a distinction between believing that a thing is good and preferring it. It also overlooks the way in which talk of grounding reasons is parasitic on talk of motivating reasons: The unrecognized value of a thing counts as a reason for pursuing it only in the proleptical sense that we can see how it would motivate conduct if it were recognized.
5. This is comparable to explaining why dropped things fall by invoking gravity, the disposition of dropped objects to fall. Dropping the object is the efficient cause of its falling; gravity the formal cause.
6. For a fuller discussion of these distinctions, see my "Aristotle's Four Becauses," cited in the preceding chapter. But ignore the mistaken discussion of motives, which I there mistakenly equate with efficient causes. I became aware of the error belatedly.
7. This account of rationality is, of course, greatly oversimplified. What a truly rational agent tries to do is weigh the value of the future outcome against the probability of its occurring and the expense of attaining it. An informative account of the mechanisms involved can be found in George Ainslie, *Picoeconomics: The Strategic Interaction of Successive Motivational States Within the Person* (Cambridge: Cambridge University Press, 1992).
8. Basic Books, 1996, pp. 93-96.
9. New York: Oxford University Press, 1986.
10. For a justification of this claim, see the chapter on Kant.
11. Stephen Darwall, *Impartial Reason* (Ithaca, NY: Cornell University Press, 1983). In his preface, Darwall speaks of a belief that reasons are *self-centered.* This ambiguous expression obscures the difference between belief that reasons are *personal* and belief that they are *selfish.* As noted in the preceding chapter, however, the first belief has to do with the *ownership* of the desire; the second with its *object.* Mother's Theresa's desires are personal; they belong to her. They are not on that account selfish, aimed at her benefit.
12. I use the word *rationalize* in its original and etymological sense, not in the somewhat narrow sense given it by Freud, who counted as rationalizations only the giving of *bad* reasons.
13. This demonstration is laid out in full in the preceding chapter.

5

How to Make Moral Judgments

Are "moral judgments" judgments properly so-called? Do they have truth values? If so, are they ever true?

This, the most vexed and difficult question in moral philosophy, is made even more vexed and difficult by the ambiguity of the word *moral*. If we use the word broadly, as was customary in ancient times, *any* evaluation of *conduct* will count as a moral judgment, the Latin word *more* being a synonym for habit, custom, or practice, as was the Greek word *ethos*. Hence, in ancient times "That was an intelligent (or brave, or considerate, or prudent, or charming, or charitable, or sensitive, or useful) thing to do" would have counted as a moral judgment, a judgment of ethics. In this broad usage, "moral judgment about conduct" is a pleonasm, "nonmoral judgment about conduct" a solecism. If, however, we use the word *moral* in the more narrow way that has become customary since Kant and was becoming so before him, only judgments regarding duties (the obligatory) and their correlatives (rights) and cognates (the permissible and the forbidden) count as moral judgments. Hence, "Doing that is obligatory" counts as a moral judgment, and so does "Doing that is forbidden, " but "Doing that is intelligent" and "Doing that is courageous" do not. In this narrow, modern usage, *moral* is a quasi-juridical word, one used to contrast *moral* conduct with *immoral* conduct—conduct that breaks the rules.

Emotivism as Obverse Platonism

Let us begin by asking, first, whether it makes sense to attribute truth values to moral judgments in the *broad* sense of the term. Consider the judgment, "That was a stupid and harmful thing to do." Is such a judgment ever true or false? To all but some philosophers, the answer will seem obvious: People sometimes do stupid and harmful things. So, it is sometimes true to say so. Therefore, some moral judgments are true; and if some are true, then some, their contraries, must be false. QED.

This straightforward and commonsensical argument will leave some philosophers unpersuaded. In their view, evaluations such as this are never true or false. In fact, these philosophers say, evaluations are not judgments at all. Despite their indicative form, they are mere expostulations, like "Bah!" and "Hurrah!," which lack the syntax and the semantics of genuine statements. These expostulations express approval or disapproval but they provide no information. This view is called *emotivism.*[1] A cousin of emotivism, J. L. Mackie's *error theory*, maintains that no evaluation is ever *true* because all such judgments are *false*.[2] There will be more on the distinction between these two theories later.

Both emotivism and the error theory appear to result from accepting an erroneous theory of truth. According to this theory, which was invented by Plato, a judgment is true or false according to whether the thing being discussed has the property that is being attributed to it, where a property is a distinctive way in which a group of objects resemble each other. Thus, a judgment of the form "x is square" is true just in case x has the property of being square, this being what squares have in common; and a judgment of the form "x is good" is true just in case x has *the property of being good,* this being what good things have in common. *Moral realists*, as they like nowadays to call themselves, believe that there are such properties.[3] Emotivists doubt it.

Why doubt that there is a property of being good? Because there appears to be no distinctive way in which all good things resemble each other.[4] Instead, some things count as good because they are pleasurable, some because they confer benefits; some behavior counts as good because it is intelligent, some because it is courageous; and so on. As this suggests, the variety of good things and actions is endless; there is no distinctive way in which they all resemble each other. That we describe all of these diverse activities and things by using the same word—viz., the word *good*—appears to mean not that that *they* are similar but that our *responses* are. Although there is no way in which all "good" things are alike, we like, admire, or otherwise approve of them. So, the emotivist concludes that the similarity denoted by the word *good* is subjective; not objective: It is in our responses, not in the things that elicit it.

Given the Platonic account of judgments as ascription of properties, and given that there is no property of being good, this conclusion is sound.[5] It is, however, also paradoxical, because it conflicts with the commonplace, and seemingly intelligible, practice of ascribing truth values to evaluations. Fortunately, the Platonic account of judgments is demonstrably false. Here are two counterexamples to it. Although the predicate "x is near Jones" is true of all objects that are near Jones, there need be no distinctive way in which these objects resemble each other. Similarly, although the predicate "x is pleasant" is true of all things that give pleasure, we count them as pleasant not because *they* are similar to each other but because they have similar effects *on us*.

Often, it is true, philosophers say that things have a certain *property,* meaning merely that these things can be described using a certain *predicate*.[6] Given this loose way of talking, which was started by Plato but persists in some regions to this day, objects near Jones do have a property in common after all, namely, the property of being near Jones. Similarly, pleasant things do have a property in common, namely the property of giving pleasure. The trouble is that this way of talking changes the meaning of the word *property*. Saying that two or more objects have the same property was supposed to mean not merely that these objects could be described *in the same terms* but also that they were *in some distinctive way alike*. If we stick with this definition of the term, the conclusion to draw is not that relations are properties but that designating a property, meaning a similarity, is not a requirement of truth.

If designating a property is not necessary to truth, what is? As Aristotle observed, it is just this: That the thing in question be as it is said to be. Thus, "x is near Jones," is true just in case x is near Jones, and "That was a stupid and harmful thing to do" is true just in case that was a stupid and harmful thing to do. There is no need to talk here of properties, and doing so just confuses the issue. Following Tarski, we may count a statement of the form "x is F" as true just in case x is F. Thus, "Snow is white" counts as true because snow is white, and "x is good " will count as true just in case x is good. If truth is the concern, evaluation presents no special difficulties.

Those who recognize this fact and get clear about its implications should no longer feel a need to choose between (1) belief that, because evaluations are sometimes true, there must be a property of being good and (2) belief that, since there is no such property, no evaluations are ever true. Instead, rejecting talk of properties as ill-defined, they will reject not only moral realism but also emotivism and the error theory. Having seen how to explain truth without talking about properties, they will see that evaluations may be true even if there is no such thing as the property of being good.

Evaluation as Description

This has an important implication. If some evaluations are true, then evaluation is not the opposite of description but a special case of it: To evaluate something is just to describe it using evaluative terminology—language that gives things a ranking on some more or less determinate scale of preferences. So, although there is a *distinction* between evaluation and description, as there is a distinction between Buicks and cars, this distinction is not a *dichotomy*, like that between Buicks and Fords. Instead, as some vehicles are at once Buicks *and* cars, so some judgments are at once descriptive *and* evaluative. An example is the judgment, "That was a stupid and harmful thing to do." At once descriptive *and* evaluative, its being the one does not preclude its being the other.

This is an unconventional claim that many philosophers will reject out of hand. Perhaps they will agree that "That was a stupid and harmful thing to do" is descriptive, but they will deny that it is also evaluative. To be evaluative, they will say, the sentence would have to do more than *describe* the behavior; it would also have to add that it was *bad*. Plainly, however, our sentence does not use the word *bad*; it uses only the words *stupid* and *harmful*. To some philosophers, this will suggest that the evaluation is not part of the description but something that has to be added on to it. This argument sounds valid, but being stupid and harmful is *one way of being bad*, not something separable from it. You cannot describe behavior as stupid and harmful without implying that it is bad. (Try it!) As this shows, the badness is not something to be added on to the stupidity and the harm, or something that results from it; it is part of it.

Why, then, do many philosophers continue to believe that describing and evaluating are not just different but also mutually exclusive activities? One reason may be that some evaluations are so vague or so imprecise that they lack *determinate* truth values. Out of all context, the generic evaluation "x is good" suffers from this defect. As just emphasized, things can be good in any of a wide variety of ways. So, describing something as good without specifying the particular way in which it has merit, is saying what needs further interpretation. In what way, specifically, is the thing supposed to be good? And how good is it supposed to be? Until we know the answers to these questions, we may feel that the evaluation has provided us with little or no information.

This consideration is real, but it does not justify the conclusion. Grant that merely calling something *good* does not specify the particular way in which it is good. This does not prove that the declaration is false, or that it lacks truth value. Consider the statement, "There is something in the next room." This is also vague, but it may nevertheless be true, and it at least supplies the information that the room is not empty. The fact that evaluations are sometimes vague does not suffice to distinguish them from other statements.

It is true that some uses of the word *good* have been so emptied of precise meaning that they may now have little but emotive content, but the same thing can happen to what purport to be evaluatively neutral words. For an example, consider current use of the word *racist*.[7] Although this word might once have had definite meaning, it has become little more than a term of abuse, to describe people who do not favor the politics of affirmative action or economic redistribution. A similar thing happened during the Cold War to the word *communist*, which people in comic strips sometimes used as a general term of condemnation equivalent to *son-of-a-bitch,* another term that long ago lost much of its precise descriptive import. There is no doubt that evaluations *can* be purely emotive, or nearly so. Still, the fact that *some* evaluations have little besides emotive content hardly fails to prove that *all* of them do.

Value as Relative but Objective

Another argument for emotivism is that evaluations do not seem be disputable like descriptions. Suppose somebody says, "This tastes good." If his statement is true, then one would expect its formal contradictory, "This does not taste good," to be false. Yet, we do not conclude that two people are contradicting each other if one affirms that licorice tastes good and the other denies it. Instead, we say that there is no disputing tastes. The emotivist has a ready explanation for this. According to him, judgments of taste are not statements but expressions of attitude. Lacking truth value they are not in opposition.

This is a good explanation, but Thomas Hobbes had a better one: Every person uses the words *good* and *bad* "in relation to himself"; so, evaluations are indexed to their speakers, like statements about location. As "The Eiffel Tower is near" is elliptical for "The Eiffel Tower is near me," so "Licorice tastes good" is elliptical for "Licorice tastes good to me." [8] Now, the same thing cannot be both near to and far from the same person, but the Eiffel Tower can be both near Jacques in Paris and far from Jack in New York, Similarly, the same thing cannot both taste good and not taste good to the same person at the same time under the same conditions, but it can taste good to you and bad to me, or taste good when you are well, bad when you are sick.

Hobbes's theory—that evaluations are indexed to persons and, we have just suggested, to circumstances—has two great advantages over emotivism. First, it enables us to see how evaluations can have truth values. If Hobbes was right, "Licorice tastes good" is true or false according to whether licorice is such as to please the palate of the person who says so in the circumstances in which he says it. Second, Hobbes's theory enables us to see how *evaluations* can be disputed even if *values* cannot. There can be no mistake in *liking* the taste of licorice, because you venture no opinion thereby, but you can mistakenly believe that you like it when in fact you do not. If so, your belief can be disputed. Again, it is like location. "The Eiffel Tower is near" is true or false according to the location of the speaker. Yet, the speaker might be mistaken in believing the Tower to be near him. So, you can dispute someone's belief about the location of the Eiffel Tower, even if you cannot dispute the Eiffel Tower.

Moral realists will not be satisfied. In their opinion, if A says "Licorice tastes good" and B replies "Licorice does not taste good," B has *contradicted* A. Often, that will be B's opinion too, but this opinion is easy to explain without supposing it to be true. A better theory is that the disagreement is purely verbal: A is attributing to licorice the power to please *his* palate, B is denying it the power to please *hers*, and each might be stating a fact of the matter. If so, there is no contradiction between them.

To insist that there must be a contradiction is to overlook the fact that, in the mouths of different persons, the same *sentence* can be used to make different *statements*, one true, the other false. Thus, "I am Max Hocutt" is true if I say it, false if you do. Similarly, "Licorice tastes good" will be true if you say it, false if I do. This important fact is often blurred by the confused Kantian notion that truth must be *universal* to be objective, but if this means "I am Max Hocutt" and "Licorice tastes good" are true whoever says them, it is patently false.

Moral realists will object that this makes truth to be a matter of opinion. In other words, it gives up truth for opinions.[9] The realist arrives at this conclusion by reasoning as follows: If the very same statement—Licorice tastes good—is true because you assert it, false because I deny it, then there is no truth of the matter, just a difference of opinions, one true for you, the other true for me, neither true absolutely.

This objection embodies three mistakes. First, as just explained, when you say and I deny "Licorice tastes good," I am not denying the statement that you are affirming. Rather, you are affirming that licorice tastes good *to you*, and I am denying that it tastes good *to me*. Second, we are not reporting a difference in our *opinions*; we are describing a difference in our *palates*. You are not saying and I am not denying "Licorice tastes good in my opinion"; you are saying, and I am denying, "Licorice pleases my palate." So, third, what each of us says is not just true in his opinion; it is true absolutely.

Again, it is like the Eiffel Tower. That its location is relative does not mean that the truth about its location is relative. Jacques says what is true when he affirms "The Eiffel Tower is near," and Jack says what is true when to denies it—*not* because the same statement is both true and false *or* because the truth about the Eiffel Tower's location depends on anybody's opinion *but* because the Eiffel Tower is in fact near Jacques, far from Jack. In short, the Eiffel Tower is not near Jacques, far from Jack, because they think so. Rather, they think so because it is true. Similarly, licorice does not taste good to you, bad to me, because we think so; we think so because it is true.

So far we have used an instance of intrinsic value to illustrate this point of logic, but it holds for instrumental goods too. In fact, these provide even clearer instances. Nothing is absolutely beneficial — beneficial independently of every person and every situation. Instead, what benefits you might not benefit, it might even harm, me. Thus, consider whether penicillin is good medicine. Taken out of all context, this seemingly simple question has no answer. Penicillin is not good *in itself*, standing there in the capsule or syringe. Instead, it is good for people with bacterial infections, not good for people with viral infections, and it is bad for people who have allergies to it.

That the utility of penicillin is thus relative ought, however, not to encourage belief that it varies with opinions. Let no one argue: If "Penicillin is beneficial" is neither true nor false as it stands, the reason must be that it is true in the opinion of some persons, false in the opinion of others. No. The reason is that penicillin benefits some people but not others. That penicillin is good for people with bacterial infections does not mean that they think so. The stuff can cure someone who does not think it beneficial, or kill someone who does.

What holds for these examples also holds for conduct. Its intrinsic or instrumental value (we shall discuss its moral value later) is also relative. Not "Courage is good" but "Courage pleases or benefits persons P under circumstances C." Not "Kindness is good" but "Kindness pleases or benefits persons Q in situations S." And so on.

Again, the explanation is not that truth is relative but that intrinsic and instrumental value are. A thing or practice does not have value V; it has value of kind K for persons P under circumstances C, and what has K for person P1 under circumstances C1 might not have K for P2 in circumstances C2.

Prescription as Description, not Command

We have learned that, since evaluation is a form of relational description, evaluations have truth values, like other indicative statements; furthermore, these truth values are absolute, although the values indicated are relative.

What about *prescriptions*, statements of the form "x ought to do y"? These also have indicative form. Do they also have truth value? Again, there is compelling reason to think so. To say "x ought to do y" is to imply that x's doing y would be a good thing, at least for x. The converse also holds, meaning that the evaluation and the prescription are logically equivalent. So, if one is true, then the other must be true too. Since evaluations have truth values, then so must prescriptions. QED.

The argument is sound, but it contradicts one of the most deeply entrenched dogmas of modern philosophy. According to this dogma, there is an unbridgeable gap between *ought* and *is*; so, you cannot derive one from the other. Many philosophers regard this principle as axiomatic, so beyond dispute. In their view, you can say how things *are,* or you can say how things *ought to be*, but you cannot do both at the same time in the same breath using the same words.

This view is sometimes attributed to David Hume, but the attribution is disputable. There is indeed a famous passage, which we have quoted and discussed in the preceding chapter, in which Hume objects to the practice, common in his day as in ours, of talking about how things *are*, then switching to talking about how things *ought to be*, without explaining the switch in terminology. But a careful reading will reveal that Hume's complaint was not about making the switch; it was about failing to explain it.

Often, however, the explanation is ready to hand. That some action would be stupid and harmful is usually good enough reason for concluding that you ought not to do it. Although this inference derives an *ought* from an *is,* Hume could not have condemned it. In Hume's understanding, one ought, other things being equal, to do what one has reason to do, but, Hume held, one has reason to do what promises to secure one's desires. Stupid and harmful behavior has consequences that are not desired; so one has reason to avoid it.

Kant, not Hume, is the source of the distinctively modern belief that you cannot derive an *ought* from an *is*.[10] Kant believed this because he maintained that the purpose of a prescription is to influence conduct.[11] So, he reasoned that a prescription must be a command, a speech act aimed at bringing about a certain action. From this, it followed that a prescription cannot also be a statement aimed at providing information. If Kant was right, the indicative form of prescriptions is misleading: "You ought to do y" means "Do y!," which is not indicative but imperative in form and is, accordingly, neither true nor false. Since imperatives lack truth values and state no matters of fact, Kant reasoned that the same must be true of prescriptions.[12]

This has been an influential line of thought, but it is fallacious. That commands lack truth values is certainly true. "Do y!" is neither true nor false. But pragmatics and semantics are not mutually exclusive.

Kant's claim is plausible only if we limit it to the second person form of address, "You ought to do y," which usually has as its aim to influence the listener's conduct. Suppose, however, that I say "Smith ought to do y," speaking of some third party who is not present. Then, whom have I commanded to do what?

Also overlooked by the Kantian argument is that nonevaluative statements of fact can influence, and be meant to influence, conduct. "You are in the path of an oncoming truck!" states a fact, but it also gives a warning, which you might do well to heed. This shows that providing information need not exclude influencing behavior. On the contrary, judgments usually influence behavior *by providing information.* Thus, "You ought to move" attempts to alter your conduct by suggesting that moving is in your interests. In this, it is quite unlike the command "Move!," which seeks to influence your behavior without giving information.

What information do statements of the form "You ought to do x" provide? It depends. As we noted in a preceding chapter on the topic, "Sam ought to do x" sometimes means "Sam's doing x would comport with *Sam's* values." At other times, it means, "Sam's doing x would comport with *my* [i.e., the speaker's] values." Sometimes it means "Sam's doing x is required by the rules of Sam's society." At other times it means, "Sam's doing x is required by the rules of my society." Nothing but confusion comes from collapsing the distinctions between these.

That a sentence does not have the same truth value on each of its many interpretations does not mean either that statements of the form "x ought to do y" have multiple truth values or that they lack truth values altogether. It means that the same sentence can be used to make different statements. Truth value attaches to the statement made, not to the sentence used to make it. Thus, just as "I am Max Hocutt" is true if said by me, false if said by you, so "Sam ought to do y" is true if said in one way, false if said in another.

This fact should not encourage belief that the same judgment might be both true and false. The point, to repeat it once more, is that mere use of the same words does not necessarily constitute the same judgment; it might instead constitute one judgment in x's mouth, another in y's. Nor is this so because what is true in x's opinion might be false in y's. It is certainly true that the same statement might be true in x's opinion, false in y's, but to say so is not to say that the same statement might be both true and false, or neither. That p is true *in x's opinion* does not mean that p is *true*; it means merely that x believes that p is true. But what x believes may be false. So, being true in x's opinion is not a way of being true.

Once again, then, there is no support here for the logically confused, if popular, doctrine that truth—including the truth of evaluations—is relative. What is relative is the values that make an evaluation true or false. Once these values are fixed, however, so is the evaluation's truth value. Again, it is like location. Location is relative, but the truth about it is absolute.

So much for moral judgments in the broad, evaluative sense of the term. Since these are indicative in form, it is natural to think of them as having truth values, and we have found no good reason not to do so.

The Juridical and the Imperative

Let us turn now to moral judgments in the narrow juridical, sense of the word. I mean judgments that some practice is *moral* or *immoral*. I call these judgments *juridical* because they are comparable to judgments as to whether a practice is *legal* or *illegal*. Because juridical judgments are also evaluative, much of what we said above will apply to them too. Let us deal with it first.

Our question is the same as before: Do these judgments have truth values? Are they ever true? As before, there is an obvious reason to think so. People often do things that are morally right or wrong, and it is sometimes true to say so. Therefore, some juridical judgments are true; and if some are true, then some (their contraries and contradictories) must be false. QED.

Unpersuaded, emotivists will reply that there is no way in which all "morally right" actions resemble each other. Describing them as morally right indicates only that we approve of them. So, it gives us no factual information about the act that is approved Therefore, emotivists conclude, juridical moral judgments lack truth values.

As before, however, the premise of the argument is false. It is true that a particular judgment *can* be an expression of approval based on no fact of the matter, but this is not necessarily, or even normally, so. As we shall see in some detail later, judgment that a practice is morally acceptable normally means that it is consistent with the rules of morality that happen to be in force in the speaker's society.[13] When that is so, the judgment has factual meaning and truth value.

Kantians will argue that moral judgments are really commands in disguise, so lacking in truth value. This view is popular, but it is also hard to square with the facts, for several reasons. First, "x is immoral" is indicative, not imperative, in form. Second, commands are always directed at the listener, while a moral judgment may concern the conduct of a third person who need be no party to the conversation. If, talking not to Smith but to you, I say "That would be the morally correct thing for Smith to do," I am informing *you*, not giving orders to *Smith*. Third, commands are given in the present and concern the future, while a moral judgment may be about the past. Thus, I may say to Smith, "What Jones did was morally correct," which will state a fact or falsehood but command nobody to do anything.

Most of these points were made above, in the discussion of evaluative judgments generally. But juridical judgments have their peculiarities, and we must now deal with these.

When Juridical Judgment is *Not* Descriptive

A fourth point is new and peculiar to juridical judgments. As you will remember, judging that some conduct is moral or immoral is comparable in point of logic and meaning to judging that it is *legal* or *illegal.* So, what makes a practice right in the juridical sense of the term is neither its intrinsic nor its instrumental features but its conformity to the relevant rules. As behavior is legal or illegal according to whether it comports with the relevant rules of *law*, so it is moral or immoral according to whether it comports with the relevant rules of *morality*.

Which law? Whose morality? According to Protestant philosopher Immanuel Kant and Catholic theologian Thomas Aquinas, the answer is the Moral Law—the law of Reason and God. Both of these pious thinkers held that to judge whether an action is morally right or wrong is to judge whether it comports or conflicts with the Moral Law, a culturally transcendent and universally binding standard created for men by God and built by Him into human reason everywhere. Practices that conform to this standard are morally right; practices that do not are morally wrong.

This is a widely accepted view, but it suffers from a fatal flaw: There is no proof of the existence of this Moral Law. So far as we can tell, all morality and law are man-made. (Since we shall argue this at length in a later chapter,[14] I will not state the argument here.) If this is right, skepticism about the existence of a culturally transcendent and universally binding Moral Law is amply justified, but it has led some philosophers to a conclusion that is not—namely, that no moral judgment is ever true. The conclusion is false, as we shall soon see, but the reasoning is valid: If there is no Moral Law, then it is either meaningless or false to declare that conduct conforms to it. Believing that there is no Moral Law, J. L. Mackie therefore held that no moral judgments are ever true and called this the *error theory*. Believing the same premise, A. J. Ayer drew the slightly different conclusion, that no moral judgment is either true *or* false and called this *emotivism*.

The difference reflects different views about judgments that are premised on falsehoods. Discussing this question, Bertrand Russell maintained that "The present king of France is bald" is false because it falsely asserts the existence of a present king of France; and so, for the same reason, is its apparent contradictory, "The present king of France is not bald." Finding it paradoxical to regard both a statement and its formal contradictory as false, Peter Strawson replied that these two statements *presuppose* but do not *assert* the existence of a present king of France; so, the question of their truth or falsity cannot arise. The difference between Mackie and Ayer parallels this. In Mackie's view, the nonexistence of a Moral Law means that all judgments invoking it are false. In Ayer's view, it means that these "judgments" are neither true nor false. According to both views, no moral judgments are ever true.

Given either view, it follows that no moral judgments can be mistaken or disputed—an inconvenient if not paradoxical claim. Are we to conclude, then, that there is no difference in point of truth between someone who says that stealing (or lying or killing) is immoral and someone who denies it? It would be good to find a way around this conclusion if we can. Fortunately, we can: Deny the premise on which it is founded.

The Juridical as Relative to Social Norms

The mistaken premise is belief that juridical judgments always invoke the same morality—namely, a single culturally transcendent and universally binding Moral Law. When we recognize instead that moral and legal judgments are indexed to a great many different moralities and laws, nothing stands in the way of assigning them truth values. Whether a given moral or legal judgment is true or false will then be determined by ascertaining whether the practice being appraised comports with the particular morality or law that is being presupposed or invoked.

Thus, to take just one example, although it is not a question of fact or falsehood whether polygamy is *absolutely* legal or moral, it is a question of fact or falsehood whether polygamy is legal or moral *in Saudi Arabia*; or *in Selma, Alabama*. Furthermore, we know the answer to this question. It is Yes in the first case, No in the second. Polygamy is legal and moral in Saudi Arabia, illegal and immoral in Selma, Alabama. Is polygamy illegal or immoral in itself, apart from the law or morality of a particular society? This question has no meaning. It is logically ill formed. One might as well ask whether the Eiffel Tower is near or far in itself, apart from its relation to anything or anybody.

The moral absolutist will object, "Is there not incoherence in saying that a practice is *both* morally permissible *and* morally impermissible?" The reply is that there is contradiction in saying this, but we are not saying it. We are so far from affirming that polygamy is *both* absolutely permissible and absolutely impermissible as to deny that it is *either*. The hypothesis being advanced is that the permissibility or impermissibility of polygamy is not absolute but relative, because it depends on the law or the morality that is in question. Thus, polygamy is permissible *in Arabia*, because it is consistent with the law and morality that are in force there, and it is impermissible *in Alabama*, because it is contrary to the law and morality that are in force there. No contradiction; just plain matter of fact.

The conclusion to be deduced from this plain matter of fact is that the expression "x is morally permissible" is elliptical for the lengthier expression "x is morally permissible in y." It makes no sense to ask whether polygamy is permissible absolutely, in itself; we can ask only whether it is permissible in this or that society.

Moral absolutists will reply that this analysis overlooks another plain matter of fact: Neither the Selman nor the Saudi thinks of himself as making a relative judgment. If he is at all typical, the Saudi will take himself to be declaring not merely that polygamy is permitted by the laws and morality of Saudi Arabia but also that it is permitted by the law of God. The Selman will have a similar opinion about his judgment. He will take himself to be declaring not merely that having several wives is forbidden by the law and morality that happen to be in force in Selma but also that it is forbidden by the law of God. How can these beliefs be squared with the proposition that moral judgments are indexed to the morality of the speaker?

By noting that the speaker's beliefs are false. Contrary to the objection, the Selman and the Saudi are *not* invoking the same transcendent Morality or Law. That may be what they *think* they are doing, but it is pretty clearly not what they are doing. When he speaks of the Law of God, the Saudi means the Law of Allah while the Selman means the Law of Jahweh, a different thing. So, it is wrong to say that the Saudi and the Selman are presupposing the same God-made Law or Morality. It is more consistent with the facts to suppose that the Saudi and the Selman are each presupposing and invoking the particular law and morality that he accepts as a member of his society. It is true that each believes this law and morality to be a universal Morality instituted by God for everybody everywhere, but the fact cuts no ice if no such Law or Morality exists.

The Empirical Meanings of Moral Judgments

Isn't the speaker the best judge of what he is saying? Doesn't he know best what his words mean? Doesn't our interpretation of his statements have to acknowledge his intentions? Don't we have to come to an understanding that is acceptable to him? That is the usual presumption, but there is good reason to take a different view.

Consider an analogous question: What was the meaning of the claim, common in the fifteenth century, that someone was a witch? More formally: What was the meaning in the fifteenth century of sentences of the form,

(1) *x is a witch?*

If we could ask a fifteenth-century speaker, he would no doubt answer that (1) means

(2) *x consorts with demons,*

and he would, if we inquired further, inform us that a demon is a *supernatural being with evil proclivities*. The trouble with this answer is obvious: Unlike the speaker, we do not believe in supernatural beings. So, we cannot take him at his word.

No matter. We can understand what he says and translate it into our lexicon if we notice the following interesting fact: Whatever people in the fifteenth century may have *thought* about those they described as witches, they generally used the label to describe heretics, Jews, gypsies, the insane, eccentrics, healers, magicians, and the like—in a word, people who were physically, intellectually, or socially deviant.[15] This entitles us to say that it was observed *deviance*, not unobserved *demons*, that determined fifteenth-century use of the word *witch*. Contrary to the understanding, belief, and intention of those who used the word, its reference was not people who consorted with demons but people who were in some way strange, mysterious, or scary.[16]

Let us express this by saying that the empirically determinate meaning of the word *witch* in the fifteenth century was not (2) but

(3) *x is in some way deviant.*

Talk of supernatural demons was just so much irrelevant and meaningless mythology. This mythology may have been part of the speaker's theory about what made someone's behavior deviant, but this theory was mistaken. It was not what determined his use of words; it was not part of the word's *observational* meaning.

Similar remarks may be made about moral judgments. As just observed, the ordinary person is likely to think that his juridical judgments reflect a God-made standard—a Moral Law—that is wholly independent of him and his culture. He is likely to think this because it is what he has been taught to think by millennia of theologians and metaphysicians—just as people in the fifteenth century were taught by such persons to think of lunatics and heretics as people in collusion with demons. We, however, need not accept this superstitious way of thinking. In fact, we ought to reject it. Like belief in demons, belief in a culturally transcendent Morality is a relic of ancient religious faith, not a product of considered reason or critical science. If moral judgments must be construed as referring to such a standard, we will have to deny, like Mackie and Ayer, that they are ever true.

Fortunately, there is an alternative. Recognize that, despite their own beliefs to the contrary, what usually causes people to describe a practice as moral or immoral is not some transcendent Morality but the consistency or inconsistency of the practice with the man-made moralities of their societies. A devout theist may think that he praises a practice because it was approved by God, but the truth is more likely that he believes the practice to have been approved by God because he has been taught to praise it. Furthermore, the "God" he has in mind will invariably be the one that is defined for him by other believers in his culture. So, whether he is aware of the fact or not, his moral judgments are best regarded as products of his acculturation to the morality of a particular society, not pronouncements on the consistency of a practice with a mythical Moral Law.

Because the judgments of other persons in the same society will also presuppose this same morality, nobody will say "x is moral in *our* society." Instead, everybody will use the shorter form "x is moral," confident that others in the society will know and accept the standard that is being presupposed. So, unless the speaker meets people from a different society, or learns that their moral judgments do not always coincide with his, he will have no occasion to recognize that his judgments are indexed to a merely provincial morality. For the speaker innocent of cultural variety, there will be only *one* morality—namely, the one that he accepts as a member of his society. If he finds somebody who does not share that morality, his first thought will not be that the two of them represent different moralities but that the other person has made a mistake about the requirements of what he wrongly believes to be the only morality there is.

We are in a different situation. We know that different societies have different moralities, as different nations have different laws. We also know that no single morality or law determines what is moral or legal in every society, only what is moral or legal in a particular society. So, a speaker who says that some practice P is morally permissible meaning that P is consistent with a culturally transcendent Morality M says what we can only regard as false or meaningless. If we are nevertheless able to treat his judgment as true in the context, it will be because we can take it to indicate that the practice comports with the morality that he accepts as a member of his society. No matter that he has another interpretation. To understand him, we must interpret his statement *in our language*, not the other way around. Hence, as talk of demons must give way to talk of deviance, so talk of the Moral Law must give way to talk of local moralities and laws.

Witches and Morality

There is an obvious objection to this comparison of witch talk with juridical judgment. If we count the Saudi's judgment as meaning

Polygamy is permissible in Arabia

on the grounds that so interpreting it will enable us to regard it as true, won't this mean that interpreting fifteenth century use of

x is a witch

as

x's behavior is deviant in a way that is strange, mysterious, or fearful

will not only enable but even oblige us to declare that it too is true? And won't this commit us to saying that there are witches? If so, our account of the truth of moral judgments entails assertions we do not wish to make—an untenable situation.

This is a powerful looking argument. Normally, declaring somebody else's affirmation to be true is tantamount to affirming the same thing. Let us call this Tarski's rule. Thus, suppose someone says, "This object is square." By Tarski's rule, to declare that what he says is true is also to affirm that the object is square. By parity of reasoning, if we affirm the truth of a fifteenth century assertion of "x is a witch," we seem to be committed to affirming that somebody in the fifteenth century was a witch, a proposition we may want to deny given the definition of a witch as someone who consorts with demons. Similarly, if we affirm the truth of the Saudi's declaration that polygamy is permissible, we seem to be committed to affirming that polygamy is permissible, even if this is something we might otherwise wish to deny. So, our position appears to be incoherent.

Fortunately, appearances can be misleading. In this case, they are misleading in two ways. First, the argument again confuses sentences with statements. Think once again of Jacques's pronouncement

The Eiffel Tower is near [me].

I may agree that the statement Jacques makes by uttering this sentence is true yet be unwilling to affirm "The Eiffel Tower is near [me]"—because by so doing I would make not only a different but also a false statement. Similarly, I may agree that the Saudi's pronouncement

Polygamy is permissible[in Arabia]

is true without being willing to use these [unbracketed] words myself—because by so doing I would make not only a different statement but also one I do not wish to affirm, namely,

Polygamy is permissible [*in Alabama*]

The puzzle is resolved.

Second, the argument misses the point. As we have already stated, the point of our discussion was to emphasize that we need not accept the fifteenth-century definition of a witch as somebody who consorts with demons. Instead, we can reinterpret fifteenth-century claims about witches as claims about deviance.

This may look like verbal sleight of hand, but we do this sort of thing all the time. Consider the statement "The sun rose." Taken literally, as meaning that the sun moved up while the horizon stayed put, this is false; but we have learned to reinterpret it as meaning that the horizon fell while the sun stayed put, that being the observational situation in which the sentence was uttered. Now consider the statement "Ruth is a witch." Taken literally, as meaning that Ruth consorts with demons, this is false, but we have learned to understand it as meaning that Ruth's behavior is deviant. That is clearly the most likely interpretation of twentieth-century use of the word—*witch* having come to mean little more than *disagreeable person.*

The proposal, then, is to interpret moral judgments in such a way as to separate observed facts from false explanations, leaving us a core of judgment that is true. Thus, suppose the Saudi says "Polygamy is permissible" intending "Polygamy is permitted by the law of Allah." Instead of declaring his claim false on the grounds that there is no law of Allah, let us recognize that it embodies a false interpretation of an observed fact—namely, that polygamy is permitted in Saudi Arabia.[17] The problem is solved.

Morality as Relative; Truth as Absolute

This way of preserving truth value for moral judgments must not be confused with another that is superficially like it but vastly different in import. What we have done is preserve truth by making morality relative This must not be confused with the attempt to preserve morality by making truth relative.

To see the distinction, compare

I. *Polygamy is morally permissible in Saudi Arabia,*

with

II. *"Polygamy is morally permissible " is believed in Saudi Arabia.*

These differ in the same way that

The Eiffel Tower is near Jacques,

differs from

"The Eiffel Tower is near" is believed by Jacques.

That the Eiffel Tower is near Jacques does not mean that Jacques believes it to be near, and that polygamy is permissible in Saudi Arabia does not mean that the Saudis believe polygamy to be permissible, or vice versa.

This last claim will seem unintelligible to those who identify a society's *morality* with the *moral beliefs* of its members. As we shall show in Chapter 7, however, a society's morality is constituted by the *practices* of its members. Roughly: That is permissible in a society which comports with its practices. Whether the action in question is also believed to comport with these practices is logically, if not practically, beside the point. Just as someone can mistakenly believe to be legally permissible in his society conduct that is in fact contrary to its law, or mistakenly believe to be mannerly in a society what is in fact contrary to its etiquette, so someone can believe to be morally permissible in his society conduct that is in fact contrary to its morality.

It is true that the people who make up a society do generally know what its rules require of them. If they did not, they could not comply with these rules, and without compliance the claim that such rules existed would lack clear meaning. Knowledge of how to behave in a society need, however, not take the form of articulate belief; people need not be conscious of the rules they obey. Indeed, obedience more often takes the form of inarticulate and unconscious habit. Few people can state the rules that determine their behavior or that of others in the society. They do what *feels* right. Their beliefs about what is right are likely to be an expression of their socially conditioned feelings. Therefore, it is a mistake to say that the permissibility of a practice is relative to belief.

Let us therefore be very clear. Moral and legal permissibility are relative; the truth about them is absolute.

Notes

1. A more cautious formulation—e.g., that of C. L. Stevenson, *Ethics and Language* (New Haven, CT: Yale University Press, 1944)—will limit this thesis to judgments about ends, final values. About the means to ends, emotivists agree that there can be real dispute over facts of the matter. A sophisticated recent exponent of emotivism is Simon Blackburn. See his "How to Be an Ethical Anti-realist," reprinted in Stephen Darwall, Allan Gibbard, and Peter Railton, *Moral Discourse and Practice* (New York: Oxford University Press, 1997), 167-179.
2. *Ethics: Inventing Right and Wrong* (Harmondsworth, Middlesex: Penguin 1977).
3. Other names for the view are Platonism, moral absolutism, and moral objectivism. For further discussion of this view, see chapter 11, "Enacting Rectitude."
4. For more on this theme, see chapter 11.
5. Whether truth is supposed to attach to statements declaring something to be bad is not clear. According to a view favored by many Platonists, evil is not a positive but a negative property. So, things count as bad not by virtue of having a property of being bad but by virtue of lacking a property of being good. This idea complicates the logical question so much that it is here being ignored. Here "x is bad" counts as an evaluative judgment, and the nonexistence of any distinctive similarity between all bad things is taken to mean that there is no property of being bad. These assumptions commit the emotivist to the view that "x is bad" also lacks truth value and the error theorist to the view that this statement is false, like "x is good." In "The Good as Reinforcing" I offer a simple solution to the puzzle.
6. Again, see chapter 11.
7. On this theme, see Michael Levin, *Why Race Matters* (Westport, CT: Praeger, 1997), 152 ff.
8. This is an oversimplification, which will be corrected later.
9. This sort of argument was a favorite with Plato. See, for just one example, his reply to Thrasymachus in *The Republic*,
10. Evidently, Kantians and other rationalists have mistakenly seized upon Hume's statement as confirmation of the very view he meant to reject.
11. The leading contemporary proponent of this Kantian view is R. M. Hare, *The Language of Morals* (New York: Oxford University Press, 1952). Hare seems to

take quite literally Kant's view that moral judgments are imperatives in indicative dress.

12. Although he denied that prescriptions have *truth*, Kant held that some have "validity," which apparently came to much the same thing.
13. See chapter 7, "Rules of Morality."
14. See Chapter 12, "The Myth of the Moral Law.".
15. See Thomas Szasz, *The Manufacture of Madness* (New York: Harper & Row, 1970) and *The Myth of Mental Illness* (New York: Harper & Row, 1974). As Szasz points out, we no longer use the word *witch* in quite the old way, but we still have a term for the people it picked out. We now use the word *mentally ill,* a term that it also fraught with myth.
16. Although I have used this word elsewhere, these persons should perhaps be called not the *denotation* but the *reference* of the word *witch.* If the denotation of a predicate is all the things of which the predicate is true; the reference of a predicate is the things it is said about, whether truly or not. Since there were no witches, and never have been, the predicate "x is a witch" is true of nothing, and was true of nothing in the fifteenth century. So, its denotation, then and now, is the null class. Be that as it may, when people in the fifteenth century described others as witches, their language referred to, and was about, the persons they were describing. Thus, "That witch who lives down the road" had reference even though it lacked denotation. Compare Keith Donnellan's "The man at the bar drinking a martini," said of a man drinking water from a martini glass. Reference without denotation.
17. That this fact itself embodies interpretation is true but beside the point. As Norwood Hanson first emphasized but most epistemologists now acknowledge, all observation is "theory laden"—invested with and influenced by existing belief. Nevertheless, as Quine has observed, we can make a working distinction between observation and interpretation. Just count as observed fact that which, in the present stage of our investigations, is not subject to dispute. The rest will be doubtful interpretation. See Quine and Ullian, *The Web of Belief* (New York: Random House, 1970).

6

The Good as Reinforcing

As a rule, one endeavors to do what is good or has good results, but there is no way to know what that is *a priori*, just by thinking about it. Instead, one must learn it from experience, either one's own or someone else's. Thus, to discover which ice cream tastes best, one must taste it, or consult somebody who has. To learn the best way to swing a hammer, one must attempt various swings, or get instruction from someone who has. To find out how to treat other people, one must experiment with many ways of treating them, or go to school with someone who has. And so on.

No doubt, some ways of behaving are innate—selected by evolution and built into the nervous system of the organism to become manifest on maturation—but which of these instinctive forms of behaving are good in the particular case must be discovered after the fact, by trial and error. It cannot be known in advance just by thinking about it. The same is true of the bad. To discover what is bad, we must try it, or benefit from the knowledge of those who have. There is no *a priori* short cut.

The explanation of this truism is roughly as follows: The right thing to do is what promises to be good or produce something that is; the wrong thing to do is what promises to be bad, or to produce what is. As B. F. Skinner observed, however, the measure of the good is its capacity to reinforce conduct that produces it, and the measure of the bad is its capacity to reinforce conduct that avoids it.[1] Described in conversational English, the good is what, once done, is more likely to be desired and done again. The bad is what, once tried, is less likely to be tried again. In the jargon of behavioral psychology, the good is positively, the bad negatively, reinforcing. This means that, to discover what is good, we need trial and error.

This holds true no matter what sort of good or evil is in question. In the conventional classification, things, events, and actions can be *intrinsically* good or bad, *instrumentally* good or bad, or *morally* good or bad. Reinforcement is the measure of all three. It is that by virtue of which they are all called *good* or *bad.*

The Intrinsically and Instrumentally Good

Begin with the *intrinsically good.* It is so-called because it is good —that is, reinforcing—apart from its effects.[2] An example is eating butter pecan ice cream. Having eaten it once, you will want to do so again; the tasting reinforces itself. So do dancing a jig, climbing a mountain on a summer day, sailing a dinghy in a fresh breeze, catching a bass on a fly rod, and listening to Mozart's *Exultate Jubilate.* Having done it once, you will be inclined to repeat it, maybe not at the moment, but on a similar occasion in the future. By contrast, being burned by a hot poker or breaking your arm is intrinsically bad. Having done it once, you are not likely to want to do it again. The act reinforces its own avoidance. In this way, it differs from getting drunk, which is enjoyable but has consequences that discourage it.

The intrinsically good may be either an unconditioned or a conditioned reinforcer; you may naturally be so constituted as to be reinforced by it, or you may have to become habituated to it. Most of us like the taste and texture of ice cream from the start, but we have to learn to like dark beer, which is too bitter the first time we try it. Association with other pleasurable things makes the difference. Just drink dark beer with friends, or use it to complement some strong cheese and hearty bread. You will soon become fond of it. The same is true in reverse of the intrinsically bad. We dislike some things from the outset, others only after they have become associated with things we dislike. A broken bone is an example of the first; the smell of food that once made us sick is an example of the second.

As these examples suggest, the intrinsically good includes the *aesthetically* good, which consists of things that taste good, look good, smell good, sound good, and feel good—in other words, things that reinforce tasting, looking, smelling, listening, and feeling. This fact has been obscured by the uncritical assumption that such words as *tastes*, *smells*, and *looks* are always epistemic, but this belief, which is based on a faulty grammatical analogy, is mistaken. What *looks* square may not *be* square, and what sounds like a loon may not be a loon, but what looks good is good to look at, what tastes good is good to taste, what smells good is good to smell, and so on. As the jazz composer Duke Ellington is reported to have said about music, if it *sounds* good, it *is* good. In the case of the aesthetic, *esse is percipi*; appearance is reality.

Not so the *instrumentally good*, that which is good as a means to some other (intrinsically or instrumentally) good thing. If it is reinforcing, the reason is that it has, or seems to have, effects that are reinforcing. An example is driving nails with a hammer. Even though we human beings are tool-using creatures, innately disposed to be reinforced by manipulating whatever objects happen to be at hand, you may get little or no gratification, only frustration, from your first attempts to drive a nail with a hammer. If, however, you have some success, your efforts will be reinforced: You will be inclined to reach for a hammer the next time a nail wants driving. By virtue of this fact, the hammer itself may also be said to have instrumental value, or *utility*, along with the activity of using it.

Given suitable conditioning, instrumental value can become intrinsic. The value of swinging a hammer is usually instrumental, but if your swings repeatedly pay dividends, you may come to value your skill with a hammer for its own sake. You will then drive nails for the sheer pleasure of it; the desire to do so will become *functionally autonomous*—independent of the utility of the act. Hence, such work as fishing, logging, rail splitting, and canoe paddling have been turned into sports and engaged in for their own sake, not just for their benefits.

To be sure, conditioned inclinations of this kind can always be extinguished, by continued absence of reinforcement, or by punishment. No conditioned response ever becomes wholly independent of the contingencies that reinforce it. Yet some reinforcers become so deeply ingrained that what stimulates them acquires intrinsic value, at least for the time being. By contrast, we avoid actions that have bad results. Thus, we dislike slippery surfaces, although, sometimes, with due practice, we may learn to use them with pleasure or profit, as in ice skating and skiing. A collective name for the instrumentally good is *utility*.

The Morally Good

Although Kant held that moral goodness is intrinsically, and G. E. Moore that it is instrumentally, valuable, its logic is more complex than that.

The morally good, or just, consists of actions that count as good not because they are themselves reinforcing but because they reinforce their reinforcement by other persons in the society.[3] Examples are acts of charity and generosity. Because we are social creatures genetically disposed to do what pleases human beings who are familiar to us, such acts can be naturally reinforcing. In the beginning, however, accommodating the wishes and welfare of strangers may have little or no value for us. Thus, a small child may get no pleasure, only pain, from being compelled to share her toy, but her playmate will get pleasure from it, and so will the child's watchful parents, who, wishing her to repeat the action in the future, will reward it, by praising her or adding some cookies to her ice cream.

After having been repeatedly reinforced in these ways and by the willingness of playmates to reciprocate when *they* have something to share, the act of sharing will itself become reinforcing. The child grown up will now *want* to share, even when there is neither thought nor prospect of reward. Having been reinforced in her formative years, her generous inclination will have become to a large extent independent of its history, if never entirely so.

Besides acts of charity, which are merely *desired* by their beneficiaries, there are also acts of duty, which are *required* by them. The former are reinforced positively, by praise and reward, the latter negatively, by condemnation and punishment. Charity was an example of the former. An example of the latter is the duty to pay taxes. Most people pay taxes not because they take pleasure in it or because they expect to be praised for it but because they want to avoid paying fines or going to jail. Of course, fear of punishment is not the only reason to do your duty. You should also do it because it contributes to the public weal. Still, what makes something a duty, rather than act of charity or generosity, is that, under the rules, failure to perform it makes you liable to punishment.[4]

To say so is not to deny that even initially onerous acts of duty can become reinforcing. Usually, it is only small children and criminals who must be punished. As Kant observed, most well-reared adults *want* to do their duty, simply because they know it to be their duty. Performance of duty being regarded as a good thing by other persons, we soon come to regard it as good ourselves. Thus, we take justifiable pride in paying our taxes or stopping at red lights, even when we know that we could avoid doing so with impunity. We behave in this principled manner because we prefer the sense of rectitude and well-being that comes from having a clear conscience and a good opinion of ourselves to the risky, transient, and dubious benefits of cheating. Still, the obligatory, or required, is distinguished from the merely desired not by the fact that it is positively reinforcing but by the fact that it is negatively reinforced.

Overlooking this fact, Kant maintained, perversely and paradoxically, that doing your duty has value only if you do it without expecting pleasure or hoping for reward. In other words, you should do your duty even if you are neither reinforced *by* it nor reinforced *for* it. Nor is this so, Kant said, because the beneficiary of the action is herself reinforced by it According to Kant, we have a duty to punish criminals even if neither we, they, nor anybody else expects to benefit from, or take pleasure in, the act. Miscreants and criminals have a *right* to be punished, it being necessary to regaining their sense of self-esteem and dignity as human beings. Kant regarded this proposition—that duty ought to be done even if nothing reinforces doing it—as a self-evident truth.

We understand this claim if it means that doing your duty has more value to the beneficiary when he need not trouble to reward its performance or punish its neglect. The landlord prefers a tenant who pays his monthly rent without having to be chased down for it. We can even understand why a criminal would insist on being punished if he thought it necessary for expiation or a feeling of self-worth. A sense of guilt being a form of anxiety conditioned by previous punishment, it can often be relieved only by getting the punishment over and done with. But if the act reinforces neither its agent, its beneficiary, nor its observer, it is not clear why anybody would regard it as good or wish to make it a duty. The whole idea is paradoxical in the extreme, and so is the companion idea that an agent might be motivated to do what is neither itself reinforcing nor reinforced by other persons. What would motivate anyone to do what nothing in nature or society encourages him to do? This is a question for which Kant had no answer, no doubt because there is none.

Unless there is an answer, we may define the good as that which either reinforces desire for it or for which desire is reinforced by others, because they are themselves reinforced by it. Briefly, the good is the reinforcing or reinforced. The bad, as we have observed, is just the opposite. It reinforces desire to avoid it, either in the agent or in others, who then reinforce its avoidance.

The Complexity of the Good

Although intuitionist philosophers, such as G. E. Moore and W. D. Ross, stoutly maintained that good and evil are simple qualities, like color, no belief could be more wrong The concept of good is complex in at least two ways.

First, when used by itself out of all context, the word *good* is ambiguous. As just noted, a thing or a practice can be intrinsically good, instrumentally good, or morally good. These ways of being good are related in various ways. The instrumentally good is so because it produces what has intrinsic value, and the morally good is so because it has intrinsic or instrumental value for those who reinforce it. So, all three goods come down in the end to the intrinsically good. Still, the same thing might be good in one way and bad in another. Butter pecan ice cream tastes good, but in large quantities it is bad for you; vigorous exercise hurts, but it can also do you good; sexual promiscuity is pleasurable but harmful, so bad, even where it is permissible.

Therefore, to ask whether something is good or bad [period] is to ask an unclear question, and to talk as though a thing or activity might be unconditionally good, or good in all ways, is to talk nonsense. It is true that we sometimes describe a thing or practice as good [period], meaning that it is good *on balance,* when its merits have been weighed against its demerits, but this way of talking is misleading. As we shall see, it is one of the ways of talking that has encouraged belief that goodness is a simple property.

Ambiguity is only one complication; here is another. Grant that the good is reinforcing or reinforced. What reinforces A may not reinforce B, and what is reinforced in group G may not be reinforced, it may even be discouraged, in group F. Thus, licorice pleases your palate but not mine; my getting the job we both wanted benefits me but harms you; having several wives is permissible in Saudi Arabia but forbidden in Selma, Alabama; and so on.

As this shows, no good thing is absolutely so. Instead, goodness is always relative to persons and, truth be told, to circumstances too. What tastes good at a picnic, or when you are hungry, may not taste good at other times or in other circumstances. A dose of penicillin will help if you have a bacterial infection but not if you have a virus, and it will kill if you are allergic to it. Driving fast on the public streets is forbidden in normal circumstances, but it is permitted in an emergency, and it is praiseworthy on a race track, where the only crime is to be slow.

This fact—that goodness, or value, is relative to people and circumstances—has been obscured by abstraction and by ellipsis. First, abstraction. Because it saves words, philosophers tend to speak collectively of "the good," or abstractly of "goodness," instead of talking concretely about the things, events, and activities that are good. Then, having abstracted from a very diverse reality, they fancy that they have discovered a single uniform entity, the "quality" or "property" that good things, events, and actions have in common. This gives an appearance of simplicity to what is really a very complex topic. Once that illusion takes hold of a philosopher, thought goes down the tubes, as he fails to notice that there is no way in which all "good" objects, or even all intrinsically good objects, resemble each other.

Now ellipsis. As noted earlier, Hobbes claimed that the word *good* is an indexical term. As Hobbes put it in his quaint but elegant way, "Each of us uses the word *good* in relation to himself," to indicate what *he* or *she* prefers. So, "Licorice tastes good" means "Licorice tastes good *to me*," "My getting the job was good" means "My getting the job was good for (that is, benefited) *me*," and "Polygamy is immoral" means "Polygamy is immoral (that is, contrary to rules of morality that are in force) *in my social group*." If reference to self is not always made explicit, it is because it can usually be taken for granted, as implied. It is only when we need to talk about the preferences of other persons that the relational form of speech becomes necessary.

Hobbes's observation was only partly right. In what might be called its default setting, the word *good* is indexed to its user, as just illustrated. In other cases, the reference may be to a second or third party. When Mama inquires rhetorically, "That tastes good, doesn't it?" she may be taken to mean "That tastes good *to me*, and I bet it tastes good *to you too*." Similarly, "Your getting the job was good" could mean that it benefits me, but it is more likely to mean that it benefits you. And, when it is asked in Saudi Arabia, "Is polygamy acceptable?" may be taken to mean "Is polygamy accepted *in Saudi Arabia*?" The exact truth is a little more complicated than Hobbes noticed.

No matter. The main point, which Hobbes got right, is that a thing does not taste good or bad *period*, it tastes good to A, bad to B; an event is not useful or harmful *period*, it is useful to X harmful to Y; a practice is not moral or immoral period; it is moral in S1, immoral in S2. In the jargon of the behavioral psychologist, a thing is not reinforcing *period*, and a practice is not reinforced *period*; the thing reinforces A, the practice is reinforced in S. In short, a thing is not good or bad. Instead, it is good in way W1 for person P1, bad in way W2 for person P2, and so on. Without the additional variable, the form of expression is incomplete and ill formed. It is like writing "x =" instead of "x =y."

Unfortunately, as we shall soon see, many philosophers insist that the formula "x =" ("The thing is equal") makes perfectly good sense as it stands, without a second variable. Because we normally say "Licorice tastes good," rather than "Licorice tastes good *to me,*" and "Polygamy is immoral" rather than "Polygamy is immoral *in this society,*" some philosophers—G. E. Moore comes immediately to mind, but he is not the only example; Plato was the first—have insisted that goodness is not relative but absolute. If, however, the good is the reinforcing, it is so relatively to those who are reinforced by it; and if it is the reinforced, it is so relatively to those who do the reinforcing.

This is true even of that which reinforces and is reinforced by practically everybody—for example, a friendly smile. Its value is also relative; it just bears this relation to every person. Universality must not be mistaken for absoluteness.

Such, in brief summary, is our account of the good. We must now consider some objections.

The Naturalistic Fallacy

An inevitable objection is that, since many people do not even understand talk of reinforcement, much less regard it as synonymous with talk of the good, equating the two fails to preserve meaning, a requirement for good definition. This, in a nutshell, was G. E. Moore's objection, in *Principia Ethica*, to all of what he called "naturalistic" ethics, meaning attempts to define *good* in empirically determinate terms. Moore said that *all* such definitions must be rejected out of hand, because they *necessarily* substitute for the word *good* an expression with an entirely different meaning—indeed, a meaning of an entirely different kind. He called doing this the "naturalistic fallacy."[5]

Moore's objection trades on an ambiguity in the word *meaning*. His complaint would be right if a naturalistic definition concerned what logicians call the connotation or intension of the word *good*, but our definition purports to give only the reference or extension. Our claim is not that whoever describes something as *good* understands himself to be referring to what he knows to be reinforcing or reinforced. Our claim is that, whether he knows it or not, he is referring to what is in fact reinforcing or reinforced.

Another way to put this point is to say that we are affirming *sameness of truth value,* not *synonymy of terms*. Let A say "x is good." Our claim is that A's statement counts as true just in case x is such as to reinforce or be reinforced. Whether this is what A *has in mind* does not matter; it will be the condition of his statement's being true. Grant, then, that the word *good* is not interchangeable for all purposes with the phrase *reinforcing or reinforced.* We maintain that it is coextensive with it. Grant that *reinforcing or reinforced* does not elicit the same thought in people's minds as *good.* We maintain that it describes the same entities.

Why the point matters will become clear if you will recall an example from a previous chapter. In the fifteenth century, people who behaved in unacceptable ways or had unacceptable beliefs were sometimes called *witches*, meaning that they "consorted with demons." Does this invocation of the supernatural mean that the word *witch* cannot be defined in empirically meaningful terms? Would there necessarily be a naturalistic fallacy in naturalistic definition? The conclusion would be too hasty. As we just observed, every person whom it was correct to describe as a *witch* could also have been described as intellectually or behaviorally *deviant.* The two terms would not have been synonymous—interchangeable in the minds of most users—but they would have referred to the same persons; they would have had the same extension; their use would have had the same truth conditions.

This entitles us to say that fifteenth-century use of the word *witch* admits of definition in naturalistic terms. In fact, these are the only terms in which the word *can* be defined. Hence, documents of the inquisition, such as the *Malleus Maleficarum*, made a point of specifying the empirically discernible signs of witchcraft in elaborate detail, warts and other skin imperfections being especially noteworthy! That empirical definition of the word *witch* fails to preserve its supernatural connotations is certainly true, but this need not concern us. The supernatural was a superfluous addition which we can disregard, if only because we could not accommodate it anyhow. For scientific purposes, what matters is a word's reference.

If the illustration of this point seems strained, consider another, one that is due to the logician Gottlob Frege. When astronomers realized that the Morning Star and the Evening Star were the same entity, namely the planet Venus, it would have been wholly misguided to object that the names "Morning Star" and "Evening Star" were not synonyms. The right reply would have been: Nobody said they were! The astronomers knew perfectly well that these two names had different connotations. That is what made their claim interesting. Despite the difference in connotation, the names had the same reference. So, the objection would have missed the mark.

Moore's objection to naturalistic definitions of *good* was also wide of the mark. He was criticizing oranges on the ground that they were not apples. The charge is true but not damaging.

Moore on Mill and Hedonism

The wonder is that Moore did not see this himself. Although he had not read Frege when he wrote *Principia Ethica*, the distinction between connotation and reference was an old one with which Moore was clearly familiar. When he denied that *goodness,* the "quality" of being good, can be defined, he was careful to add that he did not mean to deny the definability of *the good*—that which is good. Thus, in response to Mill, he proposed to grant that *the good* might be pleasure, or that which is pleasant. It will not follow, he insisted, that *good* has the same meaning (that is, connotation) as *pleasant*; it will not follow that *goodness* and *pleasure* are the same things (pp. 8f.).

Moore had a point. Although I do not wish to complicate difficult issues even further by discussing the accuracy of Moore's reading of Mill, I think it is clear that Mill, like other hedonists, did sometimes talk as though he thought that there is no difference between thinking of something as *good* and thinking of it as *pleasant*. (Moore quotes one damaging passage on p. 72.) He also seems to have held that "pleasure," meaning sensations of pleasure, is the only *intrinsically* good thing there is; everything else (for example, butter pecan ice cream or sexual intercourse) being a means to pleasure. If this way of talking represents Mill's considered and careful view, Moore's criticisms were entirely justified.

There is, however, a more charitable reading of Mill, one on which he is not vulnerable to Moore's barbs. If we read Mill as seeking to define not *goodness*, the quality of being good, but *the good*, the things that are good, then Moore's objection amounts to a complaint that Mill had failed to do what he had not attempted to do, namely, produce a *synonym*. On the new reading, Mill was not seeking a synonym; he was seeking an alternative description. In other words, he was trying to determine what it is that qualifies the things that we *call* good for this appellation, and his answer was roughly that we call good that which pleases us. On this reading, if Mill spoke of *pleasure*, he meant the word as a collective term for the pleasant; he did not, like the Platonist Moore, mean it as the name of an abstract object. I doubt whether this reading can be made to fit everything that Mill says, but it fits much, and it is more in keeping with the spirit of his empiricism.

At times Moore senses this himself, but he takes it as evidence of Mill's confusion, not his own. Thinking of passages in which Mill and other hedonists appear to argue that, because we call *good* that which we desire and find pleasant, therefore the good just is the desired or pleasant, Moore replies that this confuses the *cause* of desire with its *object*—what makes us desire and call a thing *good* with what constitutes it as such. (p. 71) He also says that this confuses ethics with lexicography (p. 11) and blurs the distinction between what is *called* good and what *is* good. Claiming "Mill's first argument then is that, because good (sic) means desired, therefore the desired is good, " (p. 73) Moore remarks that it is absurd to tell somebody that he ought to do a thing just because it is *called* good. In his view, you might as well declare "You are to say the thing that is not because most people call it lying" (p. 12).

Moore clearly regarded this as a decisive objection, but it merely posed a false dichotomy. Grant that something can be *called* good without being good *in fact*. Grant, in other words, that mistakes are made. They can only be the exception, not the rule. It makes sense to say "This has been called round, but it is not round; it is flat." It does not make sense to say "This is the sort of thing that we call round, but it is not round; it is flat." Since it is the rule to describe as round that which is shaped like a ball, it can be no mistake to do so. In that case, the mistake is to describe as round that which is not shaped like a ball, or to describe as not round that which is. Correct usage is usage that comports with the applicable rule. Grant, then, that someone tells us what is *correctly* called good, or called good *as a rule*. Then he has told us what, in our lexicon, *is* good. There is no real distinction between the two things.

This reply will also dispose of Moore's claim that identifying the good with what is called good because it is desired, either by us or other persons, is confusing ethics with psychology or sociology. Grant, that our rule is to call good that which we desire. Then saying so is defining the word *good*; it is telling us what constitutes a thing as good. That this definition is phrased in psychological and sociological terms is true, but it is no objection. If the definition is wrong, the reason is not that it is phrased in naturalistic terms but that these are not the right naturalistic terms.

In my opinion, this refutes G. E. Moore's claim that a naturalistic definition of *good* is necessarily wrong. That claim was based on a mistaken demand that definitions preserve synonymy—identity of connotation. My reply has been that definitions need preserve only identity of extensions, which naturalistic definitions are designed to do.

The Open Question Argument

Does this reply also dispose of Moore's "open question" argument? Not quite. That argument also embodies another fallacy.

What, exactly, is the open question argument? To illustrate its use, Moore considers the interesting proposition that *good* means *that which we desire to desire* (p 15f.). That this is wrong Moore takes to be evident from the fact that it makes sense to ask whether what we desire to desire is itself good; the question is open; the answer is not self-evident (ibid.). Furthermore, Moore observes, this question does not mean, "Do we desire to desire what we desire to desire?" (p. 16). We have, says Moore, nothing so complicated "before our minds" (ibid.).

Several features of this argument call for comment. The first thing to note is that it, too, depends on the idea of meaning as something that we have in mind when we use a word. To repeat: Moore has not denied that the things we call good might just be the things we desire to desire, and vice versa. Rather, he has denied that the word *good* calls to mind the same thought as the expression "what we desire to desire." He has not denied that the two expressions are coextensive. Rather, he has denied that they have the same connotation. So, we may make the same reply to the "open question" as we made to the "naturalistic fallacy," namely, that it criticizes the definition in question for failing to do what it need not have attempted to do—namely, provide a synonym.

A second thing to note about the open question is that it can also be asked about the only definition of *good* which Moore accepts, namely "Good is good" (p. 6). Moore takes this claim to be a mere tautology, but it is one only if he is using the word *good* as a noun abbreviating *goodness* and means "Goodness = goodness"—in other words, "Goodness is identical with goodness." His statement is not a tautology, however, if the second occurrence of the word *good* is an adjective and the word *is* signifies predication, as in "Goodness ε good"—in other words, "Goodness is a good thing."

So, how are we to read the claim that good is good? It is hard to say. Taking it as a definition requires reading it the first way, as a statement of identity, but the open question argument requires reading it the second way, as a statement of predication. Regrettably Moore's fumbling attempts to resolve this ambiguity merely compounded it. According to him, the word *good* is an adjective (p. 9; p. 142) that "denotes" an "object" (p. 6) namely goodness, the quality which all good things have in common (p. 2). In other words, *good* is an adjective that is a noun, because it names an object that is not an object but a quality that objects have in common. So, "Good is good" asserts both identity and predication. Clearly, Moore was confused.

Why does it matter? Because the point is central to the argument. According to Moore, hedonism, which equates goodness with pleasure, is refuted by the fact that pleasure is not self-evidently a good thing. In Moore's language, it does not necessarily have the property of being good. By contrast, Moore seems to be saying, goodness is self-evidently a good thing; it does necessarily have the property of being good. But how can it be obvious that goodness is a good thing when it is not even obvious that goodness is a thing, or what it would mean to say so? And what does it mean to say that the property of being good is itself good—that it not just *is* but also *has* the property of being good? How can properties have properties?

It did not occur to Moore to ask these questions. Trained as a classicist, not as a logician, he followed Plato in assuming that a property is necessarily its own best exemplar. Thus, he assumed, the property of being square is itself square, and the property of being good is itself good. As his colleague Bertrand Russell was later to show, however, this assumption is so far from being self-evident as likely to be false. Once we get clear, as Moore was not, about the difference between identity and predication, we are in a position to see that predicating properties of themselves has some very awkward implications. In fact, it leads to paradoxes.[6] So, grant that "Goodness = goodness." It does not obviously follow that "Goodness is a good thing." Moore's open question argument was a spit into the wind.

The Good as Desirable

The utilitarians John Stuart Mill and Jeremy Bentham were prominent among those Moore believed he had refuted by the open question argument. He had particular scorn for Mill's attempt to prove that the desirable is that which has the power to elicit desire and the admirable is that which has the power to inspire admiration, as the visible is that which has the power to cause seeing (p. 66). In Moore's view, this clever grammatical analogy confused what *is* desired or admired with what *ought to be* desired or admired (p. 67). Mill, Moore triumphantly concluded, had overlooked the existence of *bad desires* (ibid.).

This argument starts out right but ends up wrong. As Moore observes, we sometimes desire things that are not good and fail to desire things that are. I once desired to taste some absinthe, only to discover on doing so that I had made a mistake. I also once lacked any desire to buy some stocks that later tripled in value. (I have made even more embarrassing mistakes, but I won't tell you about them.) These examples prove that we cannot equate the good with the desired. That much of Moore's argument is right.

Unfortunately, when Moore went further he went wrong. Having denied that x is good = x is desired, he thought he had demonstrated the falsity of the claim that x is good = x is apt to cause desire. This was too hasty. Nothing supports this conclusion except the conviction, which Moore got from Plato, that goodness has nothing to do with desire. But what supports this conviction?

Moore offers two argument. One is that a thing has intrinsic value if it is valuable in itself, apart from its effects, including its effects on persons. In other words, Moore defines intrinsic value as the value a thing has *in itself*, considered in isolation, apart from every thing else (p. 84). Then he concludes that, therefore, the intrinsic value of a thing cannot depend on the fact that it causes somebody to desire, or admire, it; for that would make it to be relational.

Having thus begged the question, Moore goes on to buttress his claim with a thought experiment. He imagines a world in which, by hypothesis, something is good, so desirable, but not desired, because there is nobody to desire it (p. 84).[7]

This argument fails, for two reasons. First, the definition of intrinsic value is wrong. As the term is normally defined, value is intrinsic if it is not instrumental—in other words, it has value apart from its use as a means. Thus, Mozart's music has intrinsic value simply because it is good to hear, even if it does not raise your IQ or calm your cattle. On this, the standard, definition of intrinsic value, there is no contradiction in saying that the value of a thing is both intrinsic and dependent on somebody's preference for it.

Second, Moore's thought experiment is unsound, if not self-refuting. On any reasonable interpretation, saying that something is apt to cause desire or admiration means that it will cause desire or admiration *assuming that there is somebody to desire or admire it*. You do not falsify this conditional statement by presuming the falsity of its antecedent and consequent conditions. That would be like arguing that a thing is invisible when there is nobody to see it—an argument that Moore stoutly and rightly rejected when he considered the views of George Berkeley.

There is a further problem in the argument—confusion about modality. That there is no surface contradiction in "This is good but not apt to cause desire" does not mean that the sentence describes a real possibility. As we noted earlier, there is also no surface contradiction in "This is the Morning Star, not the Evening Star," but if the thing is not the Evening Star, then, necessarily, it is also not the Morning Star—not because it is a necessary truth that the Morning Star is the Evening Star but because, given that the Morning Star is the Evening

Star, it necessarily follows that anything that is the Evening Star is also the Morning Star.[8]

Similarly, if the thing *could not* under any circumstances elicit or reinforce desire, then, *necessarily*, no one will have any reason to desire it or, therefore, to regard it as good—not because it is a necessary truth that x is good = x is apt to cause desire but because, given that this equation is true, there could not be an instance of something that falsified it. It appears that Mill was right after all, or nearly so. Close enough, anyhow, for government work.

Bad Desires

What about bad desires? Did Mill overlook these? When he said so Moore did not specify the desires he had in mind, but we may choose our own examples. Think of the addict's desire to use heroin or the sadist's desire to torture small children. Moore's argument is that, since desire for these things does not suffice to make them good, *good* cannot be defined in terms of desire.

At first glance, this argument also looks conclusive, but it merely exploits ambiguities in the word *good.* To see how it does this, let us examine our two examples, beginning with the desire to use heroin. Why, exactly, is this desire bad? Presumably, it is because heroin use is detrimental to personal health and public morality. In short, it is harmful and immoral. Let us grant as much. The fact remains: If heroin were not also *pleasurable*, nobody would want it; it would not also be desirable.

Given this fact, would it not be more accurate to say *not* (a) that heroin is bad (period), as if this were true without qualifications or condition, *but* (b) that heroin is bad in one way, good in another? Not good or bad. Instead, pleasurable but harmful and immoral. We may agree that the harms of heroin use and the sins it encourages outweigh its pleasures on any just accounting; so, it should count as bad *on balance*, when the final summation has been made.[9] No matter. This accurate accounting will still not rule out the fact that heroin is in some ways good. If you ever get cancer, you will be happy to have it, or its derivative morphine. So, the case fails to constitute a counterexample. Instead, it turns out to be a confirming instance.

Now consider the desire to torture babies. At the risk of seeming morally obtuse, let us ask, "What makes torturing babies bad?" No doubt, it is the fact that the babies dislike it and are harmed by it. Torturing babies pleases the sadist; it displeases the babies, and that displeases us. In declaring it bad, we are reporting our displeasure. Yes, and rightly so. As Hobbes noted and B.F. Skinner has affirmed, the rule is "Call bad what you find aversive," and you and I certainly are averse to the torture of babies. Still, the shameful fact remains: The sadist likes it; so, he calls good what we call bad. Furthermore, given the rule just cited, his usage is as correct as ours.

Object Language and Meta-language

Is this declaring that torturing babies is good insofar as it pleases the sadist? If we may take him at his word, Mill thought so. Moore disagrees, adding that the victim's pain is not only evil in itself but made worse by the fact that "the villain," enjoys inflicting it (p. 214). Moore holds it against Bentham and Mill that they regard the sadist's pleasure as a positive good, one that is to be weighed in the balance against his victim's pain (p. 214). Most people will feel the same way. I certainly do, I expect you do too. We can attach no positive value to the sadist's pleasure, which seems to us to be irredeemably evil. Calling this an "intuition," Moore regards it as proof that utilitarianism is wrong. He has a point.

Does this mean that Moore was right and Mill was wrong after all? I wish the question were that simple, but it is not. In my opinion, both Moore and Mill were in error. They both overlooked Hobbes's point —that evaluations are indexed to their speakers. They also failed to note the important distinction, first emphasized by Alfred Tarski, between (1) the object language in which an evaluation is made and (2) the meta-language in which the evaluation's truth may be assessed.[10]

Recall Jacques in Paris. Suppose he asserts,

(a) *The Eiffel Tower is near.*

We will agree that what he says (namely [a]) is true, but we will not be willing to assert (a) ourselves. Why not? Because, as we explained in the preceding chapter, Jacques makes one statement if he says (a) and we make another; so, his statement might be true while ours was false. I maintain that the present case is similar. The sadist makes a true statement if he says

(b) *Torturing babies is good,*

because this means,

(c) *[My] torturing babies is reinforcing [to me],*

or, in plain English,

(d) *I like to torture babies,*

which is *true when the sadist says it, but not when you and I do*. So, as Moore notes, agreeing that torturing babies pleases the sadist does not require agreeing that the sadist's pleasure is a good thing. So far, Moore is right.

Goodness as a Simple Quality

Unfortunately, Moore goes on to commit the obverse error. Disliking the torture of babies, he denies that the practice has any value *for the sadist*. According to Moore, our disapproval of torture amounts to an intuition of the obvious truth that the practice is absolutely evil; so, evil even for the sadist. I confess that this conclusion seems to me to be obviously wrong. Why, then, does Moore think otherwise? And where does he go wrong?

The answer is to be found in Moore's mistaken belief that goodness and evil are *simple qualities*. Moore meant two things by this. One was that goodness—meaning *intrinsic* goodness—cannot be defined because it is not compound (p.8).[11] You can, Moore said, define a horse by enumerating its parts (p. 7). But you cannot define *yellow*, or *good*, in this way. In fact, you cannot define them at all. You can *show* somebody something yellow, or good, but you cannot *tell* him what yellow color, or goodness, is. Moore concluded that this must be so because these qualities are too simple to be analyzed, broken up into parts.

Careful thinkers no longer talk like this. Aware of the use-mention pitfalls inherent in Moore's Platonic theory of words, they no longer talk about defining horses. Instead, they talk about defining the word *horse*. Furthermore, they believe that we do this not by *dismembering* horses but by *describing* them—saying what they are like and how they differ from other herbivorous animals such as cows. It is, however, difficult to translate Moore's Platonist talk about qualities into nominalist talk of words. So let us stick with Moore's language for the time being, and let us ask, What sort of a thing is a quality?

As Moore used the term, a quality (or property) is a discernible resemblance. Thus, to use Moore's example, being yellow in color is the way in which yellow things resemble each other; it is the quality they, and only they, have in common. If Moore was right, being intrinsically good is the way in which intrinsically good things resemble each other; it is the quality they, and only they, have in common. So, the first implication of Moore's claim is that there is some way in which, despite their many differences, Mozart's *Jubilate Exultate,* eating buttter pecan ice cream, catching a trout on a fly rod, and engaging in sexual intercourse are alike.

Why did he think so? Because, like Plato, he believed that where there is a common word there must be a common quality. He says so himself. In his discussion of hedonism, he makes the following revealing remark.

> 'Pleasant' must, if words are to have any meaning at all, denote some one quality common to all the things that are pleasant; and, if so, then some one thing can only be more pleasant than another, according as it has more or less of this one quality.

Moore's Platonic prejudices are here made explicit, in a case in which they are least plausible. Contrary to Moore's confident assertion, the word *pleasant* designates not a quality but a power, namely the power to please and so, Mill had maintained, does the word *good.*

Whether Goodness is Non-relational

Moore's belief that [intrinsic] goodness is a simple quality like yellow, also had another implication: that the sentence "x is good" is more comparable in point of logical form to the simple sentence "x is yellow" than to the complex sentence "x is near y." In the language of modern logic, which Moore did not know, Moore believed that "x is good" is a monadic predicate with one subject, not a relational predicate with two or more.

What reasons did Moore give for this belief? Absolutely none. The proposition had for him not the status of a conclusion but that of an uncritical assumption. He thought it the only possible explanation of the fact that evaluations usually have monadic, not dyadic, form. Thus, we say "This tastes good," not "This tastes good to me." Taking this usage at face value, Moore confidently declared that tasting something good is like seeing something yellow in requiring an apprehension of a simple quality that attaches directly to an object independently of its apprehension.

As we also noted above, however, there is another explanation: These apparently monadic evaluations are better regarded as ellipses for relational sentences. Thus, as "x is near" usually means "x is near me," so "x tastes good" usually means "x tastes good to me." This hypothesis not only explains why we sometimes need to add a second subject, in order to say "Licorice tastes good to Jones, but not to me"; it also avoids the need to postulate unobserved similarities. For, just as two objects can be near you without resembling each other, so, we may suppose, two objects can reinforce your desire for them without resembling each other. Thus, butter pecan ice cream and back rubs are both pleasing, but they are otherwise not much alike.

That Moore could not see this explains why he could not understand how torturing babies might have both positive value for the sadist and negative value for us. In his Platonic view, a thing was either good or not; it, therefore, could not be good for you, bad for me. Saying so sounded to him like saying the earth was neither round nor flat but round for some people, flat for others—meaning that the earth is flat in the opinion of some persons, round in the opinion of others Rightly despising subjectivism of this kind, Moore wrongly dismissed out of hand the possibility that value, if not shape, might be relative to persons and circumstances.

Moore's attitude is made clearest by his discussion of what he, following Henry Sidgwick, the father of twentieth century intuitionism, called *egoism*. Disagreeing with Sidgwick, who had said that every person's own good was a good *for him* but perhaps not for other people, Moore complained that the expression *for him* lacked clear meaning and declared it the cause of many philosophical absurdities (p. 99). Setting the pattern for all subsequent discussions of the matter, he averred that the egoist is committed in spite of himself to a self-contradictory proposition—namely, that every person's *own good* is the only *absolute good* there is.

> ...when I talk of a thing as 'my own good' all that I can mean is that something which will be exclusively mine, as my own pleasure is mine ... is also *good absolutely* ...the *good* of it can in no possible sense be 'private' or belong to me;

any more than a thing can exist privately or for one person only. The only reason I can have for aiming at 'my own good' is that it is good absolutely that what I so call should belong to me—*good absolutely* that I should have something, which, if I have it, others cannot have. But if it is *good absolutely* that I should have it, then everyone else has as much reason for *aiming* at *my* having it, as I have myself. (p.99)

The mistake in this emphatic and dogmatic declaration –it can scarcely be called an *argument*—should now be clear. Moore has simply refused to see the point. Unyielding in his conviction that "x is good" more nearly resembles "x is yellow" than "x is near y," Moore thinks he sees a contradiction in the contrary view, but the contradiction is one that he has projected onto his target; not one that he has found there. You can see this by substituting the word *near* wherever Moore talks of *good.* Imagine a philosopher who said,

Things that are truly described as near must have some quality in common. This quality is undefinable; so, it must also be simple. Furthermore, if it is an intrinsic quality, it must either be in the thing or absent from it; it cannot without contradiction both be and not be possessed by it. You have claimed that what is near Jacques in Paris is far from Jack in New York, but the claim is patently self-refuting. It takes away with one hand what it gives with the other. Self-evidently, the same thing cannot be both near and far; it must be either one or the other. Such expressions as near to and far from are unintelligible and the cause of much philosophical confusion. So, do not say that what is located in one man's vicinity may not be located in another's. A location does not exist merely for a particular person; it exists absolutely, for everybody. I do not own my location as I own my head, So, when I say that a thing is in my location, I do not mean that it is in a location that exists only in relation to me. I mean that it exists absolutely in the location in which I also happen to exist.

In the end, Moore's argument is really no better than that. For any physicist who wants it, a nice way to prove Leibnitz wrong and Newton right.

Notes

1. See Hocutt, "Skinner on the Word 'Good': A Naturalistic Semantics for Ethics," *Ethics* 87 (1977): 319-338.
2. There is another use of the word *intrinsic*, to mean *inherent* in the thing itself, apart not just from its effects but from all its relations to other things. Thus, the shape of an object is intrinsic to the object, not dependent on its relations to other things. In this second usage, the intrinsic is opposed not to the instrumental or useful, as in our text, but to the extrinsic or relational. As we shall see, these two meanings are often confusingly conflated with each other.
3. This is a broad use of the word *just*, which may also be used narrowly, to describe what accords with the law.

4. The permissible is, of course, that which is not obligatory, and the forbidden, or impermissible, is that which it is obligatory, to avoid. In our jargon, the permissible is not punished; its avoidance is not reinforced. By contrast; the forbidden, or impermissible, is punished; its avoidance is reinforced, usually by condemnation or punishment.
5. The "fallacy" Moore had in mind may have been that of confusing *is* with *ought.* In Moore's view, the good is what it ought to be, but naturalistic description says only how things are. So, he thought, equating the two must be a mistake. Still, Moore did not explicitly define the fallacy in this way.
6. The first such paradox noticed by Russell was, of course, the paradox of the impredicable. Is the property of being impredicable predicable of itself? Then it is not impredicable. Is it not predicable of itself? Then it is impredicable. A paradox. To resolve this paradox, Russell forbade predicating a property of itself. The property of being square is identical with, but it does not have, the property of being square.
7. Actually, in this passage, Moore is talking about the existence of a beautiful thing that is admirable but not admired, because there is nobody to admire it. And his argument is aimed at Sidgwick's hedonism, not Mill's. The argument is, however, exactly parallel.
8. The form of the argument is that "Nec (If a=b and Fa, then Fb)" is true even if "Nec a=b" and "Nec Fa" are false. It is a point about the scope of the modal term *necessarily.*
9. Hence, when Moore discusses these matters, he makes heavy weather of discussing the value of what he calls "organic wholes."
10. For readers unfamiliar with Tarski's distinction, the object language is the language we use to talk about objects; the meta-language is the language we use to talk about the object language. Thus, "The earth is round" is in the object language, but because it is about what is said in the object language, the statement "It is true that the earth is round" is in the meta-language. One use of this distinction is being made in the text.
11. Moore did not deny that instrumental and moral goodness are definable. In fact, he thought we can define the instrumentally good as that which is a means to the intrinsically good and that the morally good is a form of the instrumentally good.

7

Rules of Morality

In *The Object of Morality*, G. J. Warnock remarks, "It is natural, I think, to entertain the idea that there are moral rules, *somewhat* as, though of course not exactly as, there are legal rules"[1] (p. 53). Explaining further, Warnock says that morality appears to resemble law in being an instrument for "social control," the main difference being that rules of morality are not "authoritatively *made* and published," like rules of law.[2] Having noticed this analogy, however, Warnock goes on to argue that it is misleading. Holding that morality differs from law in being *recognized,* not *made* (p. 54), he argues that a practice is not morally wrong because proscribed but proscribed because morally wrong (p.55). I believe that Warnock's argument fails and that the analogy between morality and law holds. Although there are differences, there are also similarities.

Rules and Enforcement

Before we expose the defects of Warnock's analysis, let us try to understand why, as he says, it is natural to compare morality with law.

The brief answer is that it fits the facts. Examine any society you like. You will find that the people in it regularly behave in some ways, rarely in others. Some part of this behavior is explainable in biological terms. It is done because it is natural, built into the genes. Another part is explainable in sociological terms. It is done because it is rewarded by other persons in the society. Because this conduct is *regular* enough to be predicted, we say that it is *regulated*—governed by rules. Officially made rules of *law* explain only part of this regulated behavior. To explain the rest, we must suppose that societies also have unofficial rules—rules of morality and etiquette.

Several features of this analysis require elaboration. Let us begin with the concept of a *rule*. Rules are often confused with laws, and laws are often confused with their verbal formulation, but although a rule can be stated in words, statement is neither necessary nor sufficient. Instead, as B. F. Skinner observed, a rule exists in the contingencies—natural or artificial—that reinforce compliance with it. In other words, a rule exists if it is complied with, and this will be so if compliance is either itself reinforcing or reinforced by other persons. Human beings are verbal creatures. So, in human societies, words will often be used to reinforce compliance with a rule, but compliance may exist without the rule being formulated, and the rule may be formulated without effecting compliance.

To see this, consider the rule governing the distance at which two people normally converse. Very roughly: Three inches is threatening if loud, confidential if soft; six inches is intimate; twelve to eighteen inches is polite; two feet is formal but correct; four feet is unfriendly; and so on. This rule, which has counterparts in every society, is not usually stated, just obeyed. (In fact, I am not at all sure my description is correct.) People conform to it because other people will become uncomfortable and make them uncomfortable if they do not. You can confirm this by watching two people from different lands carry on a conversation. One of them will keep trying to get closer while the other keeps backing away—proof that the rule exists as practice if not also as statement.

There may be little danger of confusing with its verbalization a rule of etiquette such as the one just mentioned. However, because proclamation is an efficient way of publicizing law, it is often a salient part of making it. For this reason, many people equate law with its verbal proclamation. Thus, John Austin, one of the great writers on jurisprudence, defined law as the command of the sovereign, earthly or divine. It was a mistake. Law is often proclaimed, but the important part of making any rule, including a rule of law, is enforcing it. Let the police and courts enforce a speed limit with sufficient regularity to effect compliance. Then they will have made law even if it is never formally announced. But let the legislature and governor declare a speed limit without providing the funds to enforce it. Then they will have made *statute*, but they will not yet have made *law*.

Social Conventions: Why They Exist and How They are Maintained

Different kinds of rules are distinguished by the ways in which compliance is reinforced. Compliance with the rules that we call *laws of nature* is naturally reinforcing. An example is the rule "If food is available, eat when you are hungry." Other things being equal, most of us do this naturally; so do other animals. By contrast, the kinds of rules that interest us here have to be artificially reinforced. An example is the rule "Eat large meals only at dawn, noon, and dusk." This rule exists not because compliance with it is naturally reinforcing but because it is reinforced by other persons, who find it convenient to limit eating to the hours mentioned. Such rules, which may be called *social conventions*, are the topic of the present chapter.

Social conventions are ways in which human beings control the behavior of other human beings in their group so as to make it more agreeable to them. As Jeremy Bentham emphasized, the main but not the only function of these controls is to increase *utility*—in other words, improve welfare, usually for those doing the controlling and sometimes for those who are controlled too. Some rules—for example, rules against murder and theft—do this by reducing *conflict*. When these rules are in force, people are able to devote less time and fewer resources to protecting themselves or their property and to put more energy into creating wealth or enjoying it. Other rules—for example, rules encouraging honesty and the payment of debts—enhance *cooperation*. When these rules are in force, people are enabled to make arrangements or engage in transactions that are profitable to many persons. A third sort of rule—for example, charity for the needy—insures some members of the group against misfortune by transferring its costs to those whose luck is better.

Because it is burdensome, fulfilling the requirements of social conventions is something that many individuals would prefer to avoid. They would rather enjoy the benefits of the rule without having to comply with it. Most people want other people to tell them the truth, but some are unwilling to reciprocate. They want to exploit the general expectation of honesty by being dishonest themselves. If a society has a rule, then, it is often because it is, or is thought to be, sufficiently beneficial by a sufficient number of persons to induce them to enforce compliance with it. When belief in the utility of the rule declines, however, so will efforts to comply with it and to encourage others to do so. If this trend goes far enough, the rule may eventually cease to exist. It used to be the rule to pray in times of crisis, but increasing skepticism about the utility of this practice has diminished its frequency. By contrast, new rules—for example, the rule that you should wash your hands before serving food—come into being as conviction of their value grows.

The connection with utility is not perfect. A rule may come into existence not because it is useful but because it is wrongly thought to be, and compliance with a rule that was once useful may persist out of habit long after it has ceased to do any good. The classical account of the variables that affect the making, maintenance, and unmaking of rules is William Graham Sumner's *Folkways*. There, Sumner shows how social practices depend not just on their utility but also on superstition, irrational belief, the whims of individuals, social inertia, arbitrary power, and other factors.

Reinforcement of a rule may be either positive or negative. In other words, the rule may be reinforced by rewarding compliance or by punishing noncompliance. Because withholding of reward is sometimes called punishment, the distinction is not sharp, but we usually describe behavior that is positively reinforced as *desirable* or *praiseworthy* while describing behavior that is negatively reinforced as *required* or *obligatory*. Thus, charity is praiseworthy if not always obligatory, but repaying your debts is obligatory if not usually praiseworthy. Behavior that is either praiseworthy or obligatory—for example, giving to the poor or supporting your own children—is *right*, *just*, or *fair*. Behavior that is neither praiseworthy nor punishable—for example, looking after your own interests—is *permissible*.

How Rules are Made

Societies make and maintain rules in different ways. A common, but not the only way to make law is to proclaim it, then enforce it. Thus, legislative fiat or executive edict is followed by public advertisement and judicial or administrative exaction. The Napoleonic Code is an example of law that is made in this way. Law can also be made, however, in a less formal way, by an accumulation of judicial precedent or bureaucratic practice. Common Law is the favored example. The first illustrates *enactment*, the second *evolution*. The first is usually quick, the second usually slow.

Because law has increasingly become a prominent part of modern societies, the word *law* is sometimes used as a synonym for *rule*. Thus, people speak loosely of the *laws* of morality or etiquette. This usage is misleading. Strictly speaking, the term *law* belongs only to *official* rules—rules made and maintained by officials (kings, legislatures, judges, police, etc.) acting in their capacities as officials. So, only politically organized societies have law strictly so-called. Every society, however, has *unofficial* rules of morality and etiquette — which the French call *petite morale*, meaning the morality of petty matters, a close enough characterization for present purposes, if not an entirely accurate one.[3] These unofficial rules are enforced not by officials of government acting in their official capacities but by ordinary persons in the course of their daily lives.

Since governments now regulate everything that is important and much that is trivial, clear-cut examples of *unofficial* rules of etiquette and morality are increasingly hard to come by, but we can find them in a more primitive era. In the old West, before there were sheriffs and courts, stealing someone's horse would not have gotten you arrested, but it would have gotten you hanged from the nearest tree, indicating that rustling was against the rules even before it became illegal. Without rules of morality or etiquette, there is no society, just a state of nature, but, as this example shows, societies can exist without rules of law. In fact, since rules of law are a product of political organization, they are a relatively recent invention in the history of mankind. Although men have been on the earth for perhaps two million years, they may have known nothing of political organization until perhaps six thousand years ago, when the great civilizations of the Middle East were created by roaming bandits who stayed behind to exploit those they had conquered.

Earlier societies appear to have been extended kinship groups—clans and tribes governed by patriarchs. It is sometimes said that, in such primitive societies, the word of the patriarch was law, but this literally means that there was no law, just the word of the patriarch, who ruled without making laws, according to the whim of the moment. In Plains Indian tribes, there was a hint of political organization in the fact that decisions affecting the welfare of the group were sometimes made by councils of "chiefs,"[4] but the powers of these councils were very limited. Most matters were personal, not political. If your wife committed adultery, you did not call upon a council or a chief to punish her. You did it yourself, as seemed appropriate given the customs of your tribe. A cuckolded Commanche brave beat up his wife's lover or cut off a piece of her nose. In such groups, there was no law properly so-called. Conduct was regulated in informal ways by the people most directly affected by it.

Things have changed. Not only has law—officially created rules—become the most salient kind of rule in modern societies; in some societies, it has virtually displaced traditional morality and etiquette, as officers of government have tried to subject virtually every practice, no matter how trivial, to official review. In such a society, only illegal behavior is forbidden. Everything else is permissible, because people constrained by detailed and comprehensive rules of law are not at liberty to make or observe informal rules of their own. That is one of the great differences between total and limited government. In the totalitarian societies that existed in Nazi Germany and the Soviet Union, there was, of course, not even law; just arbitrary dictatorship. Because its moral foundation has been eroded in the process, the transformation of law into dictatorship may be inevitable as government approaches total control. That is one more reason to fear the increasing power of the state.

Fortunately, the replacement of traditional morality and etiquette by officially made law is never complete. Even in what are perhaps hyperbolically called totalitarian states, people obdurately persist in behaving in ways that are not officially approved and may be officially forbidden, because they have long been deeply entrenched. In that case, officials bent on increasing or preserving their control will find to their chagrin and dismay that long-standing custom and convention stand in the way. Thus, despite its militant atheism, the Soviet government was never able to eradicate ancient religious practices, the persistence of which may yet form the basis for reconstructing the social order destroyed by totalitarian Communism.

Limits on law also exist in countries with less total political control. A frequently cited example is governmental failure to prohibit alcohol consumption. Other illustrations are drug use and gambling. Despite strenuous efforts, popular governments have been unable to eradicate them. Instead, they have begun to make them legal, so as to benefit from the profits. This sort of experience has given rise to the saying, "You cannot legislate morality." Taken literally, this is false, but it exaggerates a truth. Because customary morality and etiquette precede officially made law and form the basis for it, they are not easily displaced by it, and they may retain some authority even when they prove to be in conflict with it.

Usually, of course, the official rules are not in conflict with the unofficial rules. The society is in trouble if they are. More often, the various kinds of rules reinforce each other, as customary morality and etiquette are made into law by officials intent on buttressing them with state power. Thus, to take the more obvious examples, all governments proscribe murder, rape, and incest—not in violation of social custom but in support of it. In most cases, the intent is not to displace the old, informal rules but to strengthen them with more systematic and reliable reinforcement.

Nevertheless, there are inevitably occasions on which law contravenes customary morality. A notorious example is affirmative action. Although it has been vigorously enforced by the courts and administrative agencies of the United States for three decades, opinion polls and plebiscites show that it is contrary to principles held dear by most citizens.

Examples of the Making of Rules

As just observed, law is usually enacted by government officials in a short period of time, while morality and etiquette evolve in unofficial ways over longer periods of time. Other differences are incidental to this one. A notable difference is that, instead of being attended by publicity, like much of law, the making of morality and etiquette usually takes place without anybody noticing that it is happening until the evolution is complete, or nearly so.[5]

It works roughly like this: People do things that other people like and are praised or rewarded, or they do things that other people dislike and are condemned or punished. Then they respond themselves, with praise and reward or condemnation and punishment. Adjustments are made, and these elicit adjustments by other people, until some equilibrium is reached, at which time a rule may be said to exist. As Adam Smith showed in *The Moral Sentiments*, it resembles an informal bargaining process. People undertake to make their behavior more acceptable to others in the expectation that others will reciprocate. Then the results of these mutual accommodations are taught to others, or learned by imitation.

The two ways—enactment and evolution—of making a rule can be compared to two ways of making a path in the forest. You might set out with ax in hand to cut down the bushes and trees that stand in the way; or you might go crashing through the woods from A to B and back again, following the line of least resistance until a path comes into being. You would eventually make a path in the second way, just as you did in the first, but you would do it deliberately and quickly in the first case, by accident and slowly in the second. Law is the deliberate, morality the incidental, path.[6] Of course, a path need be neither exclusively deliberate nor exclusively accidental. You can always deliberately undertake to improve a path that came into being accidentally, and laws can be consciously enacted to buttress rules of morality that evolved without planning.

We may use Warnock's example to illustrate the making of law by enactment. Suppose it is desired to limit speeding on the public streets. To achieve this end, the city council will enact and publish an ordinance, command the local magistrates to punish speeding when it occurs, and appropriate funds for police to patrol the roads. The police will arrest people who exceed the limit, and, after reviewing charges, the courts will order these people to pay fines or endure jail sentences. When these measures become systematic enough to reduce speeding, law will have been made.

Contrast this with the way in which a society might create a rule of morality or etiquette proscribing theft. Trying to protect their personal possessions, neighbors agree to watch each other's belongings and shun or punish people who are discovered to have sticky fingers. Seeing the advantages of these practices, other people in the society imitate them. After a while, most people get into the habit of watching not only their own possessions but also those of their friends and relatives. Eventually, all but a few people learn to respect the personal property of others, while teaching their children the same attitude. When that happens, the institution of property has become a part of the group's morality, not by official enactment in a few days or months but by a process of gradual change over what may have been many generations.

Because the unofficial rules that constitute morality and etiquette come into existence in informal ways over extended periods of time, it is usually wrong to say that *we* made them. In most cases, it would be more accurate to say that they were made *for us*, by previous generations. The important work of making them having been done before our time, it is left to us merely to recognize them and comply with them. In saying so, Warnock is certainly right.

It is, however, a mistake to deny that rules of morality and etiquette are *made*. They are not made in a moment by the identifiable acts of select individuals acting for the whole society. Instead, they are created slowly, over a long period of time, by anonymous persons acting on their own behalf or that of friends and kinfolk, but they are made. The rules of morality and etiquette are not always made by the persons who have them. Instead, they are often made by previous generations, but they are made. In short, rules of morality and etiquette are not enacted, like rules of law, but they are made. Warnock has posed a false dichotomy.

The Theological View of Morality

Theologians will agree that the rules of morality are made, but they will deny that these rules are made *by men in the course of time*. In the theological view, morality is itself a kind of law, namely, Divine Law. Instead of being constituted by the datable acts of earthly officials, this Law is constituted by the eternally valid will of an omnipotent God, the creator of earth and ruler of heaven. St. Thomas Aquinas, the unofficial spokesman for medieval Christendom, said that the Divine Law, which is also called the Eternal Law, has existed, and will continue to exist for all eternity. If he was right, we do not make the rules that constitute morality, and we cannot change them. Instead, we can only recognize and obey them. To help us do that, God built these rules into natural reason, which is why they are also called Natural Law, and provided us with priests and philosophers to interpret them.

Why most people still believe this is easy to see. It has been taught them by people whose power to make the rules might otherwise be hard to justify. Unfortunately, this justification has an irremediable flaw: As we shall argue at length in chapter 12, "The Myth of the Moral Law," belief in a Higher Law is supported by no evidence. We have clear proof of the existence of man-made rules, but no proof vouchsafes the existence of God-made rules. If the theological theory is to be believed, then, it has to be taken on faith alone. One has to believe that, just as some rules are made in *visible* ways by *visible* lawmakers, so other rules are made in *invisible ways* by an *invisible*

Lawmaker, and believing this requires not only a considerable stretch of the imagination but also an unbounded faith in the persons who claim to have privileged knowledge of inscrutable powers.

Like most modern philosophers, Warnock cannot manage this leap of faith or accept the idea that law is the arbitrary will of a cosmic potentate. So, he rejects anything resembling a divine-command theory of morality. Yet, he also cannot embrace the obvious alternative, belief that all morality and law are made by men. Therefore, he concludes that morality, if not also law, is *unmade*—by either God or men. As Warnock views it, morality consists of neither man-made nor God-made rules but eternal principles of Reason which we still need philosophers, if not priests, to interpret.

This view is one that we owe to the Enlightenment. Bloody conflicts during the Protestant Reformation having convinced intellectuals that invoking God would start more fights than it settled, Enlightenment thinkers resolved not to mention the divinity when discussing matters moral and political. Instead, they would undertake to show, or they would presume, that the Moral Law is built into Reason, and theologians would have to content themselves with the thought that, since Reason was given to man by God, presuming the rational provenance of morality would indirectly acknowledge its divine origin too.

This intellectual convention is still observed. Outside of schools of theology, philosophers rarely equate the Moral Law with the will of God. Instead, they identify it with what they take to be the antecedently given ideals and convictions of what Immanuel Kant called Pure Practical Reason. In this view, which its proponents call *rationalism*, we are to find the ideals and principles of morality, not in a transcendent realm, by consulting God and his priests, but within ourselves, by reflecting on our convictions and consciences, or by consulting philosophers who will do it for us.[7] In short, we are to resort to what are nowadays call *moral intuitions*, presumed insights into the *a priori* principles of moral conduct. This shift from God to reason has led to the increasing secularization and politicization of modern society, as power has shifted from priests to politicians.[8]

The resulting changes have been profound. Since, however, reason was presumed by Aquinas to be a God-given faculty, there are those who think that the differences in theory are more verbal than real. Of this opinion was the French existentialist, Jean-Paul Sartre, who found it odd that British moralists such as Warnock continued to believe in a

God-given morality even though they no longer believed in the God who gave it. Of the same mind are Alasdair MacIntyre and Elizabeth Anscombe, British Catholics, one Scottish, the other English, who condemn as paradoxical belief in a transcendent Law without belief in a transcendent Lawgiver. They have a point. Most philosophers may no longer *be* theologians, but it is clear that many still *think* like theologians.

This is evident from what they say. Although philosophers now speak of Reason where theologians once talked of God, they still say the same things about it. They use different words, but the words have the same meaning. How, according to the theologians, are we to know the Divine Law? Not empirically, by observation of facts; instead, *a priori, by* means of *divine revelation.* How, according to Enlightenment rationalists, are we to know the Moral Law? Not empirically, by observation of facts, but *a priori,* by means of *moral intuition.* If there is more than a verbal difference here, it is hard to see.

We are, however, getting away from our story. We set out to understand why it seems reasonable to compare morality and etiquette to law, and we found the explanation in empirically discernible similarities between official and unofficial methods for regulating the behavior of people in groups. In short, we found that, in addition to man-made law, societies have man-made rules of morality and etiquette. What we have just been trying to understand is why some people want to regard these as the arbitrary commands of an invisible but omnipotent God, or as the *a priori* commands of a transcendent Reason. No good reason, we have said; just superstition and a desire for otherwise unjustifiable power, aided by the fact that the rules are not written down, giving them a mysterious air of spirituality.

Let us therefore return to the hypothesis that is favored by the evidence, namely, the theory that morality and etiquette are like law in having been made by human beings but unlike it in not having been the creation of governments. We shall call this theory *conventionalism.*

What it Means to Say that Morality is Relative to Social Conventions

Given that conventionalism is true, what follows? One thing that follows is a parallel vocabulary. Just as we describe conduct as *legal* or *illegal* according to whether it conforms to or contravenes the appropriate rules of law, so we describe it as *moral* or *immoral* according to whether it conforms to or contravenes the appropriate rules of morality. Similarly, just as we talk about legal duties, rights and justice, so we talk about moral duties, rights, and justice. And so on. The verbal parallel is complete and exact.

Furthermore, this parallel talk has parallel meaning. As you have a *legal duty* to do what you are required to do by the rules of law, so you have a *moral duty* to do what you are required to do by the rules of morality. As you get *legal justice* if you get what is due you under law, so you get *moral justice* if you get what is due you under morality. As your *legal rights* are those that other people have a legal duty to respect, so your *moral rights* are those that other people have a moral duty to respect. And so on. In these ways of talking, the law is the paradigm for discourse about all rules, including rules of morality and etiquette—which explains why people have a tendency to describe these and other rules as laws too.

Another implication of the analogy between law and morality is moral relativity. We are familiar with the fact that, since different nations have different rules of law, conduct that is legal in one place may not be legal in another. Given the comparisons just made, it is natural to draw the parallel conclusion, that since different societies have different rules of morality and etiquette, conduct that is moral and mannerly in one may be immoral or ill-mannered in another. Thus, polygamy is legally and morally permissible in Saudi Arabia but not in Selma, Alabama.

If, as conventionalists also maintain, there is no Higher Law or Morality—no rules of law, morality, or etiquette over and above those made by different groups of men—then no form of conduct will be *absolutely* legal, moral, or mannerly. No doubt, some forms of conduct—for example, incest and murder—will be prohibited everywhere, because they are everywhere unnatural, or harmful, or otherwise objectionable. However, even these forms of conduct will not be *absolutely* illegal, immoral, or ill-mannered; just illegal, immoral, and ill-mannered *everywhere*. And they will not count as illegal, immoral, or ill-mannered merely because they have been found to be objectionable. What will make these universally condemned forms of behavior objectionable is the fact that they contravene our biologically based nature. What will make them illegal, immoral, or ill-mannered is the existence of socially made rules prohibiting them.

Why Warnock's Objections Fail

Against this view, Warnock has objected that, although a practice can be made legal or illegal by the creation of man-made law, it cannot be made moral or immoral by the creation of man-made morality.

To support his objection, Warnock offers three analogies. In the first, he considers the practice of speeding in congested areas, where it is dangerous. Using a neat turn of phrase, Warnock says that this practice is not objectionable because it is proscribed; it is proscribed because it is objectionable (p. 55). He thinks that this slogan refutes the hypothesis just stated—that the legal or moral acceptability of a practice is determined by the existence of a man-made rule of law or morality prohibiting it.

Warnock's reasoning suffers from two infirmities. First, it poses a false dichotomy. Grant that practices are often proscribed because they are found to be objectionable without the proscription. It remains true that proscribing a practice makes it objectionable in an additional way, namely, as *contrary to the proscription*. Thus, speeding in congested areas will be objectionable *as dangerous* before it is proscribed by law, but it will become *illegal* only when an appropriate rule of law makes it so.

Second, Warnock makes a false assumption. It is false that a practice must be objectionable in order to be proscribed by a rule. In their folly or greed, the local magistrates may choose to proscribe speeding even in open areas, where it would be perfectly safe, simply because they want to collect the fines or demonstrate their power. If so, they will enact an ordinance making speeding illegal even where it is objectionable in no other way. Maybe governmental officials never do this sort of thing in England; they do it quite often in America. Many small townships support their governments in this objectionable way.

So much, then, for Warnock's first analogy. Believing that morality is different, Warnock also offers a second. Having compared morality to ordinances against speeding, he compares it to the game of cricket and observes that the rules of this game are not made, like rules of law. Instead, they are merely recognized and obeyed.

Unfamiliar with cricket, I will take Warnock's word that there is nobody whose *official* business it is to make its rules. Yet, it seems clear, cricket does have rules, and they have not existed forever; so, they must have been made. We may agree that the rules of cricket were never *enacted*—instituted by the formal acts of a body of persons whose official business it was to make such rules. Instead, we may presume, the rules of cricket *evolved* over time, by the gradual adoption of practices that seemed to those who played the game to make it more pleasurable. But if this is so, the rules of cricket were made after all. By emphasizing the word *made,* when he said that the rules of cricket were not "officially *made*" Warnock caused himself to forget that these rules were *unofficially* made, but made nevertheless.

Once the rules of cricket have been made, it is also true that there is no need to make them anew, before you begin to play. All that is left is to recognize and abide by the rules already in existence, as Warnock says. Pace Warnock, however, this does not distinguish the rules of cricket from rules of law. Once a rule proscribing speeding has been duly enacted by officials, it is not up to motorists to make up their own speed limits. All that is left to them is to recognize the posted limit and abide by it. The fact that, if the game is to be played, the rules of cricket must be recognized and obeyed does not imply that they were never made; it presupposes it.

Perhaps recognizing the weakness of the two arguments just refuted, Warnock offers a third. Using contraception as an example of an intrinsically and absolutely immoral practice, he attempts to show that the conventionalist view of morality has absurd implications.[9]

Suppose, Warnock says, that the immorality of contraception was a simple matter of being contrary to a man-made rule. Suppose, too, that this rule was not "authoritatively made and published, nor perhaps even formulated." Instead, it was "just generally 'recognized' in a friendly, informal sort of way," like a rule of cricket (p. 56). Then, Warnock says, it would become *a mere matter of opinion* whether the practice was wrong, and this would "yield the queer implication that morally wrong practices would actually not be morally wrong, if those concerned did not recognize moral rules proscribing them" (p.57).

This is a common objection, but its premise is false. It is not true that a rule exists in an "objective" way only if it is "authoritatively made and published." As we observed above, rules of morality and etiquette do not exist in the form of *official edicts*, but they do exist in the form of *unofficial practices*, which are just as "objective"—that is, just as real—as edicts. If the members of a society make it their practice to enforce and conform to a rule, then the rule exists, not just subjectively in their minds but also objectively as behavior.

Warnock misunderstands this because he is a rationalist, and rationalists, as Michael Oakeshott observes, can conceive of a rule only as something *written down.*[10] In other words, rationalists think of rules as verbal formulas.[11] Hence, Warnock says that a rule does not exist unless it takes the form of a command by an official of government. As we were at pains to observe above, however, verbal formulation is neither necessary nor sufficient. All that is needed is sufficiently regular and vigorous enforcement to effect compliance. So, Warnock's objection fails.

Other Misinterpretations

So do the similar objections of James Rachels. Addressing Ruth Benedict's claim, in *Patterns of Culture*, that different societies have different behavioral *norms*, Rachels accuses Benedict of confusing the question whether a practice *is* morally acceptable with the question whether it is *thought to be* so.[12] Granting that these are different questions, I shall show that it is Rachels, not Benedict, who has confused them.

Rachels begins his criticism by saying that relativists like Benedict deny the reality of "universal" and "objective" moral truth (p. 360). What does Rachels mean by "universal" and "objective" truths? Although the words are his, Rachels does not define them; so, we must guess at what they mean. A good guess is that "universal truths" means statements that should elicit agreement everywhere. Such statements are not just true *in somebody's opinion;* they are "objectively" true. In short, they are not just thought be true; they are true in fact. Rachels is claiming, then, that relativists like Benedict have replaced the idea that there is such a thing as moral *truth* with the idea that there are just moral *opinions*, each true in the opinion of the person who holds it, none true in itself.

Is this interpretation of Benedict justified? It is hard to see how. Benedict says absolutely nothing about *truth.* Her topic is *norms*, and her claim is not that there are no universal moral *truths* but that there are no universal moral *norms*. Furthermore, she supports this claim by saying not that different societies have different *opinions* but that they have different *practices, customs,* or *habits.* Her statement about the matter is admirably clear:

> We recognize that morality differs in every society, and is a convenient term for socially approved habits. Mankind has always preferred to say "It is morally good," rather than "It is habitual," and the fact of this preference is matter enough

> for a critical science of ethics. But historically, the two phrases are synonymous. (Pojman, p. 356)

Where, then, does Rachels get the idea that Benedict and other relativists reject belief that there is such a thing as moral truth? I offer the following hypothesis. Consider the sentence,

(a) *Polygamy is morally acceptable,*

which we discussed in an earlier chapter. Is this sentence true, or is it false? Although Benedict does not say so in so many words, we may reasonably suppose that she would reply, "As it stands, this statement is neither true nor false. The truth is, rather, that polygamy is acceptable in some places but not in others. For example, it is acceptable in Saudi Arabia but not in Selma, Alabama." Rachels takes this to mean that Benedict has denied the reality of moral truth; for her, there is nothing but a variety of moral opinions, each true for the person who holds it.

This is a misreading of Benedict's view. On the most plausible reading of her words, she is not denying the reality of truth; she is merely denying that it attaches to sentences like (a). Her belief is that truth attaches, rather, to sentences like

(b) *Polygamy is morally acceptable in Saudi Arabia,*

and

(c) *Polygamy is not morally acceptable in Selma, Alabama.*

Furthermore, by saying this, Benedict does not mean "Polygamy is acceptable *in the opinion* of the Saudis, unacceptable *in the opinion* of the Selmans." As her words make perfectly clear, she means "Polygamy is habitually accepted—accepted in practice—in Arabia but not in Alabama," a very different claim.

Rachels's problem is that he cannot see the difference between references to a group's opinions and references to its practices. What stands out for Rachels is this fact: If asked whether (a) is true, the Saudi will say Yes, the Selman No, and Benedict will agree that what they both say is true. So, instead of a "universal" and "objective" truth of the form (a) we will have only truths of the forms (b) and (c). That is why he says that Benedict's position amounts to a denial of the reality of universal and objective moral truth.

This reasoning has fooled many philosophers, but it is fallacious. In fact, it is backwards. If a universal and objective truth is a statement to which everybody ought to agree because it is true, then (b) and (c) are universal and objective truths, but (a) is not. Instead, if Benedict is right, (a) is not a statement but an ambiguous, because incomplete, sentence, one that, like "I am tired," has a different meaning in the mouth of every person who says it.

The conclusion? It is Rachels, who has confused "x is morally acceptable in S" with "x is morally acceptable in the opinion of the people of S," then projected his error onto Benedict. In other words, he has confused the claim that acceptability depends on a society's *conventions* with the claim that it depends on a society's *convictions*, but although Benedict makes the first claim, she does not make the second. In fact, in the passage quoted above, she explicitly rejects it, by pointing out that it does not matter what the people in a society think they mean when they declare a practice to be moral or immoral; what matters is whether the practice comports with their customs. So, Rachels's objection is aimed at a claim Benedict never made.

To say so is not to deny that some people have made this claim. College sophomores, for whom Rachels's popular text was written, sometimes vehemently insist that there is no truth, just opinions, one as good and true as another, because every opinion is true in the opinion of the person who holds it. Sophomores are especially vehement about this when the topic is morality. Their refrain is "You have your opinion and I have mine; they are both just opinions; there is no truth of the matter." This opinion, which refutes itself by purporting to be *true,* is also taught as gospel in politically correct departments of English. So, Rachels is not attacking a pure fiction. He is, however, attacking a straw man. The "relativism"—more precisely, the conventionalism—that he attacks is a much flimsier thing than that espoused by Benedict, or Westermarck, or Sumner, or any other relativist worth his salt.

Why Conventionalists Need Not Deny the Reality of Common Human Values

In addition to the criticism just refuted, Rachels accuses Benedict of having overlooked the existence of common human *values* by emphasizing the existence of uncommon social norms.

For an illustration of his point, Rachels cites reports that Eskimos living on icy tundra used to leave infant girls to starve, then remarks that, although this practice may seem peculiar, it provides no support for the view that the Eskimos have different "values." Doubting that Eskimos value their children any less than we do, Rachels concludes that the difference between us is a difference in belief. Then he goes on to elaborate this difference, saying that although girls eat nearly as much as boys, they do not make as good hunters. Furthermore, hunting, which is dangerous, eventually cuts into the supply of hunters, further threatening the food supply of the group, including the females. Rachels concludes, "So, among the Eskimos, infanticide does not signal a fundamentally different attitude toward children. Instead, it is a recognition that drastic measures are sometimes needed to ensure the family's survival" (p.363).

This is a puzzling—in fact, a self-refuting—argument. Is Rachels denying *that* the Eskimos had a different attitude towards girls? Or is he explaining *why* they had a different attitude towards them? He tries to finesse the question by inserting the word *fundamental*, saying that the Eskimos did not have a "fundamental difference in attitude." This means, I take it, that the Eskimos, who were human beings like us, would, like us, have cherished their infant girls too *if circumstances had not been different*. Let us grant the point. The fact remains: Since circumstances *were* different, the Eskimos not only preferred boys but regarded girls as a liability. This may not be what Rachels calls a *fundamental* difference in attitude, but it *is* a difference in attitude, and a very important one too! So, Rachels's explanation of this attitude, though probably right, does not refute Benedict.

Rachels believes otherwise because he thinks that Benedict has denied the reality of a common human nature and cultural universals. It is evident from his discussion that he takes Benedict to be committed to the false belief that the Eskimos had no *natural* affection for their female children; their feelings about children—their "values"—were entirely a product of culture. Does any evidence support this reading? Rachels offers none, and there is none that I can see. Benedict does say,

> We do not any longer make the mistake of deriving the morality of our locality and decade directly from the inevitable constitution of human nature. We do not elevate it to the dignity of a first principle. We recognize that morality differs in every society. (p. 356)

This may sound to Rachels like a denial of the reality of human nature; it does not sound like that to me. Benedict is not denying that

Eskimos have feelings, like other human beings, for their infant girls; she would have to be a fool to deny that. What she is denying is that these feelings suffice to determine what is morally acceptable or obligatory in Eskimo society. Rachels has missed the point once again.

How Conventionalism Differs from Cultural Relativism

Confusing conventionalism with subjectivism and the denial of human nature is only one mistake. Another is to confuse it with what is sometimes called *cultural relativism,* meaning belief that, since evaluations are relative to cultural standards, there is no declaring one culture to be superior to another; instead, every culture counts as good when judged by its own standards, the only ones that are relevant. With encouragement from Richard Rorty, who ought to know better, this line of thought is also enjoying currency in departments of English literature, but Rachels says that it is absurd, because it would forbid us to criticize not only the practices of other societies but also our own practices (p. 362). Here Rachels has a point. His mistake is to suppose that what he calls *moral relativism* entails this absurdity. I shall argue that Rachels has confused a truth with a falsehood.

The truth is this: Since there is no transcendent Morality, conduct can meaningfully be judged moral or immoral only by using the relevant local morality as a standard. Thus, as Bernard Williams has observed, you cannot sensibly equate the polygamous behavior of a pious Saudi sheik with that of a seedy London bigamist. Instead, you must judge the sheik by the standards that are applicable in his society while judging the bigamist by the different standards that are applicable in his. Nor, since there exists no culturally transcendent Morality, can anyone make sense of the claim that the Saudi institution of polygamy is itself immoral. Doing so would make as little sense as saying that the standard meter bar is more or less than a meter long.

The falsehood is this: That one society's morality cannot be compared unfavorably to another's. How this falsehood differs from the truth just stated will become obvious if you will first consider exactly analogous reasoning about law. It makes no sense to declare the conduct of a Saudi Arabian illegal on the grounds that it contravenes the laws of Selma, Alabama, and if there is no Higher Law, it also makes no sense to say that Saudi law is itself illegal. *Illegal law* is a contradiction in terms, and so is *immoral morality.* No matter. This need not prevent anybody from saying that Saudi law respecting marriage is *bad* in some other way. *Bad law* is not a contradiction in terms, and neither is *bad morality*. The claim that a society's law or morality is bad may not be true, but it can certainly make sense.

Morality and Utility

What, in the absence of a Higher Law or Morality, can it mean to say that a society has *bad* rules of law or morality? The question will be discussed at length in a separate chapter, "Must Relativists Tolerate Evil?" For now, let us notice just one thing it might mean—namely that the law or morality in question does more harm than good. Rachels has overlooked the fact, emphasized by Jeremy Bentham and other utilitarians, that we can always evaluate a rule—either one of our own or one of another society—by measuring its *utility*. For an example, consider the rule of etiquette that requires people to greet each other by shaking hands. This may once have served a useful purpose in signaling one's good intentions, but although it is still the mannerly practice, it has one great disadvantage: More diseases may be spread by handshaking than by any other practice. Good manners; bad practice.

The meaningfulness of evaluating rules in this way was first discussed by the utilitarians, whose view is all too often misunderstood. Many philosophers understand utilitarians to hold that a practice counts as moral or immoral according to whether it is useful or harmful. As is clear from even a superficial reading of *The Principles of Morals and Legislation*, however, Jeremy Bentham, the greatest of the utilitarians, had no such opinion. On the contrary, Bentham's complaint was that this proposition is all too often false. All too often, Bentham said, the existing rules require conduct that has not positive but negative utility—in other words, these rules require people to do things that are not useful but harmful. He wanted to change this by applying the test of utility to all rules, whether they be rules of law or rules of morality. For Bentham, then, utility was not the measure of what *is* lawful or moral; it was the measure of what *ought to be made* lawful or moral. The test of what is lawful or moral in a particular locale is the local law or morality.

This distinction between *justice* or *rectitude* and *utility* or *goodness* is extremely important, if usually neglected. If conventionalism is right, a society's conventions determine what, in the society, counts as just or right. A society's conventions do not, however, always determine what, in the society, should count as good, because that depends in the final analysis not on social conventions but on personal preferences, which are to a considerable extent independent of the society even when they are influenced by it. Thus, eating crow could be made obligatory in a society, either by enactment of a rule of law or by evolution of a rule of morality requiring it, but this rule could not make crow taste good or nourish those who ate it. The existence of such a rule would make the eating of crow to be legally and morally just where it was required, but it would not make the practice to be either pleasant or beneficial.

How Conventionalism Differs from Cultural Determinism

We have now looked at two criticisms of conventionalism, a variety of moral relativism. One of these interpretations confused it with *subjectivism*, belief that the morality of a practice is a matter of social opinion. Another criticism confused conventionalism with *cultural relativism* belief that one society's culture is as good as another's. A third, which we shall examine now, confuses conventionalism with *cultural determinism*—belief that human behavior is determined not by human nature but by human society.

This mistake is made by the distinguished criminologist *cum* moral philosopher James Q. Wilson. As Wilson views it in his *The Moral Sense*,[13] moral relativism, or conventionalism, is just cultural determinism, belief that, since there is no biologically fixed human nature, human beings can be molded to any shape, good or evil, that a society happens to choose. In opposition to this view, Wilson cites evidence that people everywhere have an innate sense of fairness. In *Consilience*, a distinguished biologist, E. O. Wilson,[14] advances a similar argument, claiming that moral relativists overlook such biologically rooted universals as greater male aggressiveness and the instinctive aversion to incest.

The objection is certainly valid against some views. Vulnerable to the charge of making biology irrelevant are the followers of Plato and Kant, who (1) thought of the Moral Law as a set of culturally transcendent principles inscribed on Human Reason and (2) regarded Human Reason as the only essential part of Human Nature. In the minds of these philosophers, for whom human beings might as well be disembodied intellects, biologically based desires are no part of human nature proper. That title belongs solely to a transcendent Reason, which is, by definition, the same for all human beings everywhere and has as its function to control bodily based desires in order to give human conduct the shape preferred by a transcendent divinity. In this rationalist view, the science of biology is morally irrelevant for the paradoxical reason that, having to do with the human body, *it does not treat of human nature*!

Biology is also irrelevant, or negligible, for those who follow Rousseau in believing that human conduct can be given any shape by *society*, [15] Rousseau's romantic substitute for God and Reason. On the grounds that men are naturally selfish and society is the means chosen by reason to curb their selfishness, the English political philosophers Thomas Hobbes and John Locke had defended commercial society and individual acquisitiveness. Rousseau, an implacable enemy of capitalism, replied—on no grounds that he could cite besides opposition to Enlightenment rationalism and Christian faith in the essential goodness of man—that "natural" (meaning *primitive*) men were charitable and compassionate while modern men have been made greedy and unfeeling by industrial society. Socialist readers of Rousseau, including Marx, soon drew the obvious conclusion—that, if capitalist society can corrupt man, socialist society can redeem him. In either case, they seemed to conclude, there is no biologically given human nature which society need accommodate.

As this shows, both rationalism and romanticism, which are mirror images of each other, are vulnerable to the charge of having forgotten Aristotle's reminder that human beings are *animals*—rational animals to be sure, but animals nevertheless. As such, human beings are not disembodied intellects; they are *embodied* intellects who not only use their intellects to figure out how to serve their biologically rooted needs but also structure their societies to do the same thing. Therefore, there can be no understanding of human behavior and human society that does not take account of human biology. Since human beings everywhere have similar anatomy and physiology, they also have similar instincts, needs, dispositions, and desires. Any moral philosopher who forgets or denies this dooms his view to irrelevance. Let us grant as much.

The fact remains: Nothing in conventionalism prevents recognizing that cultural diversity is premised on biological similarity; the two things are not exclusive but complementary. As even Rachels's discussion of the Eskimos suggests, a culture is best regarded as a distinctive way that a group of more or less rational beings have learned to satisfy their biologically rooted needs—for food, mates, shelter, status, love, companionship, etc.—in the particular circumstances in which they happen to have found themselves. In every case, the needs served will be rooted in a more or less fixed biology that men everywhere have in common, but these needs will exist in a range of different environments and different groups of men will have different ideas about how to satisfy them; so, human cultures will vary accordingly.

Notes

1. (London: Methuen and Company, 1971).
2. The emphasis is in the original.
3. Though questions of etiquette often concern small matters, such as the placement of forks, they may also have large implications, such as the decency, civility, or mannerliness of using certain practices in an election campaign. Furthermore, the totality of small matters of etiquette probably has greater weight taken all together than the totality of large questions of morals. Therefore, to characterize something as a matter of etiquette, or manners, is not to belittle it. On the contrary, it is to pay it the highest compliment. A book that touches on the topic is Burton M. Leiser's *Custom, Law, and Morality* (New York: Doubleday, 1969).
4. For interesting accounts of Plains Indian life, see George Bird Grinnell *The Fighting Cheyennes*; Ernest Wallace and E. Adamson Hoebel, *The Commanches: Lords of the Southern Plains;* John C. Ewers, *The Blackfeet: Riders on the Western Plains*. All are published at Norman Oklahoma by the University of Oklahoma Press. As they make clear, the plains Indians were not without leaders or recognizable rules, but they were without government and officially enforced laws.
5. Of course, the division is not sharp. What we call Common Law is not enacted; it evolves by the gradual accumulation of judicial precedent. What Amy Vanderbilt proclaims to be a rule of etiquette becomes "law" to those intent on getting everything right for the occasion. Still, even Common Law involves the actions of judges, who are governmental officials; and although she is a respected authority on etiquette, Amy Vanderbilt has no official status or power; hers is the authority of knowledge.
6. For full discussion of these topics, see the writings of Friedrich Hayek, particularly his masterful three-volume work, *Law, Legislation, and Liberty* (London: Routledge & Kegan Paul: 1973).
7. For a more complete description of this view, see chapter 8, "Rationalist Moral Philosophy."
8. For more on intuition, see chapter 9, "Sidgwick's Method."
9. This choice of example makes me think that Warnock may have been Catholic, which would falsify my earlier presumption that he is a standard Enlightenment Rationalist.
10. *Rationalism in Politics and Other Essays* (Indianapolis, IN: Liberty Press, 1991).

11. Of course, the rationalist does not require that a rule be literally inscribed on something physical. He does not even require that it be literally pronounced aloud. He is usually satisfied if the rule is metaphorically inscribed on some mind, divine or humane. In fact, he prefers it. Still, it is fair to say that the rationalist thinks of rules as verbal formulas. Well, they can be verbalized but they do not have to be; they can exist without verbalization, and they often do.
12. The arguments I discuss here are excerpted from James Rachels, *The Elements of Moral Philosophy* and reprinted in Louis Pojman, editor, *Philosophy: The Quest for Truth*,4th edition (Wadsworth, 1999): 357-365. This excerpt is conveniently preceded by one from Ruth Benedict, enabling the reader to compare them word for word. All the references in parentheses are to these two selections.
13. (New York: Macmillan, 1993).
14. *Consilience: The Unity of Knowledge* (New York: Alfred A. Knopf, 1998).
15. Benedict may be guilty here. She does say that human beings are "plastic" to their societies (p. 357).

Part II

A Critique of Rationalist Moral Theory

8

Rationalist Moral Philosophy: An Acid Portrait

Rationalist Epistemology

Orthodox moral philosophy is Rationalist moral philosophy, belief that the truths of morality are self-evident, like those of mathematics on Rationalist interpretation.[1]

This is so, if the Rationalist is right, because the truths of morality, like those of mathematics, are innate, woven somehow (by God or Nature) into the very fabric of human reason, where they can be known *a priori*, just by thinking about them. So, they are to be discovered not by induction from actions or events in the physical world but by reflection on the operations and contents of our minds. The basic truths are to be discovered by *intuition*—direct, unreasoning insight into the principles of *a priori* reason. Other truths are then to be derived from the basic ones by means of definition, deduction, and *analysis*, the preferred methods of Rationalistic philosophy. Rationalism, then, is belief in a combination of *a priori* intuition with *a priori* analysis. The Rationalist calls this combination *Reason*. Moral philosophy as the Rationalist sees it is an inquiry into Reason.

The aim of this inquiry into Reason is to discover the *a priori* rule, principle, ideal, or other standard that determines which actions and practices are to count as right and which as wrong. As the Rationalist envisages it, the use of this standard is neither to describe nor to explain conduct but to prescribe and improve it—to tell us not how people *do*, in actual fact, behave but how they *ought*, ideally speaking, to behave. Hence, the Rationalist insists, the sought-for standard cannot be discovered empirically, by observing human conduct, in order to discern the motives that guide it or the conventions that constrain it. Instead, the standard must be uncovered *a priori*, by reflecting on Reason, in order to discover the ideals that are implicit in it

According to the Rationalist, the task of reflecting on and analyzing Reason belongs to the moral philosopher, who is especially trained for it. If he does this task well, the result will be that, without gaining any great experience of the world or its affairs, he will have gained a measure of moral expertise that will enable him to advise both ordinary individuals on how to conduct their lives and ministers of state on how to reorder their societies. No doubt, the *methods* and *means* will have to be discovered after the fact, using all the instrumentalities of empirical science, but the *ends* will be known beforehand, by those especially trained to discern them.

The Rationalist Conception of Reason

What the Rationalist calls Reason should not be confused with reason, the lower case capacity for ratiocination, reasoning. As Rationalist preference for the *a priori* indicates, Rationalism is belief not in reason as such but in reason conceived in a certain way. The true Rationalist has nothing but contempt for any exercise of reason that involves an attempt to derive general truths from empirically known particulars. He prefers a higher road, direct inspection of his own share of Reason. Furthermore, as is indicated by Rationalist dependence on intuition—unreasoning insight—Rationalism does not involve a preference for ratiocination over unreasoning faith or other forms of prejudice. No. Rationalism frequently takes the form of fideism, trust in special revelation; and it invariably takes the form of foundationalism, belief in unproved first principles. Whether these first principles are given by faith, intuition, or special revelation is for the Rationalist an entirely secondary question. What matters is only that they are not acquired from experience. Rationalism is opposition to empiricism.

This fact has led Karl Popper to suggest that the name *rationalism* is misleading.[2] In Popper's view, this title ought to be reserved for the preference of reason and criticism over faith and authority. Popper suggests that the doctrine that we are describing should be called *intellectualism*, preference for the intellect over the senses. Popper has a point. In the history books written by Rationalists, David Hume, a lover of reason in all its forms, does not count as a rationalist.[3] Instead, this uncompromising proponent of the thoroughgoing use of reason is denigrated as a mere *empiricist,* often with the suggestion that this makes him to be some sort of irrationalist. Any use of terms that has this absurd implication is seriously misleading indeed. Since, however, the term *Rationalist* has become traditional, we must stick with it. To resolve the ambiguity, we shall put the word in upper case when discussing preference for the *a priori* over the empirical. When we want to talk about preference for reason over faith, we can use the lower case word *rationalist*. Hume will then count as a rationalist if not also as a Rationalist. The Rationalists will then be such as Plato and Kant.

Whatever they are called, Rationalists prefer the *a priori* to the *a posteriori* because they prefer the *ideal* to the *actual*. As we have already noted, Rationalists believe that ethics is akin to mathematics, a science that, in their view, describes not actualities but ideals. The difference, as the Rationalist sees it, is only that where mathematics treats of such ideals as the perfect square and the perfect triangle, ethics treats of such ideals as perfect goodness and perfect justice. Believing that no actual square is perfectly square, Plato denied that the concept of perfect squareness can have been derived from experience and concluded that it must be known *a priori*. Believing that no actual thing is perfectly good and no actual society is perfectly just, he denied that the concepts of perfect goodness and justice can have been derived from experience; they, too, must be known *a priori*.

The clear implication of this view is that, in the final analysis, nothing in ethics depends on actual facts of the matter. This is true of both what Plato called the Good and what he called the Just or Right. Although the Good is also said to be desirable, Plato insisted that this is *not* because the Good is, or is likely to become, an object of desire. On the contrary, he said, people frequently desire bad things; so, the only connection between the Good and desire is that the Good *ought* to be desired; it is *worthy* of desire. Whether anybody ever desires the Good is for Plato quite irrelevant. Similarly, although the Just can be defined as that which accords with the law, Plato insisted that what is just cannot be known by consulting any law that may actually exist. On the contrary, he said societies often have unjust laws; so, the true measure of justice is the ideal system of Law, the system that actual laws ought to, but all too often do not, imitate. Whether this ideal Law ever exists is, again, beside the point.

In sum, Rationalist ethics purports to be the study of ideals known *a priori* by means of a combination of unreasoning insight into self-evident truth with reasoned analysis of previously given concepts. The insights, or intuitions, supply the basic truths; the analysis spells them out. Resort to empirically known facts of the matter might help to discern the means to our ends, but the ends themselves must be known beforehand, also by intuition.

Rationalist Psychotherapy

The preceding remarks concern theoretical ethics. For Rationalists, practical ethics is *applied ethics*, the application of previously known principles to empirically given cases.[4]

What this means will become clear when you remember that the moral philosopher does not, according to the Rationalist, learn how to behave from experience, by first learning what to do in particular situations, then doing likewise in similar situations. He does not derive general formulas from present experience for use in future cases. Instead, he begins with ideals, which he knows *a priori*. Then he undertakes to bring these ideals to bear on particular cases.

The business of moral theory is to articulate the ideals, that of practice to apply them to cases. Precepts first, practice next; not the other way around. To illustrate his *a priori* precepts, the Rationalist may make use of examples, either real or imaginary, but this ought not to mislead us. Rationalist use of examples is merely heuristic, like that of the mathematician. Its purpose is to aid the reasoning, not constrain it with fact. The aim is not to enhance our understanding of cases but to facilitate our analysis of ideals or illustrate our guiding intuitions. What matters, then, is the intuitions and, of course, the ideals. Empirically known reality is of interest only to the extent to which it approximates to, or deviates from, these.

This is so whether the case at hand is private or public. In the private sphere, the Rationalist advises individuals on how they ought to behave in order to achieve the Good. In short, he looks to the good of the individual. In the public sphere, he advises rulers—executives, legislatures, judges—on how they ought to behave in order to do

Justice.[5] In short, he looks to the good of society. In both spheres, he proceeds in the same way: *not* by studying what already exists and looking for ways to improve it *but* by contemplating the ideal and looking for ways to bring it into being. Thus, in deciding what the individual ought to do, the Rationalist does not begin with her as she is, in order to see how she might secure her ends. He does not acknowledge the need to build her personality brick by brick, from the ground up, so as to insure that it will stand on the soil on which it has been constructed. No. He looks to shape her from the top down, to make her fit a preconceived pattern.

Seeking to promote individual pursuit of *the Good*, the Rationalist believes that the desires we actually have are all too often aimed not at good but at evil to be the basis of acceptable conduct. Accordingly, he believes that the main business of ethics is not to teach us how to serve our desires but how to subordinate them to the dictates of Reason. If we cannot learn how to control our passions as the Rationalist believes we should, it becomes the responsibility of more rational persons such as he to exercise control over us, for our own good.

Rationalist Politics and Economics

Nor does the Rationalist begin with the society as it is, seeking to understand its present customs and laws, or why they came into being. No. As he begins with a ready made concept of the ideally good person, so he begins with a ready made concept of the ideally just society. Then he undertakes to say what changes are needed to bring it into conformity with his preconceived ideal.

In the public sphere, then, the Rationalist seeks not to preserve moral and political tradition but to promote moral and political reform. As the Rationalist views them, the customs and conventions of a society are historically accidental affairs that serve not Justice but arbitrary power. When this is so, the Rationalist believes that the society's practices need to be not preserved but remade, so that they will comport better with the ideal of Justice, public good. Seen from this view, political and moral traditions are usually not things to be perpetuated but things to be uprooted and changed. They are candidates not for admiration but for alteration. Only the empiricist is a conservative, who wishes to preserve tradition because he thinks it likely to embody the wisdom of experience. The Rationalist is more likely to be a radical, who seeks to tear tradition out by the roots.

Furthermore, rationalists prefer wholesale reform to small-scale improvement. In other words, they favor social engineering over piecemeal melioration. Being innocent by their own choice of the rigidity of human biology and habit, Rationalists think that their *a priori* moral wisdom will enable them to devise and dictate grand social transformations without having to bother about petty details, which can be worked out later, by those who must carry out the Rationalist's orders or follow his advice. Therefore, the Rationalist wants to change society, as he changes individuals, from the top down and the inside out. Having little use for the painstaking business of piling one small advance on another, in order to build a society that will survive and prosper in the circumstances, he wants to institute a utopia now, in one fell swoop; to hell with the opposition.[6]

Having this attitude, the Rationalist is also a believer in authority rather than democracy—guidance from above, by experts, rather than decision from below, by consensus, majority vote, or (God forbid!) the unregulated choices of free individuals. Described in contemporary slang, he is an elitist rather than a republican; a paternalist rather than an anarchist. Although he may sincerely profess a high regard for the common people, and although he may genuinely believe that government ought to serve them, he opposes giving them scope to do what they believe to be good for themselves, lest they make a botch of it. Instead, he wishes to arrange things so that they will be required to do what disinterested experts like him believe to be good for them. He is therefore a devotee of centralized planning and an enthusiast of bureaucratic management, a hater of the free market and an enemy of unregulated conduct. Wanting to direct behavior in the most efficient way towards the best ends, he dislikes and distrusts anything that is not tightly organized, consciously ordered, briskly managed, and coherently directed.

For these reasons, the Rationalist abhors both consumer choice and provider competition, the market's combination of undisciplined personal preference with the disciplined struggle of producers and suppliers to make a profit for themselves by pleasing their customers. He prefers instead the discipline of socialist unity for the larger good, the management of enterprise for public rather than private ends, and the direction of consumer choice towards goals more compatible with the "general welfare." A believer in direction by the visible and heavy hand of government, he knows little of, and does not care much for, the evenhanded ways of Adam Smith's invisible hand, free individual choice. No. In his view, individual preference and greed must be curbed at all costs, and so must the inefficiency, aimlessness, and irrationality that the Rationalist thinks he sees in lack of centralized planning and direction. Therefore, in the place of individual preference for personal or selfish ends, he wishes to put the wisdom and altruism of disinterested experts working selflessly for the general welfare. In short, he wishes to substitute a managed for a free society.

This preference for regulation over choice does not, of course, prevent the Rationalist from claiming to believe in freedom. On the contrary, all Rationalists devoutly believe in what they call "true freedom." It is just that what they call freedom is not freedom but control. The Rationalist believes that the central problem of practical morality is to subordinate the loves, the hates, the fears, the ambitions, the lusts, etc. of yourself and other people to the Rational ideals of Truth, Goodness, and Justice. If this is to be accomplished, however, desire for selfish pleasures and false goods must give way to truer values. Unreasoned emotion must be replaced by deliberate ratiocination. Immoral impulse must be regulated by moral principle. Wicked practices must be replaced by virtuous ones. And so on.

If the Rationalist has his way, then, liberty will give way to law and law to personal dictate, which can be achieved in two ways. There must be internal regulation by the agent when possible and external regulation by others when necessary. What the Rationalist calls *true freedom* is the former. Thus, a man who does what he wants to do, without interference from other men, is not free in the eyes of the Rationalist. Instead, he is a slave to his desires, which he serves as his masters. The man who enjoys "true freedom" is the man who has sufficient mastery over his own proclivities, preferences, and predilections to do what he *ought* to do as he is told by those of superior intellect; no matter that it may be the very opposite of what he *wants* to do. In short, for the Rationalist, the free man is not the man without a ruler; he is the man who does not need a ruler, because he rules himself, as his Ruler would. Liberty as autonomy.

The Platonic Sources of Rationalist Belief

In two widely read books and several highly readable essays, Alasdair MacIntyre, a Scottish Catholic who blames Rationalism for most of the evils of modern times, blames the eighteenth-century Enlightenment for Rationalism.[7] In MacIntyre's account, Enlightenment philosophers went astray when they substituted an appeal to Human Reason for the appeal to Divine Wisdom that had been the defining feature of medieval (read Augustinian) fideism. Since reason is the faculty for figuring out how to satisfy your desires, MacIntyre believes that Rationalism has led to the kind of unrestrained self-seeking and social disintegration that he believes to be the characteristic evils of modern liberal society.

MacIntyre's reading of history overlooks important facts. First, although modern secular Rationalism came to full flower in the Enlightenment, Rationalism began long before that, with Plato.[8] Second, although Enlightenment appeals to Reason did indeed replace medieval appeals to God, as MacIntyre says, this was sometimes more a change in name than in substance. The ground for it had been fully prepared by the widely accepted medieval doctrine that Reason is just the voice of God within man; so, by listening to Reason, we are indirectly listening to God.[9] Hence, when Immanuel Kant undertook, in the obligatory fashion of the Enlightenment, to base his ethics on "Pure Reason," he was doing nothing that had not been legitimated by prior insistence on Reason's divine source. Finally, although Kant's appeal was to Reason, this was no longer the faculty of serving one's personal ends. Instead, as Kant repeatedly emphasized, it was the faculty of recognizing and acting in accordance with *a priori* principles.[10]

The facts needed to establish the patrimony of Rationalism are well known. As all students of philosophy are aware, the doctrine began with Plato, who taught that our ideas are not learned, acquired from experience, but innate, the results of prior acquaintance with previously existing ideals. Plato speculated that, before the soul was joined to, or imprisoned in, the wicked body, it dwelt among, and was acquainted with, these pristine ideals. The shock of birth causes temporary amnesia, but concrete objects, which imperfectly resemble the abstract ideals, can sometimes remind the soul of what it knew in its more blessed condition. Thus, an imperfect but visible square can remind us of our former knowledge of the invisible but perfect Square; and a concretely but imperfectly good thing can remind us or our prior knowledge of the perfect but invisible Good.

What Plato called the light of Reason, using a metaphor that still lives twenty-five hundred years later, was the means by which the soul achieves insight into these perfect but invisible, because immaterial, ideals. Insight into the fundamental ideals is achieved—after extended training, discussion, and thought—by *intuition,* non-inferential apprehension of the self-evident. After due reflection and analysis, such intuitive insights yield definitions, verbal formulas that can be applied to particular cases. Plato believed that this combination of *a priori* intuition with *a priori* analysis is as appropriate in ethics as it seemed to him to be in mathematics. Accordingly, he argued that knowledge of the Good and the Just is as indispensable to the moral philosopher as knowledge of the One and the Square is to the mathematician. Furthermore, because no actual entity, either mathematical or moral, ever comes up to the ideal, Plato held that knowledge of the relevant ideals cannot be gained empirically, by studying actually existing examples; instead, it must be acquired *a priori*, by reflecting on the ideals themselves. Thus, because actually existing squares are always imperfect, the mathematician cannot hope to learn, only to be reminded of, what squareness is by examining visible squares. And, because actually existing justice—that is, justice as it is embodied in the laws and moralities of actual societies—is always imperfect, the moralist cannot hope to learn, only to be reminded of, the nature of perfect Justice by observing actual societies. What is left, then, is only to examine the ideals themselves, or rather, one's memory of them.

Plato's Opponents: The Sophists

In taking this line, Plato was opposing the more common sense view of the Greek sophists, empiricists who believed that we acquire our concepts—physical, moral, *and* mathematical—from experience. The sophists took it for granted that we learn what it is for an object to be square, not *a priori* but *a posteriori*, by examining one or more actual squares; and we acquire our concepts of goodness and justice not *a priori,* by contemplating ideals, but *a posteriori*, by experiencing good things and observing the workings of justice in concretely existing societies. On this account, declaring something to be square or good was comparing it not to a previously known ideal of squareness or goodness but to objects previously designated as paradigmatically, or prototypically, square or good: A square object was one like *this*; a good object one like *that*.

It followed that we cannot expect to discover which things are square or good by analyzing our previously given concept of goodness. Instead, we must do it the other way around: We must acquire a concept of the square or the good by abstraction from concrete experience of things, which may not be the same for all of us. By the same token, we cannot discover what to regard as just or lawful merely by reflecting on a previously given ideal of justice or law. Instead, we must become concretely familiar with the workings of some society's law and morality; we must gain some experience of its practices and norms.

An obvious but important implication of this line of thought is that goodness and justice are relative. Nothing is absolutely good or just—good or just period. Instead, what is good for you is bad for me; what is just in society S1 is unjust in society S2. Here, we may suppose, are the reasons the sophists had for thinking so: First, each of us describes as *good* what *he or she* prefers, usually because it benefits or pleases. But what benefits me will harm you, and what I prefer to create, you prefer to destroy. So, what is good for me is bad for you; nothing is good or bad absolutely. Second, each of us calls *just* what accords with the rules that he knows and loves; so, *justice* is everywhere a name for what accords with law, custom, and sentiment. But what accords with the law, custom, and sentiment that are in force in *your* society might conflict with the law, custom, and sentiment that are in force in *my* society; so, what is just and lawful *here* might be unjust and unlawful *there*.

No wonder, then, that one cannot hope to discover what is good or just *a priori*, merely by reflecting on one's own conceptions of goodness and justice! If the sophists were right, to discover what is good, one must first find out what will get one what one prefers; and to discover what is just, one must learn what is required by the laws and customs of one's society. Ethics is so far from being knowable *a priori* as to be irreducibly empirical.

Although this view clearly fits the facts, Plato never understood it. Having assumed that we have knowledge of perfect ideals, he could not see how we could have acquired this knowledge from imperfect examples. He could not see how to get an idea of a perfect square by abstracting from imperfect squares, an idea of perfect goodness by enjoying imperfect goods, or an idea of perfect justice by studying imperfectly just systems of law. So, he concluded that we must already have these ideals in our minds, where they are ready to be used as standards against which to measure actually existing but imperfect objects and practices.

Furthermore, Plato assumed, these ideals must be the same in the minds of all men and women everywhere. What counts as square, good, or just for Greeks should also count as square, good, or just for Persians. Since it is a matter of logic that the same thing cannot be both good and bad and that the same practice cannot be both just and unjust, it follows that if a man regards as good what a woman thinks bad, or a Persian counts as just what a Greek believes to be unjust, one of them must be mistaken. Plato concluded that the sophists had mistaken error for relativity.

Two Opposing Concepts of "Reason"

Because Plato disagreed with the sophists about the Good and the Just, he also disagreed with them about Reason. For the sophists, practical reasoning was calculating how to satisfy your desires and achieve your ends; so, a rational human being was simply one who had the habit of doing this. In short, for the sophists, reason was the *instrument* of desire. By contrast, for Plato, to make use of Reason was to employ one's capacity for recognizing a previously given knowledge of the Good, in order to keep one's misdirected desires in check. Hence, where the sophists took it for granted, as Hume was later to put it, that reason is and ought to be the *slave* of the passions, Plato believed, on the contrary, that it is, or should be, their *master*. In short, where the sophists believed that the function of reason is to help men get what they prefer, Plato believed that the role of Reason is to direct men away from their natural preferences towards the Good.

Having different ideas about reason, Plato and the sophists also had different ideas about morality and law. For Plato, these were uncreated, so eternally changeless, principles of a transcendent Reason. Their chief function was to restrain desire for the sake of the Good. For the sophists, they were institutions created by human beings to maximize the satisfaction of desires by minimizing conflict. As human creations, law and morality were products of reason; for they were designed, or came into existence, to serve human ends. But circumstances vary even when ends do not, and different people have different ideas about how to achieve their ends. So, the sophists believed that law and morality vary accordingly. Thus, what is legal and moral here is illegal and immoral there; what was legal and moral then is illegal and immoral now.

These disagreements in moral theory were accompanied by, and served to rationalize, differences in politics. The sophists viewed society, including democratic Athens, as a more or less stable mix of competing interests striving for dominance—in short, a struggle for power. That was another reason why, in their view, there could be no *single* standard of the Good or the Just. The state of affairs praised as good or just by one group, because it seemed to serve their interests or accord with their ideas, would simultaneously be condemned as evil or unjust by another group, because it appeared to defeat their contrary interests or conform to a different ideas. Goods were therefore thought to be relative; good for A is not good for B.

And what held true of the good also held true of justice, conduct in accordance with law. Because law varied with the group that happened to be in power, which usually did what it could to serve its interests, Thrasymachus—as reported by Plato—declared that justice is nothing but the interests of the stronger. This has been interpreted as the doctrine that might makes right, but if "right" means "absolutely right," it is an egregious misunderstanding. No sophist believed in absolute right or wrong. What Thrasymachus believed was that there is no higher standard for justice than the positive law, which, he observed, is enacted by those in power to serve their interests. Since that is called just which accords with the law, it follows that that is called just which accords with the interests of those in power, or with what they believe to be in their interests. Since democracy was in force in Athens at the time, this meant that the vote of the common people was decisive in determining what counted as just or unjust. In an oligarchy, the rich would decide the matter. Statements of fact.

Again, Plato responded with a different view. No friend of Athenian democracy, which had condemned Socrates to death and removed his family from power, he wanted to reform society by restoring the rule of a rational few who, knowing what is absolutely good, would work to control the desires and passions of the common people. Democracy as Plato saw it was a political embodiment of irrationality, a form of pandering to the passions of the people. He therefore preferred aristocracy, rule by a small group of supremely wise and superbly educated persons. These "philosophers" (wise men and women) were to rule with the aid of a larger group of guardians, who would have sufficient strength of character and will to enforce the decisions of their superiors. Rule by this intellectual and moral elite would be *for* the people; but it would not by any means to be *of* or *by* the people, as in a democracy. No. What was to be done would be done for the good of the people, but it would be done without their advice and, if necessary, without their consent.

That is why justice in Plato's political order would not be determined after the fact, by discerning which laws have actually been enacted, however wisely or unwisely. Rather, it would be an antecedently given feature of the society itself, one reflecting the fact that everything had been arranged, in accordance with Reason, to achieve the public's good. In other words, justice would not be a property of individual actions determined by whatever laws happened to be in force; instead, it would be a property of the laws themselves. Thus, democratic society—which is itself inherently and irredeemably unjust when judged by Platonic standards—would have no authority to determine which actions were to count as just and which as unjust. Instead, as Plato said over and over again, justice would be the exclusive and definitive possession of a society so ordered as to give the rational persons within it control over the irrational ones.

Medieval Rationalism

Medieval Rationalism was a continuation of classical Rationalism. Following the Stoics and Augustine, Thomas Aquinas, the leading philosopher of the late Middle Ages, identified Reason with God, human reason with that overflowing share of the Divine Reason which, in his view, God had given men. In accordance with the belief that the possession of Reason is what distinguishes men from beasts, Thomas then defined justice as conduct in accordance with the Natural Law of Reason—meaning God's eternal Will and universally binding Law by two other names. Man-made law, the product of human convention and custom, Thomas declared to be a mere imitation of Divine Law and, when contrary to it, no *law* properly so-called.

Thomas, who purported to follow not Plato but Aristotle, thought of himself as an empiricist, and in some ways he was, but he did not derive his moral philosophy from an empirical study of human nature or human society. Instead, he believed that the ultimate authority in matters moral was that revelation of the divine will which we discover in a study of *a priori* reason, and although he held in theory that God had given reason to all men everywhere, he held in practice that a privileged few—namely the bishops of the Holy Catholic Church—enjoyed a special capacity for insight into God's will. So, Thomas's adoption of Christian fideism did not signal the abandonment of Platonic Rationalism. Instead, Rationalism merely took on a fideist flavor, as first principles intuitively known by philosophically trained statesmen were replaced by items of Christian faith intuitively known by priests and popes. Faith was now to be the highest exercise of Reason, and Platonic belief in following the ideals of Pure reason was to be transformed into Christian belief in obeying the will of God—something for which the precedent had been set much earlier by the Roman stoics.

Aquinas was able to effect this identification of Reason with the divine will because he had earlier effected identification of the divine will with Reason. In Aquinas's view, Reason and the will of God are not two things but two names for one thing. This thing is called Divine Law because it is commanded by God, Eternal Law because God's commands are binding forever, and Natural Law, or the Law of Reason, because, thanks to God's grace, it is the nature and glory of man to possess Reason. Therefore, in obeying God you are obeying Reason; and in obeying Reason, you are obeying God. There is no real, only a nominal, distinction between the two things.

It is this last, almost incidental, claim that inspired the historical period that we of secular conviction now tendentiously call the Enlightenment. Having gone through the bloody conflicts of the Reformation, when Protestants and Catholics were literally at each other's throats over conflicting interpretations of the divine will, intellectuals in the seventeenth and eighteenth centuries decided to bypass once unifying but now divisive appeals to God in favor of direct appeals to reason itself, in the hope that this would restore unity. We call the resulting period of comparatively peaceful reliance on reason in matters intellectual and moral the Enlightenment. Very possibly, some of this reliance on reason was due to atheist skepticism about the existence of God, or deistic doubts about our capacity to know the divine will; but most of it had nothing to do with free thinking, and it was approved by many devout theists.

And why not? According to views espoused by St. Thomas and long since endorsed by Christianity's leading philosophers, accepting the authority of Reason did not mean repudiating the authority of God. Although it would one day be revived by Kierkegaard and flourish anew, the time of Tertullian unreason was long past. It was now believed throughout Christendom that God required men neither to believe nor to do anything that was irrational. Instead, it was held, God had given us reason intending for us to use it; and what better use of reason could there be than deciding how we ought to behave? Therefore, when the Rationalists of the Enlightenment turned to Reason, they were doing nothing that St. Thomas could have condemned in good conscience, for they were not thereby intending to turn away from God.

They were, of course, turning away from previously accepted methods for discovering God's will—namely, consulting priests—and St. Thomas could not have approved of this rejection of churchly authority. At the same time, however, he could not have condemned it in principle; for, by seeking to know the will of God through the use of their God-given Reason, the men of the enlightenment were merely doing what, according to him, they ought to be doing. They were merely taking the Saint at his word, making God-given Reason to be their guiding light. Only later did it occur to anybody to notice that, if Reason will suffice, there is no need to bring God into it.

Enlightenment Rationalism: John Locke

The point could be illustrated and confirmed by discussing the works of Grotius, Prufendorf, or Hobbes—each of whom undertook to derive a system of natural law from natural reason alone. Let us look just at Locke, who continued Thomas's way of thinking while changing it. Recognizing that, where x has a duty with respect to y, y must have a right with respect to x, Locke turned medieval belief in natural (i.e., divinely instituted) duties on its head and derived the obverse doctrine, natural (i.e., divinely instituted) rights.

In Locke's understanding, these natural rights are to be contrasted with the artificial, because man-made, rights that human beings possess by virtue of their membership in society. Having been given by society, the latter rights can also be taken away by society. Not so natural rights. Having been given to us by God, they cannot be taken away by men; they are inalienable. They belong to us by virtue of our human nature, not by virtue of our membership in society. So, they are not to be infringed by society. In particular, they are not to be infringed by the state, whose main business is to protect them. Locke, echoing Aquinas, said that when the state fails to fulfill its obligation to perform this function, its citizens have the right to revolt. The state's laws, being now in contradiction to Natural Law, have ceased to be binding. Good Thomistic doctrine.

Since Locke professed to be an empiricist, it may seem strange to describe his belief in Natural Rights as Rationalist philosophy; but Locke's empiricism is little in evidence when he discusses natural rights, which he too attributes to God, a transcendent being. In this respect also, Locke resembles Aquinas, who also thought of himself as an empiricist, because he was in many particulars a follower of Aristotle. Yet neither Aquinas nor Locke made any attempt to derive the laws of nature from experience. In their view, there was no need to do so. Both thought these laws self-evident principles of an innate, because divinely endowed, Reason, and they thought that Reason is the most essential, because most distinctive, part of human nature. Locke's follower, the revolutionary Thomas Jefferson, emphasized this belief when he declared it to be *self-evident* that men are endowed by their creator with rights which it is the duty of government to preserve and protect.

It is true that Locke tried to ground what he called the natural right to property in the idea that a man is entitled to possess that with which he has mixed his labor. Locke also argued that no rational person would sign on to the "the social contract" without assurance that his right to the products of his labor would be guaranteed and protected under it. But although there may be something to the second argument, the first is entirely *a priori*. Suppose we were to ask, "Why should a man be entitled to the produce of his labor?" This question would have made no sense to Locke. That a man was entitled to the produce of his own labor seemed to him to be as evident as that 2+2=4.

What seems self-evidently true to one person may seem self-evidently false to another. Since Locke invented it, the doctrine of natural rights has been made to serve political and moral causes of which he would have disapproved most strongly. Locke's natural rights were all negative. The rights to life, liberty and property were the rights not to be interfered with in acquiring what you needed to making a living and keep it. Contemporary believers in natural rights have, however, interpreted these rights positively, turning Locke on his head. Thus, Locke's right to be left alone to make a living by your own efforts has become the right to be provided a living by others if you are unable or unwilling to do it yourself. According to this new interpretation, the needy have a right not just to the produce of *their own* labor but also to the produce of *your* labor and *mine*. This would have struck Locke as self-evidently absurd, but much current political practice is based on the belief that it is self-evidently true.[11] That Rationalist appeals to moral self-evidence can be used in this way to buttress each of two contrary points of view is proof of the unreliability of Rationalist methods, a theme that we shall develop more fully in the next chapter.

Kantian Rationalism

Immanuel Kant certainly regarded himself as a devoted child of the Enlightenment and an enthusiastic champion of its main principle, Reason. But as Kant's insistence on calling his books critiques of reason indicates, his attachment to reason was highly qualified; and it did not exist at the expense of his pietistic Lutheran faith. Kant certainly rejected rational theology and arguments for the existence of God. He did so, however, not because he doubted God's existence but because he thought that trying to reason about it undercuts faith. For Kant, God's existence and nature were matters of freely chosen faith, not topics for rational discussion. So, it seemed to him, the less philosophers had to say about it, the better.

Ethics was different. Although the main principle of Kant's ethics, the Categorical Imperative, implies his Practical Imperative, which bears a striking and acknowledged resemblance to the Golden Rule of New Testament Christianity, Kant insisted that ethics is not a matter of merely provincial Christian faith but a deliverance of "universally valid" Reason. Regarding ethics, man's duty to his fellow man, Kant thought it not only possible but also necessary to be thoroughly rational and to base nothing on contentious propositions of theology or disputable claims of faith. In short, he believed it possible to demonstrate by purely rational means why everyone ought to do his Christian duty.

It is true, of course, and not by any means irrelevant, that the "reason" to which Kant appealed differed in important ways from the more or less Aristotelian reason which Aquinas had invoked. Central to Aquinas's concept of practical reason, as it had been to Aristotle's, but specifically excluded by Kant was the faculty and habit of *prudence,* calculating how to achieve your ends. The practical reason which Kant meant to invoke was *Pure* Practical Reason, reason unmixed with things empirical. So, it was to have no truck with human desires, which Kant, like Plato before him, condemned as pathological.

This important fact has been obscured by Kant's choice of titles: He called the first of his two great works, *The Critique of Pure Reason*; the second, *The Critique of Practical Reason.* This suggests that the contrast intended was between Pure Reason and Practical Reason. Not so. The first book should have been called *The Critique of Pure Theoretical Reason*, the second *The Critique of Pure Practical Reason.* Kant's concern in both books was what he called Pure Reason. The difference is only that he was concerned with the relation of Pure Reason to *theory* in the first, the relation of Pure Reason to *practice*, or action, in the second. Here the word *practice* is used to connote a concern with action, but not a concern to secure one's ends. As Kant was careful to explain, his interest was instructing you not in how to satisfy your desires but in how to do your duty.

In fact, consciously following Plato and deliberately contradicting Hume, Kant emphasized that the business of Reason is not to *serve* the passions but to *control* them; and he postulated, with Plato, the existence of a Free Will having the ability to fulfill this miraculous office. Free will, Kant said with Plato and Augustine, is an ability to rise above your personal preferences and predilections in order to make choices determined by Pure Reason instead. Since obeying the command of Pure Reason is your duty as a rational being, Kant concluded that you must possess the capacity for it. Free will thus became the main postulate of Pure Practical Reason.

What does Pure Practical Reason command us to do? Just this, said Kant, calling it the *Categorical Imperative*: Always act in accordance with a maxim that you can will to become a universal law! More roughly: Do only what you can approve of everybody doing! According to Kant, this, the sole and sufficient principle of duty, is equivalent to what he called the Practical Imperative: Always treat mankind as an end in itself, never as a means! In other words, the central—indeed, the only—principle of duty is the Golden Rule, "Love your fellow man as yourself." Surprisingly, Christian equality is thereby revealed to be not just the provincial tenet of a peculiar religion but a universal requirement of Reason itself.

In Kant's view, what makes the Categorical Imperative (and its equivalent, the Practical Imperative) a requirement of Reason is the law of contradiction, the fundamental principle of Pure Reason, theoretical or practical. It works roughly this way. Suppose that I want to lie and cheat. By doing so I imply that lying and cheating are acceptable. But, according to the Categorical Imperative, if they were acceptable for me, then they would be acceptable for others too. But to approve of lying and cheating by others would be self-defeating. So, I cannot think that it is right for others to lie; and therefore, I cannot without self-contradiction think that it is right for me to lie.

By such logic Kant purported to derive the principles of what turns out to be Golden Rule morality from Reason alone, without making any appeal to religious faith or biblical revelation. God was therefore deliberately left out of the argument until the very end, when Kant allowed that the world would be unjust if God did not reward in the hereafter those who do His will without reward here on earth. But although this consideration is held by Kant to be persuasive, it is also acknowledged to be logically worthless. So, nothing is to rest on it.

It is this decision to exclude God from the argument that leads MacIntyre to say that, in Kant, moral philosophy made a disastrous turn away from medieval insistence on obeying God's will towards modern, secular Rationalism. As noted earlier, however, this divergence is more apparent than real. The possibility of deriving the will of God from Reason alone had already been mooted by Aquinas, who thought it possible in principle if not in practice. So, Enlightenment Rationalism was continuous with Medieval Rationalism, which was a development of the Rationalism of Plato.

Twentieth-Century Rationalism

Despite the clear influence of Kant on contemporary moral thought, many philosophers do not recognize their Rationalism. An exception is John Rawls, the most celebrated moral philosopher of our time. In his influential *A Theory of Justice*, Rawls explicitly says that he follows Henry Sidgwick, the nineteenth-century English Rationalist, in seeking to discover truths of reason that are common to human beings everywhere. Rawls then undertakes to discover these universal moral truths by reflecting on his own idea of Justice, which seems to him to establish an initial presumption for equality but to permit such inequality as can be justified by demonstration that it will make better off those who would otherwise be worst off. In reaching this conclusion, Rawls offers no argument for the proposition that people should be treated equally. Instead, this is taken as an antecedently given principle of Reason.

Rawls's Rationalism becomes even more obvious when he describes his method. According to Rawls, the "principles of justice" for a hypothetical society are to be chosen behind a *veil of ignorance* by people who know nothing about themselves. In complete ignorance of their abilities, their preferences, and their likely standing, these people are to decide what rules their society should have. Lest personal information and bias influence their decisions, they are not to know whether they are smart or dumb, energetic or lazy, strong or weak, good looking or ugly, rich or poor, healthy or sick. They are not to know whether they prefer athletics to music, philosophy to fishing, or salmon filets to beefsteak. And so on. In short, they are not to know any facts of the matter, especially about themselves. This assures that all their decisions will be decisions of principle. If this isn't Rationalism, it is hard to know what would count as such.

Similar Rationalism is evident in the writings of Rawls's most famous pupil, Thomas Nagel. In his first book, *The Possibility of Altruism*, Nagel says that if any person A has a reason to do something C, then every other person B has reason to "promote" A's doing C, including, presumably, the person who would prefer that A *not* do C. Taken as an empirical claim, this is plainly false, but Nagel does not mean it as an empirical claim. Nagel's belief in the inherent and equal worth of all human beings is a metaphysical postulate, like that of Kant and Rawls. It is not an inference from empirically known facts of the matter, and it cannot be refuted by reference to them.

If the Rationalism of these views is not clear from their commitment to *a priori* reasoning, it will be evident in their commitment to egalitarianism. Rawls, Nagel and other twentieth century followers of

Kant—such as R.M. Hare, Kurt Baier, and Ronald Dworkin—all believe, like Kant, in the inherent equality of human beings. This belief is clearly an article of uncritical *faith;* not an induction from experience, which reveals that some people are taller than others, some are smarter than others, some are stronger than others, some are better looking than others, some are more virtuous than others, and so on. It will be replied that egalitarianism means not that men are equal but only that they should be treated as if they were. Unfortunately, those who believe this have yet to explain why we should treat people as equals when we know very well that they are not. Instead, the egalitarians follow Kant in taking equality as a self-evident truth, or, as he would say, *postulate* of Moral Reason. There is irony here, in the fact that Plato, the father of Rationalism, took it to be obvious that most men are inferior. In practice, of course, it does not matter. Although all men are supposed to be treated as equals under modern socialist ideology, it will still be necessary for some to be in charge.[12] All men will be equal, but some will be more equal than others. Like Plato's *Republic*, the modern socialist state is run—not accidentally—by a largely self-anointed elite.

Conclusion

Rationalism—belief that men who may know nothing of the world can nevertheless know enough to tell men who do how to conduct their lives and manage their societies—is neither new nor dead. On the contrary, it is as old as philosophy itself and as alive as socialist belief in equality. Since the time of Plato, intellectuals have been intoxicated by the prospect of having a license to meddle in private business and manage public affairs without having to leave their armchairs, much less their cloisters.

As a result of this history, intellectuals and the politicians who have been their clients have readily convinced themselves and each other that they differ from other folk in being guided by impartial expertise and reasoned knowledge of the absolutely Good and Just rather than by narrow self-interest and habitual social prejudice like other people. That this patently self-serving belief is wholly unfounded, both in logic and in fact, we shall see in the chapters that follow; but we must acknowledge in advance that its lack of merit has done little to diminish its influence, which is attributable to other factors.

Belief that the good and the just can be known *a priori,* without benefit of practical experience, merely by reflecting on antecedently given concepts and ideals, has been one of the most popular and persistent ideas in the history of thought. As we have seen, it has been the view of philosophers as diverse in time and outlook as Cicero, Augustine, Thomas Aquinas, John Locke, Immanuel Kant, John Rawls, and Thomas Nagel—all of whom have believed that they could determine how human beings ought to behave and how societies ought to be constructed merely by reflecting on their own antecedently given ideals. If these Rationalists do not always recognize themselves as such, it is for the same reason that the character in Moliere's play failed to recognize that he spoke prose: he had no idea that there was any other way speak. For Rationalists, Rationalism is not a special *kind* of moral philosophy, it *is* moral philosophy. In the conventional view, nothing else deserves the term.

Of course, there have been dissenters from this orthodoxy. Among them were Protagoras and Sextus Empiricus of ancient Greece, Thomas Hobbes and David Hume of more modern vintage, and Michael Oakeshott and Friedrich Hayek of the present century. Critics of Rationalist philosophy have, however, usually been few in number, and they have mostly come from outside the academy, where they have generally been regarded as heretics. In the universities, moral philosophy has almost always been understood to be the business of discovering the Rational (i.e., the *a priori*) basis for conduct. Indeed, that has been its accepted *definition.*

Furthermore, it still is. Appeals to "moral intuition" and dependence on the analysis of ready-made concepts —distinguishing features of Rationalism—are still the stock-in-trade of moral philosophy. If you doubt it, try thumbing your nose at either of these in a philosophical conference. You will be met with jeers and hollers, not just for what will be regarded as unconscionable rudeness but also for your supposed incompetence. As this suggests, in the academy, little but Rationalist moral philosophy counts as moral philosophy properly so-called.

Notes

1. In what follows, I distinguish Rationalism from rationalism.
2. See *The Open Society and Its Enemies* (Princeton, NJ: Princeton University Press, 1962).

3. For an illustration see Wilhelm Windelband's classic history of philosophy.
4. This used to be called *casuistry*.
5. For a contemporary application of this idea, see Ronald Dworkin *A Matter of Principle* (Cambridge: Harvard University Press, 1985). For criticism of the idea see Robert Bork, *The Tempting of America* (New York: Basic Books, 1990).
6. Michael Oakeshott, in *Rationalism In Politics and Other Essays* (Indianapolis, IN: Liberty Press, 1991), has observed that, in modern politics, Rationalism takes the form of belief in *technique* or *expertise* rather than *skill* or *craft* —preference for methods learned from books over skills acquired from experience. In Hayek's terminology, modern rationalism takes the form of *scientism*.
7. See especially, *After Virtue* (Notre Dame, IN: Notre Dame University Press, 1981) and *Against the Self-Images of the Age* (New York: Schocken Books, 1971).
8. For the authoritative statement of Plato's Rationalism, see *The Republic*.
9. For this view see the writings of Thomas Aquinas on law and morality in *Summa Theologica*, Questions 90-97.
10. See *The Critique of Practical Reason* and *Foundations of the Metaphysics of Morals*.
11. See the United Nations *Declaration of Human Rights*, which contends that the right to a decent living, including paid vacations, free medical care, etc. are human rights.
12. See Rawls's Difference Principle, which allows some people to be more equal than others if they use their positions, power, and perquisites to make better off those who would otherwise be worst off. In other words, it is ok for some to be on top if they are busy making everybody else equal. John Rawls, *A Theory of Justice* (Cambridge, MA.: Harvard University Press, 1971).

9

Sidgwick's Method

The distinctive feature of Rationalist moral philosophy is its dependence on *moral intuition*—insights, it is believed, into the more or less self-evident truths of Moral Reason[1] In the view of the Rationalist, the function of the moral philosopher is to articulate and refine the truths revealed by moral intuition, then arrange them into a science—a systematic whole that can give detailed guidance to conduct. The philosopher who does this important task depends on moral intuition at every stage of his inquiry. It supplies his premises, checks the accuracy of his reasoning, and assures the justice of his conclusions. It is the touchstone with which he tells truth from falsehood.

W. D. Ross on Moral Intuition

This comprehensive role is described in W. D. Ross's *The Right and the Good*, one of the more celebrated works of twentieth-century moral philosophy.[2] Early in this book, Ross expresses the distinctive conviction of Rationalist moral philosophy when he boldly makes the astonishing claim that the intuitions, or fundamental convictions, of our "moral consciousness" have the self-evidence and certainty of the axioms of mathematics:

> The general principles of duty are not self-evident from the beginnings of our lives. How do they become so? The answer is, that they come to be self evident to us just as mathematical axioms do. We find by experience that this couple of matches and that couple make four matches ... and by reflection on these and similar discoveries we come to see that it is of the nature of two and two to make four. In a precisely similar way, we see the *prima facie* rightness of an act which would be the fulfilment of a particular promise ... and when we have reached

> sufficient maturity to think in general terms, we apprehend *prima facie* rightness to belong to the nature of any fulfilment of promise. From this we come by reflection to apprehend the self-evident general principle of *prima facie* duty. (p. 32)

A few pages later, Ross describes a somewhat different but equally grand role for intuition. He compares the intuitive convictions of "our moral consciousness" to the observations of empirical scientists:

> ... the moral convictions of thoughtful and well-educated people are the data of ethics just as sense perceptions are the data of a natural science. Just as some of the latter have to be rejected as illusory, so have some of the former; but as the latter are rejected only when they are in conflict with more accurate sense-perceptions, the former are rejected only when they are in conflict with other convictions which stand better the test of reflection. (p. 40)

According to Ross, intuitive convictions of both the axiomatic and perceptual sorts described in these two quotations represent not fallible opinion but secure knowledge:

> I would maintain, in fact, that what we are apt to describe as 'what we think' about moral questions contains a considerable amount that we do not think but know, and that this forms the standard by reference to which the truth of any moral theory has to be tested. (ibid.)

As these remarks make clear, moral intuition—unreflective moral conviction—is the highest authority that a philosopher like Ross knows. A Rationalist is any philosopher who thinks it appropriate to appeal to this authority. By this definition, most moral philosophers are Rationalists, even if they are empiricists regarding other matters.

Platonic Intuitionism

What is *moral intuition*, and why does it inspire such deference in the minds of Rationalist philosophers? In daily conversation, an intuition is nothing but a vague hunch or inarticulate prejudice, a hypothesis or first impression, an unreasoned and unreasoning feeling. In other words, it is what David Hume aptly and unpatronizingly called a *sentiment*. As so regarded, intuition is nothing to write home about; much less hang a theory of morality or a plan of life on. One may undertake in one's moral theory to explain, as Hume did, why people have the intuitions—or sentiments—that they do have, but one need not suppose, as Hume did not, that these feelings are authoritative revelations of Higher Truth.

This commonplace use of the word *intuition* is, however, child to an older and more freighted usage according to which an intuition is a specially privileged, exceptionally reliable, and highly authoritative if not quite infallible insight into evident and indisputable truth. According to this usage, which stems from Plato, intuitions deserve special respect because they are neither expressions of a variable passion, discoveries of the fallible senses, nor signs of brute animal instinct but dependable insights of *Reason*. In the mind of the Rationalist, it is this connection to Reason that gives intuition its distinctive authority. It is true that the word *intuition* is also used more broadly, to describe every non-inferential grasp of evident truth, including sensory observation, but it is traditional to regard even this as an exercise of Reason accompanying stimulation of the senses.

The first person to say so was Plato. Comparing intuition to sight while denying that sight itself had the authority of rational intuition, Plato declared intuition to be an intellectual insight into the obvious—or into what would become obvious after you thought about it. To know a truth by intuition was, then, to "see" that it is true without having to infer its truth from other truths. In other words, intuition was immediate, non-discursive insight—an unreasoning use of Reason. Plato thought that *all* important truths —the truths about Justice, Goodness, Beauty, and the other ideals of Reason—are known in this direct, non-ratiocinative way. In his view, serious discourse and reasoning can begin only after the basic truths have been discerned, and their purpose is not to establish but to spell out the implications of intuitively known truths, which need no proof themselves.

To Plato, the fact that intuition was *unreasoning* did not mean that it was *irrational*. On the contrary, it meant that intuition was the highest and most honorable exercise of Reason. (Holding the same view, Kant would later speak of a higher *faculty* of Reason, namely, *Vernunft*, and compare it, invidiously, to *Verstehen*, the capacity for mere understanding.) Since intuitively known propositions are self-evident by definition, Plato held that they do not themselves need, or admit, of proof. Rather, as just noted, all proof must begin with them. Therefore, Plato counted intuition as the highest exercise of Reason because he believed it to be the exercise of Reason that is presupposed and required by all other exercises of Reason. As such, Plato held, intuition is fundamental to both mathematics and ethics, the truths of which have, he believed, similar self-evidence and certainty.

It is this belief—that intuition yields knowledge of truths comparable in obviousness and certainty to the axioms of mathematics—that makes appeal to intuition the defining feature of Rationalist moral philosophy. Rationalism and intuitionism are, therefore, not two different philosophies but the same philosophy by two different names. As we shall see, Rationalists do not always make it clear just what sorts of truths they expect moral intuition to reveal, but they usually express little doubt as to its validity, dependability, or utility as a source of truth.

Sidgwick's Ambivalent Intuitionism

An instructive exception is Henry Sidgwick, whose *Methods of Ethics,* the most widely read work of Victorian moral theory, went through seven editions before its author died in 1900.[3] According to this book, which has for a century now profoundly influenced thinking about morality in English speaking countries, moral philosophy must begin with, and have its results constantly corrected by, the intuitions of "moral common sense." It must do so because these unreflective convictions are, in Sidgwick's frequently repeated phrase, "dictates of reason."

Three quarters of the way through his book, Sidgwick puts it this way:

> For we conceive it as the aim of a philosopher, as such, to do more than define and formulate the common moral opinions of mankind. He is expected to transcend Common Sense in his premises, and is allowed a certain divergence from Common Sense in his conclusions. It is true that the limits of this deviation are firmly, though indefinitely, fixed: the truth of a philosopher's premises will always be tested by the acceptability of his conclusions: if in any important point he be found in flagrant conflict with common opinion, his method is likely to be declared invalid. Still, though he is expected to establish and concatenate at least the main part of the commonly accepted moral rules, he is not necessarily bound to take them as the basis on which his own system is constructed. Rather, we should expect that the history of Moral Philosophy—so far at least as those whom we may call orthodox thinkers are concerned—would be a history of attempts to enunciate, in full breadth and clearness, those primary intuitions of Reason, by the scientific application of which the common moral thought of mankind may be at once systematised and corrected. (p. 373)

This ambivalent encomium to "the common moral thought of mankind" comes after 372 pages of dense prose in which Sidgwick tries to decide what had been learned by those English philosophers who had used *the intuitional method*, as he also called it, in replying to "the dreaded name of Hume" (p. 104). Aping Hegel's dialectic method of thesis, antithesis, and synthesis, Sidgwick had just finished surveying the first two "phases" of dependence on the intuitional method and was about to begin his account of the third phase.

"Perceptional" Intuitionism: The First Phase

What Sidgwick called the "perceptional," phase of intuitionism (p. 102) includes the efforts of two main groups. Platonists like Clarke and Stewart held that moral intuitions are exercises of Pure Reason. Followers of the "moral sense" (or "conscience") school of Hutcheson, who preceded Adam Smith at Glasgow University, held that intuitions were in some ways like sense perception. The work of both groups was vitiated, Sidgwick believed, by failure to notice any distinction between the plausible claim that intuition yields knowledge of general principles and the implausible claim that it yields knowledge of particular matters of fact. Certainty and self-evidence were claimed for both, but although Sidgwick agreed that these virtues are possessed by general convictions like "You should always do right," he did not think the same could be said of "particular intuitions" like "Lying is wrong." In Sidgwick's opinion, judgments of the latter sort could not be regarded as "dictates of reason."

Why not? Because these judgments do not command universal agreement, a requirement for anything that can be truly described as a dictate of reason, which is supposedly shared by men everywhere. Thus, human beings disagree about the morality of contraception, abortion, homosexuality, clitoridectomy, slavery, and so on. Furthermore, human beings do not just disagree *with each other*; they also disagree *with themselves*. As Sidgwick remarks, "when a man compares the utterances of his conscience at different times, he often finds it difficult to make them altogether consistent" instead, he judges one way now, another way later (p. 100).

Disagreement is easy to explain when the issues are empirical: It shows only that a mistake has been made. Freedom from gross error is, however, supposed to be what makes intuition superior to the senses as a source of moral knowledge. As an expression of self-evident reason, intuition is also supposed to be the same in human beings everywhere. So, disagreements are an embarrassment. Therefore,

Sidgwick concluded, in his understated English way, that intuitions about particular actions "do not, to reflective persons, present themselves as quite indubitable and irrefragable" (ibid.).

Sidgwick knew that the friends of intuition thought they could get around this obstacle by distinguishing real intuitions from what only seemed to the unreflective to be intuitions. He also knew, however, that many non-intuitive moral feelings wear the aspect of intuitions, making them hard to tell from the real thing. Hence, as Sidgwick observed, men are "liable to confound with moral intuitions other states or acts of mind essentially different from them" (p. 211). According to Descartes, intuitions are distinguished from their imitations by "clarity and distinctness," but this makes introspection of our states of mind to be the measure of moral right and wrong, which Sidgwick regarded as unsatisfactory.[4] And rightly so. As J. L. Austin was to point out half a century later, there is no reason to think that states of mind carry the marks of their own truth.

Dogmatic Intuitionism: The Second Phase

These reflections did not cause Sidgwick to toss the intuitional method on the scrap heap, only to conclude that it cannot deliver incorrigible dictates about particular practices, as originally promised. In Sidgwick's carefully considered view, the most that can be expected from intuition is abstract principles. Intuition will tell you that you should never do wrong; it just will not tell you whether a particular action is wrong.

Furthermore, Sidgwick thought, knowledge of general principles can be expected only if we make it our practice to correct one intuition by using another. A single, isolated intuition is not to be taken at face value; it is to be accepted only after it has been corrected by and made to cohere with other intuitions. The disagreements that were a problem for the intuitional method in its uncritical first phase are to be transformed in a dogmatic second phase into a means of testing and improving what previously lacked corroboration. Doing this is the special job of the moral philosopher. Sidgwick summed the point up as follows:

> Here, then, we have a second Intuitional Method: of which the fundamental assumption is that we can discern certain general rules with a really clear and finally valid intuition. It is held that such general rules are implicit in the moral reasoning of ordinary men, who apprehend them adequately for most practical purposes, and

> are able to enunciate them roughly; but that to state them with proper precision requires a special habit of contemplating clearly and steadily abstract moral notions. It is held that the moralist's function then is to perform this process of abstract contemplation, to arrange the results as systematically as possible, and by proper definitions and explanations to remove vagueness and prevent conflict. (p.101)

Unfortunately, after surveying this, the *dogmatic*, phase of intuitionism for nearly 250 pages, most of them concerned with what Sidgwick calls *egoism*, he again comes to a sobering conclusion: The general principles vouchsafed by intuition are all *empty tautologies,* which are certain and indisputable only because they do not provide specific guidance. In Sidgwick's words, "they are certainly self-evident, but they are also insignificant," and "The residuum, then, of clear intuition which we have so far obtained, is the insignificant proposition that it is our duty to do what we judge to be our duty" (p. 344). Thirty pages later, he adds,

> These are principles which appear certain and self-evident because they are substantially tautological: because, when examined, they are found to affirm no more than that it is right to do that which is—in a certain department of life, under certain circumstances and conditions—right to be done. (p. 375)

Examples of what Sidgwick had in mind are the tautology that one should always do right and the proposition, made popular by Kant, that what is right for one person to do must be equally right for any relevantly similar person to do in relevantly similar circumstances. As Sidgwick said, no reasonable person can deny these propositions, but nobody should expect to learn from them how he, or anybody else, should behave. That you should do what is right is certainly true, but it does not tell you what, specifically, to do. Expecting to be guided by such tautologies as this is as unrealistic as expecting to deduce the facts of the matter from the axioms of formal logic.

If we want guidance, Sidgwick thought that we can have it, but only at a price. We must give up faith in guidance by Pure Reason alone (p. 374). We must also give up talking about convictions that are "common to the whole of rational mankind." Guidance that is useful because relevant to our time and circumstances must come from a much more limited group, "educated persons of the same age and country" (p. 360). The claims to universality that were prominent in the first phase of intuitionism are surrendered in the second. We are now to favor the distinctly provincial intuitions of English gentleman educated, like Sidgwick, at Cambridge and Oxford Universities.

Philosophical Intuitionism: The Third Phase

It gets worse. Recognizing that local practices may not themselves come up to snuff, Sidgwick concludes in the third, *philosophical*, phase of his discussion, that, if moral philosophy is to provide proper guidance, the intuitional method must be "transcended" by the utilitarian. So far, intuition has assured us that we must do what is right, but it has not revealed which courses of action are right. To discover these Sidgwick believed we must discover which actions promise to do the most good. In the final analysis, intuition is to give way to general utility. Duty is to come down to other-regarding prudence.

Sidgwick did not regard this as a rejection, or abandonment, of the intuitional method. On the contrary, he was persuaded by his Hegelian logic that "transcending" intuition was validating a higher form of it. Reasoning that moral philosophy aims to provide guidance, he concluded that, to do so, it must be founded on intuitions that have substantive content. Egoism (individualistic hedonism) is founded on belief that one should do what is good for, or pleasurable to, *oneself*. Utilitarianism (universalistic hedonism) is founded on belief that one should do what is good for, or pleasurable to, *as many people as possible*. Calling these beliefs *intuitions*, Sidgwick concluded that egoism and utilitarianism, the main alternatives to intuitionism, were themselves founded on intuitions. Intuitionism, which seemed doomed, was now saved.

Unfortunately, what Sidgwick meant by this was no longer that these new doctrines are founded on self-evident truths but merely that they have foundations. Sidgwick did think that hedonism, of which egoism and utilitarianism were the two varieties, was self-evident given the close connection between goodness and pleasure, but he could not convince himself of the indisputability of either egoistic belief that one should prefer one's own happiness or utilitarian belief that one should assign equal weight the happiness of every person alike. Sidgwick favored the latter proposition, but he knew that it was neither self-evident nor provable (p. 418).[5] So, in declaring that egoism and utilitarianism were founded on intuitions, Sidgwick had changed the meaning of the word. *Intuition* now meant not self-evident *axiom* but arbitrary *postulate*. The word no longer denoted what counted as basic *because it was self-evidently true;* it now denoted simply what was taken to be basic *without regard for whether it was true*. In short, the word no longer meant an act of cognition; it now meant an act of commitment. Kant has replaced Plato.

If Sidgwick was aware of the shift, it does not seem to have mattered to him. What mattered was that other educated Englishmen would agree. As the great success of Sidgwick's book proves, his assessment of English moral opinion was correct. During Sidgwick's life, his combination of English moral sensibility with Benthamite utilitarianism justified the imposition of English authority on primitive lands throughout the world. This imposition not only promised to profit England; it also promised to bring Christianity and prosperity to the people that she conquered. How could a method of thought that promised such admirable results be wrong?

Sidgwick's Followers

Few of the philosophers who came in Sidgwick's wake thought it could. Like him, they were intuitionists, although of different varieties.

The most celebrated was G. E. Moore. Professor of philosophy at Cambridge, Sidgwick's home university, Moore was an intuitionist and a utilitarian like Sidgwick. He differed, however, in several ways. He agreed that it is always right to do what has the best consequences, but he did not think that the consequences of an action could be known by intuition, so he did not think that intuition provides direct knowledge of right and wrong. For Moore, intuition was merely the means whereby one discovered the value of an action's results once these were known by other methods.[6]

Moore also disagreed with Sidgwick's hedonism. He agreed that pleasure is good, but he denied that *good* and *pleasant* are synonyms, and he was inclined to think that Mill was right in regarding the pleasures of Socrates as superior to the pleasures of pigs. Trained as a classicist, Moore therefore accepted Plato's view that only an educated and cultivated elite can appreciate the values of finer things—beautiful music and refined manners. Unlike Sidgwick, however, Moore thought it evident that, if A's enjoyment of these things is good, then it is good absolutely; not just good *for A*. Therefore, he saw no cause to wonder, as Sidgwick had, whether one should prefer his own good to that of other people. In fact, Moore thought the idea of a proprietary good to be logically confused. We shall examine this view later.

W. D. Ross and his Oxford teacher H. A. Prichard had a more old fashioned view of the uses of intuition. Followers of Kant, they hoped to use it to distinguish right from wrong directly. They would do this by ignoring an action's consequences, which cannot be foreseen, while paying attention to the agent's intentions, which can be known by introspection. Just reflect on your intention. If it is honorable, you will know it; what Ross called its *prima facie* goodness or evil will be evident. Anyhow, it will be evident to the right persons. Although Ross started out, like Sidgwick, touting the moral intuitions of "plain men," he soon explained that this expression did not include just anybody anywhere.[7] Instead, it meant educated persons in civilized societies—again, Cambridge- and Oxford-educated gentlemen.

Why should we put our lives and social orders in the hands of these persons? Ross explained the reason as follows:

> The existing body of moral convictions of the best people is the cumulative product of the moral reflection of many generations, which has developed an extremely delicate power of appreciation of moral distinctions; and this the theorist cannot afford to treat with anything but the greatest respect. The verdicts of the moral consciousness of the best people are the foundation on which he must build; though he must compare them with one another and eliminate any contradictions they may contain. (p. 40)

Ross's Emphatic but Qualified Intuitionism

A reader of this remark and our opening quotations from Ross might be forgiven for supposing that Ross had never read Sidgwick, whose survey of intuitionism had started out to defend it but ended up undermining it without recognizing the fact. Given that he had been well schooled in Sidgwick's book, how can we explain Ross's claims? By noting that they die the death of a thousand qualifications. Actually, there was just one qualification, but it was fatal. Ross said that what we can know by intuition is not really whether a particular action is right or wrong; only whether it is *prima facie* right or wrong.

What did this mean? That we cannot know whether it is wrong to lie, only that it is wrong to lie *unless some consideration makes it right*. In other words, what we can know by intuition is the kind of empty tautology that Sidgwick warned about. Ross virtually admitted this himself when he added that moral intuition provides not knowledge of how to behave in particular situations but knowledge of the general principles that ought to guide behavior. What Ross did not admit, or even appear to notice, is that he had thereby taken back with one hand what he had previously given with the other. Principles general enough to guide all behavior can provide specific guidance to none.[8]

Ross concealed this fact from himself and his reader by altering his definition of the original project. That project was to show how moral intuition gives us knowledge about the morality or immorality of conduct. When push came to shove, however, Ross said that we cannot appraise *conduct*, only *intentions*. Hence, Ross's attempt to revive intuitionism drove a stake in its heart.

Intuitionism after Moore and Ross

The death certificate was issued by A. J. Ayer, a Welsh disciple of the Viennese positivists.[9] Impressed like Sidgwick by disagreements between persons invoking contrary intuitions, Ayer renewed Hume's contention that moral judgments are not dictates of reason but expressions of personal, cultural, and instinctual feeling. In Ayer's view, to call an action right or wrong was not to state a self-evident truth. It was merely to express one's approval or disapproval. In America, C. L. Stevenson took the same line.

For a brief time, this skeptical doctrine had a considerable following, but the influence of Hume and positivism did not last. Having been shocked into dismayed silence or provoked into outraged protest by the skepticism of these unkempt empiricists, genteel English philosophers soon recovered their composure and reverted to their former ways: finding confirmation of their moral convictions and political practices in their "moral intuitions," confident that, if they felt strongly about a proposition, it *must* be true; let others prove them wrong. American philosophers soon followed suit. As a consequence, you cannot now raise an issue, or make a claim, in moral philosophy without having it tested in the acid of "moral intuitions." Once again, intuition is king. It has risen from the dead. The only difference is that, now, few philosophers admit to being intuitionists.

One who does is John Rawls, the most celebrated moral philosopher since Kant. In his massive *A Theory of Justice,* Rawls observes that his "method of reflective equilibrium," is merely a version of the intuitional method of Sidgwick, who, says Rawls, "thought of the history of moral philosophy as a series of attempts to state 'in their full breadth and clearness those *primary intuitions of Reason,* by the scientific application of which *the common moral thought of mankind* may be at once systematized and corrected'" (Rawls, p. 51, emphasis added).[10] Then Rawls goes on to confirm this description of his method by seeking to discover the principles that define justice "behind a veil of ignorance" which, by concealing all empirical facts of the matter, enables one to focus on an antecedently given concept of Justice.

That Rawls is one of the few who admit to being intuitionists does not mean that intuitionists are few in number.[11] If an intuitionist is one who rests his moral philosophy on intuition, then most anglophonic moral philosophers are intuitionists. They may not be intuitionists in theory, but they are still intuitionists in practice. If you have any doubt about it, attend any conference on, or read any issue of a journal in *applied ethics*, the only growth industry in late twentieth-century philosophy.[12] You will observe philosophers busily declaring this or that practice to be either contrary to or consistent with their moral intuitions, and you will see their opponents answering them in like manner. Thus, in a debate on abortion, some disputants will argue that abortion is self-evidently murder, while others will reply that it is self-evidently an exercise of the right to determine who uses one's body. Use of the term *applied ethics* to describe these tiresome exchanges indicates that those who engage in them think of themselves as deciding particular cases by invoking general principles that are self-evident.

That few academic philosophers in the English-speaking part of the world *call* themselves intuitionists proves only that faith in intuition has become so commonplace that it has ceased to distinguish one moral philosopher from another.[13] For most anglophonic moral philosophers, intuitionist moral philosophy is not merely one *kind* of moral philosophy; it *is* moral philosophy. Such philosophers speak the language of intuition as Moliere observed that most people speak prose without knowing it, because it does not occur to them that there is another way to speak. Consistency with intuitive moral conviction is still the accepted standard of moral truth —so much so that, under prevailing, if unofficial, rules, you may not thumb your nose at your critic's moral intuitions. Instead, you must either accede to them or oppose them with contrary intuitions of your own. To reject arguments from moral intuition out of hand is regarded as both a breach of philosophical etiquette and a proof of philosophical incompetence.[14]

Theoretical Uses of Sidgwick's Method

The same holds true when you come to moral theory. As our quotation from Rawls shows, Sidgwick's method is used in constructing one's own moral theory, but a still more popular use of the method is criticizing other people's theories. Propose an account of morality—claim that x is morally right if and only if x is F. The first thing that an English- speaking philosopher—British, American, or Australian—will do is try to think of a "counterexample," something that is F but not, in his view, morally right. If he succeeds, he will regard himself as having shown your formula to be logically or morally absurd.

The favored objects of this style of philosophizing are Sidgwick's other two "methods," *egoism* and *utilitarianism.* Both doctrines are invariably criticized in the same way. First, they are described, not in the words of their authors but in the words of their critics, who define them in such a way that they refute themselves. Thus, "egoist" belief that it is *rational* to do what serves your personal but possibly unselfish interests is redefined by critics as belief that your sole *duty* is to be unrelentingly selfish, even if that requires you to behave in ways that are plainly immoral.[15] Then this new doctrine is refuted by noting that it cannot be your moral duty to do what is plainly immoral. Similarly, utilitarian belief that maximizing good is *best* is redefined as belief that maximizing good is *morally obligatory*, even if this means violating established rules of morality. Then this new belief is refuted by observing that it is self-evidently immoral to do what violates the rules of morality.[16] Refutations of straw men.[17]

So entrenched has this style of argument become that even its victims have sometimes been browbeaten into accepting it. The century-old campaign against "egoism" that Sidgwick started has been so effective that the only sensible version of the doctrine is now confined almost entirely to economics, where, under the less prejudicial heading *methodological individualism*, it is central to accounts of not morality but rationality.[18] Only Ayn Rand, a romantic novelist, has had the chutzpah and the naiveté to praise "the virtue of selfishness" in defiance of philosophical convention. Others either sensibly reject the pejorative label or try to gain favor with their critics by arguing, futilely and falsely, that common-sense morality makes duty to one's self to be primary. The whole debate is an embarrassment. It cannot compare in acuteness to the careful and sensible discussions of "self-love" by Bishop Butler and other eighteenth-century figures.

Similar confusion has muddled intuitionist discussions of utilitarianism, causing even those who think of themselves as utilitarians to miss the point of the doctrine. Sidgwick did so when he presumed that there is a Moral Law (an absolute standard for Right and Wrong) that can be discerned using the method of utility (p. 411). If one thing is clear, it is that Jeremy Bentham, the greatest of the utilitarians, did not share Sidgwick's belief in an antecedently given Morality. As his *Principles of Morals and Legislation* makes clear, Bentham believed that morality and law are *man made*. His point was that, if we want good (meaning satisfactory) law or morality, we will use utility as our guide when making it. For Bentham utility was a method of *decision*; in Sidgwick it becomes a method of *discovery*, a very different thing. The result is a utilitarianism that only an intuitionist could love.[19]

Bayles on Moral Intuition

The situation just described is paradoxical. Moral philosophers no longer call themselves intuitionists and no longer defend belief that their "moral intuitions" provide reliable knowledge, but they still treat moral intuition as if it were authoritative, both in practice and in theory. How can these two stances be reconciled?

A recent paper by Michael Bayles contains an answer. Citing Rawls, Bayles admits that appeals to intuition cannot always settle the moral issue, but he maintains that these appeals are nevertheless appropriate, *because we have nothing better to go on*. Besides, Bayles adds, moral intuitions must be respected even when they can be disputed, because they have "heuristic" value. In other words, we may presume that our moral intuitions are right if they have not been proved wrong, because they are suggestive even when they are not conclusive. Hence, admissions of the fallibility of moral intuition do nothing to diminish its authority.[20]

Bayles's view is now orthodox, but it is also puzzling. When intuitions were thought to be unerring revelations of self-evident truth, it was obvious why they had to be trusted: They were trustworthy by definition. You do not doubt the truth of what you take to be an intuition of Reason. Once grant, however, that "intuitions" are inherently doubtful and it becomes wholly mysterious why they should be believed. How can intuition have the epistemological defects that Sidgwick reluctantly exposed and Bayles grudgingly admits yet deserve our respect? If intuition is still authoritative despite being unreliable, what makes it so?

If there is an answer to this question, it is that, despite the concessions and qualifications, intuitions are still being regarded as insights, however fallible, into *a priori* truths of *Reason.* Rawls explicitly says so, quoting Sidgwick, and Bayles must think so too if he believes that we have no other source of moral knowledge. That claim is true only if morality cannot be known by empirical means, and this is true only if morality is a transcendent entity, like the Will of God. If that is what Bayles's is assuming, however, he has begged the main question, which is whether there is a transcendent Morality. As we shall show in detail in a later chapter, no evidence supports belief that there is. The intuitionist will reply that his moral intuitions support this belief, but this begs the question twice. The evidentiary value of moral intuition is urged on the ground that it provides evidence of a transcendent Morality; then belief in a transcendent Morality is justified on the evidence of moral intuition.

A tighter circle would be hard to find. The nearest analogy is theological argument. In fact, this is not merely an analogy; it is an identity. Appeal to moral intuition is not merely *like* theological argument; it *is* theological argument transposed to a new key. The claims made for intuition by Rationalists are a secular rephrasing of the claims formerly made for special revelation by theologians. Why do the theologians believe in God? Because they believe in special revelation, which they accept because they believe it comes from God. Why do Rationalists believe in moral intuition? Because they believe it to be the only source of knowledge of the Good and the Right, in which they believe because of their moral intuitions. The same closed circle in both cases.

Do Moral Intuitions Evince Universal Principles of Reason?

This circular epistemology is only one of the problems with moral intuition; there is a another. Grant that the existence of certain moral convictions is evidence of *something*. It remains an open question just what that is. The intuitionist believes that his intuitions evince a transcendent Moral Law that is self-evident and indisputable because it is built into Reason, which is the same in men everywhere, like the capacity to understand mathematics. Once this belief has been clearly stated, however, the main objection to it also becomes clear: There are very few things that men disagree about more than morality, which commands nothing like the universal assent enjoyed by the truths of mathematics.

Ask about almost any practice: polygamy, slavery, homosexuality, clitoridectomy, infanticide, or abortion. You will find it praised in some places, condemned in others. This well-known fact is hard to reconcile with the conviction that moral opinions are self evidently true expressions of a universal Reason. As J. L. Mackie has urged, it is more readily and plausibly explained by the hypothesis that most moral convictions are socially inculcated prejudices. It is true that some things—for example, the unacceptability of incest and gratuitous killing—do occasion agreement everywhere. "Cultural universals" like these cannot be put down to social prejudice, which varies with the society, but they are more plausibly attributed to *animal instinct* than to Reason. In this respect, they are more like the universal taste for sugar and universal dislike of loud noises than the proposition that 2+2=4.

Belief in the insights of a privileged elite has been thought to save moral intuition from the fact of moral disagreement, but it does the opposite. It may be true, as Hegel argued, that Reason has been developed further in some societies than in others. This is certainly true if we are talking about the institutionalization of reason which we call *science*, and I do not know why it could not be true of the institutions of law and morality too. If the health, happiness, longevity, and prosperity of their members are any measure, some societies are very much better ordered than others. In other words, some cultures, including some moralities, are superior to others. I would be the last person to deny it.

The fact remains: Our "intuition" that our culture is superior to others constitutes no proof that it is so. If it did, every society would have proof that its own morality is superior to every other; for this is the natural conviction of the members of every society. Thus, Moslems think that Muslim culture is superior to Christian, and Christians have the reverse opinion; city dwellers believe that life in town is superior, and country folk have the contrary view; and so on. No phenomenon is more familiar. What it proves is not that cultures cannot be compared but that this cannot be done in the simple-minded way in which the intuitionist supposes—by sitting in his armchair and reflecting on his antecedently given convictions. The intuitionist may find out something by engaging in his armchair reflections, but it is not likely to be truths of Reason. It is more likely to be his society's provincial prejudices.

Cultural Universals as Expressions of Human Biology

Are there no cultural universals? Certainly. As just noted, one is the taboo against incest. Another is the existence of rules against gratuitous killing. If you want a third, still another is patriarchy, male dominance. Every society known to man has all three, and it is probably safe, if not politically correct, to say that every viable society will continue to have them. The existence of these universals does not, however, confirm belief that they are expressions of a common Reason. As suggested briefly above, a better explanation is *animal biology*.[21]

To see why, consider incest. Aversion to it is found in human beings everywhere, but close inbreeding is also avoided by other mammalian species, such as dogs. To account for this, we need not suppose that dogs and other mammals also share in reason; the phenomenon is better explained by invoking animal instinct. For this instinct, there is an obvious evolutionary explanation: By emphasizing harmful traits that might otherwise remain recessive, inbreeding reduces genetic fitness. A similar hypothesis explains the universal disapproval of gratuitous killing. If social animals, which depend on cooperation with others, were not reluctant to kill members of their own group, they would soon reduce their genetic fitness. So, nature has built into them an aversion to killing their own kind. Again, instinct, not reason. The universality of patriarchy has a similar explanation. As Steven Goldberg has shown, male dominance, which is also not limited to human beings, can be attributed to larger male size and greater male aggressiveness, both functions of male testosterone.[22]

Somewhat different remarks must be made about James Q. Wilson's observation, in *The Moral Sense*, that there is an innate sense of justice, one that children everywhere develop very early.[23] Grant that this claim is true. It does not support Rationalist belief in self-evident principles of morality. What it shows is merely that human beings are social animals; they are innately adapted to internalize and conform to the rules that, in their society, happen to determine and define what counts as acceptable conduct. It is only in this highly restricted and highly general sense that a preference for and understanding of justice can be claimed to be innate.

No evidence supports the hypothesis that we all know instinctively, without instruction, which specific acts are just and which unjust. Furthermore, that hypothesis is plainly contrary to fact. The rules defining justice vary from society to society. Thus, it is just in Saudi Arabia but not in Selma, Alabama, to cut off the hands of thieves. Similarly, it is just in Saudi Arabia but not in Selma, Alabama to have several wives. So, although a "sense of justice" may be innate and universal, its specific content varies with the society. You condemn as unjust what conflicts with an idealized version of your society's rules; I what conflicts with an idealized version of my society's rules.

In this connection, the most illuminating analogy may be language. Human beings have a unique capacity for speech that is almost certainly innate. As linguist Noam Chomsky has emphasized, this capacity becomes manifest early in the life of virtually every human child, no matter what the culture. Children learn to speak their language at such an astonishing rate that Chomsky takes it to be evidence that they already know it and need only to be reminded of it, as Socrates reminded the slave boy of the principles of geometry. Chomsky holds that the human brain is like a computer hardwired with the syntax of a universal Language. Particular languages, such as Chinese and English, are variations on this language. They differ in their diction but not in more important ways. Or so Chomsky believes.

When all the evidence is in, Chomsky's linguistic Rationalism might prove to be true, but it has yet to be proved, and it is not entirely plausible. Grant that the capacity for language is innate. It does not follow that all languages are variations on a single, innately known but as yet unspecified, Language. Furthermore, the more reasonable hypothesis is that specific languages are cultural products, which is why they have to be learned. Children are quick to learn a language, but birds are quick to learn how to fly. The same is true of morality. Grant that the disposition to behave "justly" is innate. It means that most human children will be easy to socialize—indoctrinate in and condition to the morality of their society. It does not mean that moralities are all variations on a single, innately known but as yet unspecified, Morality.

Moral Intuitions as Ambiguous Sentiments

To say so is not to deny that our moral intuitions yield insights into moral truth. It is only to question whether they constitute insights into self-evident, because antecedently given, truths of *Reason.*

Considering the evidence just summarized, a better hypothesis is that moral intuitions are *ex post facto* expressions of either biological *instinct*, socially inculcated *feeling*, or personal *preference*—in short, expressions of *sentiment*. Some of these sentiments—for example, the disgust occasioned by incest—have their roots in biological instinct. Others—for example, the acceptability of abortion or polygamy—

have their origin in social conditioning. Still others—for example, dislike of authority or the preference for being alone—may have a purely personal basis. In all of these cases, "moral intuition" will indicate some fact, as a fever indicates illness; but without further evidence, we will be unable to determine whether a particular intuition evinces animal instinct, social conditioning, or personal preference—just as we are unable to tell without further evidence whether a fever indicates a viral or a bacterial infection.

If this is right, moral intuition lacks the kind of evidentiary value that is usually attributed to it by Rationalist philosophers, who are merely engaging in special pleading for privileged authority. When they invoke it, they are saying, "Do what people like me tell you to do, because we know best. Listen to us because we speak for God." Why the intuitionist might want this kind of authority is clear. Why the rest of us should give it to him is not.

Notes

1. In other times, this has been called *the moral sense*, *conscience*, *Pure Practical Reason,* and a variety of other names.
2. (Oxford: Clarendon Press, 1930).
3. *Methods of Ethics*, 7th edition, with a foreword by John Rawls (Indianapolis, IN: Hackett, 1981).
4. Unfortunately, Ross did not share this feeling. In the end, he made introspection of one's intentions to be the test of rectitude, as G. E. Moore made it the test of goodness.
5. No doubt, Sidgwick had long since recognized like everybody else that Mill's famous attempt to prove this proposition—by arguing that the pleasure of every person is a good for all because pleasure is desired by all—had committed a fallacy of composition.
6. The source of these observations is Moore's *Principia Ethica* (Cambridge: CambridgeUniversity Press, 1962).
7. As Ross's disciple W. T. Stace was later to explain, the moral intuitions of African "Hottentots," were not to be accorded the same weight as the intuitions of graduates of Cambridge and Oxford Universities. No doubt, he felt the same way about the intuitions of Indian fakirs, Welsh coal miners, and American frontiersmen. See, *The Concept of Morals* (New York: Macmillan, 1962), pp. 1f.
8. If Ross thought otherwise, it is perhaps because he believed that one should do one's *prima facie* duty unless one can show that not doing it is justified. This seems reasonable until one notices that Ross defines a *prima facie* duty as a conditional duty—in other words, a duty one has unless one does not have it. As this shows and Ross eventually acknowledges, a *prima facie* duty is not a *kind* of duty. So, it is not something one is obligated, even conditionally, to do. Instead, it is a conditional statement about one's duty, and such a statement provides no categorical guide to conduct.
9. See *Language, Truth, and Logic.*

10. *A Theory of Justice* (Cambridge, MA: Harvard University Press).
11. Recently Rawls seems to have changed his view. Apparently repudiating his former Rationalism, he has become what he calls a *constructivist.* See his "Kantian Constructivism in Moral Theory," reprinted in Stephen Darwall, Allan Gibbard, and Peter Railton, editors, *Moral Discourse and Practice* (New York: Oxford University Press, 1997), 247-266.
12. The old name for this was *casuistry.*
13. The term usually preferred is "analytic" ethics; but it names the same thing. The idea is that moral philosophy provides an *analysis* of the main terms of ethics—a list of the distinguishing characteristics of items known by intuition to be describable by the term.
14. I know this from personal and bitter experience, having once read a paper criticizing dependence on the authority of intuition in moral philosophy only to be challenged by someone who rested his case against me on his "moral intuitions," then got extremely angry when I replied that I did not find his appeal to intuition persuasive.
15. Less of a straw man would be the view that it is *rational* for an individual to act in ways that promise to advance his interests, which may be selfish or unselfish.
16. Utilitarianism as Bentham advocated it is not the view that it is everybody's duty to do what produces the greatest good for the greatest number but that we ought to make rules that make it everybody's duty to behave in this way—quite a different proposition.
17. Gilbert Harman calls this dissuasive definition. For examples of its use, you need only look at almost any of the hundreds of "refutations" of "egoism" and "utilitarianism" that have been produced since Sidgwick.
18. The difference is that the cagey individualist claims only that it is *rational* to do what promises to advance your interests, not also that it is your *moral duty* to behave in this way.
19. Failure to see the point is characteristic of most textbook accounts of utilitarianism. It is also the cause of the pointless debate over whether "rule" or "act" utilitarianism comports best with our commonplace moral intuitions. Bentham emphatically repudiated the absolutist presumptions behind this debate.
20. "Intuitions in Ethics," *Dialogue* XXIII (1984), 439-455.
21. The cause of error here may be a Platonic misreading of Aristotle's definition of man as a rational animal. Because it is the possession of reason that distinguishes man from other creatures, human nature is equated with reason. So, Rationalists forget that we are animals and think of us as disembodied bits of reason. This leads to the fallacious idea that, if it is universal, it is attributable to human nature; so to Reason. Such thinking overlooks the fact that human beings also share certain needs, dispositions, and instincts with other animals.
22. See *Why Men Rule: A Theory of Male Dominance* (Chicago: Open Court, 1993).
23. James Q. Wilson, *The Moral Sense* (New York: Macmillan, 1993).

10

Platonic Semantic Theory

In the final analysis, Rationalist moral theory is premised on Platonic semantic theory, a particular view of words. In order to see, then, what is wrong with the moral theory, we must see what is wrong with the theory of words. Let us therefore take a look at it.

Words as Names

The central ideas of Platonic semantic theory were conceived by Plato, who appears to have regarded words—including verbs, adverbs, prepositions, and adjectives—as names.[1] Some of these names (for example, *Socrates*) denote *objects* or *things*. Others (for example, *snub-nosed*) designate *attributes*, *properties*, or *qualities*.[2] What a word names is its *meaning*; so, the person Socrates is the meaning of the word *Socrates*, and the attribute of being snub-nosed is the meaning of the word *snub-nosed*. Sentences, which are composed of names, are themselves names. They name facts or falsehoods. For example, "Socrates was snub-nosed" names the fact that Socrates had a certain relation to the attribute snub-nosed.[3]

What relation was this? It is never entirely clear. Often Plato said that the object *possesses* its qualities; at other times, that it *participates* in them. These are both metaphors, the exact meaning of which is a subject for endless debate by scholars, and Plato never offered a single definitive explanation. On many occasions, however, he suggested an interpretation by describing the relationship in question as *exemplification, manifestation*, or *resemblance*. This usage has two main implications, both of which have been important in subsequent thought. One implication is that a thing counts as possessing a certain quality just to the extent to which it manifests, exemplifies, or resembles that quality. The other implication is that every quality is its own best exemplar. Thus, that Socrates was snub-nosed means that the shape of his nose approximated to the paradigmatically Snub Nose, the very ideal of, and standard for, a snub nose.

The clearest statement of this view is in the *Phaedo*, where Socrates, presumably speaking for Plato, bases an argument for immortality on the principles just adumbrated. According to this argument, to be alive is to possess *psyche*, meaning *life.*[4] Socrates reasons that, since every attribute is its own best exemplar, Life (the attribute of being alive) must itself embody Life; it must itself be alive. Indeed, since Life is the essence and paradigm of life, it must be the most truly alive thing there is. Therefore, Socrates reasons, Life will never admit of Death, its opposite; for to do so would be to bring about *dead life*, a contradiction in terms. Accordingly, he concludes, life must be immortal, and so, in a way, must every thing that, being alive, has, participates in, or manifests Life. In short, living things cannot die; they will live for ever.[5]

If we take this reasoning literally, as Plato seems to have meant us to do, several important conclusions follow. First, to *describe* something is to *evaluate* it; there is, in fact, no distinguishing the two activities. This is so because a thing is to count as an instance of kind K if and only if it resembles the *ideal,* or *paradigmatic*, K—this being K-ness itself, the best, or most perfect, example of K there is. So, every genuine K is a good, or exemplary, instance of K, and whatever is so defective as not to be like the ideal K is not to count as a K at all but as something else. A bad house is not a house but a shack or hovel, a poor substitute for a house; wicked and irrational men are not men but beasts in the bodies of men; bad poetry is not poetry but doggerel, an attempt at poetry that failed; an irregularly shaped square is not a square but a bad imitation of a square; and so on. Evil is unreal; the real is good, and the good is real.[6]

Second, Plato appears to have believed that, because an object has the attribute that makes it a thing of kind K only in so far as it resembles the ideal K, there must be some way in which all objects described as K resemble each other. This resemblance need not be evident to the senses, like yellow color or square shape. It may be evident only to the mind, like the attribute of being two numbered or the quality of being just. If, however, there is a name for it, it must exist; all objects described by this name must have something in common.

Third, Plato appears to have believed that, since no object detectable with the senses ever perfectly manifests a given quality, a concept of that quality cannot be acquired inductively, by abstracting from observed instances. Thus, because all visible squares are imperfect, we cannot hope to get a concept of the perfect Square by examining visible and tangible squares. Yet we have the concept; we use it whenever we recognize some object as square, and the geometer defines it when he spells out what this recognition means. Plato therefore reasoned that, if the concept Square is not learned, it must be innate; so, known *a priori*.

To explain how this *a priori* knowledge is possible, Plato speculated that, before birth, the human soul exists apart from physical things in a realm of perfect ideals or paradigms—the Square, the One, the Two, the Good, the Just, and so on. When a soul is put into its body at birth, it comes ready equipped with knowledge of these ideals, from prior acquaintance. The shock of birth causes the soul to forget these ideals until it is reminded of them by physical objects and events that resemble them, and this fact causes us to believe that the ideals are learned by abstracting from things, but Plato had the reverse opinion: In his view, we know the ideals first; their physical manifestations second. All of this is made explicit in the *Meno*, where Socrates tries to show that, with a little judicious prompting, a slave boy could prove a theorem of geometry he had not been taught.

The Four Transcendental Concepts

The Platonic theory of words just spelled out has special implications for what are called the *transcendental* concepts: Truth, Beauty, Goodness, and Justice. With minor variations, the story is the same for each of them.

Begin with Truth. According to Platonic theory, all truths manifest or exemplify Truth, the attribute of being true. Indeed, it is possession or manifestation of this attribute that makes them true and enables us to recognize them as true. In this respect, then, all truths resemble each other. Despite the differences between them, the truths "2+2=4," "The earth is round," and "Water freezes at 32 degrees Fahrenheit" are in some discernible and distinctive way alike. That this likeness cannot be detected by means of the senses is true, but Platonists believe this proves only that Truth is an "intelligible," not a "sensible" object. In other words, we know it by thought, not by sensation.

The same holds for Beauty. Are Arizona sunsets and Mozart's music both beautiful? If Platonic theory is right, this is so because there is some attribute—namely, Beauty—that the two things have in common. Despite their many differences, they are in some way alike. Since you *see* one and *hear* the other, this resemblance is not known by means of the senses, but it must exist; else it would be wrong to describe both things as beautiful. Because, however, we do so describe them and understand the description, Plato thought we must be talking about something real. Beauty must exist—not just in beautiful things but apart from them as an ideal and standard for aesthetic judgment.

Next take Goodness—the attribute of being good—and think of clam soup and sexual intercourse. In their different ways, both are good. So, according to Platonic theory, they must resemble each other. It does not matter that you *taste* clam soup and *feel* sexual intercourse. If they are both good, the Platonist believes that they must have something in common; there must be some way in which they are alike. That this common factor cannot be discerned by the senses proves, again, only that we did not acquire the concept of Goodness by abstracting from sensible objects. We had the idea beforehand; it is known *a priori*.

Finally Justice. A concept of perfect Justice could not have been acquired by observing imperfectly just actions and societies. So, the Platonist reasons, the concept of justice must be innate; we must come into the world knowing what Justice is and how to recognize it; the idea of Justice must be built into Reason. (Or, as we would say in this computer age, it must be hard wired in the brain.) If that is so, however, there must be some way in which every just act resembles every other. Since keeping your promises and giving alms to the poor are both just actions, they must be in some distinctive way alike. No matter that their resemblance cannot be detected by the senses. It, too, is known by an act of pure thought.

Platonists agree that, some people are incapable of the necessary acts of thought. In fact, they insist on the point, figuring that, as the inability of the blind to discern a distant object's color or shape casts no doubt on the reality of these qualities, so the inability of some persons to discern Truth, Beauty, Goodness, and Justice casts no doubt on the reality of these qualities. In the Platonic view, it merely argues a need for suitably trained experts. We shall want scientists to tell us what is true, aestheticians to tell us what is beautiful, lawyers to tell us what is just, and so on. In short, we shall want philosophers.

Plato was eager to train them. He set up the Academy to do it and argued in the *Republic* that either its graduates should be made kings or kings should become its graduates. The argument has ever since been the standard apology for authoritarian rule—rule by persons who would tell others what is good for them.

How Rationalist Moral Philosophy Embodies Platonic Semantic Theory

Rationalist moral philosophy and the authoritarian politics that it was designed to support are straightforward deductions from Plato's theory of words. To see how, let us take a look at a small but important sample of Rationalist theories of goodness and justice.

Begin with *justice*. It has both a broad and a narrow meaning. In the original sense of the word, the just is what comports with law; it is the lawful. In the broader sense that has become increasingly common, the just (or fair) is what comports with the rules of morality and etiquette as well as those of law strictly so-called. In this broader usage, justice is divided into *legal justice* and *moral justice*. This way of speaking confusingly treats non-legal rules of morality and etiquette as if they were themselves a kind of laws, namely "laws" of morality and etiquette. Nevertheless, we shall accept it for the moment.

Suppose, then, that you want to decide whether a practice is just, in either the narrow or the broad sense of the word. In either case, you would need to discover whether the practice comports with the relevant rules (or "laws"). But these vary with the society, Greeks having different rules than Chinese; so, what comports with one may conflict with the other. Therefore, to find out whether a practice was just in Greece, you would need to study the law, morality, and etiquette of Greece, but to find out whether the same practice was just in China, you would need to study the different law, morality, or etiquette of China. Or so it would seem.

But not if you are St. Thomas Aquinas, for whom the diversity of law was largely an illusion. It is true, the Saint agreed, that law is the "rule and measure" of justice, but, he added, there are two kinds of law: (1) man-made law, which varies with the society and is itself sometimes unjust and (2) God-made law, which does not vary and is itself necessarily just because it is, by definition, the "rule and measure" of justice. Where there is a conflict between these two "laws," Thomas believed that God-made law takes precedence. In fact, he said, man-made law counts as law truly so-called only insofar as it comports with, exemplifies, or manifests God-made law. In other cases, it is merely a bad imitation of law—a failed attempt at making law. So, in the final analysis, there is just one "rule and measure" of justice, and it is the invariable law of God, not the variable laws of human societies.

How are the provisions of this Divine Law to be known? Certainly not, Thomas said, by observing human practices. That may be how you discover the man-made laws of Greece or China. It is not how you discover the eternal Law of God. Because the Divine Law is an ideal entity only very imperfectly embodied in the laws of any actual human society, and not at all manifest in some, it cannot be discovered by empirical means. No matter. God has built a knowledge of His Holy Law into Human Reason, where it can be discovered by all who will take the time and the trouble to think about it. Any person who has trouble figuring it out may call on the philosophers of the Holy Roman Church to help with the task, but it is within the capacities of men everywhere. Hence Chinamen are as answerable to God as Frenchmen.

Compare this account of the Divine Law with our earlier account of Justice, one of the four transcendental concepts. You will see that Thomas's theory of law and justice presupposes Plato's theory of words and is unintelligible without it. (We shall soon inquire whether it is intelligible with it.)

The same is true of G. E. Moore's theory of goodness. Professor of classics and philosophy at Cambridge University in the first half of the present century, Moore held that describing something as good is saying that it has a certain quality. This same quality is also possessed, Moore believed, by every good thing. But since we cannot perceive this quality with the senses, Moore reasoned that it must be a "non-natural" quality, one that can be discerned only by an act of intellect. Moore also reasoned that, because this quality contains no parts, it must be a "simple" quality, which cannot be defined. It is, he said, like the color yellow. Those who can perceive it know what it is like, but there is no explaining it; so, people who cannot see it will have to take the word of those who can.[7]

Moore's counterpart at Oxford, W. D. Ross, said very similar things about what he called moral rightness, meaning not the fitness of actions to ends but the performance of duty—in other words, rectitude. In Ross's view, that we describe actions as right means that these actions have something in common; there is some way in which they are alike. That this common feature cannot be discerned by the senses is true, but Ross denied that this proves its unreality. Instead, he thought, it proves that apprehending the rectitude of an action requires an act of *moral intuition*, a special exercise of what Kant had called Moral Reason. Presumably, every rational being has the latent capacity for the requisite moral discrimination, but Ross believed that this faculty is fully developed only in educated persons in civilized societies; "plain men" will need to be instructed in their duties.[8] So, according to Ross's follower and former foreign service officer Walter Stace, will the savages of Africa, India, and other backward lands. Clearly, all of this is straight from Plato.

Equally Platonic, if less obviously so, is John Rawls's more recent account of justice. As Rawls, professor of philosophy at Harvard University, makes clear, his celebrated *A Theory of Justice* is meant as a detailed explanation of an ideal that he believes to be inherent in human Reason.[9] Like Thomas Aquinas, Rawls intends this *a priori* ideal to be used in deciding not what is just according to existing rules but what form the rules themselves ought to take. So, empirical investigation plays no role in Rawls's account. The requirements of justice as he understands them are discovered not by studying law books and anthropological field reports but by thinking about an antecedently given concept of justice. Conceptual analysis displaces empirical inquiry, and no mere facts of the matter are allowed to disturb the results. To make sure of this, Rawls stipulates that the analysis is to be conducted behind a "veil of ignorance," through which no empirical information will be visible. Not incidentally, Rawls also provides, with his Difference Principle, for an elite few to occupy positions of power and privilege in order to carry out the equalization of welfare in the rest of the population that he believes our *a priori* idea of justice will require.[10] No way of proceeding could be more Platonic.

Also Platonic in word and spirit are the theories that philosophers nowadays like to describe as forms of *moral realism*, meaning belief that intrinsically good things, or morally right actions, have some attribute, property, or quality in common. We shall discuss this belief more fully in the next chapter, "Enacting Rectitude." For now, we need note only how the theory depends on Platonic belief that general terms designate attributes, qualities, properties or the like. As moral realist use of this terminology makes clear, the doctrine is drenched in the terminology and presuppositions of Platonic semantic theory.

The Falsity of Plato's First Principle

This dependence on Platonic semantic theory needs emphasizing because few philosophers acknowledge it.[11] With regard to Platonic assumptions, most are like the husband who is ashamed to be seen in public with his wife: Although he cannot do without her, he does not wish to acknowledge that she is his.

This attitude is understandable: The tenets of Platonic semantic theory cannot withstand examination. To see why not, begin with the first and most distinctive of these tenets—that a common name designates a common property. Plato proposed this as an explanation of predication, but it is circular. We understand the claim " x has the property of being F" only if we already understand the claim "x is F" Thus, we know what it means to say "x has the property of being yellow" only if we already know that it means "x is yellow." As this shows, talk of properties does not explain predication; it presupposes it. Plato's principle gets the cart before the horse.

Plato's principle is also demonstrably false. Objects are sometimes described using the same word not because they have something in common but because they have what Wittgenstein called *family resemblance*: Sister Sue has eyes like brother Bob's, whose ears resemble father Fred's, and so on. Wittgenstein's example was games. Although every game resembles some other, there is no way in which all games are alike.

Eleanor Rosch has shown how this can happen. Somebody starts out using a word to describe what she calls a *prototype;* then the word's extension is increased by successive analogies.[12] Thus, someone calls object y F because it resembles prototype x in way W1; then someone calls object z F because it resembles y in different way W2;

and so on. As a result, each successive item is described as F because it resembles some other item that was previously so described, but there is no way in which all similarly described items resemble each other. There is a network of similarities, but no single similarity common to all cases.

Words indicating family resemblance are not the only exceptions to Platonic belief. That we use the same word to describe an object sometimes means not that *it* is like other objects of the same name but that it has like *effects* on us or other things. Thus, things are called attractive, nourishing, irritating, pleasant, likable, helpful, curative, useful, fattening, frightening, tiring, dangerous, enervating, boring, magnetic, explosive, and so on—not because they resemble each other but because they affect us in the same way. Of such things, it is more accurate to say that they have similar *powers* than to say that they have similar *qualities*.

Analogous remarks apply to dispositions. We call things brittle or fragile because they are easy to break, delicate because they are easy to harm, soft because they are easy to scratch or compress, tough because they are hard to wear out, and so on. There need be no discernible way in which the things so described resemble each other. Thus, clear glass is brittle and so is dark charcoal; eggs are delicate and so are silk stockings; orange juice is nourishing and so is beefsteak; alcohol is intoxicating and so is cocaine. Often, the similarities that do exist are metaphorical. Rocks are hard and so are puzzles; paths are crooked and so are politicians; the meat is rotten and so is something in Denmark; the milk is spoiled and so is the child; the iron bar is magnetic and so is the lady's personality; sadists are cruel and so are thorn bushes.

Finally—to end, but not complete this sampling of ways to use a word—objects are often called by the same name not because they have either similar qualities or powers but because (a) they have the same relation to something else or (b) they have the same function, use, or role. Examples of the first sort are "located in Shanghai" and "shorter than Wilt Chamberlain." Examples of the second are *chair* and *valve*. None of these uses is consistent with Platonic belief that a common name always means a common property.

Platonists sometimes reply that powers, dispositions, relations, and functions are also properties, but this makes mere predicability—a grammatical category—to be the defining mark of a property, which trivializes the original thesis. We certainly do attribute powers, dispositions, relations, and functions to things, just as we attribute qualities to them; but saying that two objects have the same property was supposed to mean more than "They are describable by the same terms." It was supposed to mean that they are in some discernible way alike, because each of them is like a common paradigm. If, however, there is a way in which all irritating things—or all fragile things, or all things located in Shangri-La, or all values, or all truths—resemble each other, it is hard to see, or say, what it is.

This fact has never bothered the Platonist. In his view, your inability to perceive a quality does not prove its unreality; it proves your lack of acumen. That the blind cannot see the colors and shapes of things, does not mean that these qualities are unreal; it means that the blind must depend on the guidance of the sighted. Similarly, the Platonist believes, that you cannot perceive the "moral quality" of an action does not mean that there is no such quality; it means that you must depend on the guidance of those who can. In this way, the Platonist neatly makes the absence of evidence for common qualities to be a reason for accepting his authority: "You think the coin I just gave you is base metal? How ignorant of you! Take my word; it is pure gold."

This plea for uncritical trust is as bogus as it sounds. Some people do indeed have capacities that others lack, but if what one person perceives is real, it can also be detected by other persons and in other ways. Thus, the shapes of things can be felt as well as seen, and the light waves that determine colors can be detected with appropriate laboratory instruments. So, the blind need not take the word of the sighted. When their money is at stake, they are entitled to independent confirmation by collateral information and to decline the offer if it is not forthcoming. We have the same right when the more important questions of ethics are at issue. In this matter as in others, the burden of proof is on those who make the positive claim, not on those who doubt it.

Defects in Plato's Second Principle

As questionable as Plato's first principle is his second—that the paradigm supposedly designated by a predicate is its own best exemplar: Squareness is the squarest thing there is, Beauty the most beautiful; Justice the most just; Truth the truest , and so on. As that superlative logician Bertrand Russell pointed out nearly a century ago, this proposition is not just untenable; it is also incoherent.

To see why, consider the attribute *predicable of itself.* If Plato was right, every attribute has this attribute. If there is such an attribute, however, there is also its complementary attribute, *not predicable of itself.* But if this attribute is predicable of itself, as Plato assumed all attributes to be, then we get the following contradiction: The attribute of not being predicable of itself both is and is not predicable of itself. The existence of this contradiction shows that there is no such attribute as *predicable of itself.* Unrestricted self-predication is incoherent. [13]

Plato suspected as much himself. Perhaps because of criticism by his pupil Aristotle, who was a better logician, Plato knew that his theory gives rise to paradoxes. One such paradox involved the number two. On Plato's theory, this number should itself be two-numbered; it should itself be a *pair* of numbers—in fact the paradigmatic pair. As the most perfect instance of Twoness, it should manifest Twoness above all other things; it should be the truest Two there is. Yet, the number Two is itself just *one* number—a paradox. Plato never resolved this paradox, but its existence is fatal to his whole theory.

So is another. On Plato's principles, there ought to be an attribute, *Visibility*, that all visible objects manifest, exemplify, or have in common. What is more, this attribute ought to be *the most visible object there is*; it ought to be the easiest to see. But, according to Plato, an abstract entity cannot be *seen*; it can only be *thought* about. It is an intelligible, not a visible object. So, contrary to the principle that every attribute is its own best exemplar, Visibility must be invisible. Ditto Tangibility, the property that all tangible objects have in common. Although it ought, given Plato's principle, to be *the most tangible object there is*, it cannot be touched—a straight out contradiction.

It does not follow that visibility is invisible or that tangibility is intangible. What follows is, rather, that, since there is no such thing, visibility is *neither* visible nor invisible; tangibility is *neither* tangible nor intangible; and so on. The lesson of modern logic is that predicates are well-defined only for a certain restricted domain. Outside that domain, they lack clear meaning. Thus, the domain of the predicates *even* and *odd* is numbers. Ducks and tempers, which fall outside this domain, can be even or odd only in metaphorical senses of these words. Similarly, the domain of the predicates *visible* and *invisible* is physical things. Abstract entities, which fall outside this domain, are themselves neither visible nor invisible.

Why Laws and Other Rules Cannot be Unjust

Every philosopher worth his rum knows this when he is talking about visibility, but when philosophers come to law and morality, they seem to forget it. Yet, the relevant point of logic is the same. The domain of the predicates *just* and *unjust* is actions falling under the law. So, asking whether the law is itself just or unjust is asking an undefined, because ill-formed, question. Law is the standard for the justice or injustice of acts falling under it; it is itself neither just nor unjust.

Confusion about this has been caused by belief that there is a Higher Law by reference to which we may decide whether man-made laws are themselves lawful, so just. It is supposed to be like the Constitution of the United States, the supreme law of the land. Laws contrary to it are null and void; only laws that comport with the Constitution are to determine what is lawful or just. According to the doctrine of Higher Law, even the Constitution can contain unjust provisions, so even it is not the final authority. That function is reserved for the Higher Law. In the final analysis, then, if you want to do what is lawful or just you must conform to the Higher Law. Or so it is believed.

The trouble, as we show in "The Myth of the Moral Law,"[14] is that no evidence supports belief in a Higher Law. Instead, the relevant evidence favors belief that man-made law is all the law there is. Man-made laws exist in the sense that they are obeyed where they are enforced, so there is empirical evidence of the fact. If a Higher Law existed, there would also be evidence for it. Higher law would be obeyed everywhere because it was enforced everywhere. So far as we can tell, however, the only "laws" that are everywhere "obeyed" are the laws of nature. These, however are laws only in a metaphorical sense of the word. As Hume noted, the "laws" of nature are regularities, not regulations. Things do not literally "obey" these laws; they illustrate them.

The reply will be that the lack of empirical evidence is of no consequence, because the Higher Law is not an *actual* but an *ideal* law.

Unfortunately for this reply, a merely ideal but not yet actual law is no law; at best it is merely an *ideal* for law. Perhaps such an ideal could determine what everywhere ought to be *made* just or unjust by the enactment of appropriate laws It cannot anywhere determine what *actually is* just or unjust. Only actual law can do that.

If some moral philosophers have a different view, the reason may be that they have confused saying that a rule of law is *good* or *bad* with saying that it is *just* or *unjust*. These are, however, different claims. The rules that determine what practices are to count as just cannot themselves be intelligibly regarded as unjust, but they can certainly be bad, in either of two ways. First, a rule of any kind can be *useless* or *harmful*. An example is minimum wage law. By creating unemployment among the poor, which it is supposed to help, it does more harm than good.[15] Second, a rule of law can be *immoral*. An example is law permitting infanticide where the practice occasions widespread disapproval. Sometimes bad and immoral laws are described as unjust, but the term is at best loose, as worst misleading.

The defect of this way of talking is only partly relieved by saying that the laws in question are *morally*, if not also *legally*, *unjust*—meaning that they are contrary to morality if not also to law. There is no difficulty with the idea; it is the choice of words that is problematic. Rules of law can certainly be contrary to morality; if there is no Higher Law, they cannot be contrary to law. The same is true of rules of morality. They can be good or bad, but if there is no Higher Morality, they cannot be immoral.

This is sometimes obscured by using the word *law* as a synonym for *rule*–as in *the laws of morality*, but this way of talking is misleading. It implies that there is a single transcendent Morality that we can use as a standard in judging man-made moralities and that this Morality is itself a kind of law—namely, the Moral Law. But there is no transcendent law if there is no transcendent lawgiver, and the existence of such a lawgiver is an article of faith supported by no evidence. Furthermore, law strictly so-called consists of official, morality unofficial, rules—making "moral law" to be the contradiction *rules that are both official and not.* [16]

An Alternative View of Moral Language

We have been discussing the incoherence of Rationalist belief that the man-made rules that define justice and injustice for us can themselves be just or unjust. We have found that this commonplace belief makes a misleadingly broad use of juridical language, unjustifiably assumes the existence of a Divine lawgiver (or mistakenly takes metaphors literally), and wrongly assumes that a merely ideal law or morality is itself an instance of law or morality But if we reject the Platonic view of language that produces these unhappy results, what is our alternative?

The alternative that I prefer has been most fully and carefully worked out by Willard Quine, in *Word and Object* and elsewhere.[17] Taking the sentence to be a more basic unit of speech than the words that make it up, Quine holds that the meanings of individual words depend on how they are used in sentences, the meanings of which depend on their place in the language. Thus, the meaning of the word *snub-nosed* is fixed by sentences like "Socrates was snub-nosed" and "This is a snub-nosed revolver." In these sentences, the word *snub-nosed* is a predicate of Socrates and the revolver, not a name of a property that attaches to these. Therefore, instead of saying with the Platonist that Socrates has the property of being snub-nosed, we say that the predicate "x is snub-nosed" *is true of* Socrates.

In general, when asked for the *meaning* of a predicate, we will not reply that it means a certain property. Instead, we will divide the question and reply that the predicate *describes* or *denotes* the objects of which it is true and *connotes* the other predicates that are, or are thought to be, true of these same objects. The objects described are the predicate's *extension* or *denotation*; other predicates that describe these same objects are its *intension* or *connotation.* Thus, the denotation of the predicate "x is snub-nosed" is all the entities that can truly be said to be snub-nosed—Socrates, 38 revolvers, and so on. The connotation of this predicate is the other predicates—for example, "x has a short or flat nose"—that can substitute for it or go into explaining it. Dropped out of the picture is what Plato called the meaning of this predicate—namely, the property, attribute, or quality of being snub-nosed. All that is left is snub-nosed things and the predicates that describe them—a much simpler view of language.

This view differs from the Platonic view in two main respects. First, as already noted, a predicate of the form "x is F" is to be regarded as denoting not some abstract entity F but some concrete entities describable as F. Second, describing an entity x as F will not mean that x resembles some abstract entity that is the paradigmatic F, as in Plato. It may not even mean that x resembles some concrete entity that is the prototypical F, as in Rosch. Instead, as noted in our sampling of the many exceptions to Platonic belief, it may mean that x has an effect on us that is like the effect y has on us, or that x is related in a certain way to y; and so on. What it means cannot be known in advance, only after the fact, by examining the case at issue. That is what makes this an empiricist theory of language.

Empiricism in Moral Theory

That abstract ideals play no role in an empiricist account of language means, in particular, that there is no use for the transcendental ideals Truth, Beauty, Goodness, and Justice. Instead of talking about these, the empiricist will talk about the predicates "x is true," "x is beautiful," "x is good," and "x is just"; and if he does talk for convenience sake about the "properties," he will mean the predicates. This will make for both greater simplicity and greater clarity. Nobody ever understood what sorts of things these "properties" were supposed to be anyhow. Now, we do not have to worry about the question.

The resulting advantages are considerable. Suppose that some object or event x has been described as *good.* As noted above, the Platonist will insist that this means: "x resembles other good things because it resembles the Good, the paradigm of Goodness, by comparison with which all things are to be described as good." Unencumbered with Platonist ontology, the empiricist will make no such assumption. He will not even assume that describing x as good means that it resembles some other concrete thing described as good. In fact, he will make no *a priori* assumptions about the meaning of the word. Instead, as Wittgenstein recommended, he will *look and see.*

When he does, he will find that, contrary to Platonic prejudice, describing something as good is *never* a matter of saying that it has a distinctive quality, for the fact is that *there is pretty plainly no way in which all and only good things are alike.* Instead, things are called good for a limitless variety of reasons. Foods count as good if they are nourishing or pleasant tasting, craftsmen if they are skilled, means of transportation if they are fast and cheap, omens if they portend desirable events, and so on. So far as anybody can tell, then, there is no distinctive way in which all good things resemble each other. Instead, as Aristotle observed, *good* "is predicated in all the categories." That is why Westermarck suggests that *good* may be not a single word but a set of homonyms.[18]

If we do not think of *good* as a set of homonyms, it is because we know that something ties the word's many disparate uses together. As we saw in an earlier chapter, prototypical use of the word is to describe things that reinforce the speaker's preference for them.[19] In this usage, saying that things are good is not saying that there is some way in which *they* are alike; it is saying that they have like *effects*, often on *us*. Contrary to Platonic presumption, goodness is not a *quality*; it is a *power*. Furthermore, this power is not transcendent but empirically knowable. We know that a thing *can* reinforce preference when we see that it *does*.

Justice is also not a quality. Instead, it is a relation. As just noted, what makes an action just or unjust is its relation to the law—or (in a looser sense that we shall ignore for the moment) the rules that constitute morality. Roughly: That is just which comports with the law; that is unjust which does not. Nor is this law a transcendent ideal knowable only by means of Pure Reason. Instead, it is an empirical entity discoverable by observing the practices of officials, who enforce it by punishing what does not comport with it and by rewarding what does. Sometimes, it is true, the laws instituted by officials are themselves said to be unjust, but, as we have just noted, this usage confuses injustice with evil, for which there is a different test.

The essential point is that there are empirical tests for both goodness and justice. We have been prevented from seeing this only by Platonic insistence that these are simple qualities that can be discerned only by privileged persons using esoteric means. But this Platonic doctrine is a prejudice coupled with a plea for arbitrary authority—the power to decide what is to count as good and just.

Qualities and Truth

The standard reply is that denying the reality of the properties *Goodness* and *Justice* is denying the "objectivity" of evaluation, making it a question of opinion rather than fact whether some thing should count as good or some act as just. The usual argument for this claim is an attempt at *reductio ad absurdum* that goes as follows: If there are no such properties as goodness and justice, it makes no sense to assert that things have or lack these properties. In other words, it makes no sense to say either that some things are good or that some actions are just. Such judgments will state no objective matters of fact; instead, they will express mere attitudes or feelings. In short, they will lack truth values. Finding this implication absurd, the Platonist concludes that, since things do sometimes count as good and actions do sometimes count as just, there must be such properties as *goodness* and *justice*. Thus do truisms give rise to metaphysics. Because the argument for this conclusion is metaphysical, not empirical, the Platonist remains unmoved by the lack of evidence for it.

The main error in this line of thought has already been identified. It is the Platonist's belief that there must be such entities as properties. Let us be very clear about this. If the Platonist were right, the predicate "x is F" would be elliptical for, "There is a property F which is possessed by object x." Hence, every statement about *one* thing would really be a statement about *two* things—a visible and tangible object and its invisible and intangible property. The statement would amount to the claim that the object is related in a certain way to the property, and so the Platonist believes. As we have already seen, however, there is no reason to accept this account. In fact, it represents a needless complication. Since we understand the claim that object x has property F only if we already understand the statement "x is F," it is going in circles to say that "x is F" is true just in case x has property F.

For the sake of the discussion, however, let us adopt the Platonist's way of speaking. Let us say that every predication ascribes a property. In fact, let us regard talk of properties and predicates as interchangeable. Saying that some object x has property F will just mean that x is describable using predicate 'F.' In other words, saying that object x *has* property F will just be a convenient way of saying that predicate 'F' is *true of* object x. As we have also been at pains to show, however, this will not secure the Platonist's original claim—which was that an object x has a property F only if x resembles all other objects having that same property because it resembles the paradigm F.

The Platonist who thinks that it does follow has confused *properties* with *qualities*—common predicates with discernible similarities. As noted earlier, use of the same predicate sometimes means not that the things described have a certain *quality* but that they have a certain *power*. Thus, saying that something is good is saying that it has the power to reinforce desire for it. Also, use of the same predicate sometimes means not that there is a common quality but that there is a common *relation*. Thus, describing a practice as just means that it comports with the rules of law or morality that we happen to have in mind. That is why it serves nobody's cause to reply that powers and relations are also properties. Grant that this is true. It will not settle the question that is at issue—namely, whether a common *predicate* indicates a discernible *resemblance*.

Furthermore, if that is the Platonist's claim, it is pretty clearly mistaken. So far as we can tell, there is no way in which all good things or all just actions resemble each other. Belief that such resemblance is required for objective truth is a mistake. Grant that a thing has the power to reinforce desire for it. Then the claim that it is good must be true. Not just true in somebody's opinion, but true. Grant that a practice conforms to the relevant law or morality. Then the claim that it is just must be true. Not just true in somebody's opinion, but true. The only mystery is why the Platonist believes otherwise.

Properties and the Paradoxes of Relativity

We have explored one of the reasons above, in "How to Make Moral Judgments." It is that, unless goodness and justice are regarded as qualities, the truth values of "x is good" and "x is just" appear to be relative, the first to persons, the second to societies. This has encouraged philosophers who doubt the reality of Goodness and Justice to believe that whether a thing is good or a practice is just is a matter of opinion, and it has encouraged Platonists to insist that, since "x is good" and "x is just" are not matters of opinion, the qualities Goodness and Justice must be real. The mistake, which is the same in both cases, is to think that the existence of Goodness and Justice is necessary for the objectivity of ethics.

To see, once again, why this is an error, consider the sentence,

> C: *Clam soup tastes good.*

If we have been right up to now, C will be true if A says it; false if B does. As a matter of logic, however, the same statement cannot be both true and false. Assuming that we know this, the Platonist reasons that we must be saying *not* that C is both true and false but that A thinks "C is true" and B thinks "C is false," a real possibility. In short, since saying that C is both true and false would be obviously self-contradictory, the Platonist reasons that we must be saying "C has no truth value; it is just an opinion."

As we explained above, this overlooks the distinction between a sentence and the statement it is used to make. It also overlooks the fact that sentence C is indexed to its speaker, so elliptical for

C': *Clam soup tastes good* to me,

which makes one statement (a true one) if A says it, a different statement (a false one) if B says it. Therefore, although there would be a contradiction in saying that *the same statement* is both true and false, there is none in the fact that C is true if A says it but false if B does. Nor does this mean that A thinks that C and B does not. It means that clam soup pleases A's palate but not B's.

Similarly, although there would be a contradiction in saying that "Polygamy is legally and morally acceptable" is both true and false, there is no contradiction in the claim that "Polygamy is legally and morally acceptable" will be true if said by a Saudi Arabian, false if said by a Selma, Alabamian. Nor does this mean that the Saudi and the Selman disagree about the legality and morality of polygamy. It means that polygamy is permitted in Saudi Arabia, forbidden in Selma Alabama. So, the Platonist's attempt at reducing relativism to subjectivism fails. Values are relative, but truth—including the truth about value—is absolute.

I have explained this before. What I have not yet explained is why this is so hard for the Platonist to understand. I suspect the explanation is the Platonic theory of words. Once someone is transfixed by the idea that predication is ascription of properties, and properties are qualities which things either have or lack, he will have difficulty understanding predicates that do not fit this Procrustean mold. A perfect illustration is Plato's befuddlement over the fact that an object x can be both small and large, because smaller than y and larger than z. How, Plato wondered in all seriousness, can the same thing manifest both Smallness *and* Largeness, two mutually exclusive qualities? He concluded that, since nothing can be both large and small, relative size must be a matter of false opinion engendered by perceptual illusion. Just find the correct standards, Small and Large, and this illusion will be dispelled.

Twenty-five centuries later, Plato's followers are still drawing the same conclusion about goodness and justice. Not seeing how a thing can both have and lack a quality, they reason that the relativity of goodness to persons and justice to societies must be illusions engendered by contrary opinions. All we need to do, then, is identify, or have someone else identify, *the Good* and *the Just*—the "objective" (that is, absolute) standards by which to determine whether a thing is to count as good or an action as just. Then the illusion of relativity will be dispelled once and for all. People will then see that, just as it is a muddle to believe that the truth values of "x is square" and "x is yellow" vary with speakers, so it is a muddle to say the same thing about "x is good" and "x is just."

Reinforcement with Irritation

If the error is still not obvious, perhaps it can be made so with an analogy. Consider the predicate "x is irritating." Among the things describable by this predicate are frustrating tasks, uncooperative children, incessant noise, and speeches by politicians. If there is any quality which these irritating things have in common, no one can identify it. Should we say, then, that being irritating is a "simple" but "non-natural" quality discernible only by a special power of irritable (or would it be irritating?) intuition possessed by only a privileged few persons who should be given authority to decide what is irritating and what is not? The ludicrousness of the suggestion is patent, and so is the fact that being irritating is not a quality but a power.

Yet, what irritates A may leave B unruffled; so, the power to irritate is relative, not absolute. Does this imply that you say nothing true if you say that something is irritating? Only a very befuddled person might think so. We can imagine such a person—call him Pseudo-Platonist—arguing as follows. "If being irritating is not a quality, then it will be meaningless to say that something has or lacks this quality; so, it will be meaningless to ascribe truth value to the statement that something is irritating. Since what irritates A might not irritate B, it will follow that whether a thing is irritating is a question not of fact but of opinion. A thing will be irritating to A if A thinks so, not to B if B disagrees." Pseudo-Platonist will regard this as proving, by *reductio ad absurdum*, that being irritating must be a quality—this being, in his view, necessary for statements of the form "x is irritating" to have "objective" truth value.

It proves no such conclusion. Although it attributes no quality to anything, the statement "Small children and loud noises are irritating" has truth value. Grant that its truth value will vary with the speaker, the statement being true when A says it, false when B does. This does not mean that the question whether something is irritating is a mere matter of opinion; so, a thing is irritating if you think so, not otherwise. It means only that the sentence "x is irritating" is indexed to its user and that the same thing can irritate A but not B.

In summary, the Platonist's attempt to reduce relativism to subjectivism embodies a series of mistakes. First, thinking of predication as ascription of properties, and thinking of properties as qualities, the Platonist mistakenly assimilates all statements, including "Clam soup tastes good" and "Keeping your promises is just," to the subject-predicate form exemplified by "This lemon is yellow." Interpreting the latter as meaning "This lemon has the property of being yellow," he therefore interprets the former as meaning "Clam soup has the property of tasting good" and "Keeping your promises has the property of being just." Then he compounds his error by construing "This soup tastes good *to Smith* " as meaning "This soup has the property of tasting good *in Smith's opinion*" and "Polygamy is immoral *in S*" with "Polygamy has the property of being immoral *in the opinion of the people of S*." Finally, having thus completely misunderstood the claim that goodness and justice are relative, he congratulates himself that he has reduced this claim to the absurd proposition that there is no truth about goodness and justice; merely opinions.

The irony is that it is the view of the Platonic absolutist, not that of the relativist, which leads to this pessimistic conclusion. To see how, grant the Platonist's belief that there are absolute but transcendent standards for goodness and justice. Since these standards are not empirically known, it is also not known whether anything conforms to them. But that there is no known fact, merely a variety of opinions, is what is normally meant by saying "It is just a matter of opinion." Grant that one of the opinions in question might be true. If it cannot be known, the fact can be of no practical use to us. By contrast, the claims that a thing is good if it reinforces desire and that a practice is just if it comports with the rules provide us with empirically determinate tests of goodness and justice. In the final analysis, it is the availability of these tests, not unknown ideals, that gives us reason to believe that our talk of goodness and justice belongs in the realm of the true and the false.

Notes

1. What is here called Platonic semantic theory should not be confused with Plato's semantic theory. What Plato's considered opinions on these matters may have been is a question for the dispute of scholars better equipped than I to deal with the ambiguities and obscurities of Plato's complicated dialogues. My concern is not to offer an authoritative interpretation of Plato's philosophy. In fact, I doubt whether such a thing is possible. My aim is only to spell out the main implications of a doctrine that is prominent in Plato's writings, was apparently invented by him, and has had an important influence on Western thought. It is a doctrine that, rightly or wrongly, has often been thought to be Plato's, but whether it was in fact his is irrelevant for present purposes.

2. I am told that the Greek word is *eide*, which is sometimes translated as *ideas.* The same word is, however, often translated as *forms*, although it has no connotation of shape, the Greek term for that being *morphe*. Perhaps the basis for talk of forms is the belief that Plato was trying to say that everything of a given kind satisfies, or is describable by, a certain *formula*, one that defines it as an object of that particular kind. The question exceeds my competence.
3. This particular example is not Plato's but Aristotle's. Plato preferred mathematical examples, e.g., squareness.
4. This word is usually translated *soul.*
5. Of course, this did not imply that what we loosely call living bodies never die. In Plato's view, bodies are not alive. They merely have life (a thing) in them; they merely resemble or manifest Life. What survives the death of the body is, then, not the body but only the life that it possessed. What, exactly, this can mean, if it means anything, has ever since been a source of speculation and debate. Since I do not accept Plato's premises, I have absolutely no wish to engage in this debate, which I happily leave to the theologians and metaphysicians.
6. Again, the examples are mine.
7. All of this is laid out in Moore's *Principia Ethica*, which we discuss at length elsewhere.
8. For the source of these remarks, see Ross's *The Right and the Good;* also, his *Foundations of Ethics.* For criticism see next chapter, "Enacting Rectitude."
9. *A Theory of Justice* (Cambridge, MA: Harvard University Press, 1971).
10. Since Rawls is usually seen as, and sees himself as, an egalitarian, this claim may come as a surprise, but the whole point of the Difference Principle is to provide for inequalities. The principle says that positions of prestige, power and privilege will be allowed to exist whenever they are necessary to make better off those who might otherwise be worst off. If that is not a provision for an elite group, I do not know what would be.
11. A notable exception is George Bealer, whose *Concept and Quality* is a very sophisticated and powerful explanation and defense of a Platonic theory of words.
12. See Eleanor Rosch, editor, *Cognition and Categorization* (Hillsdale, N J: Lawrence Erlbaum, 1978).
13. This claim of incoherence could not be sustained against the vaguer idea that things *possess* and *participate in,* but do not *manifest, resemble*, or *exemplify* their attributes. The trouble with the first idea is not that it is incoherent but that, without further explanation, it is meaningless.
14. Chapter 11.
15. Of course, minimum wage law does protect the jobs of union workers, which they regard as a good thing.
16. If there is no transcendent Morality, how can the rules that constitute a society's morality be bad rules? By failing to advance, or by defeating, the interests of those who created these rules and enforce them or must live by them. The test of goodness and badness is not moral; it is utilitarian. Good rules are rules that achieve our purposes; bad rules are rules that frustrate them.
17. *Word and Object* (New York: Wiley, 1960).
18. Edward Westermark, *Ethical Relativity*, (Paterson, NJ: Littlefield, Adams, & Co., 1960).
19. As talk of good thieves and good murderers illustrates, however, use of the word *good* is not limited to things reinforcing. In these two examples,, *good* means *efficient*—usually a desirable characteristic, but not always.

11

Enacting Rectitude

Among philosophers, a *realist* is someone who affirms the reality of what *skeptics* have called into doubt.[1] Thus, a *unicorn realist*, if there were such a person, would be someone who believed in unicorns, the reality of which we *unicorn skeptics* doubt. A *moral realist*, then, is someone who believes in the reality of what he calls morality, which he takes some *moral skeptic* to have doubted. Since "moral skeptics" are not all cut from the same cloth, this means that there are many different varieties of "moral realism," some inconsistent with others. The precise form that moral realism takes therefore depends on the particular variety of moral skepticism to which it is thought to be the answer.

Property Realism

The oldest and purest version of moral realism is *moral absolutism*, belief that all good things, or all morally right actions, have something in common—namely, a "property" of goodness, or rectitude, as the case may be. If the moral absolutist is right, it is possession of this property that both makes things good, or actions just, and enables us to recognize them as such. Plato invented this theory, which he held in opposition to sophist belief that good and bad are relative to persons, justice and injustice to societies.

The chief difficulty in appraising Plato's doctrine is to understand its central concept. What sort of thing is a *property*, and what does it mean to say that something *has* one? In the final analysis, only one answer makes sense, namely:

(1) *Object o has property P,*

means

(2) *Object o is P.*

For example, "This table has the property of being square" means "This table is square," and "That book has the property of being interesting" means "That book is interesting." In each case, we understand the first, verbally inflated, sentence only if we understand the second, shorter, sentence—which the first was supposed to clarify. Talk of properties does not *explain* predication; it *presupposes* it. Trying to explain predication by talking of properties is trying to clarify the clear by mixing it with the obscure.

If some philosophers persist in talking of properties despite the obscurities of the concept, the reason is probably their belief that it is merely a convenient way of talking about *predicates*. (Perhaps we should call this the *semantic*, or *redundancy*, theory of properties?) According to this belief, (1) is a substitute not for (2) but for its metalanguage counterpart,

(3) *The predicate "x is square" is true of object o,*

which does not fall so trippingly off the tongue.

Unfortunately for this belief, talk of properties cannot be reduced to talk of predicates. It is true that we can make some sense of "x has the property of being square" by regarding it as a rough equivalent for (3), but what will we do when someone speaks, as Platonic-minded philosophers are wont to do, of the property that some objects *have in common*? If, as is naturally supposed, this means that there is some way in which these objects *resemble* each other, it cannot be merely a way of saying that the same predicate is true of them. The predicate "x is near y" is true of all objects that are near y, but there is no reason to believe that an examination of these objects would reveal a distinctive way in which they are alike.

This sore spot cannot be healed, only irritated, by treating relations as properties. Saying that objects near y have in common the "relational property" of being near y will not secure their resemblance. If similarity is what is wanted, a more precise term for it is *quality*.

Goodness and Rectitude as Primary Qualities

Unfortunately, the word *quality* also suffers from ambiguity. Since Galileo, most philosophers have distinguished *primary* qualities, such as shape, which things have independently of perception, from *secondary* qualities, such as color, which things have in relation to perception. So, we must ask, "Which kind of qualities are goodness (the quality of being good) and rectitude (the quality of being morally right) supposed to be?"

Although he did not know the term or the distinction on which it would be based, Plato's view was that goodness and rectitude are both *primary* qualities, which things and actions have independently of perception.[2] Twenty-five centuries later, G. E. Moore and W. D. Ross were still espousing this view—Moore about goodness, Ross about rectitude—although they confused the issue by comparing both qualities to color, which is a secondary quality.[3] As Ross eventually explained, however, the comparison with color was meant only to emphasize that goodness and rectitude are *simple* qualities. To emphasize that goodness and rectitude are independent of perception, Moore and Ross described them as *objective* rather than *subjective*, or as *intrinsic* rather than *extrinsic*, meaning that they inhere, like shape, in things and actions themselves, apart from their effects on us.[4] To make this point as clear as he could, Moore declared that an admirable, so good, thing would be admirable even if there were nobody to admire it, and Ross said the same thing about a morally right action: It would be right "even if it existed quite alone."[5]

How were the intrinsic goodness of things and the intrinsic rectitude of actions to be known? Except to insist that they were not known by means of the bodily senses but in some other way, Moore and Ross did not really say. According to Moore, goodness was a "non-natural" quality detectable only by means of a special, but otherwise undefined, faculty of "intuition," by means of which it could, however, be known more less infallibly, because of the quality's absolute simplicity. Ross said the same thing about rectitude, explaining that "'*right*' does not stand for anything we can point out to one another or apprehend by one of the senses" (p. 2). It, too, was a simple quality, like yellow color, known by a more or less infallible and mysterious faculty of "moral intuition." Why did Moore and Ross believe that they had such faculties? Because they could think of no other way in which they might discern goodness and rectitude. The faculties were needed to detect the qualities, which were needed to explain their detection by the faculties.[6]

Not only was this circular epistemology unsatisfactory, it also undercut the idea that goodness and rectitude are primary qualities, like shape, which things have independently of perception. If shape counts as a primary quality, it is because there is an independent test of its reality. Having discerned the coin's circular shape by using your eyes, you can confirm it by using your fingers; you need not depend on sight alone. If that were not true, shape would have to count as a merely secondary quality, like color, which can be verified only by means of sight, not also by touch, or sound.[7] Since "intuitions" of goodness and rectitude cannot be confirmed in other ways, the same must be said for them. They are at best secondary qualities, and, as we shall see later, they may not deserve even that status.

Harman and Brink on the Best Explanation

Gilbert Harman and J. L. Mackie were making essentially this point when they argued, over twenty years ago, that there is no need to assume the existence of the qualities *goodness* and *rectitude* in order to explain normative judgments.[8]

Harman's illustration was the act of setting a cat on fire. To account for our disapproval of this act, we need not suppose that it has a distinctive and discernible *quality* of being morally wrong. Instead, said Harman, our aversion to the act can be explained more simply by noting certain facts about *us*—namely, that we are disposed by biological evolution or cultural conditioning to dislike cruelty. In this respect, said Harman, the case compares unfavorably to the physicist's observation of a disturbance in a cloud chamber. To explain this event the physicist must suppose that it was caused by a passing electron. No facts about him will suffice.

In a dense, difficult, disorganized, and dilatory book, David Brink has replied that the evil of torching cats is not well explained by talking about our likes and dislikes, however we came to have them.[9] In Brink's view, a better explanation of our disapproval is the fact that the act is wrong; in other words, it has an objectionable moral quality. Brink is persuaded that Harman's denial of this proposition is self-refuting. By objecting to the act of torching cats, Harman appears to

Brink to have accepted the judgment "Torching cats is wrong," which, Brink believes, can be true only if the act of torching cats has the quality of being morally objectionable, the existence of which Harman denies.

This attempt at *reductio ad absurdum* is vitiated by a failure to observe the distinction between (a) the claim that a normative judgment is true and (b) the claim that it is true because it ascribes a quality to something. Like other moral realists, Brink repeatedly collapses this distinction. Grant, however, that torching cats is wrong. It does not follow that you must also grant Brink's metaphysical explanation of this fact—that the act is wrong because it possesses a distinctive quality that it shares with other wrong acts. To *assume* that this does follow is only to beg the question, which is precisely whether normative judgments are intelligible only if they are made so by the existence of the qualities goodness and rectitude.

It will be replied that Brink is not trying to refute Harman's theory; just trying to show that Harman has failed to refute his. Grant that "We dislike cruelty" could explain our aversion to torching cats, as Harman avers. Brink's reply is that this does not rule out the proposition that we dislike the act *because it is wrong* or the proposition that the act is wrong *because it has an objectionable quality.* In Brink's view, this means that Harman has failed to show what he tried to show—that there are no such qualities as goodness and rectitude.

Although this attempt to shift the burden of proof has been widely celebrated as a refutation of Harman, it has two fatal flaws. First, as emphasized above, no one has identified the quality which Harman is being expected to disprove. It has been named, but no dog has answered to the name. No one has shown by independent means that there is any way in which, say, honesty and charity—both virtues—resemble each other. Second, as the popular saying goes, you cannot expect someone to prove a negative. We do not doubt the existence of unicorns because we can prove their unreality. We doubt it because we lack good evidence of their reality. Here an argument from ignorance suffices. It is an application of Occam's principle of parsimony: Don't multiply entities beyond necessity.

Empty Explanations

There is a third difficulty with Brink's reply. To say that moral judgments are best explained by acknowledging the reality of such qualities as rectitude and goodness is to suppose that invoking these qualities explains something. In fact, the explanations Brink offers are empty. Saying that we regard torching cats as wrong *because it has the quality of being wrong* is like saying with the Learned Doctor in Moliere's *Hypochondriac* that opium puts people to sleep *because it has a soporific virtue*. As Aristotle observed regarding Plato's analogous claim that a thing is beautiful *because it participates in Beauty*, this merely duplicates terminology without increasing understanding. Renaming the thing does not explain it. It merely gives us a new word for the same phenomenon.

John McDowell has replied that Harman is demanding the wrong kind of explanation,[10] seeking a causal mechanism when what is wanted is an explanation of a radically different kind, one that makes its explanandum "intelligible," somewhat as "We laughed because it was funny" makes our laughter intelligible. Unfortunately, this reply has two problems. First Harman and Mackie were refuting Moore and Ross, who undoubtedly *did* suppose that they were specifying causes. Except that it involved no bodily sense, Moore regarded intuition of the good, and Ross regarded intuition of the right, as an act of *perception* caused, they insisted, in much the same way as a ripe lemon causes us to see its color or shape. Second, McDowell makes no effort to explain how "We laughed because it is was funny," makes our laughter intelligible if not because being funny is a *cause* of laughter.

We shall return to this question later, when we take up McDowell's view that "value," or goodness, is a secondary quality.

Goodness and Rectitude as Supervenient Qualities

The main defect in the moral realism of Moore and Ross besides the circularity of their epistemology was their failure to identify other than by name the distinctive way in which good things or "morally right" actions are supposed to resemble each other. Let us say more about this.

Since the arguments are parallel, we may save space and avoid repetition by considering just Ross on rectitude. Wrongly taking *obligatory* as a near synonym for *morally right*,[11] Ross once suggested that morally right actions all have in common the quality of being *obligatory*, but the claim is hard to credit when you look at the cases. I am obligated to pay my taxes, do my job, care for my children, tell the truth, keep my promises, be faithful to my wife, contribute to the welfare of the community, be kind to animals, help the needy, and ever endlessly on. If there is a single distinctive quality of *obligatoriness* tying all of these very diverse obligations together, it is hard to see.

The reason will be obvious to anybody who thinks about the issue for more than two minutes. As Ross himself acknowledged when he faced the question head on, actions are described as right for a great and irreducible variety of reasons—some because they are beneficial, others because they are brave; some because they are generous, others because they are kind; some because they are principled, others because they are flexible; some because they are useful, others because they are pleasant; and so on. If there is any *one* quality that makes all of these actions right, nobody has been able to identify it.

Ross had a reply. He said that rectitude is a *resultant* quality, which actions have by virtue of having some *other* quality. Thus, action A is right because it is brave; B because it is generous; C because it is kind; and so on. Between these cases there is no obvious similarity, but Ross believed that the rightness of the action is discernibly the same in every case; only its cause varies. Here, again, Ross followed Moore, who had tried to resolve the exactly parallel difficulty about goodness by claiming that the quality which good things have in common *supervenes on* a great variety of diverse base properties, yet continues to be exactly the same quality in every instance. If Moore was right, butter pecan ice cream and sexual intercourse have a common quality, the quality of being good. That this quality is not discernible by means of the senses proves only that it supervenes on qualities that are.

What does it mean to say that a property P *supervenes* on another property Q? Roughly: That object x has property P if it has property Q. Thus, suppose that G is the property *made of gold* and E is the property *expensive*. Then, since things made of gold are also expensive, E supervenes on G. E also supervenes on S, the property *made of silver*; for whatever is made of silver is also expensive; and so on. In fact, E supervenes on every property—for example, the property of being *rare*, or the property of being *painted by Picasso*—possession of which makes an object expensive. The properties on which a property supervenes are called its *base properties*. The property of being expensive supervenes on a great variety of base properties.

Because supervenience is a many-one relation, Moore and Ross thought that invoking it would enable them to acknowledge both the diversity of good things and right actions and the unity of the qualities, goodness and rectitude, which they believed to be possessed by these things and actions. Our example shows why they were wrong. That otherwise dissimilar objects have in common a merely supervenient property of being expensive does *not* mean that there is some discernible way in which these objects are alike, merely that they all count as expensive despite their lack of resemblance. In this case, a common predicate does not denote a common quality. No dog answers to the name because there is no dog to answer.

If Moore and Ross did not notice this fact, it is because talk of supervenient properties has an ambiguity that they overlooked. As we observed in the beginning, saying that two objects have the same property can mean either that they are both *describable using the same word* or that they are *in some discernible way alike*. Since the first claim would be trivial, we have presumed that the second was meant, but adding that the property in question is merely supervenient must give us pause. As we have just remarked, a merely supervening quality is only nominally a quality—as a sea horse is only nominally a horse. (Here the names are syncategorematic.) Therefore, calling goodness and rectitude supervenient qualities is taking away with one hand what was given with the other.

In short, to admit that goodness and rectitude are merely supervenient qualities is to admit that they might not be qualities at all. What purported to be a defense has amounted to a confession of guilt on all counts. Moore and Ross have shot themselves in the foot. That is why Mackie, who doubted the reality of these "qualities," agreed that they are merely supervenient—this being, in Mackie's view, just another way of saying that they are not part of "the furniture of the world." As Hume insisted, they belong instead to our way of responding to the world, a topic to which we shall recur later.

Goodness as a Secondary Quality

Lately, little has been said on behalf of the kind of intuitionist moral realism that was hatched by Plato and cultivated by Moore and Ross. Recently, however, a number of her brood have taken her place. These chicks are in some ways like their parent, in other ways different, and each differs from its sibling, complicating the problem of finding a single description that fits them all. Since there is a family resemblance, we will refer to them under the heading *new moral realism*, but we shall not be able to ignore differences between them.

One new idea being advanced under the banner "moral realism" is McDowell's hypothesis that goodness (or "value") is a quality but not, as Moore supposed, a primary quality, like shape; instead, a secondary quality, like color—the quality with which Moore and Ross confusingly compared it while talking about it as if it were logically on a par with shape. Ross's parallel belief that rectitude is a primary quality has also been largely abandoned by moral realists. Although he does not use the term, what W. D. Falk, a leading new realist, has said about rectitude could also be summarized as belief that it is a secondary, rather than a primary, quality. [12] Unfortunately, the central concept of this new realism is also ambiguous, like the concept of supervenient qualities.

First conceived by Galileo, the idea of a *secondary quality* was more elaborately explained by Locke, who rightly and acutely noted that secondary qualities are not *qualities* but *powers*—capacities to affect suitably endowed perceivers in familiar ways. In Locke's words, a lemon is yellow not "in itself" but in the sense that it has the power to produce a sensation of yellow "in us." Locke's colleague Isaac Newton had shown that this power resides in the lemon by virtue of the molecular composition of its surface, which enables the lemon to absorb some parts of light while reflecting others. As Locke and Newton realized, however, color perception depends on the peculiarities of our perceptual apparatus.[13] So, color has to be *seen* to be *known*; there is no independent means of discovering it. Hence, Locke concluded that color is an illusion, which belongs as much to our way of perceiving the world as to the world itself. In the ambiguous jargon of moral realists, color is as "subjective" as it is "objective."

This makes it uncertain just how we should interpret McDowell's and Falk's claims. What does it mean to say that goodness and rectitude are "objective" yet not "primary" qualities? In saying this, do McDowell and Falk mean to affirm, or do they mean to deny, that things are good and actions are right *in themselves,* apart from their effects on persons? Calling them objective qualities suggests affirmation, but adding that they are merely secondary qualities suggests denial. What was given with the right hand is taken away with the left.

This ambiguity is not resolved but compounded when McDowell explains that although secondary qualities are *phenomenal*, not *physical,* they count as real because they belong to what Wilfred Sellars called the *manifest,* if not also to what he called the *scientific*, image. On the most natural understanding of McDowell's words, a physical property is one that objects *really* have, whereas a merely phenomenal property is one that they merely *appear* to have. Thus, in Sellars, the scientific image represents the world as it really is according to our best science, while the manifest image represents the world as it is wrongly taken to be by uncritical common sense. To say, then, that values and rectitude are merely phenomenal properties, or that they exist in the manifest but not the scientific image, is not to affirm their reality but to deny it. Under which shell is the pea located?

Language Games, Ontology, and Truth

If McDowell regards this as a misguided question, it is because he has a view of reality that would never have occurred to such Platonic absolutists as Moore and Ross.

McDowell takes from Wittgenstein's *Investigations* the belief that questions about reality are meaningful only in relation to a particular "language game." Grant, then, that the terminology of color plays no part in the canonical language of physicists. This indicates to McDowell only that colors do not belong to the ontology of physics; they are not part of the scientific image. No matter. What matters if McDowell is right is that color words *do* belong to the diction of workaday discourse; so, colors do belong to our common sense ontology. In McDowell's view, this suffices to justify the claim that colors are real.

This view begs the question by changing it. Grant that colors *are* part of the ontology of ordinary discourse. The fact remains that they *are not* part of the ontology of science. So, we are still left with the original question. Should colors, which count as real in the largely unreflective discourse of common speech, also count as real given the more rigorous standards of physical science? Once the question is clearly asked, the answer is also pretty clear. Considered from the point of view of physics, colors are not realities; they are illusions. Nor, read closely, does McDowell say otherwise. True, he says that colors are real, but, as he explains, he does not mean that colors satisfy the standard of reality that is in force in rigorous science; only that they satisfy the standard that is in force in daily discourse. But to say this is not to *refute* Harman and Mackie; it is to *agree* with them. Such is the ambiguity of McDowell's new realism.

Instead of taking this ambiguity as an objection, however, McDowell appears to regard it as an advantage, because it enables him to walk a middle path between extreme objectivism and extreme subjectivism, both of which he wisely deems implausible. In McDowell's view, old realist attempts to preserve the objectivity of value ended up implausibly denying that human preferences have anything to do with it.[14] By contrast, subjectivists go to the other extreme, making value to be nothing but a matter of individual preference, leaving it unexplained how someone can be mistaken about a thing's value. McDowell hopes to avoid both the Scylla of Platonic objectivism and the Charybdis of Protagorean subjectivism by acknowledging that value is relative to humanity while denying that it is determined by the opinions of individuals.

McDowell's comparison of value with color is an attempt to walk this verbal tightrope. Granting that things have color only in relation to the cones of human vision, McDowell says that this does not deprive color of "objectivity," because it does not rule out the possibility of making mistakes. You can still get a thing's color wrong, because the standard for correctness is not the color perceptions of arbitrarily chosen persons but the color perceptions of normal human beings. For normal perceivers, McDowell holds, there is no distinction between the real and the phenomenal. Here *esse* is *percipi*. Red is, by definition, the color that red things seem to normal perceivers to have. Believing that the objectivity of color is secured by this fact, McDowell hopes to preserve the objectivity of value, or goodness, in the same way—by making it relative to "normal" perceivers.

This argument also seeks to win the debate by reformulating the issue. It is again pertinent here to remember that, when Moore declared goodness to be an objective quality, he meant that it is independent of perceivers. Given this definition, only primary qualities are objective. To acknowledge that value, or goodness, is not a primary but a secondary quality is, then, not to defend Moore but to concede that he was wrong. The concession is merely concealed by using the old word "objective" in a new way.

"Normal" Perceivers

What is worse, this new usage is completely undefined. How are we to identify "normal" perceivers of value, and why should we accept their judgments as authoritative? McDowell never tells us.

In the case of color, we have a physiological test. Normal color perceivers are the ones with the usual contingent of cones. They can also be identified statistically, as the largest group whose color discriminations agree with each other. Furthermore, these discriminations have an objective physical correlate in the wave lengths of light to which color-sensitive persons respond, giving colorblind persons a reason to believe that other folks can see differences undetectable by them.

Nothing like this is true in the case of value. There is no known physical organ for perceiving the value of things, and if we counted heads, we would have to say that, because more people prefer Mick Jagger, he has greater musical value than Mozart—a proposition that we lovers of Mozart have no good reason to accept. Nor can the problem be solved by defining normal perceivers as those who appreciate the real value of things, as you and I appreciate Mozart. Since the original proposal was to determine the real value of things by consulting normal perceivers, this would merely take us in a circle, back to where we started. Not a way to run a railroad.

Falk's account of rectitude, as the power of some actions to elicit "natural" feelings of approval, is subject to similar criticism. Grant that Saudis approve of polygamy and Selmans do not. Which response is to count as more "natural," and why should it be made the test of moral correctness? Is the basis of "naturalness" to be biological? Then polygamy is morally superior to monogamy, because it is in better accord with the biologically based impulse of males to mate with as many females as they can and with the biologically based impulse of females to acquiesce to the wishes of dominant males. Although it is favored by some socio-biologists, the argument is less than compelling.[15] Why should biological impulses, however natural, be regarded as *morally* authoritative when we know that much morality has as its purpose to curb and control these impulses? Falk conveniently leaves this difficult question for others to ponder, but his proposal is empty unless the question has an answer.

McDowell does not help either his case or Falk's when he makes a point of comparing value to such qualities as being amusing, irritating, and disgusting—qualities once described by George Santayana as not secondary but *tertiary* qualities, because our only indication of their reality is their effect on perceivers. Things count as amusing, irritating, or disgusting not because *they* are alike but because they have similar effects on *us*. If it amuses, irritates, or disgusts, us, then it is amusing, irritating, or disgusting; there is no independent test of the matter, by means of which that which amuses, irritates, or disgusts might be discovered not to be amusing, irritating, or disgusting.

Acknowledging that this is a common view, McDowell thinks that he can refute it, by noting that someone might say "That isn't funny" about something that has made us laugh. He seems to think that the possibility of correcting someone in this way proves the necessity of admitting the reality of a quality of being funny, which things either have or lack, as they have or lack square shape. But a different analysis is suggested by the way in which we correct misapprehensions: "I did not laugh because it *amused* me; I laughed because it *embarrassed* me." Where there is no mistaking the explanation of our laughter, we always have available to us the reply, "Well, it may not be funny *to you*, but it certainly amuses *me*," which seems quite irrefutable. True, one can always be rebuked by the remark that one should not be amused by such things, but this will be criticism of our *laughter*, not our *judgment*. If we were amused, it remains true that the thing was amusing, at least to us on that occasion. That it should not have amused us will in no way alter that fact.

If there were some independent test of what is funny, this would not be so; but there isn't. And there is no independent test of goodness or rectitude. These "qualities" are also discoverable only from their effects on persons.

Goodness and Rectitude as not Qualities but Powers

The explanation of this fact is simple and obvious: These "qualities" *are* their effects on persons—or, more accurately, they are the capacities to have these effects on persons. Though real, goodness and rectitude are not *qualities* but *powers*. As I have explained at length in a preceding chapter, goodness is the power to reinforce preference; rectitude is the power to reinforce its reinforcement. In other words, goodness is the power to strengthen desire; rectitude the power to elicit approval. The good is what I want again; the right is what other people want me to do again.

If McDowell and Falk resist recognizing this truth, it is for the same reason that other moral realists resist it. They are aware that powers such as these are not absolute or "objective" but relative to individuals and to circumstances. Thus, the taste of licorice has the power to reinforce you but not me, and it has the power to reinforce you on only some occasions, not also on others. In short, the goodness of licorice depends on taste: You like it; I do not. Similarly, polygamy has the power to elicit disapproval in Alabama but not in Arabia, where it is tolerated, making its rectitude to be not absolute but relative to custom, which varies with time and place. Very misleading is the apparent simplicity of the question whether an act is permissible or not. The right question is more complicated—namely, whether the act is permissible for persons P in location L at time T under circumstances C.

Contrary to the beliefs of some critics, this does not mean that there are no "universal values."[16] Some things—for example, food and sex—have value for practically everybody everywhere. However, there are also things—for example, a lock of my true love's hair—that have value only for particular persons at particular times. So, despite appearances, the logical form of evaluation is not "x is F" but " x is F to y in circumstances z" In this respect "x is good" is comparable not to "x is square" or to "x is yellow" but to "x is irritating," which is short for "There is some y such that x has the power to irritate y." That some irritants are universal means merely that the x in question has the power to irritate *every* y. In other words, it means "For every y, x irritates y."

Something similar is true of morality, the measure of which is social approval. Grant that there are cultural universals —for example, prohibition of incest[17] and a sense of fair play.[18] The fact remains: Practices that are prohibited in A may be permitted in B, indicating that the seemingly absolute statement "x is permissible" is elliptical for the relational statement "There is a society y in which x is permitted." That there are cultural universals just means that some practices are permitted in *every* society.

In short, the logic of value and the logic of morality are relational.

Railton's Naturalistic Moral Realism

Half of this, if not all of it, has been recognized by Peter Railton, a self-proclaimed moral realist who says that there are objective moral *truths* if not also objective moral *qualities*.

This distinction will puzzle most moral realists. Because the existence of "objective" truths is wrongly thought to presuppose the reality of "objective" qualities, it is often taken for granted that these are the same things. But although "My wife is nearby and beloved" is an objective truth, it would be a mistake to think that it is so because she possesses the qualities *nearbyness* and *belovedness*. Railton avoids this kind of mistake.[19] Like others who describe themselves as moral realists, he sees the issue as a question about "objectivity," but he realizes that objectivity does not require objective *qualities*, only objective *facts*—truths that are independent of thought (p. 142).

Railton also doubts that objectivity entails transcendence, getting away from the empirically known facts. He is a naturalistic moral realist, who wisely proposes to keep his feet on the ground. Commendably dividing the question, Railton begins with *value* before taking up *morality*. In the case of value, he says that the necessary objectivity can be secured in more or less naturalistic fashion by idealizing an individual's "subjective" interests and beliefs. Consider person A, who has interests I and beliefs B. Given that some of his interests and beliefs will be misguided, A can be mistaken about what has value, even *for him*. We, however, can imagine a counterpart to A, namely A+, who has a more perfect knowledge of both his interests and the means to serve them.

In Railton's view, the judgments of this idealized A+ can provide a standard of truth about what A "would want himself to seek if he knew what he were doing" (p. 143). That this would be a standard for A alone does not, in Railton's view, diminish its "objectivity," which is preserved by the possibility of making and subsequently correcting mistakes about what is in A's interests (p. 146). That this standard would also depend on idealization does not, Railton thinks, distinguish moral philosophy from physical science, which frequently makes use of idealizations—for example, "perfect vacuums" or "friction free surfaces."

Whether this provides the much desired "objectivity" could be debated, but it is an interesting and insightful idea, which captures many of the features of common-sense deliberation about what an individual ought to do in order to behave in a way that she will find to be reinforcing. To give such an agent advice that we can expect to influence her conduct, we begin either by assuming that, as a person of a given type, she is likely to have certain interests and beliefs or, in the more favorable situation, by trying to discover her actual interests and beliefs as these are revealed in her past and present behavior. That done, we can then undertake to improve the resulting picture in ways that the agent would regard as acceptable if she were more fully rational. To resolve conflicts between interests, we can attach greater weight to some than to others, and to enhance the chances of success we can add new information and subtract old misinformation.

Railton realizes that, if it is to remain relevant, the new and improved picture must not depart too far from the agent's actual interests and beliefs, but to serve as a basis for good advice, it must also go beyond them to accommodate likely projections and modifications of these interests and beliefs into the future. This requires a tricky balancing act the success of which can never be assured in advance. That there is no guarantee of success does not, however, mean that there are no means and methods for correcting mistakes after we see how things have gone wrong.[20] These are all important insights, for which Railton deserves much credit.

Given that morality has to do with relations between individuals in social groupings, you might expect a self-proclaimed naturalist to propose a parallel idealization regarding it. The general idea would be to start with observations of the practices, verbal and non-verbal, of various members of some group; then abstract from these the norms and ideals that are implicit in them, insofar as these norms are deemed to be consistent and workable. Individuals within the group would then be advised to behave in accordance with these norms, in order to bring their conduct into maximum conformity with the wishes of other members of the group.

Since the practices of different persons in the group may be in conflict with each other, the task of discovering the group's norms will not be purely descriptive; it will also assign norms different weight, in order to secure greater coherence. It might also try to predict changes in norms that can be expected to result from new information—all in all, a tricky business that can go wrong in many ways and yields, at best, only an idea of what is morally acceptable *in a given society*; not knowledge of what is moral or immoral absolutely. Such would be the naturalistic approach to morality.

Unfortunately, Railton does not take this naturalistic line when he comes to morality. Instead of trying to advise individuals on how they are to discover what obligations they actually have as members of their societies, he undertakes to tell them how they ought to act as human beings among indefinitely many other human beings in a highly idealized world in which every person takes into account not only how she can serve her idealized interests but also how she can accommodate the idealized interests of *all* other persons who might conceivably be affected. According to Railton, the morally right thing to do will then be what "would be rationally approved of were the interests of all potentially affected individuals counted equally under circumstances of full and vivid information"(p. 150).

This proposal is hard to appraise, first because it is vague, second because it detaches moral deliberation from empirically determinate circumstances, a thing no real naturalist would ever do. We can have *some* idea how to serve our foreseeable interests in ways that comport with our obligations as members of a society. We can have *no* idea how to aggregate the idealized interests and beliefs of all persons who might conceivably be affected. Does Railton have a magic formula—a hedonic calculus—to use in making the necessary computations? Or is the thing to be done by political means—say, by democratic procedures? Railton gives us not a clue.

The problem is not with using idealizations; it is with using idealizations that are both ill-defined and lack determinate relation to realities. Railton expresses hope that his proposal will enable us to understand "how moral values and judgments might be 'objective' without being cosmic or absolute." He also says that it supposes "nothing more transcendental than facts about man and his environment, facts about what sorts of things matter to us, and how the ways we live affect these things" (p. 155). In fact, Railton's insistence that equal weight be given to the interests of all conceivably affected parties invites us to take up not the point of view of an actual individual with definite interests and limited knowledge but the point of view of an omniscient and impartial deity—which is as "cosmic and absolute," so other-worldly and useless, as any ideal gets.

Does Railton achieve the "objectivity" he seeks. Who can tell? This honorific concept, which was never very clear, has now lost all meaning.[21]

Objectivity versus Absoluteness

The solution to the puzzle is to recognize that defending the "objectivity" of goodness and rectitude does not require denying its relativity. Licorice really does taste good, but only to some persons on some occasions; not also to others, or on other occasions. Polygamy really is permissible, but only in some countries at certain times, not also in others, or at other times. Once stated, this truism is so obvious that it is a mystery why some philosophers insist on denying it.

A very real possibility is that they fear the breakdown of social order and the resurgence of barbarism once it is admitted that the rules of morality are not eternally engraved on tablets of stone handed down from an omniscient and benevolent Dictator. The emotional tone of many conservative animadversions against "moral relativism" can be explained only on this belief. To such criticism, only two responses are possible here. One is that we are touting moral relativism—more exactly, conventionalism—not on moral but on factual grounds. The other is that, if moralities are human constructs, knowledge of the fact should enable us to do a better job of constructing them and provide a more realistic basis for complying with them when compliance is rational. Granting that moral norms are neither divine commands nor principles of *a priori* reason but products of contingent circumstances, historical accident, arbitrary choice, and ignorance should enable us to think more clearly about how to improve them.

That having been said, let us return to the error of logic that is embodied in absolutist objections to relativism. They are mostly based on failure to distinguish *relativity* from *subjectivity.* Many philosophers—especially many who call themselves moral realists—are convinced that the one reduces in the end to the other. In their view, to say that goodness and rectitude are relative does not differ from saying that it is a matter not of fact but of opinion whether a thing is good or an action is right. In other words, the action is right or wrong according to whether you think so. Thus, suppose the relativist reports that (1) licorice tastes good to Smith but not to Jones and (2) polygamy is permissible in Saudi Arabia but not in Selma, Alabama. The absolutist will take him to mean (1)' "Smith thinks that licorice tastes good but Jones disagrees" and (2)'"Saudis think that polygamy is permissible, but Selmans do not." Convinced that the relativist cannot mean exactly what he says, the absolutist will suppose that he must mean something entirely different.[22]

The absolutist's error stems from his uncritical acceptance of the Platonic presumption that statements always attribute qualities. Therefore, when you say that x has value for A but not for B, he supposes you must mean that A believes and B doubts the proposition "x has value," the latter being the only form of proposition which he recognizes. Then he solemnly and rightly assures you that a difference in opinion is irrelevant to the facts of the matter, even when these are facts about value. Entranced by the truth of this observation, he never notices its irrelevancy. He makes the same mistake when he turns "Polygamy is permissible in Saudi Arabia, not in Selma, Alabama" into "Saudis think that polygamy is permissible; Selmans disagree." Plato can be excused for having made this mistake. He thought and wrote when there was no understanding of the logic of relations, which he found confusing. The same excuse is not available to our contemporaries, who really ought to know better. Multivariate quantification theory, which includes the logic of relations, is now a well-developed branch of mathematics.

Not that it takes familiarity with mathematical logic to see the error we are discussing. A simple example will make it clear. Suppose someone were to point out that the Eiffel Tower is near Jacques in Paris but far from Jack in New York. Confusing objectivity with absoluteness, the *location realist* would take this to mean "Jacques thinks that the Eiffel Tower has the property, or quality, of being nearby; Jack disagrees." The typical moral realist makes a similar mistake about goodness and rectitude. Mistakenly supposing that relativity entails subjectivity, he seeks to avoid the latter by denying the former.

Summary

We have learned several things from our limited sample of moral realist thought. One is that talk of *properties* is so obscure as to be otiose. It explains nothing to say that a thing is good *because it has the property of being good.* In fact, such claims are meaningless if good things are defined only as things having the property of being good.

Meaning attaches to talk of *qualities* when these are defined as ways in which things are discernibly alike, but we have no good reason to believe that there is any distinctive way in which all good things, or all right actions, resemble each other. Therefore, we have no good reason to believe that there are such qualities as goodness and rectitude. Moral Realists often suppose that our ability to distinguish good things from bad ones, or right actions from wrong ones, is itself sufficient basis on which to claim that similarity is the basis of the discrimination, but this overlooks the need for an independent test. In the absence of such a test, claims to "objectivity"—independence of persons—become highly doubtful. They are on a level with explanations invoking soporific virtues.

Such explanations have some utility if the soporific virtues in question are construed as not qualities but *powers*. Thus, opium does put people to sleep because it has the power to do so, and jokes make people laugh because they have the power to do so. To take advantage of this insight, however, what must also be recognized is that the relevant powers, though "objective," are not absolute but relative, both to human beings and to circumstances. Contrary to realist belief and superficial grammatical appearance, "x is funny" does not have the simple logical form of "x is square" or "x is yellow"; it has the complex logical form "x has the power to amuse y in circumstances c."

Moral realist belief in such qualities as goodness and rectitude is the result of failing to see that these supposedly simple qualities have the forms of complex relations. "Thing x is good" has the form "Thing x has the power to reinforce person y in circumstances c" and "Action x is morally right" has the form "In society s at time t under circumstances c, action x has the power to reinforce acts of reinforcing x by persons p." Once we realize these facts of logic, most of the pseudo-puzzles that have perplexed moral philosophers since Plato will evaporate in thin air. What is left will be only the very real questions "How, given one's circumstances and the norms of one's society, ought one to behave?"

Notes

1. In the high Middle Ages, a realist (from the Latin *res* for *things*) was someone who believed in abstract universals, the reality of which was denied by nominalists and conceptualists.
2. Plato had this view because he thought that *all* properties, including relations, are primary qualities. A person was tall if he participated in *tallness*. So, Plato could not understand how B might be taller than A but shorter than C. For how could B participate in both tallness and shortness at one and the same time? An insoluble problem arising from a false presumption.
3. See G. E. Moore, *Principia Ethica* (Cambridge: Cambridge University Press, 1962) and W. D. Ross, *The Right and the Good* (London: Oxford University Press, 1930).

4. Ross confusingly but consistently used the word *intrinsic* not only as an opposite to *instrumental* but also as an opposite to *extrinsic*, or *relational*. Thus, the value of pleasure was said to be intrinsic not just in the sense that pleasure is prized for its own sake but also in the sense that it is *inherent in* pleasure, as one of its attributes, whatever that piece of Platonic gobbledygook might mean.
5. Ross, op. cit. p. 69. Actually, Ross is here talking about the related but different quality of being *morally good,* but he is trying to define the sense in which this quality too is *intrinsic*. Notice that the word *intrinsic* is here used not just in its ethical sense as the opposite of *instrumental*, but also in its metaphysical sense as the opposite of *extrinsic* or *relational*. Ross and Moore never noticed the distinction.
6. This claim—that goodness and rectitude are as directly and easily discerned as color —will seem less astonishing when you notice that Moore and Ross end up insisting that these qualities belong not to *things* and *actions* but only to *states of mind*. Thus, Moore held in the final analysis that goodness is exclusively a property of such states of mind as refined *pleasure*, and Ross said that rectitude is exclusively a quality of honorable *intentions*. What is good is not the butter pecan ice cream, but the pleasure you get from eating it. What is right is not your act of charity but your intention to help your fellow man. According to the Cartesian epistemology which Moore and Ross both accepted quite uncritically, the qualities of one's own states of mind are knowable immediately and infallibly, by introspection. So, one can know intuitively—that is, directly and infallibly—that one's pleasure is good and one's intention is honorable, but one can have no such intuitive knowledge of the physical thing or act. This means that Moore and Ross end up being as skeptical as Hume about the possibility of knowing what they set out to explain—namely, the goodness of things and the rectitude of actions themselves. Such knowledged precluded for them, as it was for Kant, by the impossibility of having intuitive knowledge of the physical world, the existence of which was acknowledge to be was not self-evident and irrefutable but fallibly inferred as the unobserved cause of our introspected states of mind. Significantly, neither Moore nor Ross ever undertook to make clear how there could be a state of mind without somebody to have it. That this makes incoherent their account of the "objectivity" of goodness and rectitude was very conveniently ignored, as it has also been ignored by commentators.
7. The light rays that cause the perception of color can, of course, be detected by means of suitable instruments, but wave lengths of light do not correlate exactly with color differences. It is apparently the combinations of cones stimulated that explain color distinctions. See the article on color in R. L. Gregory, editor, *The Oxford Companion to the Mind* (Oxford: Oxford University Press, 1987).
8. See Gilbert Harman, *The Nature of Morality* (New York: Oxford University Press, 1977) and David Mackie, *Ethics: Inventing Right and Wrong* (Harmondsworth: Penguin, 1977).
9. See David Brink, *Moral Realism and the Foundations of Ethics* (Cambridge: Cambridge University Press, 1989)
10. McDowell, "Values and Secondary Qualities," and "Projection and Truth in Ethics," reprinted in Stephen Darwall, Allan Gibbard, and Peter Railton, editors, *Moral Discourse and Practice* (New York: Oxford University Press, 1997) 201-226.
11. The morally right also includes the permissible and the praiseworthy.
12. W. D. Falk, *Ought, Reasons and Morality* (Ithaca, NY: Cornell University Press, 1986).

13. Specifically, it depends on how the ambient light affects the three light sensitive cones of the retina. Each of these cones responds to light from a different region of the spectrum, and the color seen is the result of a summation or mix of the three.
14. This claim was made all the more paradoxical by Moore's further insistence, and Ross's agreement, that only states of consciousness have intrinsic value. How can there be a state of mind without somebody to have it? And how could it have value without somebody to prize it?
15. See Robert Wright, *The Moral Animal.* (New York: Vintage Books, 1995).
16. Belief to the contrary has been encouraged by Kant's confusion of "objective truth," meaning fact, with "universal validity," meaning what everybody believes. We can see a relic of this idea in McDowell's and Falk's ill-considered notion that the objective is what accords with the perceptions of normal persons, who are in the majority.
17. See E. O. Wilson, *Consilience: The Unity of Knowledge* (New York: Alfred A. Knopf, 1998)
18. See James Q. Wilson, *The Moral Sense* (New York: Macmillan, 1993).
19. See Peter Railton, "Moral Realism" in Darwall, Gibbard and Railton, pp 137-163.
20. Here, I suspect, we see the influence of Charles Peirce's idea that truth is the ideal result of indefinitely prolonged inquiry using methods that are self-correcting. This is the wrong view of *truth*, but it is not a bad view of *knowledge*.
21. The term *objective* has had an interesting, and confusing, history. When Descartes said that something has "objective reality," he meant only that it is an object of thought. In this way of speaking, the pink rats hallucinated in *delirium tremens* have "objective" if not "formal" reality. Later on, thinking of "subjective" reality and truth as reality and truth according to the thinking subject, Kant equated "objective truth" with "universal validity," that which everybody believes. In this way of speaking, "The earth is flat" was objectively true when everyone believed it but is "objectively false" now, although no geological cataclysm has taken place. This Kantian idea is manifest in the kind of moral philosophy exemplified by Thomas Nagel, in which the "objective" is the impersonal. After Kant, Hegel further confused the topic by arguing that, since *objective* and *subjective* are correlatives, you cannot have one without the other. So, even subjectivity has objectivity in it, and conversely. This has encouraged belief that every belief, however wrongheaded, has a measure of objective truth. The moral of the story is that when philosophers start talking about "objectivity," you would be well advised to grab your wallet.
22. Examples are endless. We have cited some in previous chapters.

12

The Myth of the Moral Law

Two Views of Rules

Different societies have different rules, and it is these that determine, in a society, what counts as legal, moral, or mannerly.[1] So, conduct that is legal, moral, or mannerly in society S1 may be illegal, immoral, and ill-mannered in S2, where the rules are different. Thus, having several wives is legal, moral, and mannerly in Saudi Arabia; illegal, immoral, and ill-mannered in Selma, Alabama.[2] Furthermore, conduct that is legal, moral, and mannerly at time T1 may be illegal, immoral, and ill-mannered at different time T2, because the rules have changed. Thus, semi-nudity is legally and morally acceptable, if not always good manners, in twentieth-century America; but it was contrary to law and morality, and it would have been unthinkable in polite society, in colonial times. In this sense, legal and moral relativity is a plain, and well-verified, fact of the matter.

Few people dispute this fact of the matter, but moral absolutists are anxious to add to it, qualify it, and reinterpret it. In their view, man-made rules of law, morality, and etiquette are not the only rules of law, morality, and etiquette there are. Nor are they even the most important. Absolutists believe that, over and above these, there are also some changeless and universally binding rules—a *Moral Law*—to which local and variable rules are subordinate, somewhat as the laws of the various states are subordinate to the Constitution of the United States. If absolutists are right, it is the Moral Law, not local custom and convention that determines what, in the final analysis, should count as legal, moral, or mannerly. Local and contemporary practice is decisive only on the condition that it is consistent with the universal and eternal standard. Or so absolutists believe.

What follows is an argument against this belief. The gist of the argument is that if there exists a universally binding Moral Law, it must exist and be binding *in essentially the same sense of these words* as local laws and moralities. Local laws and moralities, our empirical paradigms, *exist* in the sense that behavior comports with them, and they are *binding* in the sense that conformity with them is *required.* But although we have clear evidence that members of different societies comply with and enforce different rules of law, morality, and etiquette we have no good evidence that people everywhere comply with, or require compliance with, a single uniform Moral Law.

Absolutists try to get around this by saying that the Moral Law determines what *ought* to be done, not what *is* done; so, actual practices are irrelevant. But this usage detaches the legal and moral vocabulary from the empirically discernible practices that give it objective meaning, with the result that it becomes entirely subjective, emotional, and arbitrary. The present chapter is an attempt to recover the objectively determinate, but culturally relative, meaning of moral discourse.

How Rules Exist

What, then, does it mean to say that a rule *exists*? To see, let us look at an example. Although our interest here is in rules of law, morality, and etiquette, our example need not itself be such a rule. In fact, since rules of law, morality, and etiquette not only exist but are also binding, it will be better if we find a rule that exists but is not binding; and, for this, we may use not a rule of law, morality, or etiquette but a rule, or law, of *nature*—for example, the rule, "If food is available, eat when hungry!" This rule exists; many people have it. So do most animals. What does it mean to say so?

One thing it clearly does *not* mean is: The rule has been formulated in words; those who have it are conscious of it. Not so. Because rules can be stated, we are liable to confuse them with their statement, but this is a mistake. Most animals have the rule, "Eat when hungry," but we may not presume that they could state it in so many words, or that they are conscious of it. That the rule exists does not mean that it has been formulated, or even that it has been thought of. It means only that the rule is complied with; behavior conforms to it. Thus, that a dog has the rule "Eat when hungry!" means that the dog eats when hungry; doing so is its tendency, disposition, habit, practice, or custom.[3]

It will be replied that there is a use of the word *exist* in which there exist rules with which nobody complies, somewhat as there exist shapes—for example, million-sided polygons—of which there are no examples. These rules may be said to exist "in the mind," if not also in reality. The trouble with this is that what exists only "in the mind" does not in any substantive sense *exist.* Existing "only in the mind" is not a way of existing; it is a way of *not* existing. Hence, we say "It exists only in his mind" when we want to *deny,* not *affirm*, that the thing exists. Only what exists "in reality" truly exists. Thus, unicorns exist "in the mind" and "in literature"; for they have been described, imagined, thought of, and written about. But unicorns do not exist in reality; so they do not exist. Neither do rules that are nowhere embodied in practice. For a rule to exist, it must be complied with; there must be conduct in accordance with it.

How Rules are Binding

For a rule to be in the relevant sense *binding* somewhat more is needed. In that case, the rule must not just exist; it must also be *socially instituted and enforced*; conformity to it must be *required of some persons by others.* In short, it must be the sort of rule that we call a *regulation.*

All rules exist because conduct that complies with them is either reinforcing or reinforced. Hence, B.F. Skinner once observed that a rule exists in the contingencies that reinforce it—in other words, the circumstances that maintain compliance with it. Some rules—for example, "Eat when hungry"—are naturally reinforcing. Relief from hunger keeps these rules alive. By contrast, other rules—for example, "Eat only three times a day"—need artificial support. Social convention keeps these rules alive. When the convention is buttressed by punishing people who violate it, compliance has been made a socially enforceable *requirement*, or *obligation.* When that happens, we may say that the rule exists because conformity to it is *binding.*

Rules of law, morality, and etiquette are all in this sense binding; their being so is what distinguishes them from other rules, such as laws of nature, or rules of prudence. Compliance with socially imposed rules is not *optional* but *obligatory*: You can be *compelled* to comply with these rules, even if you do not wish to do so. Thus, compare the wearing of hats to protect yourself from the sun to the wearing of hats as a sign of modesty or social decorum. The first practice is optional; it exists because people want to avoid sunburn. The second is obligatory; it exists as a requirement of good standing in the social order.

In this case, the requirement is an obligation of etiquette. In other cases, it might be an obligation of morality, or law. Which it is depends on whether the requirement is official or unofficial. Rules of law strictly so-called are *official* rules—rules made by officials acting in their capacities as officials. The requirements imposed by these rules are therefore also official. Rules of morality and etiquette are *unofficial* rules—rules made by ordinary persons in the course of their daily affairs and interactions with each other; and the requirements imposed by these rules are also unofficial. To call a rule or requirement unofficial is not to denigrate it. The unofficial requirements of etiquette and morality are just as real as, and may be even more binding than, the official requirements of law.

As before, there is no need for verbal formulation. Imagine that a prominent person in the community wears a hat on a solemn occasion. Soon somebody will imitate her conduct; then somebody else. After awhile, the practice will become so common that those who do not wear hats on such occasions will begin to feel odd. Eventually any who are so indifferent to fashion or so careless as to go hatless will be frowned on, perhaps even ostracized from polite company. If so, a rule of etiquette will have come into being, perhaps before anyone has become sufficiently conscious of the fact to state it. This rule will become a rule of morality when those who go hatless are regarded as not merely gauche or awkward but also insensitive and wicked. It will become a rule of law when the police start arresting and the courts start jailing or fining people who have forgotten their hats. Formulation of the rule need neither precede nor accompany any of these events.

Many people will acknowledge that rules of morality and etiquette need no formulation, but lack of verbal articulation is sometimes taken to be evidence that there is no rule of law. This is a mistake. What scholars call customary law, which is still the basic law of most societies, consists not of explicitly formulated rules but of unstated rules that are implicit in precedent and customary practice. Where there is explicit statement, it is usually a late development, which follows, summarizes, and justifies the rules that are implicit in practice. Thus, arrests of the hatless will not always follow the command to wear hats. Instead, the command to wear hats will often follow arrests of the hatless—when courts try to justify the arrests by announcing that hats must be worn on solemn occasions.

Not only is proclamation not necessary; it is also not sufficient. Law has often been equated with statute, executive orders and the like. In short, it has been equated with verbal commands; but law is not command, it is obedience. Let some official or legislature command, "Everyone will drive under 60 mph!" By itself, this will not suffice to make law. If such a command is to become law, it will have to be obeyed; and if it is to be obeyed, it will have to be enforced. Thus, the speed limit that is posted on the highways is not the real limit. The real limit is the one that drivers may not exceed without risking warning, fine, or jail. In other words, it is the limit that drivers are *bound*—that is, *obligated,* or *required*—to obey.

The same is true of rules of morality and etiquette. Although honesty in business is desirable even when it is not obligatory, there exists a rule making honesty obligatory only where honesty is required of businessmen by those who trade with them, go to church with them, marry them, and so on.

We may say, then, that a rule R of law, morality, or etiquette *exists* in community C and *is binding* on persons P at time T just in case conduct in accordance with R is *required* of P, or is *obligatory*, for P, in C at T; and we may say that conduct in accordance with R is required, or obligatory, in C just in case there exists in C a practice of enforcing, or reinforcing, compliance with R. Less formally, you have a binding rule—a regulation—where, and only where, people are required to, and do, conform their conduct to the rule in order to avoid condemnation or punishment or to secure praise or reward.

This may, of course, not be what most people have in mind, or intend, when they speak of obligation; but it is the empirically determinate condition for counting their statements as true, and our concern here is to preserve not meaning but truth value.

The Nonexistence of Divine Law

If we have been right so far, our original question—*Is there a Moral Law?*—can now be rephrased as follows: *Are there any rules that human beings everywhere comply with because compliance with them is everywhere required by other persons?* If the answer to this question is Yes, then a culturally transcendent and universally binding Moral Law may be said to exist; otherwise not.

It will be objected that thus construing the issue misunderstands it, in at least two ways. First, when absolutists assert the existence of the Moral Law, they do not mean that some rules are *in fact* everywhere enforced and complied with; they mean that some rules *ought to be* everywhere enforced and complied with. Second, in saying that compliance is required, absolutists do not mean that compliance is required *by other people;* they mean that it is required *by God, Nature, or Reason.* We shall now show that this objection is incoherent if taken literally.

Begin with the second claim—that the Moral Law consists of requirements by God, Nature, or Reason. The trouble with this is obvious: Reason and Nature are not persons; so they cannot make literal requirements. It is only in the case of God, who is generally regarded as a person, that one can speak literally of requirements.

Consider, then, the claim of the theological absolutist—that there is a Moral Law that ought to be everywhere obeyed *because obedience to it is everywhere a divinely imposed requirement, or obligation.* For the sake of the discussion, ignore the inconvenient fact that there is no proof for the existence of God. Grant that God exists. Grant, too, that God has issued some commands that He wants all human beings everywhere to obey. Grant, even, that people everywhere *ought* to obey these commands.

Having granted all of that, we may still reasonably doubt whether God has everywhere made obedience to His will a requirement, or obligation. Here is why: As J.L. Austin would have said, *require* is a success word; and so is *obligate.* You can *command* people to do what they nevertheless fail, or refuse, to do; but if you require, or obligate, them to do it, then they must in fact do it. Therefore, it is incoherent to suppose that people are everywhere required, or obligated, to behave in a certain way but do not in fact do so. Saying this takes away with one hand what it gives with the other. If the thing is required everywhere, it is done everywhere. If the practice is obligatory everywhere, it is observed everywhere.

Don't people sometimes neglect, or refuse, to fulfill their obligations? Yes, certainly. For example, people sometimes fail to pay their taxes. This does not prove that they lack the obligation to do so. No, but if people are obligated to pay their taxes, failure to pay them cannot be the rule; it must be the exception. In the absence of regular compliance, we might be justified in saying that payment of taxes had been commanded, but we could no longer justify saying that it had been required, or made obligatory. In the absence of compulsion to pay taxes, it means little to say that paying taxes is an obligation, something one is required to do, whether or not one wishes to do it.

If this reasoning is right, it is meaningless to say that payment of taxes is required when the "requirement" is not enforced with sufficient effectiveness or reliability to effect more or less regular compliance. The truth is, rather, that the strength of the requirement is measured by the effectiveness of the enforcement, which is measured by the degree of the compliance that it effects. So the greater the obligation, the greater the compliance. Although compliance may certainly be obligatory without being inevitable, it becomes obligatory only to the degree to which enforcement suffices to make it regular. As its etymology indicates, an obligation is a metaphorical bond; but "bonds" that do not bind are not bonds.

This is as true of the commands of God as it is the commands of men. We have no obligation to obey the commands of *any* person, earthly or divine, who lacks the power of enforcement or the will to exercise it. Let God issue commands all day long, in as loud a voice as you please. In that case, God may be said to have "given voice" to His will. If, however, He has not begun to *enforce* His will, He has not yet created any obligation to comply with it. But God has not begun to enforce His will unless people have begun to comply with it. So, if God's commands are not everywhere observed in practice, they are not everywhere in force. And if they are not everywhere in force, it is not true that people are everywhere obligated to comply with them. That statement may seem counterintuitive, but it is the merest tautology.

Shouldn't we obey God's Holy Will just because it is holy, not because it is backed up by force? And is it not true that people often neglect to do what they ought to do? Yes, but the question at issue here is not what we *ought* to do; it is what we are *obligated* to do—a very different thing. Although it is certainly true that one ought to do God's will because it is holy, to say so is to say only that obedience to the divine will is *fitting*, not that it is *obligatory*. Furthermore, obedience is not obligatory unless the threat of divine punishment makes it so. But if obedience is in this sense obligatory, then obedience exists. So, there is still no sense in the idea that obedience to God's will is everywhere obligatory but not everywhere in evidence.

What follows? That it is an empirical question whether the Divine Law exists, just as it is an empirical question whether Turkish law exists. If, per hypothesis, God has imposed the same Law on all men everywhere, then there must everywhere be evidence of this fact in their conduct. If the Divine Law is everywhere enforced, we may expect that men will everywhere demonstrate its reality by obeying it, most of all when they prefer to do otherwise. But observations of human behavior lend no credence to the theory that men everywhere obey the same divinely instituted law, morality, or etiquette. Instead, as noted in the beginning, the evidence comports better with the contrary hypothesis—that human beings in different societies obey not the same but different laws.

The Metaphorical Character of Laws of Nature

Different remarks apply to the doctrine of Natural Law. This doctrine was planted in ancient Rome by Stoics and cultivated in Paris by Christian thinkers of the middle ages before being pulled up by its theological roots in Germany and Britain during the eighteenth century, when philosophers started talking of Reason and Nature instead of God.[4] The new idea differs from the old, however, only in terminology, not also in substance. So, it is vulnerable to the very same objection: It detaches the word *obligation* from the empirically determinate practices that give it meaning; and this threatens to make of the word largely an arbitrary expression of indeterminate emotion.

The problem, we should say at the outset, is not that there are no culturally transcendent and universally observed rules, or laws, of Nature, or Reason. On the contrary, there are many such rules. An example is the rule mentioned earlier, viz., "If food is available, eat when hungry." This "law of nature" is "obeyed" everywhere, not just by human beings but also by dogs, centipedes, chickadees, and other animals. The problem is that this so-called law of nature is not in any literal sense *law*, and "obedience" to it is not in any literal sense *obedience.*

Talk of obedience to natural law is a dead metaphor, one left over from ancient belief that the patterns of behavior which we can discern in nature are responses to divinely instituted commands. The defects of this theological mode of thought become obvious when you try to take it literally. Gravity is a "law of nature," but try to take literally the idea that falling stones are "obeying" the "law" of gravity, perhaps out of fear that God will punish them if they do not. Everybody in the twentieth century will agree that this once popular idea is ludicrous, but it is only slightly less so than the analogous but still popular idea that hungry animals eat in literal obedience to a law laid down for them by God or Mother Nature.

As empiricist philosophers have long insisted, this way of thinking confuses *regularities* with *regulations.* The so-called laws of nature are not regulations, just regularities. The natural behavior of stones and centipedes does not obey these so-called laws; it manifests, illustrates, or exemplifies them. But if laws of nature are not in the literal sense laws, then it is not in any literal sense true that human beings or dogs, much less stones, are obligated to obey them. What is true is merely that we, and dogs, and stones are disposed by our natures to behave in accordance with them.

Believers in the doctrine of Natural Law have obscured this important distinction by talking as though stones were compelled to fall by Gravity and hungry animals were compelled to eat by their Hunger—somewhat as a dirty child is compelled to wash by its mother, often against its will. As Hobbes and Hume pointed out, this confuses causation with compulsion—causation by means of threats. The difference is roughly this: Causes can be impersonal; threats, which are symbolic gestures, cannot. But gravity and hunger are not persons. So, although they can cause, they cannot literally compel, anything or anybody to do anything.[5] Belief to the contrary requires taking metaphors literally and falling in with the crudest animism.

It will be replied that this misses the point—which is not that animals are compelled to eat by their hunger but only that, other things being equal, they ought to eat when hungry, because doing so is good. When phrased in this way, the doctrine of Natural Law is, of course, entirely unobjectionable. Indeed, it embodies a profound truth: Other things being equal, an animal ought to do what is natural. Thus, other things being equal, a hungry animal ought to eat; a tired animal ought to sleep; and so on.

Of course, other things might not be equal. Perhaps the animal is already too fat; or perhaps sleeping will put it in danger. In that case, it ought, all things considered, not to eat, or sleep; instead, it ought to fast, or flee. Still, as a general rule, animals—including human beings—ought to do what comes naturally. That is one reason why the ancient Greeks held that our conduct ought to accord with nature. The other reason was that our conduct ought to take account of, and be accommodated to, the facts of nature.

But to acknowledge that our conduct ought for these reasons to accord with nature is not by any means to say that acting according to nature is our obligation. It is just to say that failure, or refusal, to act in accordance with nature has its costs. Thus, failure to eat nourishing food results in hunger or ill health; failure to flee from harm results in injury; and so on. But while such circumstances can make eating or fleeing advisable, they cannot make it obligatory.

Only a socially imposed rule can do that. Let it be made a rule that I must eat, or sleep, or flee under certain circumstances, even if I have no natural inclination to do so. Then, and only then, may it be said that eating, sleeping, or fleeing has become an obligation. What we ought to do may, in the final analysis, be determined by nature; but, as the sophists of ancient Greece insisted, what we are obligated to do is determined by convention and custom.[6]

This important distinction has also been obscured by loose use of the word *punishment*. It is sometimes said that a person who is so foolish as to eat unhealthy foods will be punished by ill health. Taken as a metaphor, this way of talking is unobjectionable, but taking it literally confuses naturally occurring evil with socially imposed evil. A child who is spanked for eating too much candy has been punished. A child who gets sick from eating too much candy has merely suffered the natural consequences of its foolishness.

As this shows, not every form of harm or evil is punishment. Like threats, punishment requires another party, somebody, or something, with a will of its own. So, literal punishment exists only in a social context, and only when one person's unpleasant conduct causes another to respond in ways that are also unpleasant. Again, belief to the contrary is a relic of theological (i.e., metaphysical) modes of thought, or a consequence of taking metaphors literally.

The Metaphorical Character of Laws of Reason

Exactly analogous remarks must be made about the obligations, or requirements, supposedly imposed on us by Reason.

Literally speaking, there are none. Despite the Germanic practice of personifying her, Reason is not a person, so she cannot make requirements, impose obligations, or punish those who disobey her. It is certainly true that there are rules of reason and that these are independent of any particular society's conventions and customs. An example is the rule "If you prefer A to B and B to C, then, other things being equal, you should prefer A to C." Another is the rule, "Help those who are willing to help you." People everywhere comply with these rules. Their doing so is an indication not that they are members of a particular society but that they are rational beings, who try to do what serves their ends.

This fact has recently been obscured by claims that the meaning of the word *rational* varies with the society. This is false. Although conduct that is rational for one person in a given place and time may not be so for another person, or in another place and time, this is not because the meaning of the word *rational* has changed; it is because the persons in question have different ends, or must pursue them in different circumstances.

Grant, then, that there exist universally valid rules of reason. It still cannot be concluded that conformity to these rules exists because it is in any literal sense obligatory. Speaking metaphorically we may say that Reason requires conformity to her laws, but to take this way of talking literally is again to fall in with the crudest form of anthropomorphism.

It is true that the philosopher Immanuel Kant spoke in this misleading way when he talked of our duty to obey the commands of Pure Reason, but even Kant's authority cannot confer legitimacy on this way of talking if we are expected to take it literally. Although Kant invariably used a proper name in speaking of it, reason is not a person but a capacity. So, reason cannot literally command, much less obligate, anybody to do anything. Furthermore, people do not "obey" the "laws" of reason because they are required, or compelled, to do so; they do it because doing it serves their ends.

It follows that universal adherence to the "laws " of nature and reason provides no grounds whatsoever for belief in a Moral Law, a set of universally binding, because universally enforced, rules of behavior. Furthermore, such evidence as we have comports better with the simpler hypothesis—that universal compliance with the "laws of nature" exists because compliance is natural or rational even where it is *not* obligatory.

Cultural Universals and the Moral Law

We have been emphasizing that, if a case for the Moral Law is to be made out, there has to be a showing that compliance with some determinate set of rules exists everywhere because compliance is everywhere obligatory—a socially imposed requirement. In short, it has to be shown, by citing relevant empirical evidence, that some determinate rules of law, morality, or etiquette are *in force* everywhere.

Can this be shown? Some absolutists believe that it can, by documenting the existence of what are called *cultural universals*, rules that are essentially the same in all societies. Frequently cited as examples are such universals as prohibitions of incest, murder, rape, theft, and so on. Other universals are language, a sense of modesty, a sense of justice, pecking orders, patriarchy, and so on. According to some absolutists, the existence of these universals constitutes proof of the existence of a culturally transcendent and universally binding Moral Law.

In replying to this argument, we need not deny either that cultural universals exist or that they are important. Instead, we may freely admit both claims. Let us stipulate at the outset that people everywhere are obligated by law, morality, and etiquette to refrain from incest, murder, rape, and so on. Let us also stipulate that human beings everywhere have language, a sense of modesty, a sense of justice, a desire for status, differentiation of status by sex, and so on. In short, let us agree that all human societies institute many of the same rules. We may still doubt whether any rules exist that are, as we shall say for short, *in force* everywhere.

To see that the contradiction in this assertion is merely apparent, begin with an example: the universal enforcement of rules prohibiting murder. Every society has such rules; prohibitions of murder are universal; they exist everywhere. Furthermore, the fact is no accident; it is hard to see how a society could exist without prohibiting murder. If the members of a society could kill each other with impunity, it would soon cease to exist; it would disintegrate into a disunited mob. So, it seems clear that, if societies are to exist, they must prohibit murder. Therefore, all human societies do prohibit murder. Rules against murder are a cultural universal.

No matter. The universal existence of binding rules prohibiting murder does not suffice to guarantee the existence of a universally binding Rule prohibiting murder.[7] Furthermore, we have no reason to think that any such rule exists. On the contrary. Although indiscriminately killing other persons in one's own society is everywhere forbidden, indiscriminately killing people in other societies than one's own may be permitted, even required. So, although every society has a rule prohibiting murder, there is no Rule prohibiting murder in every society. Yet, the existence of such a Rule is just what the moral absolutist is eager to assert and must be prepared to prove.

The absolutist might think to get around this difficulty by holding that there is in force everywhere a universally applicable Rule of the form "Do not murder the members of your own society." In other words, he might attempt to treat the universal prohibition of murder as the enforcement everywhere of a single Rule with a universally quantified variable, one that relativizes applications of the rule to one's own society. Thus to represent the situation is, however, to misunderstand its logic. As just noted, each society's prohibition of murder concerns its own members; no rule in force in any society concerns, or has application to, the members of every society. In fact, in some societies—for example, head hunting societies—the rule is to kill members of other societies. So, although it can almost certainly be said that rules against murder are universal, it cannot be said that there is a universally binding Rule against murder. Furthermore, it seems clear that there is not.

If the distinction is still elusive, perhaps it will help to note that, in this respect, law and morality are very much like language. As noted earlier, language is a cultural universal: Every human society has language. From this fact, however, it does not follow that there is a universal Language, one that people in every society speak. Instead, the French speak French, the Chinese speak Chinese. Despite Noam Chomsky's claim to the contrary, there appears to be no Language that the French, the Chinese, and all other human beings speak. In short, language is universal, but there is no universal Language. Instead, all language is local, and so, it appears, are all law, morality, and etiquette.

Why There is No Universally Binding Moral Law

Once this purely logical point has been understood, the reason for it should be clear too. Laws and moralities belong to, and are applicable only in, the groups, communities, or societies, that create and enforce them.[8] Thus, Chinese law and morality binds Chinamen; Mexican law and morality binds Mexicans, and so on.

For there to be a single worldwide Morality or Law, there would have to be a single world-wide community with a single set of laws that binds everybody. In fact, we know that there is no such community. Instead, human beings can be divided into distinguishable, if not always distinct, groups, each with its distinctive customs, institutions, and rules. So, there is no worldwide community for the allegedly universal rules of the Moral Law to be the rules of, and, therefore, there is no universally binding Moral Law.

Why should the lack of a unified community matter? Because distinct societies could be governed by *similar* laws or moralities, but they could not have *the same* Law or morality. This is, again, a simple point of logic. To see it, imagine that there exists somewhere in the cosmos (say, on a planet of the star Sirius) a nation with a constitution exactly like that of the United States. It would make sense to say that this nation was governed by a constitution *just like* ours. It would not make sense to say that this nation was governed by *our* Constitution. No. Theirs would be theirs and ours would remain ours, even if theirs were a word-for-word copy of ours. Here as elsewhere talk of *sameness* is ambiguous. Qualitative sameness (i.e., similarity) of law or morality between distinct societies is real; numerical sameness (i.e., identity) is not.

This simple and obvious fact has a simple and obvious explanation: Rules, which are abstract entities, can exist (i.e., be instantiated) in many different places and times. So, you can have two societies with similar rules, as you can have two objects with similar shape. But, as we emphasized earlier, rules considered as abstract entities do not exist —no more than do shapes. What exist are the concrete embodiments of these rules in the practices of various human beings.

As we have also been at pains to emphasize, however, to say that a binding rule (i.e., a rule of law, morality or etiquette) exists means two things. First, it means that the members of some society make it their practice to conform their conduct to the rule. Second, it means that they do so because they are required to do so by other members of the society. But this means that they must be members of *one and the same society*; they must belong to a single *community*. Otherwise, they would not be able to influence each other's behavior in the way that is required. Failure to see this is the product of thinking in too abstract a way about rules; it comes from failure to see that a rule is just an abstraction from a practice.

If this is right, membership in the same community is an essential condition of being governed by the same rule; similarity of rule in separate and disconnected communities will not do. People in separate, distinct, and unrelated communities do not influence each other to behave in accordance with a common rule. So, the well-documented existence of social disunity is incompatible with the existence of a single, unitary Morality or Law. Since there exists no world-wide community to be governed by a culturally transcendent Law or Morality, there exists no single, world-wide Law or Morality to govern it. But the human species does not constitute a single, unified community. Instead, human beings divide up into distinct societies, many of which do not as yet form any community with even closely neighboring societies, much less with all other societies on the surface of the earth.

What exist, then, are locally limited communities with their locally binding laws and moralities. These local moralities and laws need not be limited to one particular place. They can be spread, even gerrymandered, throughout the world—as Muslim culture is spread throughout much of the East and even into Britain and the United States. A community can also encompass people in very distant places, as Christian community includes not just Presbyterian churchgoers in the United States but also Catholic missionaries and their proselytes in China and Africa. So far, however, no community exists everywhere or encompasses everybody. Therefore, there is no Moral Law—no universally binding rule of law or morality.

What Unity Under A Single Moral Law Would Entail

The situation would be otherwise if there were a single, world-wide Moral Authority—a single person, or group of persons, to make and enforce the rules on all persons everywhere.

Suppose that a single omnipotent and omniscient God were in charge of the whole world. Then He might undertake to enforce a single, world-wide Morality or Law. Of course, he might not. Being intelligent, He might instead devise a different morality for each group, according to its particular circumstances. Let us, however, set that possibility aside. Suppose, as St. Thomas Aquinas did, that God has made just one highly abstract set of moral rules, or principles, then allowed each society to adapt this set of rules to its particular situation. In that case, talk of a culturally transcendent and universally binding Morality or Law would have reasonably clear meaning.

The trouble is that this hypothesis, though widely believed, is empirically unfounded. As we have already noted, the existence of a single God with the power and disposition to enforce His unitary Will on human beings everywhere is vouchsafed by no evidence that anybody has been able to produce. Instead, such evidence as exists contradicts the hypothesis. If there is a God, and if He intends to exert His will, it seems clear that He is waiting until the hereafter to do it; for there is little evidence that He is doing it now, by means sufficiently well chosen to effect worldwide compliance. Thus, consider the injunction to love your fellow man as yourself. If that is a divine command, as Christians maintain, then it has yet to be universally enforced; for it is certainly not universally complied with. So, if it is to be believed, the whole proposition has to be taken on faith; it certainly cannot be proved, and it is hard to square with the facts.

Even without a God, there might be a single, overarching Morality or Law if human beings everywhere formed a single, unified community and either shared a single, harmonious set of moral conventions or were ruled by a single authority who promulgated and reinforced the very same rules everywhere. But although a world-wide community is certainly developing very rapidly, along with a world-wide morality, law, and etiquette, there is as yet no reason to believe that it exists at the moment.[9]

On the contrary, the evidence supports the contrary hypothesis. For the most part, what we still have is what we have always had: not a single, world-wide society with a single, world-wide Morality or Law, but so many local societies with their local, and locally binding, moralities and laws. That these social conventions and customs are in many ways alike is certainly true; just as it is true that languages are in many ways alike. It is, however, still not true that everybody everywhere obeys the same Moral Law; just as it is not true that everybody everywhere speaks the same Language. Neither thing will happen until the many diverse communities in the world are united into one.

It is possible, of course, that a world-wide community will eventually develop, as people everywhere increasingly acquire the means of communicating with and influencing each other, either by trade and negotiation or by war and conquest. In fact, there is evidence that such a community is already developing. As societies everywhere come into contact with and begin to influence each other, they will learn to speak each other's language, and they will adopt each other's customs; or devise new ones. Since it is in the interests of people everywhere to increase trade and avoid fights, we may expect the pace of this development to accelerate. If we human beings do not destroy ourselves and our planet first, we may eventually manage to mold ourselves into a single world-wide community, one governed by a single world-wide law or morality. Perhaps it will even be a democratic community with a free market, one that gives people everywhere both liberty of choice and the means to prosperity. One can always hope.

As yet, however, no one sensitive to the facts can claim that anything of the sort has happened; and perhaps it never will. Instead, mankind, which is now concentrated in large political units, may once again be divided up into increasingly isolated and alienated groups, each armed with terrifying weapons of destruction. Nobody can say. All that is clear is that humanity is presently divided. Instead of constituting a single community that is governed by a single set of rules, it is divided up into a countless variety of communities, groups, and classes, all governed by different rules.

The Myth of Human Unity

This fact has been obscured by the ancient idea that mankind is not just a single *species* but also a single *family,* the members of which have familial obligations to each other.

Again, the main perpetrator of this talk has been theistic—specifically Christian—religion. According to belief which Christianity took from Stoicism, we should love each other because we are all brothers —children of a powerful and peremptory God whose holy will we are all obligated to obey, as all children are obligated to obey their fathers.

One hesitates to criticize this hoary proposition, which has inspired many persons to admirable acts of charity and still guides much of our political thinking, but it takes only a second to see that the proposition is false if it is taken literally. If God is our father, it is in some wholly figurative and obscure sense of the word that can hardly serve as a basis for the claim that all human beings are literally obligated to each other in the way that brothers are obligated to each other.

Mainly for this reason, belief in the brotherhood of man has been a religious faith, not a scientific hypothesis. In the course of its history, however, Western philosophy, performing its customary role as the buttress for religious (or, more recently, political) faith, has produced both metaphysical and empirical arguments in support of this theological proposition.

The metaphysical argument is that human beings belong to the same family because they all have a share in the same human nature—namely, their God-given capacity for reason. According to Christian theology, God, the Father of all mankind, is himself the perfect embodiment of Reason, but men also embody this faculty imperfectly. Hence, love of God, or oneself, entails love of other human beings; it makes us all brothers. Or so St. Thomas Aquinas maintained. Leaving God out of it in accordance with the fashion of the Enlightenment, Kant tried to secure the same conclusion by arguing that human beings, who are by definition rational, are, in consistency, obligated by their respect for their own rationality to show the same, or a similar, respect for other rational beings.

The defects of this argument are multiple. First, the premise is false. The plain fact is that all human beings are not rational. Indeed, some are quite irrational, and of those who are rational, some are clearly less so than others. These, it seems clear, should be treated differently. Second, even if all human beings were rational, it would not follow that they were all literally brothers. That human beings are alike in being rational does not mean that they all have the same father. Furthermore, it seems clear that they do not. So, contrary to Christian belief, not all men are brothers.

What is meant, of course, is that we should treat all men as if they were brothers, because they are alike in respect of their possession of reason. But why should we treat as brothers those who are not in fact our brothers?

Shouldn't like cases be treated alike? Yes, but human beings are not disembodied bits of Pure Reason. They differ in ways that make a difference to how we should treat them. Even brothers differ in various ways. Some are weak and some are strong, some are good and some are evil, some are young and some are old; some are talented and some are not; some are beautiful and some are ugly; and so on. We should certainly have regard for the rationality that many human beings have in common, but we should also take into account the many ways in which they differ. To the extent that human beings are alike, they should be treated alike; but to the extent that they are different, they should be treated differently. So, the mere fact of their rationality cannot secure the conclusion that they should all be treated in the same way.

Furthermore, even if it could secure this conclusion, the postulate of human rationality could not secure the further conclusion that we are obligated to treat all human beings as if they were our brothers. As we have emphasized before, nature and reason may determine what we ought to do; they cannot by themselves determine what we are obligated to do. In the final analysis, what determines that is social convention, which usually requires favoring our literal over our merely metaphorical brothers, in disregard of the fact that our metaphorical brother may in many ways be more like us.

The Argument from Evolution

So much for the metaphysical argument. In modern times, this argument has been buttressed by another that purports to be more scientific. According to the Leakeys, all human beings are descended from a common humanoid ancestor that originated in tropical Africa, by evolving from a branch of the tree of apes. If this hypothesis is right, we are all members of the same extended "family," even if we are not literally children of God. So, some philosophers believe that we ought to treat each other accordingly.

One such philosopher, James Rachels has taken this line of thinking even further, arguing that our biological kinship with, and similarity to, other animals, obligates us to treat all animals, including cats and centipedes, as brothers. According to Rachels, our genetic relatedness and our similarity to cats makes us members of their families too. Not only is Joe Smith the Englishman a brother to Huang Wu the Chinamen;

he is also brother to Tabby the cat. This leads Rachels to the conclusion that eating cats is as immoral as eating kinfolk.[10] For some unaccountable reason, Rachels does not draw the same conclusion regarding plants, which you are permitted to eat in spite of your biological kinship with them.

This view has the same defects as the one just examined. First, its premise may be false. Against the Leakeys, some anthropologists believe that human beings descended from a variety of humanoid ancestors; and we simply have no proof that every living creature belongs to the same evolutionary line. Secondly, even if the premise is true, the conclusion does not follow. Grant that all animals are members of the same extended "family." It follows only that we are "brothers" in a metaphorical, not a literal, sense of the word.

So, thirdly, it cannot be concluded that we ought to treat all animals, or all human beings, alike. Indeed, fourth, given the differences between one species and another, and between one human being and another, it seems clear, that we should not. Finally, fifth, the obligations that we have to our literal and metaphorical brothers are determined not by biology but by social conventions, and these usually require treating human beings one way, cats another. Thus, you are forbidden to eat your brother, but the eating of cats is permitted, if you have a taste for it.

If Rachels and other absolutists have come to a different conclusion, it is not on scientific but on metaphysical grounds. What is required for their view is the *a priori* postulate that, however they may differ in other ways, all human beings, or all animals, are "equal in the eyes of God"—or its secular counterpart, that every person has the same "intrinsic" value; so deserves the same treatment. Unfortunately, this postulate not only lacks clear basis; it also lacks clear meaning. What is supposed to be the measure of a thing's, or a person's, "intrinsic" value? On what grounds are we to say that the life and comforts of Tabby the cat are equal in intrinsic value to the life and comforts of your older brother Sam? None that I can see.

For the sake of the argument, however, grant that our brothers are *intrinsically* no better than our neighbors or their cats. The fact remains that they are more important *to us*; and it is the importance a thing has for us that determines how *we* ought to treat it. This is so because what one ought to do is what one has reason to do, and that depends on what one values. Because I value my brother more than I value my neighbor, or his cat, I have reason to behave accordingly. It is not intrinsic value but relative value—value for us—that determines how we ought to treat a thing.

Furthermore, here as elsewhere, what one ought to do must be distinguished from what one is obligated to do. Suppose that I love my cat more than I love either my neighbor or my brother. Then, other things being equal, I ought to behave accordingly. The fact remains that, under the legal and moral conventions presently maintaining in this society, my obligations go in the reverse direction: I owe more to my brother than to my neighbor, and more to my neighbor than to my cat. If the rules were different, the ordering would be too.

The Reality of Human Nature

Notice that these arguments neither deny the existence of a common human nature nor belittle its importance.

It is clear that human beings everywhere have similar anatomy, similar physiology, similar genetic coding, and so on. Because of this they also have similar needs, similar emotions, similar preferences, and similar dispositions. Accordingly, human societies are much alike. In every society, people cooperate and compete for food, sex, power, status, excitement, and other goods; and they require each other to behave in ways that they can tolerate. We ignore all this at our peril.

Marxists and other disciples of Rousseau sometimes argue that human nature is a product of human society, not the other way around. Anxious to undertake the reshaping of behavior, they believe that human nature puts no limits on the forms it can take: Just alter the society, and you will transform human beings. Or so it is believed. The enormous evils caused by the resulting attempts to subordinate biology to sociology ought, however, to give us pause. Human nature, which is rooted in the genes, cannot be ignored and will not be altered simply by tinkering with social structures. The attempt to suppress biological instincts in the cause of political ideology can only do great harm without achieving the result intended. We will all be able to rest more easily, then, when belief to the contrary is recognized for the delusion it is and politicians quit using it as an excuse to meddle in our lives and loves. In the meanwhile, we should hold fast to this evident fact: There is indeed such a thing as a biologically rooted human nature that everywhere finds expression in similar, or functionally equivalent, forms of behavior.

No matter. The existence of a culturally transcendent human nature does not suffice to guarantee the existence of a culturally transcendent and universally binding Law or Morality. We know that because, although there is a common humanity, each society has its own rules, and it is these that determine, in a society, what conduct is to count as moral or legal. It may be thought that, because human beings everywhere have a similar nature and needs, they ought all to have the same laws and moralities, even if they do not in fact do so. But even this claim is doubtful. Although is doubtless true that all human beings have the same basic needs, different groups of human beings exist under different circumstances, and the rules that would serve their needs under one set of circumstances might defeat them under others. So, social variation is itself a natural outcome of a common human nature. Important as biology is, then, we cannot deduce from biology alone what rules societies ought to have. Furthermore, if we could, it would not settle the present question. It is one thing to say that human beings *ought* all to live by the same rules; it is quite another to say that they are *obligated* to do so. Even if the first proposition were true, it would do nothing to show that the second was true too.

Conclusion

Our question was whether there is a culturally transcendent and universally binding Morality or Law. In other words, Is there a single Morality or Law that all human beings everywhere are obligated to obey. On the grounds that being obligated means being required, we have argued that there is not, if only because there is no evidence of the existence of a single Moral Authority to do the requiring. It has been claimed that Nature, or Reason, constitutes such an authority, but this personifies both Nature and Reason. It also confuses what people *ought* to do with what they are *obligated* to do. Nature or Reason may determine the first of these; social convention determines the second.

There is no Moral Law. The whole idea is a myth created by priests and perpetuated by politicians seeking a justification for their authority, but the justifications so far constructed are tissues of fallacies. Such is the cleverness of philosophers that these justifications seem plausible on the surface, but examination reveals that they detach the moral and legal vocabulary from the empirical circumstances that give it determinate meaning. Thus, pious philosophers suffer from the delusion that legal and moral obligation have to do not with force but with divine holiness or Pure Reason. They also confuse what people ought to do with what they are obligated to do, with the result that we are left no objective standard by which to determine either. No wonder, then, that appeals to a transcendent and universally binding Moral Law often appear to be nothing but arbitrary expressions of personal preference and socially inculcated prejudice! That is often what they are.

Notes

1. That a practice is *legal* means here that it is permitted, or required, by the rules of law that happen to be in force and applicable. That the practice is *illegal* means that it is forbidden by these rules. And so on.
2. More exactly, having several wives is legally and morally permissible, as well as mannerly, for *some* persons in Saudi Arabia, for *no* persons in Selma, Alabama. This is a complication that we can safely ignore for the moment. Its general importance is to remind us that evaluations of law, morality and etiquette are not so simple, or absolute, as they appear to be on the surface. Instead, they are complex relational judgments. Not, "x is immoral" but "x is immoral for persons P in society S at time T under other conditions C... "
3. This need not mean that they are conscious of the rule. People can comply with a rule without being aware of the fact. Most of the time they do.
4. The connection, of course, is that reason is supposed to be the nature of human beings.
5. Actually, it is somewhat misleading even to say that gravity causes; but this is a point that can be ignored in the present context.
6. On this theme, see Richard Taylor, *Good and Evil* (Buffalo, N. Y.: Prometheus Books, 1984).
7. Logically, a sentence of the form "(x) (Ey) Fxy" is not to be confused with one of the form "(Ey) (x) Fxy." In English, "For every society x there is a rule y such that x has y" should not be confused with "There is a rule y such that every society x has y."
8. *Create* is in many cases an inappropriate term. It wrongly suggests that the thing is done deliberately, in a definable period of time. More often, the rules of a society simply *evolve*—come into existence gradually, over a long and indefinite period of time, without anybody noticing that it is happening until the process is complete. On this topic see Friedrich Hayek's *Law, Legislation, and Liberty*.
9. Something approaching what was mistakenly thought to be a world wide community existed in Western Europe in the Christian Middle Ages, and this may have given credence to the idea that all men everywhere are subject to the same divinely instituted law.
10. See James Rachels, *Created from Animals: The Moral Implications of Darwinism* (Oxford: Oxford University Press, 1990).

13

Kant on Practical Reason

Kant's Claim

Many philosophers believe that Immanuel Kant showed how to derive a version of the Golden Rule from reason alone, without benefit of divine revelation or religious authority. Kant himself fostered this belief by making two claims. First, he purported to have derived the main principle of his morality, the Categorical Imperative, from what he called Pure Practical Reason. Second, he said that the Categorical Imperative is equivalent to the Practical Imperative, his technical version of the Golden Rule. Taken together, these two contentions amount to a claim to have deduced something very like the Golden Rule of New Testament Christianity from reason alone; and, therefore, it is widely believed that this is what Kant did.

I believe, on the contrary, that Kant did no such thing. As we normally conceive it, being *rational* means calculating how best to achieve your own ends. Following the Golden Rule means helping other people to achieve their ends. Therefore, in order to have shown that being rational entails behaving in accordance with the Golden Rule, Kant would have had to show how it serves *your* ends to help other people achieve *theirs*. But, of course, Kant never showed any such thing. He never even tried. Others before him—for example, St. Thomas Aquinas and Joseph Butler—had tried to prove this, by arguing that helping others is the best way to serve yourself. But Kant vigorously and repeatedly repudiated all such arguments as not just misguided but also pernicious.

What Kant did was quite different: He *redefined* reason, so as to make it accord with his Christian morality. Defining the rational as the *nonempirical*, and observing that the Categorical and Practical Imperatives are not derived from experience, he concluded that they must be known *a priori*. Then he called this fallacious inference a proof that these principles were an expression of not just the Christian religion but also universal human Reason. In other words, Kant began by assuming an essentially Christian morality. Then he sought a conception of reason that would vindicate this assumption and declared the result a proof—a transcendental deduction.

In my view, one might as well try to prove that cats are dogs by redefining a cat as a canine animal. Clearly, this would prove nothing, not even if it was called a transcendental deduction. So, in my view, the question worth discussing is not whether Kant proved the rationality of Christian ethics. As I shall try to show, he did not. What is worth discussing is why he mistakenly believed that he had done so. As we shall see, the answer to this question is to be found in Kant's conception of reason. He defined reason in such a way that uncritical faith and feeling turn out to be forms of reason. Indeed, they become its paradigms, its highest forms.

Kant's Platonic Redefinition of Reason

To see that this is what Kant did, compare his metaphysical work, *The Critique of Pure Reason*, with his moral work, *The Critique of Practical Reason*. As is indicated by the similarity of their titles and by the correspondence between their outlines, Kant took himself to be doing the same thing in the second that he thought he had done in the first—namely, engage in an inquiry into the necessary conditions of knowledge. The difference was only that, where his topic in the first book had been knowledge of *theory*, it was in the second to be knowledge of *practice*. Kant did not in either book undertake to demonstrate the truth of the knowledge in question. In both cases, he uncritically took it as given and inquired into its "transcendental conditions." In other words, he asked: Given that I have this knowledge, what makes it possible?

Thus, to take the paradigm case first, Kant began the *Critique of Pure Reason* not by proving the truth of the Newtonian physics that was then current but by taking it for granted and asking what Reason would have to be like for it to be true, as he had previously assumed. Then he argued that, because space and time, the fundamental concepts of Newtonian physics, could not be known empirically, by observation, but would be presupposed by and made use of in all observation, they would have to be regarded as *a priori* (i.e., innately given) features of Reason. Finally, he declared this to be a kind of proof—a transcendental deduction—of space and time. In the second *Critique*, Kant proceeds in exactly the same way. He starts not by questioning but by assuming the soundness of what he calls the ordinary moral consciousness, meaning the moral convictions of the unlettered German (i.e., Lutheran) peasant. Formulating these convictions technically, as the Categorical and Practical Imperatives, he asks what Reason would have to be like for them to be "valid," as he has antecedently assumed. Then he infers that, because obeying these imperatives sometimes requires acting in ways that defeat one's desires, one must have free will—a capacity for making choices undetermined by desire. This capacity, he adds, must be regarded as an *a priori* (i.e., antecedently given) feature of human reason. Finally, he declares this a kind of proof—a transcendental deduction—of free will.

Of course, Kant did not use the English word *reason*. Instead, he used two German words, *Vernunft* and *Verstehen. Vernunft*, or Pure Reason, the highest form of Reason, is *a priori* reason, reason before it has been mixed with and polluted by consideration of facts known empirically. This form of reason is contrasted with understanding, or *Verstehen*, the procedure whereby we use our *a priori* knowledge of space, time, and the categories (the *a priori* principles of judgment) to order and interpret the empirical information that comes in through our senses. In ethics, *Vernunft* is to be contrasted with prudence, the habit of calculating how best to satisfy one's empirically given desires. In both cases, *Reason* means *Pure Reason*, reason unrelated to the empirically known world, reason as existing apart from the natural (i.e., the physical) order of things.

This fact would have been clearer if Kant had not titled one of these books the *Critique of Pure Reason* and the other the *Critique of Practical Reason*. These titles suggest that the opposition intended is between pure and practical reason. But the two titles really should have been *Critique of Pure Theoretical Reason* and *Critique of Pure Practical Reason*. Both were about Pure Reason, the first about its uses in theory, the second about its uses in practice.

As this demonstrates, in Kant's thought, the *rational* is opposed not to the *irrational* but to the *empirical*—that which relates to the senses. Following Plato, Kant excluded from the rational everything learned *a posteriori*, from experience, and included only what is known *a priori*, before experience. Thus, the "rational" component of science for Kant was geometry and arithmetic, the mathematics of space and time; and, in his view, the "rational" component of ethics would have to be something equally abstract and formal, something equally devoid of empirical (i.e., sensory) content, the Categorical and Practical Imperatives.

In ethics, our present concern, Kant's identification of morality with Reason and his separation of the rational from the empirical meant two things. First, it meant that morality ceased to have any relation to empirically discoverable social conventions. Thus, in Kant's view, your moral duty cannot be discovered by ascertaining the rules or practices that happen to be in force in the society to which you happen to belong. It has to be learned instead by gaining insight into the culturally transcendent and universally binding principles that define your innate sense of duty. Second, the separation of the rational from the empirical meant that reason ceased to have any relation to empirically known desires. Thus, in Kant's view, reason was not to be regarded as the slave of the passions, as Hume had erroneously claimed. Instead, as Plato had rightly affirmed, it was to be their master. In other words, the most important use of Practical Reason was not to calculate the means to your ends but to enable you to disregard your ends for the sake of duty.

Duty is defined by Kant's two imperatives. The Categorical Imperative commands, "So act that you can will the maxim of your action to be a universal law."[1] In other words: Do only what you can wish everybody to do. The Practical Imperative commands, "Treat every rational being as an end only; treat none as a means." In other words: Respect your fellow man as yourself. As Kant realized, neither of these two imperatives can be derived from experience. So, he argued, they must be known *a priori*. Because he took it to be evident that both principles are "valid"—a term he never defined—the only question that concerned him very much was, How are we able to conform to these principles in spite of our desires? And, to this self-posed question, he replied: We have *free will*, a capacity to rise above our empirically given desires, in order to do our Holy Duty as it is made known to us by Pure Practical Reason.

Such, in brief summary, was Kant's derivation from Pure Practical Reason of what turns out to be essentially Christian morality. Such, in other words, was Kant's proof that behaving in accordance with the Golden Rule of New Testament Christianity is rational—not in the usual workaday sense of the word but in a higher and more honorific sense.

The New and Paradoxical Nature of Kant's Claim

In thus contending that behaving in accordance with Christian morality is rational, Kant was claiming nothing novel. The same conclusion had been urged many times before, by many other philosophers. In fact, belief in the rationality of Christian morality was a commonplace of medieval theology, one explained by the proposition that, because God had created human reason, He would not command men to do anything irrational.

What was new in Kant was the meaning that was now to be assigned to this belief. Before Kant, when anyone said that doing your duty was rational, he meant that it would serve your interests and make you happy, if not directly then indirectly, as a result of divine rewards and human reciprocity. Kant, however, meant no such thing. Instead, he maintained that doing your Christian duty is rational even when it does not serve your interests—even when it defeats them. In the end, Kant, who was a devout Protestant, did acknowledge, even insist, that God will reward you with happiness in heaven if you do your duty here on earth. But Kant also insisted that considerations of heavenly reward should play no part in your deliberations as to how to behave here on earth. What matters, he said, is only that you do your duty. You ought to do it even when you see no prospect that it will make you happy. In fact, if you do not disregard your earthly happiness, all promise of reward in heaven is null and void.

This, I think, is a new and different claim, one that nobody before Kant ever made, or would have thought of making, because it turns everything on its head. Even previous Christian thinkers made no such claim. When St. Thomas said that doing your duty is rational, he was using the word *rational* in its workaday sense, to describe actions that serve your ends. By contrast, when Kant said that doing your duty is rational, he meant that it will conform to the Categorical and Practical Imperatives, a different thing. In short, Kant so changed the meaning of the word *rational* that what once counted as paradigmatic rationality—namely, calculating how to achieve your ends—no longer does, and conduct that used to count as paradigmatically irrational—namely, acting in ways that disregard or defeat your ends—now counts as its opposite. A stunning redefinition of terms!

In case you think I have made this up, I invite you to look at Kant's text again. Here, somewhat compressed and simplified, but in more or less his own words, is what he said: What we normally call reason is merely *Verstehen*, the faculty for understanding (i.e., perceiving and analyzing) the physical (i.e., the phenomenal) world to which our souls happen, for the moment, to be unhappily consigned. We use this faculty whenever we do natural science or carry on our daily business. So, it is pragmatically important; but it is not Reason properly and strictly so-called, for it deals only with illusion and evil, the appearances of corruptible things. True reason is *Vernunft*, our capacity to comprehend the spiritual and ideal reality that lies behind the corruptible world of physical appearances, so as to apprehend and do our Holy Duty.

Having in this way explained what Pure Reason meant to him, Kant then drew the following moral. He said in so many words: If we look at things from the this-worldly point of view of *Verstehen* (i.e., scientific and technological reason), we will get the mistaken idea that rationality consists in calculating how to satisfy our selfish desires. In other words, we will confuse rationality with unprincipled self-seeking. Making the same mistake as the ancients, who believed that all of our behavior is determined by our desires, we will forget that each of us has a Free Will with which to control his desires and a Reason with to recognize the path of righteousness. To see things rightly, we must switch from a personal to a transcendental point of view; we must switch from *Verstehen* to *Vernunft*. When we do, we will achieve a position of detachment from our social condition and bodily desires that will enable us to rule them instead of letting them rule us. In Kant's words, we will cease to be *heteronomous* and become *autonomous*.

Kant believed that, once we gain this position of spiritual detachment, we shall see that, contrary to appearances, there is no "objective" (i.e., *impersonal)* reason why our personal interests should count for more than, or come before, the interests of other persons. It will become evident to us that one person is as worthy of respect and consideration as another. We will see that preferring ourselves to others, by seeking to advance our personal desires [perhaps] at their expense, is not rational but wrong. In short: We will see that true and pure Reason—reason rightly regarded—rules out self-seeking and requires impartiality, equal consideration for everybody, friend or foe. In a word, we shall see that Reason commands us to obey something very like the Golden Rule.

It follows, if Kant was right, that what people usually think of as practical reason, because it makes use of reasoning (i.e., calculation or ratiocination) in the service of empirically discovered social conventions and individual desires, is not reason at all but the empirical semblance of reason. Pure Reason—reason truly and strictly so-called—neither makes use of reasoning nor appeals to the empirical. Instead, it depends on faith and intuition, unreasoning insight into *a priori* truth. In short, if Kant was right, we get the following two paradoxes. First, Pure Practical Reason is *reason* not because it makes use of reasoning but because it does not; instead, it apprehends truth and duty without benefit of reasoning, by what some philosophers would call *intuition*, meaning immediate, unthinking insight. Second, Pure Practical Reason is *practical* not because it aims at serving your desires but because it does not; instead, it aims at controlling and suppressing your desires in the service of an intuitively known and antecedently given duty. Anyhow, so Kant reasoned.

By means of this style of reasoning, Kant was able to convince himself and his many followers that he had founded the convictions of his Pietist Lutheran conscience on Pure Reason, without invoking divine revelation or religious authority. In other words, he thought he had provided a strictly rational basis for something very like Christian morality; he thought he had proved that Christian belief in the Golden Rule is not just the provincial faith of a particular religious sect but an instance of *a priori* insight into the fundamental and most evident principle of universal human reason.

In my view, Kant proved no such thing. What he did was merely to avoid basing his moral principles on an empirical study of Christian social practices. Instead, he arrived at them by reflecting on his own socially inculcated moral prejudices. Then he mistook this for a proof. Because he had not derived the principles of his ethics *a posteriori*, by the use of "empirical intuition," he believed that he had got them *a priori*, by considering an antecedently given idea of duty. In other words, because he had not got his moral principles from empirical psychology or cultural anthropology, he believed that he had got them from Pure Practical Reason. The more obvious explanation—that he had got them from a wholly unreasoned and unreasoning Lutheran faith—was dismissed by postulating that faith is itself the highest form of reason, because it contains nothing empirical.

The Relevance of Kant's Fideism

This last remark may come as a surprise. Kant thought of himself as a thoroughgoing rationalist, and that assessment is generally accepted by other philosophers. If, however, a rationalist is someone who believes in reason rather than faith, this opinion could not be more wrong. As the briefest look at his biography reveals, Kant's first commitment was to faith.

To see this, begin with Kant's life. Born a son of Pietist Lutherans, he began adulthood by studying for the ministry. He never completed his training, and he quit attending formal church services as a mature adult. Like other Lutherans, he also had doubts about rational theology—the attempt to prove God's existence by rational means. But he never gave up his faith in New Testament morality, which he, like other Pietists, took to be the most essential part of Christian religion. So, although Kant gave up belief in the saving power of church ritual and in the possibility of rational theology, these were things in which Lutherans were never inclined to put much stock anyhow. Like Luther himself, the Pietists associated ritual with the hated Roman Church and regarded reason as "the whore of Babylon." What mattered to them was Christian community, the love and respect of one man for another, and it was these same things that mattered to Kant.

This piece of *ad hominem* information is generally thought to be philosophically irrelevant, but I do not believe that it is. As Kant's writings make clear, he never doubted a single article of his Christian faith. Although he doubted that any proposition of his *theological* faith could be proved true, he was certain that no such proposition could be proved false. His strategy, therefore, was not to attempt to bolster his faith by means of reason, as Aquinas and others had tried to do, but to protect his faith from what he believed to be the excesses of reason as these had found expression in the work of such unbelievers as David Hume. So, Kant described his philosophical program as a *critique* of reason, meaning not that it was a rejection of reason but that it was an attempt to show that reason has limits. And, because some people had missed the point, he once remarked (to his butler, it is said) that he had written his critique of reason "in order to make room for faith."

As this remark confirms, Kant was no rationalist—not if that means someone who believes in the supremacy of reason. No. He was a fideist, one who believes that reason must be kept in its proper place, subordination to faith. If he nevertheless sincerely regarded himself as a rationalist, it is only because he knew that he was no *irrationalist*—no Tertullian thumbing his nose at things rational while declaring the superiority of things irrational.[2] Furthermore, although he emphatically denied that theological truths can be derived from reason, he was not as pessimistic about moral truths. Hence, despite his distaste for unbridled reason, especially in matters theological, he regarded himself as a thoroughgoing rationalist, meaning that he was as much of a rationalist as he believed that any sensible person could be.

The Fallaciousness of Kant's Alleged Proof

Be that as it may, in my view, Kant's alleged proof of the rationality of Christian morality is no such thing. Instead, it is just a philosophically fancy bit of double talk. Behavior that is demonstrably rational is merely made to seem rational by adopting a new and different definition of reason. But one cannot prove irrationality to be irrational by redefining the word *rational*—no more than one can prove that cats are dogs by redefining the word *cat*. Even when it is dignified as a transcendental deduction, this procedure proves nothing. Instead, it just confuses the issue and begs the question. When, in a normal tone of voice, we ask whether behaving in accordance with Christian morality is rational, what we want to know is whether it is rational in the sense that it is *not irrational*. To reply, as Kant does, by telling us that such conduct is rational in the sense that it is *not empirical* is not to answer our question but to change the subject.

As I see it, then, Kant's so-called proof is not a proof, just a bit of double-talk. It has, of course, been a very successful bit of double-talk. Instead of rejecting this way of talking, historians of philosophy influenced by Kant have for over a century and a half been poisoning the intellectual wells by denying the honorable title *rationalist* to such uncompromising champions of reason as David Hume, while conferring this same title on such unremitting enemies of reason as Hegel.[3] So, the double-talk has done its work. Still, it is just double-talk.

If it is just double-talk, why have so many intelligent philosophers fallen for it? No doubt, part of the answer is this: Kant's reasoning confirmed prior religious conviction; it reinforced what people of Christian sentiment wanted to believe anyhow. Because most of us are Christian in sentiment, having been Christian in upbringing, this means that most of us are not disposed to examine very critically the means by which Kant secured his result; few of us want to look his gift horse in the mouth. Instead, we prefer to accept it gladly, grateful like Kant, to be assured that what we already believe on faith without benefit of reason can, after all, be not just reconciled with but even derived from reason. It does not matter that this "reason" is now a very much compromised and tainted lady—hardly the chaste and austere maiden that David Hume adored so shamelessly. In our hearts, if not in our heads, we believe that she is still the loveliest bride to be had. So, we will hear nothing against her; and we will regard everything said in her praise, no matter how extravagant, as the simplest and most obvious truth.

Credulity is, however, only part of the explanation. Another part is this. Double talk though it may be, Kant's talk of "reason" contains a grain of truth. As Plato noticed and Kant reaffirmed, we do regard as intemperate and irrational the man who spends his life in uncritical service to his every desire. Accordingly, we also regard ability to control one's impulses and passions as one of the most important indices and measures of rationality. That we do so gives powerful support to the Platonic belief, which Kant shared, that the essence of reason is not service to but mastery of desire. Like Plato, Kant traded heavily on this important fact.

Unfortunately, both Kant and Plato misunderstood the fact. Both understood it as representing an inherent conflict between reason and desire, two separate faculties of the mind. This was a mistake. The need for control of desire arises, rather, from the existence of conflict *between desires*. I want the extra glass of wine, but I also want to be clear-headed tomorrow. Reason offers a solution: sacrifice the less important to the more important desire. This means that being rational in practice does indeed require controlling your desires, as Plato and Kant maintained. But, contrary to their belief, being rational does not consist in that alone. It consists, rather, in controlling some desires in order thereby better to satisfy other desires. Because it would be an effort without a purpose, a cost without a compensating benefit, self-control for no good end would be an exercise not of reason but of unreason. The mistake of Kantian, as of Platonic philosophy generally, is to overlook this fact.

Kant on the Irrationality of Immorality

So far, I have argued that Kant's ethics were based not on reason but on faith. I have, however, not yet said anything about Kant's attempt to reinforce his moral faith by showing that people who behave immorally thereby behave illogically. If Kant proved this, he made his case. So, I must now discuss whether he proved it. And since the central item in Kant's case is the Categorical Imperative, I must discuss the meaning of this principle.

I do so with extreme reluctance. In my opinion, the Categorical Imperative is one of the most obscure and ambiguous doctrines in Kant's writings, which are exceeded in obscurity and ambiguity only by the writings of two of his followers, Hegel and Heidegger. Two things make the Categorical Imperative ambiguous. First, Kant formulated it in several slightly different ways. Second, each of these formulations is itself ambiguous in several ways. Thus, consider the formulation, "So act that you can will the maxim of your action to become a universal law." This makes use of five concepts: *universal law*, *action*, *maxim*, *will*, and *can*. As the subsequent history of philosophy has revealed, each of these concepts can be interpreted in *at least* two ways. This means that this one formulation alone has more than 2^5 (= 32) distinguishable meanings. So, we are talking about ambiguity of a very high order indeed.

Such ambiguity is not calculated to ease the task of a critic. Somebody once said of J.S. Mill, "He wrote so clearly he could be found out." The only people who have ever accused Kant of writing clearly are his disciples, who unwittingly refute themselves by chastising other people for misunderstanding passages that they pronounce incapable of misinterpretation.[4] In my opinion, Kant rarely said anything clearly. As C.D. Broad once wittily remarked, Kant contrived to be technical without managing to be precise. So, he can never definitely be refuted, or found out. Since nobody can be sure what Kant meant, nobody can prove that it was wrong. This makes criticism unprofitable.

The task of criticism is made even more onerous by the attitude of Kant's devotees. Kant's philosophy serves such sacred religious and political cows that, in some quarters, to criticize him is to risk being charged with sacrilege. One may pillory heretical Hume with impunity, but nothing disrespectful must be said about pious Kant. German intellectuals are particularly prone to this kind of hagiography. For them, Kant is to be revered and interpreted like the Bible, not read and criticized like *The Treatise on Human Nature*. We are not to ask what Kant meant, then decide whether it is true. Instead, we are to assume that it is true, then ask what it means. For such worshipers, Kant is a holy oracle, and we do not demand that oracles say things clearly. Instead, we take their word as a holy text, while regarding its ambiguities and obscurities as evidence of not muddle-headedness but profundity.

For these reasons, I would rather pass by in silence Kant's Categorical Imperative; but, given my larger aim, which is to criticize Rationalist moral philosophy, I cannot afford to do so. Kant is the most influential moral philosopher of our times—not in spite of his ambiguities and obscurities but because of them. In philosophy, as in politics, vagueness and ambiguity are not always bars to acceptance. Quite the contrary: Obscure and ambiguous texts usually have the most devoted followings, perhaps because every reader can find a way to read his own views into them. So, Kant cannot be ignored.

In what follows, then, I shall consider various readings of Kant's Categorical Imperative. I shall do this *not* in order to establish that one of these interpretations is correct *but* in order to show that *there is no obvious reading on which Kant can be said to have proved that Christian morality is the product of reason.* As I shall show, and you shall see, there are interpretations on which the Categorical Imperative can plausibly be regarded as a principle of *practical logic*; but on these it ceases to distinguish morality from immorality. There are also interpretations on which it can plausibly function as a test of *morality*, but on these it can no longer be regarded as a rule of logic. Unnoticed ambiguity has made it seem that the Categorical Imperative is both a principle of logic and a criterion of morality, but there is no single and obvious interpretation on which it turns out to be so.

Pointing this out will, of course, not definitively prove that Kant was wrong. Rather, since Kant cannot be definitively interpreted, he cannot be definitively refuted. My criticism will, however, shift the burden of proof. After all, the question under discussion here is whether Kant *demonstrated* that Christian morality is a matter of pure reason. In order to demonstrate something you must make its truth clear and unequivocal. If Kant did not do that, then he did not prove what he claimed to prove.

Kant's Argument

Central to Kant's argument as I understand it is his Categorical Imperative. Exactly what this might mean, we shall consider later. For now, what we need to do is understand its place in Kant's argument. The first point to grasp is this: According to Kant, the Categorical Imperative is a purely formal principle of practical logic; it has much the same relation to practice as the law of non-contradiction has to theory. Indeed, Kant implied that the Categorical Imperative is nothing more than a law of non-contradiction for practice. He said that to violate it is to beak a rule of practical logic; it is to act in a way that will involve you in something that is very like a contradiction. Our question is whether he proved that.

On the most obvious and charitable reading, Kant's argument goes like this: The fundamental principle of Practical Reason is that whatever is right for one person must be equally right for every other. So, we may test the morality of an action by ascertaining whether it comports with the following rule: So act that you can will the maxim of your action to become a universal law. In other words: Ask yourself, "Could I will that everybody do that?" If you cannot answer affirmatively, your action is forbidden. Kant called this test the Categorical Imperative.

Kant never explained this principle. Instead, the philosopher who once excoriated examples as the "go cart of judgment for those deficient in natural intellect" was content to indicate the meaning of his most revered principle by using examples. In his text, we find three: lying, reneging on your promises, and committing suicide. Let us begin, by summarizing what Kant had to say about these.

Suppose, first, that you are thinking of telling a lie. Could you "will" everybody to do the same? No. If everybody lied, nobody would believe anybody; lying would soon lose its advantage, even for you; the policy behind it would defeat itself. So, Kant concluded that, by choosing to lie, you would involve yourself in a self-contradiction. Suppose, second, that you are thinking of reneging on your promise. If it were permissible for you to renege, then it would be permissible for everybody else to do so too. But if every promisor reneged, promising would soon lose its utility and the institution would cease to exist. So, Kant concluded that, when it is universalized, the policy of reneging on promises cancels and destroys itself, proving that it is self-contradictory. Suppose, finally, that you are considering suicide. Ask yourself what would happen if everybody did it. Obviously, the human species would be eliminated and, with it, the practice of suicide. So, Kant concluded, this practice also embodies self-contradiction.

It is hard to say just what these examples are supposed to show. Each is supposed to make clear how there is contradiction in immorality; but, if there is, where, exactly, is it? Each case suggests a different answer. In the first, the "contradiction" is located in the fact that the motive of your lying would be defeated if other people were to reciprocate. Here, the suggestion is that lying sets a precedent which, when followed by others, makes the action *pointless*, without purpose. In the third case, the lesson seems to be different: Suicide, the action in question, becomes not pointless or futile but *impossible*. When everybody is dead, nobody *can* kill himself. In the intermediate case, the practice becomes *first pointless, then impossible*. When everybody reneges, promising loses its point, then ceases to exist. So, we are left wondering whether practices are to count as illogical because universalizing them makes them pointless, impossible, or both. So far as I know, Kant never noticed this difficulty. Exactly what he meant by declaring immorality to involve self-contradiction therefore remains unspecified.

All that is clear is that Kant believed immorality to be in some way *irrational because illogical*. This point is easy to miss when you look at his examples. These may tempt you to suppose that Kant was saying no more than, "Telling lies or reneging on your promises causes people to mistrust each other, and that is a bad thing, which nobody wants; so is suicide." But Kant was emphatic that he had no such utilitarian considerations in mind. Kant was not arguing that misbehavior produces *undesirable results*. As he saw it, that would have been an empirical claim, and therefore morally irrelevant. As a self-conscious Rationalist, he was claiming that immorality produces *self-contradiction*; no other objection would suffice. Therefore, Kant believed, and repeatedly said, that his was not a *utilitarian* but a *logical* test of morality—one rooted not in empirically discoverable facts of the matter but in *a priori* reason. The question, once again, is whether Kant proved this.

It may seem churlish to raise this question. Who wants to reject a proof that lying and reneging on your debts (if not also suicide) are immoral actions? Who wants to look such a splendid animal in the mouth? As the influence of Kant's ethics on Western philosophy shows, the obvious answer is: Not many people. Nevertheless, we must inspect this Kantian gift horse very closely. It is not quite the dashing animal it seems. On the contrary, it has some very bad faults. One of its main faults is this: Despite Kant's rejection of empirical considerations, his argument makes assumptions whose truth can be known empirically or not at all. An obvious example is the presumption that, if I lie, I will set a precedent that other people will imitate. If we believe his assumption, it is not because it is self-evident, like "2+2=4," but because experience of human behavior attests to its truth.

But let us overlook this difficulty. Important as it is, there is an even more serious problem: There are interpretations on which the Categorical Imperative is plausible as a principle of logic, and there are interpretations on which it is plausible as a criterion of morality, but there does not seem to be an interpretation on which it is plausible as both. Rather, when we interpret it as a rule of logic, it ceases to function as a plausible criterion of morality; and when we read it as a test of morality, it ceases to resemble a principle of logic.

To see this, let us look at some examples; but where Kant considered *wicked* actions, let us consider an *innocent* action. Suppose, that a young man wants to be a professor. On the face of it, this seems like a perfectly innocent desire. But let us put it to Kant's test. Let us have the young man ask: "Would I (could I) will that *every* person become a professor?" Anyone who asks this question will soon realize that, if we all became professors, there would be no farmers—no producers or gatherers of food. But without food, we would all soon starve to death, leaving us with nobody to be either professor or farmer. When universalized, the resolution to become a professor cancels itself by becoming impossible of fulfillment. So, according to Kant's argument, we should none of us (including Kant!) become professors.

We get a similar result *no matter what action we consider*. Even the most praiseworthy is ruled out. Consider the practice of feeding the hungry. If everybody were to feed the hungry, there would soon be no hunger. But where there is no hunger, there can be no practice of feeding the hungry. When universalized, the practice nullifies and cancels itself, like lying, reneging on debts, and suicide. On Kant's reasoning, it follows that it is immoral to feed the hungry —a patently absurd result and one that Kant would not have wished to produce. This suggests that the Categorical Imperative rules out such immoral actions as lying, reneging on your debts, and suicide only because it also rules out such innocent actions as becoming a professor and such virtuous practices as feeding the starving. The Categorical Imperative rules out immorality because it rules out everything.

Ambiguities in the Categorical Imperative

Have I misunderstood the Categorical Imperative? Very possibly. As noted earlier, the principle is highly ambiguous. It enjoins you to act only on maxims that you can will to become a universal law. (Elsewhere, this is a law of nature.) But what does this mean? What is a *maxim*? What is involved in *willing* something? What is the test of whether you *can* do that? And how *universal* does a law have to be?

Let us begin at the end and work backwards. What does it mean to will that a maxim be made a *universal law*? On the most obvious interpretation, it means that you should do nothing that you could not will *everybody* to do. As we have just seen however, when it is so interpreted, the Categorical Imperative has the absurd implication that nobody should become a professor unless everybody should. But that cannot be right. Perhaps, *everybody* does not really mean everybody.

Does it mean *every relevantly similar person in every relevantly similar circumstance*? Perhaps. The principle is certainly more plausible when it is so limited. Unfortunately, Kant himself never limited it in this way. On the contrary, when he applied his principle to actual cases, he usually placed no restrictions of any kind on it. Thus, in his old age, he made it quite clear that he thought it immoral for *anybody* to lie under *any* circumstances for *any* purpose, good or bad. For him, white lies were as bad as black ones; morality forbids all lying, without exception. It appears that, by *everybody*, Kant did indeed mean everybody.

In what follows, however, I propose to overlook this. For the sake of the argument, I propose to assume that Kant meant to limit generalization to relevantly similar cases. This will strengthen his case by weakening his claim. Unfortunately, it will at the same time expose his principle to a very different objection. To see what this is, ask yourself: How is anyone to decide what counts as a *relevant similarity*? For example, how is one to decide just which persons should become professors? The obvious answer is that we must ascertain who is and who is not suited to become a professor, and we must ask how many professors we need. But doing this requires us to engage in empirical inquiries, which Kant has declared irrelevant. As this illustrates, the Categorical Imperative is empty without some empirical measure of relevant similarity; but if we add such a measure, it ceases to be a test of the purely logical kind that Kant took it to be.

Clearly, the concept of a universal law raises as many questions as it answers. The concept of *willing* also raises questions: What does it mean to *will* something, and how are you to decide whether you can will something to become a universal law or not?

Some of Kant's remarks suggest that by *willing*, he means *choosing*; but on this interpretation, Kant's principle is not very plausible. For, while it makes sense to say "I choose to lie," it does not make sense to say "I choose that you lie." In the nature of the case, I cannot be the agent of your actions as I am of mine. But if I cannot choose *your* actions, how am I going to choose *everybody's*? Kant's answer is that, in choosing for myself, I *legislate* for others. In his view, every agent is a *moral legislator*, who implicitly enacts a law for the whole of mankind whenever he chooses a course of action for himself. Since Kant counts a law as a command, this suggests that "willing" means not choosing but *commanding*: In "willing" an action, you are commanding everybody else to choose it too. Thus, suppose that I choose to lie. I would thereby be commanding you and every relevantly similar person in every relevantly similar situation to lie too.

So understood, the concept of "willing" may seem to make clear and precise sense; let us grant that it does. For the sake of the argument, let us grant that one can *choose* to do something oneself and *command* everyone else to do it too. There is still a problem. Why should it follow that, in choosing to lie, I thereby command you and every relevantly similar person to lie too? Why does Reason require me to command you to do what I choose to do, especially when my doing it would advance my interests but your doing it would defeat them? If Reason is as intelligent as she is supposed to be, why does she not require, instead, that I choose to lie and command you to tell the truth?

It is not enough to answer, "Because what is right for me must be equally right for everybody sufficiently like me in circumstances sufficiently like mine." We may freely grant that this is so. We may even grant that it is self-evident. No matter. It will not settle the present question. *Acknowledging* that lying would be right for everybody and *commanding* everybody to lie are not the same things, and it is not at all clear that doing the first entails doing the second. So, the argument fails.

Admittedly, there may yet be an interpretation of Kant on which the argument succeeds. So, let us try again. Consider lying one more time. At times, Kant suggests that the practice is illogical because its universalization would render it self-defeating: If everybody lied, lying would become useless to everybody, including the liar—a result the liar could not want. This suggests a new interpretation for the word *willing*: Willing everybody to lie is *wishing* them to do so, and Kant's point is that wishing such a result is not just psychologically but also logically impossible—not just something we are psychologically incapable of desiring but also something that it is logically impossible, because self-contradictory, to desire.

Is this true? I confess that I cannot see how. Remember: We are not discussing whether I contradict myself unless I *think* that you would do right to lie, like me. We have already granted that this attitude would be incoherent. The question at issue is a different one. It is whether I contradict myself unless I *want* you to lie, like me. Grant that I would contradict myself if I believed that lying would be right for me but wrong for you. It is hard to see how I contradict myself by lying to you and hoping that you will not to lie to me in return. That there is *immorality* in this attitude is certainly true; that there is *contradiction* in it is not by any means obvious. But Kant is arguing that the attitude is immoral *because it is illogical*, and this he has altogether failed to prove.

Isn't such an attitude—lying to you while hoping that you won't lie to me—also unreasonable as well as immoral? Certainly; but we are discussing *rationality*, not *reasonableness*. Although they are frequently confused with each other, these are very different things. A rational man is one who reasons; a reasonable man is one who can be reasoned with. A man is rational provided only that he takes due regard for his own interests, needs, desires, and preferences; he is reasonable only if he responds to the pleas, arguments, needs, importunings, and demands of others.[5] In short, rationality is individual; reasonableness, social. Thus, Robinson Crusoe alone on his island had many opportunities to be rational, but until his man Friday arrived he had no opportunity to be reasonable. Kant's Categorical Imperative makes a great deal of sense when regarded as a standard of reasonableness. It makes no sense at all when treated as a criterion of rationality.

We have now looked at the concept of a *universal law* and at the concept of *willing*. There remains the concept of a *maxim*. What sort of a thing is a maxim? So far as I can recall, Kant does not say. He sometimes describes a maxim as a principle, or motive, of an action; but that does not help much. At what level of abstraction is this to be determined? If I tell a lie to gain an advantage over my enemy, what is the principle, or motive, of my action: To tell a lie? To tell a lie in order to gain an advantage? To tell a lie in order to gain an advantage over an enemy? It makes a difference. One might willingly universalize the last, highly restricted, maxim while disapproving of the other, more general, principles.

Important as it is, Kant did not go into this difficulty, and neither shall I. Obviously, the term *maxim* needs interpretation; but, so far as I can see, no interpretation of this term will solve any of the difficulties just noted. So, even without guessing at what Kant meant by his talk of maxims, we are justified in saying that Kant did not demonstrate—that is, make it clear—that actions are immoral because they are in some way illogical or irrational. As John Stuart Mill once remarked in this connection, Kant failed "almost grotesquely" to prove what he set out to prove, namely that doing your Christian duty is a requirement of Pure (i.e., *a priori*) Reason.

Conclusions

Kant failed to prove that the Golden Rule is a principle of reason. That he did so should not surprise anybody, for two reasons. First, to expect that one and the same principle will serve as both a self-evident truth of formal logic and a substantive standard for conduct is to expect too much. Despite Kant's belief in *a priori* synthetic truths, no principle is both formally correct and possessed of concrete content. Thus, knowing only that it cannot both be raining and fair outside, we do not yet whether to carry an umbrella; and knowing only that no one can both lie and tell the truth at the same time in the same act, we do not yet know whether anyone should lie or tell the truth. Second, there is no way in which one *can* know what one should do until one knows what results are both possible and desirable; but there is no way to know either of these things without engaging in empirical investigations of the kind which Kant eschewed.

If this reflection were not reason enough to doubt the feasibility of Kant's project, there is another. Even if Kant had succeeded in discovering a purely formal test of what we should do, he would not have discovered therein a purely formal test of duty. Contrary to Kant's belief, oughthood and obligation are not the same thing. As we have seen in earlier chapters, there are times when you ought, rationally speaking, to do what you have no obligation, of either law or morality, to do; and vice versa. This is so because you ought, rationally speaking, to do what serves your personal interests, but you are obligated by law or morality to do only what the rules require you to do, and these may not coincide; they may even conflict. Thus, other things being equal, a hungry man ought to seek food; but it does not follow that he has a duty to eat it when he finds it. Conversely, a slave in a slave holding society has a duty to obey his tyrannical master; but it does not follow that he ought, all things considered, to fulfill this duty.

All of this is so because, contrary to Kant's belief, there are empirical conditions both on what one ought, rationally speaking, to do and on what one is obligated by law or morality to do. What one ought, rationally speaking, to do is determined by one's personal ends, whereas what one has a legal or moral duty to do is determined by the conventions that happen to be in force in one's society, and each of these can be known empirically. That there is also a purely logical condition on both obligation and oughthood—namely, consistency—is true, as Kant noticed. But while this condition is always necessary, it is never sufficient. So, there is and can be no purely formal criterion of *either* oughthood *or* obligation. Kant's search for such a criterion was bound to fail.

Notes

1. Just why and how Kant thought this could be regarded as a principle of Pure Reason will be explained later. Briefly, he thought that it involved no empirical facts of the matter. As in pure mathematics, it involved only logical consistency.
2. Tertullian, as is well known, had declared a *credo quia absurdum*: I believe because it is absurd; it is true because it impossible. Kierkegaard notoriously took the same line fifteen centuries later. Like most Christian theologians, Kant was unwilling to go that far.
3. For a history of philosophy from a Kantian point of view, see Wilhelm Windelband, A History of Philosophy, vol. I, vol. II (New York: Harper & Brothers, 1958). For more on Hegel's irrationalism, see Karl Popper *The Open Society and Its Enemies*, vol. II (Princeton, NJ: Princeton University Press, 1962).
4. A perfect example is Julius Ebbinghaus, "Interpretation and misinterpretation of the categorical imperative," in Robert Paul Wolff, *Foundations of the Metaphysics of Morals: Text and Critical Essays* (New York: Bobbs-Merrill, 1969), 97-116. Ebbinghaus begins by declaring Kant's concept of a categorical imperative "easy to explain. It means a law valid for the will of every rational being and therefore valid unconditionally. This is in no need of interpretation; it can hardly be misinterpreted. Kant has stated it in the clearest and most intelligible terms." Then Ebbinghaus immediately goes on to complain of the many ways in which a great many philosophers, including John Dewey, have misinterpreted this concept. Ebbinghaus never pauses to notice that if this gibberish were impossible to misunderstand, nobody would have misunderstood it.
5. I do not mean that a man is rational only if he takes regard for his *selfish* interests. The word used above is *personal*. Although personal interests are often confused with selfish interests by followers of Kant, they are not by any means the same. Suppose I desire to advance the welfare of mankind. Since, it may not be shared by others, this is my personal interest; but it is not, on that account, a selfish interest. More on this elsewhere.

Part III

Applications and Implications

14

Must Relativists Tolerate Evil?

The Argumentum ad Nazium

The standard objection to moral relativism is that it wickedly or self-defeatingly entails tolerance of what even the relativist regards as evil.[1] Thus, suppose a relativist encounters ritual torture or Nazi genocide. Even if he is appalled, he may not say so. Instead, his principles require him to wink at evil by declaring such practices morally and legally right as judged by the standards of those who engage in them. Or, anyhow, so say critics.

In a justly famous paper, Gilbert Harman has provided a partial answer to this *argumentum ad Nazium* (as George Graham calls it); but Harman's answer needs to be supplemented.[2] Harman points out that many of a society's moral and legal standards are subject to *internal* criticism as inconsistent with other moral and legal standards also accepted in the same society. Thus, says Harman, Nazism was subject to criticism on the grounds that Nazi practices violated standards of conduct basic to a civilization which the Nazis themselves professed to accept. Harman admits that there are some ways in which the Nazis were beyond the pale, but he maintains that there were objections to their behavior that ought to have given even them pause. Harman has made a valid and important point, but it does not suffice to answer the feeling that relativism seems to forbid *external* criticism. Grant that we may sometimes condemn a society's moral or legal standards using more basic moral and legal standards of that same society. The question remains whether a relativist can condemn a society's most basic moral and legal standards themselves. Critics believe that he cannot.

In what follows, I shall show that he can. If intolerance is a virtue, I shall show that a relativist has as much capacity for it as anybody. Specifically, I shall show that there is nothing to prevent a relativist from condemning as either (1) contrary to reason or (2) contrary to his personal preferences or the values of his hearers an action he acknowledges to be in accord with conventional morality and law. Therefore, there are at least two ways in which a relativist may criticize actions he admits to be legally and morally permissible. To be sure, these two forms of criticism will not please the absolutist, who wants absolute moral condemnation or none at all; but to object to relativism on the ground that it precludes that form of criticism is to beg the question.

Relativism as not Subjectivism but Relationalism

There are many forms of relativism, and some of them cannot be defended in the way just indicated and soon to be explained. One that cannot is *subjectivism*, the doctrine that moral or legal *truth* is relative to societies because statements believed true in one are believed false in another. According to the subjectivist, "Polygamy is legal" is true in Saudi Arabia because believed or affirmed there, and it is false in Alabama because doubted or denied there.

As has often been shown, this doctrine is a muddle. That a statement is believed does not make it true; and that it is both believed and doubted does not make it both true and false. It is a principle of logic that no single statement can *be* both true and false. If the fact seems otherwise, it is because what appears to be one statement with contrary truth values is really two statements, one true the other false. Thus, a Saudi saying (in English; God forbid that we complicate this by having him talk in his own language!) "Polygamy is legal," means "Polygamy is legal *here in Saudi Arabia*," whereas an Alabamian denying "Polygamy is legal" means to deny "Polygamy is legal *here in Alabama*." Although he same *sentence* is used in both cases, its use by different speakers in different contexts makes different *statements*.

Somewhat more defensible than subjectivism is *conventionalism*, the doctrine that actions that are legal or moral in one society may be illegal or immoral in another, because an action is legal or moral in a society according to whether it is consistent with that society's customs or conventions. Thus, according to conventionalism, having more than one wife is legal and moral in Saudi Arabia but illegal and immoral in Alabama, because permitted by Saudi law and custom but forbidden by Alabama law and custom.

Like others, Fred Feldman criticizes conventionalism on the grounds that the concept of a *society* is ill-defined.[3] And like others, Feldman is wrong to do so. The premise is certainly true. There is some indeterminacy in the concept of a society—enough, anyhow, to make it hard sometimes to count how many societies there are in a given region or population. However, from this premise, it does not by any means follow that conventionalism is false. Rather, what follows is that there must also be indeterminacy to law and morality—enough, anyhow, to make it unclear sometimes whether a particular action is legal and moral in a given context. But, when we examine the facts, this is just what we find. Thus, there is often much room for disagreement in any given region or population as to the legality and morality of particular practices. If the sociological facts were otherwise, they would disconfirm conventionalism. In fact, since no other theory accounts for them so well, they confirm it.[2]

A far more worrisome problem for conventionalism than the vagueness of the concept of society is the referential opacity of descriptions of actions. *Whose* possession of many wives do we have in mind when we say "Polygamy is legal in Saudi Arabia, illegal in Alabama"? Do we mean that Saudi law permits everybody to have many wives while Alabama law forbids everybody to do so? Then, what we say is false. Saudi law addresses Saudis, not Alabamians; so, it does not permit (though it also does not forbid) any Alabamians to have many wives. Alabama law addresses Alabamians, not Saudis; so, it does not forbid any Saudis to have many wives.

Much closer to the truth is the statement that Saudi law permits certain Saudi men to have several wives while Alabama law forbids any Alabamian to do so. However, when the facts are thus stated, the discussion is no longer about a single abstractly specified action, *the having of many wives* that is legal in one place, illegal in another. Instead, we are now talking about two quite different actions: (1) *certain Saudi men having many wives*; (2) *any Alabamian's having many wives*. We no longer have a single abstractly specified action – having many wives—that is both permitted by Saudi law and forbidden by Alabama law. Rather, we now have two different actions, one permitted by Saudi law, the other forbidden by Alabama law.

This difficulty is quite general. It is hard, if not impossible, to equate any action in one society with any action in another. Thus, as Bernard Williams has observed, we cannot equate the possession of several wives by a pious Saudi sheik with the practice of bigamy by a seedy London insurance salesman.[4] Not only does the difference in culture make these two things hard to compare evaluatively; it also makes them hard to compare descriptively.

This fact does not refute relativism, but it does refute naive conventionalist belief that *one and the same action* can be both legal or moral in one society and illegal or immoral in another. That form of conventionalism, it turns out, will not do. The trouble is not that it is too relativistic. Rather, the trouble is that it is not relativistic enough. It naively presupposes the descriptive equivalence of actions in different cultures, denying only their moral and legal comparability. Evidently, a defensible relativism will have to take a more sophisticated stance and question this assumption.

For this reason, the most defensible formulation of relativism is probably one like that chosen by Harman, whose relativism is about neither beliefs nor actions but the logical forms of statements of moral and legal appraisal of actions.[5] According to Harman, such statements are not of the simple subject-predicate form which they seem to be. Rather, they are elliptical for longer statements containing many terms, including most prominently a term referring to the relevant moral or legal customs and conventions. Or, anyhow, their fully articulated and analyzed equivalents are. Thus, "Polygamy is morally and legally permissible" is short for what would be more accurately and completely expressed by saying, "The conventions and customs (Harman calls the sum of these "the social contract") C of society S permit certain persons P to have many wives of description W under circumstances Z at times T." Feldman, whose carefully done textbook I have cited above and will cite again, calls this *conceptualism*; but perhaps a better term would be *relationalism*.

Whatever it is called, the doctrine does not mistakenly make the truth of moral and legal claims relative to societies, as does subjectivism. Instead, it leaves truth absolute by putting the relativity in the statement itself. It also neatly if quietly solves problems of referential opacity by reminding us that referentially transparent talk of action makes tacit or explicit reference to particular persons, times, and circumstances. So, we need no longer worry whether the action permitted by one society is the very same action as that forbidden by another. Instead, we can now see that the question was an artificial one produced by talking in a too abstract and insufficiently relational way.

There remains, of course, the *argumentum ad Nazium*. But before we answer that, there are some other details to be taken care of.

How the Relativist Defines Moral and Legal Terms

So far, we have stated the relativist's view of the *logical forms* of statements as to the morality or legality of actions, while saying little about the *meanings* of the legal and moral terms used in such statements. What we need to do now is to make a little clearer what, from a relativist point of view, is and is not meant by saying that an action is legally or morally right or wrong.

We may do so in one fell swoop as follows: Considered from the relativist's point of view, a kind of action A is legally or morally *right* for persons P in society S if and only if P's doing A is either permitted or required by legal or moral norms N of S. If doing A is permitted, it is *permissible*, a moral or legal right; if doing A is required, it is *obligatory*, a moral or legal duty. If doing A is neither permitted nor required but forbidden, it is a moral or legal *wrong* and avoiding it is a duty. That the norm in question is *legal* means that it was made or is enforced by officials (legislatures, judges, police) of a political state; that the norm is *moral* means that it was made or is enforced by ordinary persons in unofficial ways, as are the norms that go under the heading of etiquette, good manners.

For an illustration, consider the action of Xing. According to the relativist, saying that Xing is *legally* wrong means simply that Xing is contrary to (that is: expressly or implicitly forbidden by) the laws in force in the political state in question. Similarly, saying that Xing is *morally* wrong means that Xing is tacitly or explicitly forbidden by the moral conventions of the society in question. Normally, the discussants will be thinking of their own state and society. So, "Xing is morally and legally wrong" will normally be elliptical for "Xing is against the moral and legal rules prevailing in our country and in our society." Lacking reference to some state or society, the claim that Xing is morally or legally wrong has no clear meaning. Thus, it would make no sense on relativist principles either to say or to deny that killing is legally or morally wrong in a Hobbesian state of nature, where there is neither established law nor accepted morality. What must rather be said is that the question has not yet been assigned any definite meaning.

The Difference Between the Right of Morality or Law and that of Reason

We now understand what a relativist means by describing an action as legally or morally right in a given society at a given time: Like the conventionalist, he means that it is consistent with the relevant legal or moral conventions and customs. What we must also understand is that this is all he means. In particular, he does not mean that the action in question is what the agent ought, everything considered, to do. To state the point differently: His remark is purely descriptive; it is utterly devoid of prescriptive force. As we shall soon see, this is what saves relativism from the *argumentum ad Nazium*. So, let me explain it a little more fully.

Let us begin with the difference between calling an action *right* and calling it *morally right*.[6] Absolutists invariably use these two terms interchangeably, as if they were synonyms. The relativist does not. For the relativist, talk of moral and legal right is not pleonastic for talk of right *simpliciter*. Rather, in the relativist's view, the modifiers "morally" and "legally" limit the universe of discourse to morality and law, which are constituted by custom and convention. (That was the truth in conventionalism.) So, to ask whether an action is legally or morally right is merely to ask whether it is consistent with custom and convention. By contrast, to ask whether an action is right, everything considered, is to raise the much broader question whether the agent would do well to prefer it after taking into account not just law and morality but everything of relevance. No longer do we want to know merely whether the action is consistent with convention. Now we want to know whether it is consistent with *reason*.

That these are different questions is indicated by the fact that an action satisfying all applicable legal and moral standards may not satisfy the requirements of reason. Thus, marrying out of one's religion is legally and morally permissible in our society, but it is not on that account also advisable or sensible. And the converse is also true:

Actions that seem best, when all has been said and done, do not necessarily comport with existing legal and moral convention. Thus, a slave in a slave holding society might find escape or rebellion the better part of reason, in spite of the fact that either course of action would be contrary to the law and morality of his society.

The same point holds if we switch from permissibility to obligation. That an action is morally or legally *obligatory* means only that it is required under the relevant legal or moral conventions and customs. Thus, a legally and morally held slave is under legal and moral obligations to obey his master. Nevertheless, the existence of such slavish obligations does not mean that all who have them should respect them. Perhaps not. Perhaps they should escape or rebel instead. Whether they should or not is a question not of morality or law as the relativist understands them but of practical reason; and although a man of reason will duly respect the conventions to which he is bound, he will not necessarily be guided by them in the final analysis.

Normally, of course, there is no conflict between the requirements of convention and those of reason. Normally, it is rational to do the legal and moral thing. Hobbes explained why: Practically everything a man values depends on his being a member of a legally and morally ordered society; so, a rational man will place the greatest possible weight on adhering to the requirements of morality and law. That is why describing an action as morally or legally right seems to be an act of endorsement; often it is. Nevertheless, it need not be. There can come a time when the demands of convention conflict with those of reason. Therefore, a relativist can intelligibly affirm that an action is morally and legally right while denying that it is what the agent ought, everything considered, to do.

On what grounds can a relativist advise someone not to do what he is under legal and moral obligation to do? On the grounds that doing it is contrary to the agent's interests. There is a standard conception of rationality according to which acting in a way that is contrary to one's interests is irrational, by definition. And there is also a standard use of the word *ought* according to which one ought to do something if and only if doing it is rational. Put the two together, and it will turn out that one ought sometimes not to do what one is obligated to do.

How the *Argumentum ad Nazium* Begs the Question

It is true that this amoral conception of rationality is not accepted by absolutists, who traditionally equate reason with morality. Thus, according to Kant, who is the most influential absolutist of modern times, an action is morally obligatory if and only if it is what the agent ought to do; and self-interest is not the measure of what one ought as a matter of reason to do. Rather, the test of that is consistency with the Moral Law. If Kant was right, there can be no conflict between reason and morality, which are one and the same thing looked at in two difference ways. And since only morally acceptable law is law properly so called, there can also be no conflict between reason and law: If the Moral Law requires it, you must do it; and if you ought to do it, that is because the Moral Law requires it.

The Relativist rejects this identification of morality with reason while insisting on an identification of morality with convention. What we are considering here is whether the relativist contradicts himself when he declares to be inadvisable an action that he acknowledges to be morally or legally binding. Absolutists claim that he does, but they cannot prove their claim merely by pointing out that the relativist's conceptions of rationality and morality are unacceptable to them. That is certainly true, but it proves only that the relativist's views contradict those of the absolutist. It does not prove that the relativist's views contradict themselves.

If they nevertheless seem to the absolutist to do so, it is because he is blurring some distinctions that the relativist makes. Thus, consider another of Feldman's objections to conventionalism. Defining conventionalism as belief that an action is *morally right* if and only if it is permitted by the conventions of the agent's society, Feldman criticizes it on the grounds that it requires praising as *right* all and only actions that accord with convention. Here Feldman overlooks the distinction between describing an action as "right" and describing it as "morally right." Then, Feldman takes the conventionalist to be saying, "we *ought* to conform to the conventions of our own society."[7] Feldman never notices that in thus interpreting relativism, he has turned it into its opposite. By sliding from "morally right" to "right" and then it "it ought to be done" he has blurred the distinction between describing an action as consistent with a given set of social conventions and recommending it as the most rational course of behavior. So, he has turned what was meant to be a purely descriptive account into a set of moral prescriptions.

Of course, considered from the absolutist's point of view, Feldman has made no mistake. According to orthodox absolutist doctrine, there is no important distinction between the requirements of morality and those of reason; so there is none between what you ought to do as a matter of reason and what you ought to do as a matter of law and morality. Therefore, when the absolutist hears the relativist declare an action to be morally and legally obligatory in a given society, he automatically takes him to mean that it is what people in that society ought, all things considered, to do. And that seems to the absolutist to constitute a recommendation of various forms of evil.

Well, it does not. To construe it so is just to miss the point and beg the question, by attributing to the relativist the very use of words which it is his purpose to reject as meaningless. No wonder that, so interpreted, relativism seems to defeat itself! So understood, the relativist is accepting the very absolutism he thought he was repudiating. So regarded, he is contradicting himself by condemning as immoral (when he declares to be irrational) the behavior he has earlier praised as moral (by saying that it is in accord with custom and convention.) Well, the blunt but accurate reply is that the contradiction is wholly in the absolutist's mind. The relativist does not use moral and legal terms as the absolutist dies. He thinks absolutist usage misguided.

It is possible, of course, that the relativist is wrong about this and the absolutist right. I do not think so, but my immediate purpose is not to prove that relativism is true. I am at the moment merely trying to rescue it from the tiresome *ad hominem* charge that it deprives its holders of the right to criticize as wrong actions that they acknowledge to be legally and morally correct. My answer to this charge has been that it confuses describing an action as morally or legally right with praising it as rational. That these are not different things from the point of view of the absolutist is true, but to assume that the absolutist is right is to beg the very question that is at issue.

How the Relativist Can Criticize Moral and Legal Conventions

It is now clear how a relativist can advise an individual not to obey the legal and moral conventions of his society. Can he also advise a society that its legal or moral institutions are bad ones, which they ought not to have? I don't see why not. Consider a society in which the practice of slavery is in accord with established morality and law. The relativist's principles require him to agree that slaveholding is legally and morally acceptable in that society, but they do not require him to agree that the practice is a good one. On the contrary, having acknowledged its legitimacy, the relativist remains perfectly free to question its advisability.

Here is why: Like everything else that human beings do, the making of rules can be done badly or well. It is done well if the rules advance the aims of those who make them; otherwise it is done badly. So, although the existence of a rule of morality or law settles the moral or legal question, it does not settle the question whether the rule is itself a good one. There is another test of that. If it helps to advance the aims of those who made it or must live by it, the rule is a good one; otherwise not. Therefore, acknowledging that an institution is legally and morally permissible in a given society does not require agreeing that the law and morality which make it so are themselves good law and morality. On the contrary, using the interests of those it affects as the standard of good and bad practice, one may declare to be bad rules that one agrees define what is to count as moral and legal.

There is, of course, ambiguity in the last remark. Conduct that is in the interests of some people might not be in the interests of others. Thus, slavery might be in the interests of slave holders if not in the interests of slaves. However, this is precisely the sort of fact which a relativist can easily accommodate. Moral complexity and ambiguity of this kind are hard for the absolutist to fathom, but they are right down the relativist's alley. Indeed, that is one of the things that makes relativism seem to the absolutist to be so morally slippery and slimy.

Is the relativist who judges an institution as good or bad not appealing to a transcendent standard of morality and law, something he is forbidden by his principles to do? No. He is appealing to reason; so, he is appealing to a standard that transcends the legal and moral conventions of any society. However, it would be wrong to say that he is invoking transcendent standards *of* morality. It would be more accurate to say that he is using transcendent standards *for* morality. According to the relativist, convention and custom are the only standards determining what is to count as moral and legal. However, to say so is not by any means to say that they are the only standards determining which laws and moralities count as good ones. Not so. To decide that, we must appeal not to convention and custom but to the interests of the people involved.

These distinctions are necessary because absolutists have confused things by assuming that judging a practice to be morally or legally valid and binding is equivalent to judging it to be good. Thus, Aquinas, the spokesman for medieval absolutism, denied that there are any such things as bad laws proper so-called. According to Aquinas, all laws are good laws. Evil laws—laws contrary to God, Reason, or Nature—are not laws but human imitations of law. Seen from this idealistic and proleptical point of view, the idea that someone can have a legal or moral obligation to engage in bad practice is a contradiction in terms—which is why the relativist seems to the absolutist to be contradicting himself if he says that such an institution as slavery might in fact be morally and legally binding but not on that account good.

The answer to this, however, is simply that the relativist need not accept absolutist usage. In the relativist's view, a legal or moral standard is binding if it is *valid*, and there are other measures of an institution's validity besides its goodness. According to H. L. A. Hart, the main test is whether it is consistent with more fundamental (first order) legal and moral conventions.[8] Thus, slavery was legally valid in the United States before the civil war, because the laws protecting it had been constitutionally enacted. If slavery had also been consistent with Christian ideals of human equality, it would also have been morally valid in the United States, as it was morally valid in ancient Greece, which made no assumptions of equality. Whether slavery was also a good practice in either Southern or Greek society is a legitimate question but a different one. So, acknowledging its legal and moral validity need not prevent a relativist from criticizing it.

How a Relativist Can Condemn a Society's Conventions as Evil

So far, I have argued that a relativist can criticize as contrary to the interests of the society or its members institutions that are, according to him, legally and morally binding. Criticism of this kind does not object to one institution on the grounds that it is contrary to another institution. However, since it appeals to the interests of people in the society, it can still be regarded as a kind of internal criticism. So, you may wonder whether the relativist is capable of genuinely external criticism. I shall now show that he is. Besides condemning a practice as contrary to the interests of those it affects, the relativist can condemn it on the grounds that it is contrary to his own values or to those of his hearers.

For an illustration, let us consider slavery once again. And, for the sake of discussion, let us grant that there is a hypothetical society in which its practice is legally and morally valid and benefits everybody as well as would any other workable arrangement. Then, having made these highly implausible assumptions, let us ask whether there is anything left for the relativist to say in criticism.

The answer, I think, is that there will not be much left to say that will (or should) interest any person in the society in question. The stipulations just made provide that every person in that society has good reasons to be satisfied with it. However, there is still plenty that can be said outside the society by and to people who do not share its values. Someone else can always object, "Well, *they* may like it; but *I* do not. Serving the will of others demeans people in ways that seem to me to be inhumane. I prefer societies of free men and women." In a word, there is nothing to prevent a relativist from condemning a social institution or a social order simply on the grounds that it is not the sort he prefers.

Is not this an appeal to a moral standard? Well, to invoke a distinction made earlier, it is a standard *for* morality; but that does not make it a standard *of* morality. By using it, the relativist is not appealing to any principle or rule that is a constituent part of any morality. Rather, he is simply judging a morality by appealing to what Hume aptly called sentiment. The point I wish to make here is simply that there is nothing to prevent him from doing that. He cannot, like the absolutist, appeal to a Higher Morality; for he does not believe that any such morality exists. However, that need not prevent him from harshly judging a principle of morality simply on the grounds that he does not like it.

Why should others care what he likes? No reason, unless they either share his values or value his opinions. However, they might. In thus expressing his own personal sentiments (as Hume called them), the relativist might succeed in invoking what Hume aptly called human sympathy. He might even find that everybody shares his sentiments. If so, he will be giving all his listeners good reason to disapprove too. Like him, they will have all the reason they need to regard the institution of slavery as evil.

To be sure, the relativist's sentiments won't be good enough for the absolutist, who thinks he has a better basis for judgment—namely, Moral Law. And what the absolutist means when he says that relativism undercuts itself and encourages evil is that relativists cannot stand on this solid absolutist ground to combat what the absolutist regards as unconditional evil. However, thus to criticize the relativist is obviously to beg the question. Whether the absolutist is standing on the solid ground of an impersonal and culturally transcendent moral standard or on the shifting sands of personal sentiment and appeals to human sympathy is precisely what is in dispute.

How the Relativist Can Accommodate Social Conflict

I believe that the *argumentum ad Nazium* has now been decisively answered, but it sometimes takes a peculiar form that we had better look at separately before we conclude.

According to Fred Feldman, relativism not only entails tolerance of evil; it also makes "social conflict" impossible.[9] This is not very clear language. What does it mean? To show us, Feldman imagines a society where the police poke out the eyes of voyeurs. A visitor declares this practice immoral. Natives affirm its morality. Here, says Feldman, is real conflict. Yet, on the relativist's view, the native means "Poking out the eyes of voyeurs is immoral in society S_1" while the visitor means "Poking out the eyes of voyeurs is immoral in society S_2," and there is no reason why both statements cannot be true. Feldman regards this as a *reductio ad absurdum* of relativism.

Like other versions of the *argumentum ad Nazium,* this argument just begs the question. To see how, look at the premise—the contention that our native and visitor have a real conflict. What, exactly, does this mean? Presumably: That one of them thinks true, while the other thinks false, the absolute (unrelativized) statement, "Poking out the eyes of voyeurs is immoral." Perhaps. Let us admit as much. What will it prove? If the relativist is right, it will prove merely that the native and the visitor are both mistaken. Each is an absolutist, who wrongly thinks that, in judging an action to be moral or immoral, he is appealing to a higher morality than that of his own society. But, if the relativist is right, there is no Higher Morality; so, there is none to be used in deciding whether poking out the eyes of voyeurs is absolutely moral or immoral. Of course, the relativist may be wrong about this; but, as we noted before, you cannot prove it by assuming it.

Summary and Conclusions

I have done nothing in this chapter to prove that relativism is true. The proof of that, if the relativist is right, is to be found in the plain facts: Different societies have different moralities and laws, and there exists no morality or law that is demonstrably binding on all societies alike.

What I have tried to do here is rebut attempts to prove that a relativist is precluded by his view from criticizing practices that even he regards as evil. I have argued that he can criticize institutions as contrary either to the interests of those who have them or to the interests of those who are obliged to obey them, and he can criticize institutions as contrary either to his own preferences or to those of his audience. These two forms of criticism will not satisfy the absolutist, who will accept nothing less than criticism appealing to a transcendent morality. But to suppose that that refutes relativism is to assume what is in dispute.

If critics wish to do more than beg the question, they are going to have to do more than point with a sense of outrage and shock at the fact that the relativist denies the existence of culturally transcendent standards of morality that seem to the absolutist to be self-evident. That fact goes without saying. There would be no point to relativism if it did not. However, to point it out is not by any means to prove either that such a transcendent morality exists or that the relativist lacks non-moral grounds on which to criticize institutions he admits to be legally and morally valid. It is merely to say: Relativism is wicked and false because it denies the truth of absolutism.

Notes

1. Thus, Robert C. Solomon begins his textbook *Ethics: A Brief Introduction* (New York: McGraw Hill, 1984), p. 9, by wondering whether relativists can condemn evil. And the same question is central to the discussion of relativism in Fred Feldman, *Introductory Ethics* (Englewood Cliffs, NJ: Prentice-Hall, 1978), pp. 160-172. For an earlier statement, see W. T. Stace. *The Concept of Morals* (New York: Macmillan, 1962), p. 58. For more recent comment, see David Lyons, "Ethical Relativism and the Problem of Incoherence: and Geoffrey Harrison, "Relativism and Tolerance," in Jack W. Meiland and Michael Krausz, editors, *Relativism: Cognitive and Moral* (Notre Dame, IN: University of Notre Dame Press, 1982), pp. 205-243.

2. "Moral Relativism Defended," reprinted in Meiland and Krausz, pp. 189-205.
3. Feldman, *op. cit.*, p. 164. See also Stace, *op. cit.*, pp. 52-56.
4. "The Truth in Relativism," reprinted in Meiland and Krausz, p. 179.
5. "Moral Relativism Defended" in Meiland and Knausg, 189-205. Also see Gilbert Harman and Judith Jarvis Thompson, *Moral Relativism and Moral Objectivity* (Cambridge, MA: Blackwell, 1996).
6. The best short discussion I know of the distinctions to be made in this section are to be found in C. H. Whiteley, "On Duties," in Joel Feinberg, editor, *Moral Concepts* (London: Oxford University Press, 1969).
7. Feldman, *op. cit.*, p. 164, emphasis added. The same confusion is evident in Stace, *op. cit.*, p. 10 and p. 28.
8. *The Concept of Law* (Oxford: Clarendon Press, 1961), pp. 97-107. Hart here addresses positive (i.e., conventional) law alone, but his concept extends naturally to positive (i.e., conventional,) morality as well.
9. Feldman, *op. cit.*, p. 170.

Appendix

Relativism and Moral Judgments: A Reply to Sullivan

I

Professor Sullivan's critique of my paper raises many interesting and important issues. I shall take them up in approximately the order in which Sullivan raises them.

Sullivan begins by attributing to me two intentions: One is to advance and defend a *normative*, but relativistic, ethical theory; the other is to claim that this theory is true because *analytic* of the intentions, or thoughts, of speakers. To the first, Sullivan objects that my account does not cohere with our "moral intuitions," the traditional test of normative ethical theories. To the second, he objects that my view, a form of moral relativism, ignores the absolutist convictions that most people have about their moral judgments. When Sullivan has finished making these two objections, he adds a third, by criticizing as inconclusive my suggestion that relativism is confirmed by the diversity of social customs.

II

Let me begin with the claim that I was advancing a normative ethical theory. This claim is hard for me to understand. I began my paper by explaining that my concern was not what people *ought* to do because they have certain interests, inclinations, or dispositions but what they are *obligated* to do because they are subject to certain rules. Then I said that, because different rules are in force in different societies, people in society A may be obligated to do what people in society B are not obligated to do. Finally, for the sake of clarity, I added that this thesis "is purely descriptive; it is utterly devoid of prescriptive force" (p. 192). I do not know how I could have made my intentions plainer.

Having stated my intentions, I then went on to acknowledge their implication: Relativists cannot criticize the morality of a society on the grounds that it is itself *immoral*—contrary to morality. If relativism is right, such criticism is nonsensical—as nonsensical as declaring that the rules of law are themselves illegal, contrary to law.[3] No matter, I hastened to add. It does not follow that moralities cannot be criticized. It merely follows that they must be criticized in *non-moral* terms. Thus, even where it cannot sensibly be described as immoral, the institution of slavery can always be condemned as inhumane or inefficient, contrary to human feeling or human interests.[4]

To this, Sullivan objects that declaring conduct inhumane and inefficient is itself a form of *moral* criticism. This is a verbal dispute. Sullivan counts all evaluations as moral evaluations, provided that they are evaluations of conduct. I do not. For me, moral evaluation is a special kind of evaluation of conduct. Which of us is right? Both of us. The word *moral* derives from the Latin word *more*, for conduct, habit, or custom.[5] So, as Alasdair MacIntyre has reminded us, in classical times a moral concern was any concern with conduct; the moral was distinct only from the physical. Therefore, Sullivan's usage has a long history and respectable credentials. But words change their meanings. In modern times, the words *moral* and *ethical* have increasingly been used in a way that makes the moral to be the counterpart of not the physical but the legal.[6] Therefore, my usage is also legitimate. You pays your money and you takes your choice.

Whether my choice is best, I will not undertake to argue here. More to the point here is the fact that I made my usage clear from the very beginning. As I plainly said, my paper was an attempt to point out that a relativist, who denies the possibility of moral evaluation of diverse moralities, because he denies the existence of a Higher Morality, may nevertheless recognize the possibility of non-moral evaluation of these same moralities. If Sullivan wants to say that these evaluations also count as moral judgments in his lexicon, he is certainly entitled to do so; but they will continue to count as non-moral evaluations in my different lexicon.

Whichever lexicon you prefer, the substantive point holds. At the risk of beating a dead horse, let me state this point once again: There are several ways to evaluate conduct. One is to evaluate it as consistent with or contrary to the relevant rules, the ones that happen to be in force. To avoid verbal disputes and charges of begging the question, call this *dooble* evaluation, meaning evaluation of conduct as dooble or imdooble. My point was that no rules of dooble are in force everywhere. Instead, different rules are in force in different societies. So, what is dooble in A might be imdooble in B. Does Sullivan wish to dispute this? I doubt it. The fact is too plain to be denied. Sullivan's objection is, then, not to my substantive thesis but only to my way of stating it, and to the relativistic conclusions that I deduce from it.

III

So much for Sullivan's first point. Now for the second, Sullivan's belief that my thesis is meant to be analytic of the meanings, or intentions, of speakers. Here I must take some blame for Sullivan's misunderstanding. I should have explained that my analysis was purely extensionalist: It concerned only *denotations*, not also *connotations*. What I was trying to do was state the truth conditions for moral judgments—to spell out the circumstances under which they count as true or false. I was not trying to state, or to explain, what people have in mind when they make such judgments.

This distinction is important, because denotation may vary even when connotation does not. Thus, consider the sentence "Having several wives is immoral." If moral relativism is right, the existence of different conventions in the two places makes this sentence true in Selma, Alabama, where it is routinely affirmed; false in Saudi Arabia, where it (or some Arabic counterpart) is routinely denied. Yet to speakers in both places, this sentence may connote, or intend, a comparable thought, viz., "God has forbidden the having of several wives." It is just that Selmans affirm this thought while Saudis deny it.[7]

It is this similarity of connotation together with the dissimilarity of affirmation that gives rise to the illusion—which Sullivan takes to be a reality—that Selmans and Saudis are disagreeing with each other. Each group believes that it is interpreting the will of God, and it assumes that the other group is doing so too, only wrongly. In short, the two groups think that they have contrary opinions about the same thing. That is their common theory of the meanings of their diverse moral judgments. It is also Sullivan's theory.

Relativists like myself have a different theory. We believe that neither group is expressing or interpreting God's will; so, *a fortiori*, neither group is expressing or interpreting God's will rightly. Instead, although neither group realizes it, each is articulating or interpreting the peculiar conventions of its own society; and, for the most part, each is doing so correctly. It is true that neither group realizes this, but the fact is also irrelevant. What matter to moral theory are the different circumstances that cause different groups of people to make dissimilar judgments, not their own misguided beliefs as to what cause them to make these judgments.

Dismissal of the beliefs and intentions of speakers may seem arbitrary, but it is standard practice in behavioral science. Consider, for example, the belief that guided those misguided souls who conducted the Spanish inquisition. According to this belief, when someone was condemned as a witch, it was because she was "in league with the devil." We, however, have a quite different theory. We believe that what once caused some people to condemn some other people as witches was not that the latter were allied with the devil (who does not exist) but that they were allied with unpopular social groups—Muslims, Jews, gypsies, heretics, etc. We do not regard as relevant the fact that this interpretation of the word *witch* does not comport with the beliefs of those who used the word.

Sullivan objects that this attitude shows insufficient regard for moral intuitions. Not so. Like absolutists, we relativists take moral intuitions seriously; we just attach different significance to them. Where absolutists regard moral intuitions as insights into a culturally transcendent and universally binding Morality, relativists regard most moral intuitions as expressions of locally prevailing moralities. Relativists take this attitude because we have clear evidence that moral intuitions vary with locality but no evidence that they are the same everywhere. Thus, Selmans disapprove of polygamy, while Saudis see nothing wrong with it.

IV

This brings us to Sullivan's third point. In the final analysis, what really offends Sullivan is my skepticism about the existence of a culturally transcendent Morality. Although the purpose of my paper was not to prove relativism but to rescue it from the charge that it is pragmatically self-refuting, I finished by indicating why relativists believe that local and variable morality is all the morality there is. The reason, I said all too briefly, is that, whereas we have much empirical evidence of the existence of diverse local moralities, we have no evidence whatsoever of the existence of a Higher Morality that is the same for everybody everywhere.

In reply, Sullivan notes that many philosophers believe that "cross-cultural moral diversity is consistent with underlying agreement on basic moral principles." Sullivan is right; many philosophers do believe this. The trouble is that no philosopher has been able to identify the unobserved, because underlying, agreement or explain how it gives rise to the observed, because evident, diversity. That fact seems to me to be very damning.

Here, briefly stated, is why. As I understand it, to say that certain rules are *in force* is to imply that these rules are being enforced or reinforced with sufficient effectiveness to ensure more or less regular compliance with them. But people could not readily or regularly comply with a given set of rules if they did not know them. Therefore, in a given society, where given rules and principles are in force, there is widespread unanimity as to what the rules are. Furthermore, where it exists, this unanimity is usually evident right on the surface, in the deeds and words of virtually all members of the society. Now, to come to the present case, if there were a culturally transcendent and universally binding Morality, it too would presumably be evident right on the surface, in the words and deeds of men everywhere. Therefore, the fact that it is not thus evident constitutes pretty convincing proof that it does not exist.[8]

It will be replied that this is an argument from ignorance, but so is our reason for being skeptical about unicorns. In all relevant respects, the two arguments are analogous. We have no convincing evidence that unicorns exist; there is neither a trace nor a fossil. So, we do not believe in unicorns. This inference may seem invalid, but it is saved by the fact that, if unicorns did exist, there would be some evidence of the fact. Just so, that we lack proof of the Moral Law in worldwide uniformity of word and deed, means that the Moral Law does not exist; because, if it did, so, in all probability, would the proof.

V

Sullivan does not address this problem. Instead, in a last ditch effort to undermine my view, he cites Lyons's distinction between appraiser group and agent group relativity. Then he observes that "Hocutt's version of relativism is evidently of the *agent's*-group type" and, after some explanatory remarks, goes on to ask, rhetorically, "how can it be legitimate... to move from an *appraiser's*-group descriptive relativity to an *agent's*-group relativity?"

This question seems to me to betray a failure to understand Sullivan's own observation that my theory concerns agent-group moralities. Lyons's distinction assumes that agent and appraiser have different moralities. If so, however, they are from different groups; and, in my view, the morality of one group is irrelevant to the moral evaluation of the conduct of people in a different group.[9] Saying so is, in fact, the central point of moral relativism, which maintains that, to make sense, distinctively moral appraisal of an agent's conduct must be done in terms of the morality that is in force in *her* community, not in somebody else's.

This claim will strike Lyons and Sullivan as arbitrary, but it is no more so than the exactly comparable idea that legal appraisal of an agent's conduct is relevant and meaningful only when it is done in terms of the law to which *she* is subject. Thus, it is fallacious for someone in Arabia to reason that people in Alabama are doing something illegal because it would be illegal if done in Arabia, where the rules are different. By my reasoning, it is equally fallacious for someone in Alabama to reason that people in Arabia are doing something immoral because they would be doing something immoral if they were doing it in Alabama, where the rules are different. That a good many people *do* reason like this is certainly true; but if moral relativism is even approximately right, they are wrong to do so.

VI

Sullivan's critique is an attack not on my view but on what he supposes that any view of morality ought to be—namely, an attempt to accommodate absolutist moral intuitions and convictions. That my view contradicts these Sullivan sees and holds against me. That my view contradicts them by intent he does not seem to understand, so transfixed is he by the presumption that any account of morality must intend to comport with his antecedently given convictions. Accommodating absolutist moral convictions is, however, no business for a relativist, who needs only to be able to explain them. So, Sullivan's critique reduces to the argument that my view is wrong because it does not agree with his; but, although the premise is true, the conclusion does not follow.

Notes

1. This essay, now very slightly revised for clarity and terminological consistency, first appeared in *The Philosophical Forum*, XVII, 3, (1986): 188-200. The "Reply to Sullivan" appeared, with Sullivan's critique, in *Philosophia* 24, 2 (1994): 203-210.
2. An illustration is the present uncertainty in the United States over the morality of abortion.
3. Compare the claim, "The standard meter bar is not a meter long."
4. Sometimes, of course, slavery can sensibly be criticized as immoral. That was certainly the case in the United States, where slavery was clearly contrary to a Christian morality that holds all men to be equal in the eyes of God. Slavery was, however, pretty clearly not contrary to the morality of ancient Greece, which had no such egalitarian beliefs.
5. The same is true of the word *ethical*, which relates to the Greek word *ethos*, for conduct.
6. That the word *moral* has narrowed in this way, becoming a correlative of the word *legal*, is noted (and protested) by MacIntyre, in *After Virtue*. This narrower usage probably stems from ancient Hebrew practice, in which morality was an extension of divine law.
7. Actually, I am uncomfortable with this talk of common thoughts. In the final analysis, nominalistic talk of sentences would be better; but here, I believe, it would only complicate things.
8. When evaluating this argument, you should remember that it concerns the rules that determine what people are legally or morally *obligated* (i.e., required) to do. It does not concern the rules that determine what people *ought*, rationally speaking, to do. In my opinion, these are quite different. Unlike the rules of morality, the rules of rationality are the same everywhere. This is so because the rules of practical reason are virtual tautologies like "You should do what promises to get you what you want," whereas rules of morality are socially dependent injunctions like "Do not have intercourse with another man's wife."
9. In my view, disagreements within a group mean either that somebody has got the group morality wrong or that the group morality is indeterminate, perhaps because it has yet to be, or is no longer, settled.

15

Rights: Literal and Proleptic

Rights and Duties

What are *rights*, and what does it mean to say that someone has them? A correct but incomplete answer is that your having a right means that someone else has a duty. With one exception, that A has right R with respect to B means that B has duty D with respect to A.[1] That my wife has a right to my fidelity means that I have a duty to remain faithful; that your children have a right to your support means that you have a duty to support them. Nobody has rights unless somebody else has duties.

The converse proposition is also true. If B has duty D with respect to A, it is because A has right R with respect to B. My having a duty to be faithful means that my wife has a right to my fidelity; your having a duty to support your children means that they have a right to your support. Rights and duties are two sides of one coin; you do not have either side without the other.

Yet we go in a circle if we define rights in terms of duties, then define duties in terms of rights and stop there. To define both, we need a third term which we know how to define independently. In the case of *legal* rights and duties, which are paradigmatic, the needed term is *law*. That your children have a legal right to your support means that some rule of law confers this right on them; that you have a legal duty to support them means that the same rule of law imposes this duty on you.

To define rights and duties more inclusively, we need the broader concept of a *rule,* which encompasses not just rules of *law* but also rules of *morality* and *etiquette.*[2] That your friends have a moral right to your aid in times of need means that the rules of morality confer this right on them and impose that duty on you. That participants in a game of cards have a right to a fair shuffle means that the rules of etiquette that govern card playing give them this right and impose the correlative duty on dealers. In general, person A has right R and person B has correlative duty D if and only if some rule of law, morality, or etiquette LME confers R on A and imposes D on B.

Rules

Only one task remains: to tie these verbal formulas down to determinate realities. In other words, we need to explain, in empirically meaningful terms, what is meant by saying that a rule of law, morality, or etiquette exists and confers a right on A while imposing a duty on B. More precisely: We need to specify the verifiable circumstances under which this claim would be true.

I suggest the following hypothesis as an account of the claim that a rule R *exists*, or is *in force*, in a social group G: Within G there is a *regular practice* of permitting, enabling, or encouraging some persons P to behave in one way while requiring other persons Q to behave accordingly. Where that is so, we may say that group G *has* a rule of law, morality, or etiquette LME that confers a right R on persons P while imposing a duty D on persons Q. Thus, suppose that wives in group G are routinely permitted, enabled, and encouraged by praise or reward to demand fidelity from their husbands, and husbands are routinely required by censure or punishment to comply with these demands. Then we may say that, *under the rules in force in G*, wives have a right to fidelity and husbands have a duty to provide it.

As this should make clear, the reality of a rule is evident in the existence of the behavior of reinforcing conformity with it by using effective sanctions. If these sanctions are provided by officials of government, then the rule belongs to *law*; otherwise to *morality* or *etiquette*. Thus, two kinds of rules are relevant to the determination of rights and duties: *official* rules of law and *unofficial* rules of morality or etiquette. The former are made and enforced by officials of government acting in their official capacities, the latter by ordinary persons in the course of their daily lives.

Rules ought not to be confused with their verbal formulation. A rule of law is not the statute that proclaims it; nor is a rule of etiquette what Miss Manners says. Instead, a rule, whether of law, morality, or etiquette, is a practice maintained by sanctions—social reinforcement. Things are done in a regular way because people in the group are regularly praised and rewarded for doing them in that way, or routinely condemned and punished for not doing them in that way. A correct statement of the rule merely describes this state of affairs, or announces the intention of bringing it into being.

Given this understanding of rules, we can define not just rights and duties but also the related terms *desert* and *justice*, or *fairness.* The prize is deserved by the runner who finishes the race first having obeyed the rules that govern the contest; punishment is deserved by the criminal who robs a bank in violation of the law. Justice is done, and the game is fair, when the winning runner gets the prize and the bank robber gets the punishment that are due them, these being the results that are prescribed by the rules. Persons charged with enforcing these rules have duties to behave accordingly, and others have the right to demand that they do so. In short, a person *deserves* what is prescribed by the rules, and *justice* is done when he gets what he deserves under the rules. Reference to the rules is essential. To talk of desert or justice where the concept is not defined by some rule of law, morality, or etiquette makes no determinate sense.

Rights: Artificial and Natural

We have seen that a right exists if and only if it is conferred by an applicable rule, which exists if and only if there is a regular practice of protecting the right by enforcing the duties that, under the rule, are correlative to it. This may not be what people have in mind when they say that a right exists, but, in cases where talk of rights has determinate truth value, it indicates the empirical conditions for the statement's being true.

It will be objected that these remarks apply only to *conventional*, or *man-made,* rights and duties. According to the doctrine of *natural law*, which was invented by Stoic jurists in ancient Rome and given its definitive formulation by Thomas Aquinas in the high Middle Ages before being made modern by John Locke,[3] there is also another kind of rights and duties—namely *natural* rights and duties—to which the empirical test just described does not apply.[4]

Why not? Because conventional rights and duties are created and conferred on us in obvious ways by visible men, while natural rights and duties are supposed to be created and conferred on us in mysterious ways by an invisible God, or by Nature.[5] Hence, to find out whether a conventional right exists, we need only observe behavior, but no such test works for natural rights. To discover that citizens of Communist China have no *man-made* right to criticize their government, you need only note that arrest and incarceration are the fate of those who do. Yet, it is said, citizens of the People's Republic do have a *natural*, or God-made, right to criticize their leaders. That this right is systematically violated in practice does not mean that it is unreal, just that it is not respected.

This raises a question. How, if there is no empirical test for them, are we to know what natural rights we have? The traditional reply is that, since natural rights are not known *a posteriori*, by observing human practices, they must be known *a priori*, by using the Natural Light of Reason. Before going on to enumerate the rights to which he thought this claim applied, Thomas Jefferson expressed this view when he declared, "We hold these truths to be self-evident..."

Difficulties in the Doctrine of Natural Rights

Jefferson's famous proclamation, which faithfully echoed Locke's, has inspired many a political upheaval, but it faces an insuperable intellectual difficulty. Evident truths ought to be evident to all rational men; there ought to be no dispute about them—else it is not clear what is meant by saying that they are evident. Yet disagreements about natural rights are both commonplace and intractable, that which is "evident" to A being at the same time evidently false to B.

If you have any doubt about it, consider just Locke's famous list: life, liberty, and property. Even those who agree that these are natural rights disagree as to what this means. In Locke's view, your having a right to life meant that other people were not permitted to cause your death by stealing your food; it did not mean that other people were required to keep you alive by feeding you.[6] Even when Locke expressed this view, however, many people had the opposite belief—that, if A needs food and B has more than he needs, then A has the right to demand that B share, and B is obligated to comply. Even in Locke's day many people regarded this proposition as not just true but also self-evidently and indisputably so. It is, however, not clear how two opposed views can both be self-evidently and indisputably true.

This difficulty arises for the following reason. As we saw earlier, rights are the correlatives of duties: But although rights are nice things to have, duties are irksome, and this is a cause for dispute. Where there is a reasonably clear empirical test of a right and its correlative duty, there is room for hope that such disputes can be resolved by rational debate; not so where the right in question is a merely natural right, for which there is no empirical test. Thus, it has been clear since *Roe v Wade* that women in America have a *legal* right to get an abortion in the first trimester of pregnancy. It is, however, not clear whether there is such a right under *natural* law. Invoking their self-evident right as women to determine the use of their own bodies, some say Yes; invoking the fetus's self-evident right not to be killed, others say No. That neither they nor anybody else can say what it would take to settle the issue indicates that the question is unclear. We know what is meant by saying that a conventional right exists. What is meant by saying that a natural right exists is not so obvious.

Closely connected with this epistemological problem is an even more serious ontological difficulty. Saying that natural rights exist where they lack protection detaches the concept from the very thing that gives it such determinate meaning as it has for us, making it largely emotive. As we have emphasized, that someone has a right means that, under the rules, exercise of this right is protected by enforcement of the correlative duties. This is not a merely incidental fact about rights; it is of their essence. Where there is no protection for a right, it is not clear what is meant by saying that the right exists.

Some Standard but Unsatisfactory Replies

There are two replies to this objection, one very old, the other comparatively new. The old reply was that natural rights *are* protected—in invisible ways by God, if not also in visible ways by men. Consider Communist China again. Grant that its leaders do not protect those who criticize them. Locke believed that, because God has promised to punish wicked leaders in the hereafter, the right to criticize even them enjoys protection—the invisible protection of an invisible God.

Unfortunately for this reply, *protection* is an example of what J. L. Austin inelegantly but accurately described as a success word.[7] You can try to protect something and fail, but if you protect it you succeed. If the "protection" is not effective, it is not real. But it is clear to all who will take the trouble to look, that the invisible protection supposedly being provided natural (or "human") rights by God is not effective in China, whose rulers share neither Locke's theistic religion nor his liberal politics. To protect the people of Communist China from their wicked leaders, God would need to punish those leaders now, in the present era, not wait until we and they are all dead, when punishment can do nobody any good.

This difficulty is not solved, merely exacerbated, when talk of natural rights is divorced, as it has increasingly been since the Enlightenment, from its theological provenance. Because irresolvable disagreements about the will of God caused bloody conflicts during the Protestant Reformation, Enlightenment thinkers resolved to forego appeals to theology in discussions of morality and politics. The result has been that few philosophers since Locke claim a divine origin for natural rights. Nowadays, natural rights are said to be given to us not by God but by Nature. So, although they are not always evident in the behavior of human beings, they are implicit, somehow, in human reason, the most distinctive part of human nature. That is why, it is said, we can discover our natural rights merely by reflecting on what it means to be human. Reflection on reason will make it obvious that human beings have certain rights even where—as in the People's Republic of China—they lack effective protection. Or so it is believed.

Unfortunately, to embrace this belief is to jump from the frying pan into the fire. Talk of natural rights at least had some semblance of meaning when these were conceived as gifts of a divine lawgiver. In that case, natural rights were held to be parallel to man-made rights and could be understood accordingly, as having some protection, however nominal. As soon, however, as you say that natural rights differ from conventional rights in not needing protection, either human or divine, you take away even the nominal parallel and raise the following question: In what sense are "natural rights" *rights*? So far as man-made rights are concerned, an unprotected right is a contradiction in terms. Without protection, man-made rights do not exist; they are not rights. How, then, can you say that a natural right is unprotected without implying that it too is not a right? Why isn't that a contradiction in terms?

It will not do to reply that natural rights are rights in a special sense of the word, being *moral* as opposed to *legal* rights. This reply is unsatisfactory in two ways. First, if "natural rights" are not rights in the *same* sense of the word as conventional rights, then they are not rights in the sense of the word that is at issue. Nor are they rights in the standard acceptation of the term. So, they are not rights properly so-called. Trying to make them rights by redefining the term is like trying to make a dog into a cat by defining a dog as a feline animal. That it attempts to do precisely this is the central defect in the doctrine of natural rights. Second, rights of morality and etiquette *are* rights in the same sense of the word *rights* as legal rights and are just as much in need of protection. Where there is no protection for your "right" to a fair shuffle or to honest business dealing—where that "right" is never respected—then your claim to have it is empty.

It appears that Bentham was right: Talk of *natural* rights is nonsense on stilts. To repeat: a right is something for which there is protection. So, if there is no God to protect the rights that men don't—and there might as well not be if He is going to wait until the hereafter to do anything—then these "rights" are unreal; they do not deserve to be called rights. All rights are conventional.

Natural Rights as Proleptic, Not Literal

If the doctrine of natural rights is nonsensical, why is it popular? Because the doctrine is nonsensical only if it is taken literally; it makes sense on a different reading, which I shall now try to explain.

As we have already noted, empirical fact about social practices is not and never has been the test of natural rights; the test of these is desire. Rights are good things to have, so people want them. Wanting them, they are easily persuaded that they ought to have them, this being one of the common (if loose) ways of expressing belief that having them would be a good thing. Once people think they ought to have something, however, they are prone to conclude that other people owe it to them; in other words, they have a right to it. In this way, wish turns into demand: I want it, so you owe it to me. But since I cannot prove this by citing empirical evidence, I infer that its truth must be self-evident—a truth of reason if not empirical fact. Others may disagree with this claim, but in the absence of an empirical test for rights, they cannot hope to refute it.

If this hypothesis is correct, talk of natural rights is best understood as not *literal* but *proleptic* or *protreptic* speech—an attempt to make something true by saying that it already is true.[8] Roughly, "X has a natural right to R" means not "X has a right to R" but "Since X's having R would be a good thing, X ought to have a right to R; therefore, behave as if he did."[9] Considered as such, claims to natural right are not so much attempts to *report* rights as to *anticipate* and *create* them. Thus, saying that citizens of Communist China have a natural but unprotected right to criticize their government means "Although they do not in fact have this right, their having it would be a good thing; so, behave as if it were already so." Disagreements over whether a natural right exists, then, are not so much disagreements about facts as disagreements in attitude. In other words, they are contests of wishes.

This theory not only explains why people believe that their claims to natural rights are evidently true; it also explains why other, equally rational, people regard these same claims as evidently false and why there is no way to settle the resulting disputes without a fight or compromise. Thus, A, who covets a share of B's food, money, or power but cannot establish his claim by citing clear principles of man-made law or morality, asserts his self-evident natural right to it, secure in his belief that, although he cannot prove this claim, nobody, including B, can disprove it. Not wanting to share, B merely counters by asserting her self-evident but equally unproved right to keep her food, money, or power and is equally secure in her belief that nobody, including A, will be able to refute this claim either. In each case, the claim to self-evidence means only that neither claimant can support his position with argument. For each, it is not a conclusion but a premise—not a deduction from facts but a prejudice, presumption, or presupposition from which to make deductions. This makes disputes about natural rights intractable in a way that disagreements about conventional rights are not.[10]

This interpretation also explains why intelligent and learned believers in natural rights say things that, literally interpreted, are plainly false. Locke repeatedly said that, because life, liberty, and property are conferred on us by natural right, no man *can* take them away. Yet Locke knew perfectly well that men were killing, enslaving, and robbing each other even as he spoke. Unless, then, we are to regard

Locke as a simpleton who wrote without thinking, we must regard his political philosophy as not literal but proleptic discourse. Although that is what he said, he did not literally mean "Nobody *can* take away another's life, liberty or property." He meant, and should have said, "Nobody *should* take another's life, liberty or property"—an evaluation that might be true even if the claim of empirical fact were false.

Secular Forms of the Doctrine of Natural Rights

If this analysis is correct, what Locke called natural rights may be regarded not as rights that people *do in fact have* but as rights that he thought they *ought to have* because their having them would be a good thing. If Locke expressed himself by saying that people already *have* these rights, it is not because he believed that what he said was literally so but because he knew that it was not so and hoped to help make it so by saying it.

That is why Locke thought of natural rights as divine, rather than human, gifts. By thus making them transcendent, he exempted them from the usual empirical requirements, making his claim irrefutable by evidence. For such ideal entities as natural rights, only ideal protections are needed; real protections are necessary only for real rights. Political authority is thereby made otherworldly; politics is turned, as in the middle ages, into theology—a highly convenient outcome for a theorist eager to deny final authority to some earthly king or legislature.

As noted earlier, the doctrine of natural rights has since Locke been detached from its theological moorings, as talk of God has given way to talk of Reason. This leaves only the doctrine's attachment to wishes as an anchor, but this attachment, which was the most important thing all along, is as strong as ever.

The writings of political philosopher Alan Gewirth provide unintentional illustration of this fact. Making no reference to God, Gewirth argues that people have a right—a natural right—to whatever they need. Never mind that there may be no guarantee for this right in law or custom. If the right is needed, Gewirth thinks that it exists; people have it. The fact is evident, Gewirth thinks, from an analysis of the concept of agency. Gewirth puts the analysis this way: Since human beings are by nature agents, they are entitled to the rights that are necessary for agency.[11] In plain English, people have a right to what they need.

The claim is mistaken. Although confusion of the two things has become commonplace, needs and rights are different; in fact, they are logically independent. That I need a car does not mean that I have a right to take one of yours, not even if you have more cars than you need. Nor does the situation change when the need is rooted in nature. Arguably, men have a biologically based, so natural, need to copulate with as many women as they can. Like the males of other mammalian species, some of them certainly try. It does not follow that every man has a right to a harem. Of course, Gewirth does not specifically say anything so clearly false. He is content to argue, more vaguely and abstractly, that we have rights to the "generic freedom," etc. that we need for "agency." But to resort to these metaphysical abstractions is to obscure absurdity with opacity.

The absurdity and the opacity are multiplied when Gewirth adds that, once we claim title to what we need for agency, we must be prepared to grant a similar title to every other prospective agent. On the most obvious interpretation, this adds to the claim that an agent has a right to what he needs the claim that everybody else has the same right. But although the new claim enjoys the authority of Kant, it too is false. To sail the high seas in comfort and safety, I need a large yacht with crew, but I may not on that account alone take forcible possession from the present owner, and if I did, the act could hardly be understood as an implied declaration that every other person who needs something has the right to take it.

Why Prolepsis Has Increased

I am arguing that, since rights exist only where they are protected by enforcement of the duties that are correlated with them, talk of natural but unprotected rights must be regarded as not literal but proleptic discourse. It is claiming what you want, or think you need, in the expectation that your claim will be treated as if it were true. You are saying that it is true in the hope of making it so.

Why anybody might do this is easy to see. Claims to rights have a distinctive power. Because they are subject to protection by enforcement of the correlative duties, rights are not merely things that people *want* or *need*; they are things that people have standing to *demand*. Furthermore, respecting rights is not a mere option, like granting wishes. When rights exist, respecting them is a binding obligation. You *must* respect someone's rights even when you do not wish to do so; it is a *requirement*, one subject to enforcement. Mere wishes have no such binding force. So, people are more likely to get what they want if they demand it as a right rather than request it as a wish. Therefore, people are tempted to claim a right even when they know that their claim is not true, in order to benefit from the power of the falsehood.

For this reason, people now make it a regular practice to say that they have a right to whatever they happen to want. As a result, everything you can mention is made an object of a claim to right. Thus, the local chiropractor declares on TV, "You have a *right* to feel good," meaning merely that he wants to help you feel good—for a fee. Similarly, the advocate of socialized medicine declares, "Everybody has a right to governmentally provided medical care," meaning merely that he wishes somebody would pay his medical bills, so that he will not have to pay them himself. And the United Nations *Declaration of Human Rights* declares that everybody has a *right*—a "human" right—to a well-paid occupation of his choice (We can all be rich brain surgeons.), to paid vacations (We can all spend three weeks each year in luxury hotels in Bermuda.), and so on. Name it, and if anybody wants it, somebody has said that he has a right to it. Claims to rights have become both ubiquitous and indiscriminate.

How Proleptic Discourse Poisons Politics

Though risible, this practice has been endorsed by distinguished philosophers of law. Calling it *manifesto speech*, Joel Feinberg acknowledges that much talk of rights is misleading if it is taken literally, but he defends it on the grounds that it helps people to get rights that they need or want.[12] Ronald Dworkin, a noted philosopher of jurisprudence, has argued in a different way to similar effect. Describing rights claims as moral and political trump cards, he has urged selected groups to play these cards whenever they want something, and he has made a career of urging judges in courts of law to grant their wishes when they grow insistent enough.[13] It appears not to matter that the claims in question are false, or that lying is an underhanded way to get what you want. A little inaccuracy is permissible if it serves a good cause.

The deception often works, but it has costs. When people get into the habit of claiming rights to everything they want or think they need, claims to rights will cease being demands and become merely plaintive or querulous expressions of wishes. Discourse that once belonged to the peremptory mode will then be transferred to the optative mode and lose much of its force. Instead of indicating an objective necessity, it will express a merely subjective desire, to which other persons will increasingly become indifferent or hostile. The resulting skepticism will extend not just to claims of natural right but also to other claims of right, including those that may be well-founded. In fact it has already happened. Having become endless and indiscriminate, demands for "rights" have begun to fall on deaf ears, like the shepherd boy's mischievous cries of "Wolf!"[14]

The harm done has not been limited to the concept of rights. We cannot degrade the way we talk about rights without degrading the way we talk and think about law, duty, desert and justice —the other members of the family. As a result, our understanding of *justice* has suffered degradation along with our understanding of rights. Once the word meant getting your due as that was defined by the rules. Now it means getting what you want or think you need, no matter what the rules may prescribe. That you did not win the Heissman trophy, succeed in business, or marry the woman you adored now means that "life is unfair"; never mind that you were a poor athlete, a lazy businessman, or a desultory suitor. In accordance with this whining usage, every personal failure or bit of bad luck has been made the basis for a claim of victimization by villains—society, racism, sexism, capitalism—of an abstract, so indeterminate, nature. Such thinking demoralizes those who engage in it and alienates everybody else.

It also causes great and lasting confusion. Whether other people are obligated to respect rights that you already have is one question; whether other people ought to give you rights that you want is another. The first question concerns *application,* the second *creation*, of a rule. "Do you *have* the right to smoke marijuana?" means "Does some rule confer this right on you?"—a question of empirical fact calling for an inquiry. "Should you be *given* the right to smoke marijuana?" means "Should we create a rule conferring this right on you?"—a question of social policy calling for a decision. By blurring the distinction, proleptic discourse causes people to talk past each other, A claiming that he already has a right while B wonders whether A's having it would be a good thing. So, there is no clear recognition of the issue between them, and where this is so there can be no satisfactory resolution.

Consider a not so hypothetical case. The members of a sailing club are meeting to discuss the claim, enthusiastically asserted by some and emphatically denied by others, that members have a "right" to bring pets into the clubhouse. Each side feels very strongly about the matter. How is the question to be settled?

To say, we shall first have to decide how the question is to be interpreted. There are two possibilities. It could be regarded simply as a straightforward factual question: Do the club's rules grant the right, either explicitly or by implication? If so, the issue is easy to settle. Things get harder, however, if the question is understood differently, as asking not whether the right already *exists* but whether it *ought* to. Here, the terms of the debate must be different. It must now be asked not what the present rules provide but whether new rules making such a provision ought to be enacted. No longer a question for lawyers and judges, it has become a question for legislators.[15] Getting this distinction clear may not suffice to settle the issue, but it is certainly necessary to doing so.

How the Rot Spreads

When Locke ascribed to men natural rights to "life, liberty, and property," the duties he associated with these were purely negative. Your having these rights meant that other people had the duty to refrain from killing you, enslaving you, or taking what you owned; it did not also mean that other people had the duty to provide you with the property you might need to sustain your life and enjoy your liberty. By insensible degrees, the understanding of natural (or "human") rights has changed. Now your having a right to life is often taken to mean that other people are obligated to supply you with the means to sustain your life if you are unable or unwilling to do it yourself. Thus, a moral right to unlimited medical care at government expense is frequently urged solely on the grounds that it is inherent in one's "right to life." In short, where "natural rights" once imposed merely negative duties, they are now thought to impose positive duties.

This change in the meaning of the word *rights* is momentous in two ways. First, being more burdensome than their negative counterparts, positive duties are more likely to be rejected by those who must bear them. As a result, political disagreement has become both more commonplace and more acrimonious. Second, the more duties you impose on A for the benefit of B, the less liberty you leave A. So, this transformation in the meaning of "natural rights" has done much to diminish *liberty* and increase the power of the state, which Locke would have regretted, because his doctrine of natural rights was intended to extend and protect liberty by limiting the power of the state.

Yet Locke would have no right to complain. If the only test for a natural right is desire or need, expansion of the term's meaning was inevitable. It is indeed good to be left alone to pursue life as you wish, but it is also good to be supported by others while you remain carefree. If the first, purely negative, good is to be claimed as a right merely because of its desirability, then why not also the second, positive, good? There is nothing in the doctrine of natural rights to prevent this. On the contrary, it encourages it. Given the lack of empirical test for "natural rights," debasement of the language of rights was inevitable.

Some philosophers—for example, John Hospers—believe that we could stop the rot by returning to Locke's practice of describing as rights not everything that may be desired or needed but only what would increase liberty. Unfortunately, it is not clear that this will work. Where there is no *empirical* test for an alleged right, the only test that remains is desire, or need, which has no clear limits. This makes inevitable endless extension of the notion of rights. The slide from negative to positive duties was certainly momentous and, all things considered, regrettable, but everything in the doctrine of natural rights encourages it. Better, then, to end the doctrine than to undertake the hopeless task of mending it.

Are Rights Inherently Normative?

I have argued that talk of natural rights is proleptic discourse, which confuses wishes with facts and corrupts even our understanding of conventional rights, our prototype. The same point could be put by saying that belief in natural rights and the resulting prolepsis confuses what *ought to be* with what *is*. People are reasoning that if x *ought to have* right R, then x already *has* right R; there is no real, only a verbal, distinction between the rights you ought to have and the rights you do have.

One believer in natural rights, political philosopher Jan Narveson, has said as much in correspondence. According to him, "Rights are inherently normative. If you ought to have them, you do." In his view, that you have the rights you ought to have is a pleonasm; that you lack them a solecism.

The first point to notice about this portentous claim is that it violates a rule of grammar and logic. In the normal case there is a great and obvious difference between sentences of the form

(1) *x has y.*

and their counterparts of the form

(2) *x ought to have y.*

Thus, "x has a horse" reports that there is a horse among x's possessions, where "x ought to have a horse" editorializes that it would be a good thing if there were a horse among x's possessions," a very different claim. By parity of reasoning, "x has a right to y" should mean "A right to y is among x's possessions," whereas "x ought to have a right to y" should mean "It would be a good thing if a right to y were among x's possessions," also a different claim.

This conclusion is reinforced by observing that equating (1) and (2), as in

(3) *x has a right to y = It ought to be the case that x has a right to y,*

uses the *definiendum* to define itself, which produces what Hobbes quaintly called insignificant speech. This indicates that the fundamental notion is the indicative one, *having a right*. Trying, as Narveson does, to explain this notion using its normative counterpart is asking the cart to pull the horse. The same conclusion is indicated by repeated substitution of equals for equals, which turns (3) into (4),

(4) *x has a right to y = It ought to be the case that it ought to be the case that ... x has a right to y,*

a self generating infinite regress that is patently absurd.

How Narveson Might Reply

Despite these arguments, Narveson holds that natural rights are inherently normative. He does not say why he believes this. So, we must guess.

One possibility is that he has confused two different things that his claim might be taken to mean. First, we might interpret it as meaning "Given that a right exists, it ought to be respected." On this interpretation, the claim is indisputably true. Grant, for example, that x has a right to say what he thinks. Then y has the obligation to let him. This, however, is not Narveson's claim. His claim is the converse—that a right exists if it ought to—and this claim is demonstrably false. Grant that citizens of the People's Republic ought to have the right to criticize their government. The sad fact is that they do not. If they had it, their leaders would be bound to respect it; but since their leaders do not respect it, we must conclude that they do not have it. Rights are "inherently normative," but only when they are real.

Narveson's belief to the contrary may also be the result of reasoning as follows. Since natural rights are good things, they ought to exist. But if they ought to exist, then we have an obligation to behave as if they did, but saying this is all it means to claim that the right exists. So, granting that right R *ought* to exist is granting that it *does*; rights are inherently normative. Or so it may be thought, but the thought confuses saying that a right *ought* to exist, because its existence would be a good thing, with saying that there already exists an *obligation* to respect this right, because it is already in force.

Because argument of the kind just examined and found wanting attempts to deduce the existence of natural rights from their definition, we may call it *ontological argument* for the reality of natural rights. As such, it has all the defects of comparable arguments for the existence of God. Most analysts agree that ontological argument proves that *if* anything has the name *God*, then God exists, but ontological argument fails to prove that anything has the name *God*; so, it fails to prove that God exists. Similarly, ontological argument for the existence of rights proves that *if* something is correctly called a right, it ought to be respected; but such argument does not prove that anything is correctly called a right.

Ideals Mistaken for Realities

If believers in natural rights remain unpersuaded, it will be because they do not accept the fundamental premise of my argument—which has been that the prototype of rights is not natural but man-made rights, the measure of which is visible protection. Taking natural rights as his paradigm, the believer is unimpressed by their lack of protection. Seeing their desirability, he takes this to be the measure of their reality, while ignoring the lack of empirical evidence.

Aquinas, the medieval spokesman for natural law set the precedent for this attitude when he said that man-made law is law properly so-called only insofar as it exemplifies, imitates, or manifests the superior law of God. In other words, law in the true and primary sense of the word is Natural Law, the divinely made law from which our natural rights are derived. Conventional law, its human counterpart, counts as law only by courtesy and only in an attenuated sense of the word. So, the argument goes, it is not just true that the citizens of Communist China have a natural right to freedom of speech; it is also true in the sense of the word *rights* that counts for most in the final analysis. In short, it is man-made rights, not natural rights, that are the poor cousins.

This view is refuted by the evidence. Being discernible in the practice of protecting them, man-made rights are the rights that we experience first. Indeed, they are the only rights that we experience. Hence, explanations of natural rights, which we do not experience, necessarily consist in comparing them to the man-made rights with which we are already familiar. If, then, we have any understanding of the concept of natural rights, it is only by analogy with man-made rights. Thus, we are told that, as man-made rights are made in visible ways by visible rulers, so natural rights were made in invisible ways by an Invisible Ruler, or by Nature. This comparison is supposed to make natural rights intelligible to us by telling us how they resemble conventional rights.

The trouble is that the comparison tells us more about differences than about similarities. Thus, we are not only told that natural rights are conferred on us by an *invisible* ruler while man-made rights are conferred on us by *visible* rulers; we are also told that the invisible Ruler differs from the visible one in every respect that can be imagined. He is not only invisible where the other is visible; He is also perfect where the other is imperfect, infinite where the other is limited, far away in heaven where the other is close at hand on earth, and so on. Furthermore, His law is uncreated, perfect, metaphysically necessary, valid everywhere, eternal, and known by means of divine revelation while the laws of earthly rulers are created, imperfect, historically accidental, applicable locally, temporary, and known by means of the senses.

These familiar contrasts, which were meant to emphasize the superiority of natural rights over their man-made counterparts, should make us wonder whether the comparison leaves a sufficient resemblance between the two things to justify calling them by the same name. Because officers of the law visibly protect speech in the United States, we understand what it means to say that citizens of the U. S. have a right to criticize their government. This gives us, however, no good idea what it means to say that citizens of Communist China have a comparable right when we know perfectly well that officials in China not only do not protect speech but punish it.

Such talk uses the word *rights* in the acknowledged absence of the very condition—namely, the existence of effective protections—that is normally required for its justification. Since these newly invented "rights" no longer need protections, like the old ones, we no longer know how to verify or falsify the claim that they exist. In fact, we no longer know what this claim is supposed to mean; we no longer understand the claim that these are rights. The aroma is still there, but the bottle has been emptied.

A different error vitiates the idea that, since some forms of behavior are *natural* for human beings, they must also be *rational*, and if rational, then *obligatory*. Thus, to take just one example, seeking food and mates is natural, so rational. But—so the argument goes—you *ought* to do what is rational; and, if you ought to do it, then you must have an obligation, and a right, to do it. Hence, seeking food and mates must be not just a natural *disposition* but also a natural *obligation* entailing a natural right. Males are duty bound, so have a right, to copulate with as many females as they can, by force if necessary. Or so it would seem.

As the *reductio ad absurdum* suggests, the reasoning is erroneous, in several ways. The source of these errors is the claim that it is necessarily rational to do what it is natural to do, because the essence of human nature is reason. This commits several errors. First it overlooks the fact that human beings are also animals with biological needs that are no part of reason but that it is the business of reason to serve. Second, there are clear exceptions to the claim that it is always rational to do what is natural. It may be natural, but it is not always rational, to eat as much as you can.

A third and more important error is the argument's confusion of *ought* with *obligated*. Grant that you ought to do what you are obligated to do. The converse is not true. I ought to get more exercise and eat less fat, but this does not mean that I am obligated to do these things. If I ought to do them, it is out of self-interest, not because doing them is my duty.[16]

Grant, then, that it is natural for human beings to seek food and mates. Grant, too, that human beings ought to do what it is rational for them to do. It does not follow, and it is not true, that human beings are *obligated* to seek food and mates. So, contrary to the argument, the existence of such an "obligation" cannot be cited as the basis for a claim to have a right.

Why Moral Intuitions are not Trustworthy Here

I have argued that detaching rights from the human practice of protecting them deprives them of clear meaning. Trusting to their "moral intuitions," many philosophers will disagree. In their view, some rights lack protection; yet exist anyhow. Since this proposition seems to them to be intuitively correct, they suppose it must be. In other words, it feels right; so, they conclude that it is.

For an example of this kind of reasoning, consider a dying man's wish to be told the truth by his physician. Some philosophers I know insist that everybody has a right to this kind of disclosure. They regard this proposition as confirmed by their "moral intuitions." No matter that it is not confirmed by empirical evidence of enforcement of the correlative obligations. In their view, this proves only that the right lacks protection; not that it is unreal.

Let us examine this view. We must concede at once that the occurrence of occasional violations of a right is consistent with its existence —as the occurrence of occasional speeding on the highways is consistent with the existence of a speed limit. That much of the philosopher's "moral intuition" is correct. But what could it mean to say that a speed limit was in force where exceeding it was the rule, because the limit was rarely or never enforced? That such a limit was prescribed by the governing statute and posted on the highways would not suffice to bring it into existence. For that, enforcement is essential. An unenforced *statute* is possible; an unenforced *law* is a contradiction in terms. If the law is not enforced, it is not *in force*; if it is not in force, it does not in the relevant sense *exist*. So, if it is not enforced, it is not a law, and the philosopher's "moral intuitions" won't make it to be one.

Suppose, then, that physicians who declined to make full disclosure faced neither lawsuits, fines, time in jail, nor suspension of license. Under that hypothesis, what would it mean to say that patients of these physicians had a *legal* right to full disclosure—a right which their physicians were bound by law to respect? It is true that a physician's patients might have a *moral* right to that to which they had no *legal* right, but suppose that this alleged right also lacked enforcement. Suppose, in other words, that nobody ever censured or avoided physicians who failed to make full disclosure. Under that hypothesis, what would it mean to say that their patients had even a *moral* right to such disclosure? Grant that disclosure would be a good thing. Good things are not always required, and in the absence of a requirement to respect a right, we may doubt that it exists.

If this conclusion violates some philosophers' "moral intuitions," perhaps they ought to reconsider their faith in intuition as a source of moral truth. Contrary to widespread belief, uncritical feelings are not always expressions of self-evident truth or data of Pure Reason. Instead, they are more likely to be expressions of socially inculcated prejudice and personal preference.[17] This fact does not deprive them of evidentiary value as indexes of existing practices, but it does mean that they lack the presumptive authority that is usually attributed to them.[18]

This conclusion is buttressed in the present case by a further fact. If I have been right so far, the moral intuitions of many people, including many intellectuals, have been corrupted by an increase in proleptic discourse. As a result many people—including many intellectuals—now have great difficulty discriminating real rights from merely desired ones, and even see no need to observe the distinction. This fact, which is amply illustrated and confirmed above, makes an appeal to moral intuitions especially dubious in the present context.

Conclusion

Much talk of rights, particularly talk of natural rights, is prolepsis, which describes as a right whatever seems desirable, in the expectation of causing others to behave as if the right already existed. The main casualty of this usage, which detaches talk of rights from its empirical moorings, is a regard for truth. Debates about rights become contests of wishes rather than inquiries into facts; so, remain intractable.

Notes

1. This generalization applies to three of the four kinds of rights recognized by W. N. Hohfeld in *Fundamental Legal Conceptions* (New Haven, CT: Yale University Press, 1964—namely, permissions, powers, and privileges. The exception is *liberties*. In *Leviathan* Hobbes said that men in a state of nature have a right to everything, including one another's body. Yet, Hobbes also said, nobody in a state of nature has duties. What Hobbes meant was that men in a state of nature are *at liberty* to do anything they can get away with. There being no government to "overawe them," nobody has a duty to refrain from doing anything he wants to do.
2. More precisely, we need the concept of a *regulation*, a socially imposed rule. We shall, however, permit ourselves a certain looseness here, while counting on the context to resolve any ambiguity.
3. Thomas emphasizes the *duties* men have under the natural law, Locke the *rights*, but as duties and rights are correlatives, this difference, though important in practice is of no consequence in theory.
4. *Conventional* rights are sometimes called *positive* rights, but the term is better reserved as a contrast for *negative*.
5. Traditional doctrine is that natural rights are God given, but natural rights have since the Enlightenment become disconnected from theology. Few people any longer claim that natural rights are God-made. Still preserved, however, is belief that knowledge of natural rights is inherent in Reason. It is merely held that this knowledge was built into Reason by Nature rather than God.
6. To put his point using the usual jargon, Locke thought that all natural duties are *negative*—duties to refrain from doing something to others. In his view, nature imposes no *positive* duties—no duty to do something *for* others. That was to be left to *charity*, for which there can be no obligation.
7. A related success word is *enforce*. If a rule is enforced, it is in force; if in force, then complied with in practice. So, to enforce a rule is to secure compliance with it.
8. I have had difficulty deciding which word is most apt. The speech is proleptic in the sense that it anticipates, protreptic in the sense that it urges, future developments.
9. I do not claim that this rendition captures the speaker's thought, just the truth conditions of his statement.
10. This is not to say that disputes about conventional rights are always easy to resolve. Sometimes, there is vagueness or ambiguity, so indeterminacy of truth value, even about these. The point is that it is *only* well defined conventional rights that we know how to verify, not that we *always* know how to verify them.
11. Alan Gewirth, *Reason and Morality* (Chicago: University of Chicago Press, 1978).
12. Joel Feinberg, *Rights, Justice, and the Bounds of Liberty* (Princeton, NJ: Princeton University Press, 1980), 141, 152.
13. See his *Taking Rights Seriously* (London: Duckworth, 1978).
14. For more on this theme, see J. R. Lucas, *On Justice* (New York: Oxford University Press, 1980).
15. If ordinary folk have trouble making this distinction, so do many philosophers. Much of the debate between "deontologists" and "utilitarians" is vitiated by confusing the question "What duties and rights do people have under the rules that are already in force," with the question "What rules imposing what duties and

rights should we enact?" As the title of his major work, *The Principles of Morals and Legislation* indicates, Bentham was asking the second question, and his answer was that we should enact rules that maximize utility. Yet Bentham is usually read as if he were offering an answer to the first question. But Bentham was a moral *reformer*. He proposed utility not as a test of what already *is* just given present rules but as a standard for what would be *made* just by a better law and morality—quite a different thing.

16. For more on this distinction, see chapter 4, "What One Ought to Do."
17. For an extended discussion of moral intuition as a method in moral philosophy, see chapter 9, "Sidgwick's Method."
18. Philosophers in the Rationalist tradition used to attribute to their "moral intuitions" the same self-evident authority as the axioms and definitions of elementary mathematics. Contemporary claims are sometimes more guarded, but even these presume that moral intuition provides insight, however fallible, into *a priori* truth—a belief that confuses presumption, personal preference and prejudice with self-evidence.

Index